THE RISE OF CENTRAL AMERICAN FILM
IN THE TWENTY-FIRST CENTURY

Reframing Media, Technology, and Culture in Latin/o America

THE RISE OF CENTRAL AMERICAN FILM IN THE TWENTY-FIRST CENTURY

Edited by
Mauricio Espinoza and Jared List

UNIVERSITY OF FLORIDA PRESS
Gainesville

Publication of this work was made possible by a Sustaining the Humanities through the American Rescue Plan grant from the National Endowment for the Humanities.

Copyright 2023 by Mauricio Espinoza and Jared List
All rights reserved
Published in the United States of America.

28 27 26 25 24 23   6 5 4 3 2 1

Library of Congress Cataloging-in-Publication Data

A record of cataloging-in-publication information is available from the Library of Congress: https://lccn.loc.gov/2022058904
ISBN 978-1-68340-371-5 (cloth)
ISBN 978-1-68340-408-8 (pbk.)

University of Florida Press
2046 NE Waldo Road
Suite 2100
Gainesville, FL 32609
http://upress.ufl.edu

UF PRESS

UNIVERSITY
OF FLORIDA

Contents

List of Figures   vii

Acknowledgments   ix

Introduction: A New Cinema for a New Century   1
  Mauricio Espinoza and Jared List

Part I. Postwar and Memory

1. "¿How Many Deaths?": Official Silence, Subversive Memory, and Death's Performativity in Abner Benaim's documentary film *Invasión* (2014)   27
   Jared List

2. Illuminating from the Darkness: Transitional Justice, Testimonies and Archive in Salvadoran Postwar Documentary (2011–2018)   46
   Lilia García Torres

3. Memories and Critical History: Documenting the Past in Nicaragua and El Salvador   69
   Juan Pablo Gómez Lacayo

4. *Palabras mágicas* and *Heredera del viento*: Two Diagnoses of the Sandinista Revolution's Decay   96
   Tomás Arce Mairena

Part II. Migration, Movement, and Place

5. Borders, Body, and Violence: The Representation of the Central American Migrant in Contemporary Cinema   113
   María Lourdes Cortés

6. Migrant Credence in Marcela Zamora's *María en tierra de nadie*   131
   Esteban E. Loustaunau

7. Longing for Missing Memories: Journeys of "Return" and Postmemory in *Children of the Diaspora,* by Jennifer A. Cárcamo (2013)   152
   Patricia Arroyo Calderón

Part III. Re/presenting the Nation, Counter Cinema, and Popular Culture

8. Panamanian Cinema in the Twenty-First Century: *Panama Canal Stories* 175
   Carolina Sanabria, Translated by Carla Ros

9. Costa Rican Exceptionalism: Nostalgia, *Costumbrismo*, and Extreme Patriotism in *Maikol Yordan de viaje perdido* 193
   Liz Harvey-Kattou

10. The Games We Play: Forging and Contesting National Identities in Central American Sports Films 209
    Mauricio Espinoza

11. Toward a Central American Counter Cinema: The Films of Tatiana Huezo and Julio Hernández Cordón 234
    Júlia González de Canales Carcereny

Part IV. The Oppositional Lens: Minorities and Gender Issues

12. Tangible Afro-Indigenous Heritage: Land and Sea in *Garifuna in Peril* 251
    Jennifer Carolina Gómez Menjívar

13. ¿No que muy machito pues? Alternate Masculinities in Twenty-First-Century Guatemalan Cinema 275
    Arno Jacob Argueta

14. Film and Gender in Central America: Five Voices 292
    Daniela Granja Núñez, Interviews by Mauricio Espinoza and Jared List, Translated by Mauricio Espinoza, Jared List, and Ana Pérez Méndez

Central American Filmography: 2000–2021 309
   María Lourdes Cortés, Mauricio Espinoza, and Jared List

List of Contributors 319
Index 323

Figures

6.1. Doña Inés speaks with microphone (*María en tierra de nadie*)   138
6.2. A small altar with photo of Jazmín, cosmetics, and statues of the Virgin Mary (*María en tierra de nadie*)   141
6.3. Marta shows the prayer card while walking near train tracks (*María en tierra de nadie*)   145
6.4. Janeth and Irma cooking (*María en tierra de nadie*)   146
12.1. Ricardo at Miguel's door (*Garifuna in Peril*)   261
12.2. Facing the no trespassing sign (*Garifuna in Peril*)   261
12.3. A conversation with the next generation (*Garifuna in Peril*)   262

Acknowledgments

We thank the volume's contributors for their diligence in the editing and publishing process—a process that spanned a global pandemic. We appreciate their analytical acumen and the scholarly contributions that they each bring to this volume. We would like to particularly thank María Lourdes Cortés for her help in compiling the filmography. When one thinks of Central American film, she inevitably comes to mind. Her scholarly dedication to the region's cinema is unparalleled, as noted in the volume's continuous references to her book *La pantalla rota* (2005). We also greatly appreciate the filmmakers interviewed in this volume and their willingness to share about their work. A special note of gratitude is needed for our editors, Stephanye Hunter and Eleanor Deumens. We thank them for their time, guidance, and patience throughout the process. We would like to recognize the volume's reviewers and the series coeditor, Héctor Fernández L'Hoeste. As evidenced in their helpful and generous feedback, we thank them for the time and attention with which they read our manuscript. We would also like to thank the University of Cincinnati's Taft Research Center and the Niehoff Center for Film and Media Studies, as well as Doane University's Ardis Butler James Endowed Chair for the Advancement of the Liberal and Fine Arts, for their valuable research funding. Finally, we thank our colleagues, families, and friends for their support during the publication process.

Introduction

A New Cinema for a New Century

MAURICIO ESPINOZA AND JARED LIST

Central American cinema has experienced an unprecedented growth in local production and international exposure in the twenty-first century. Since 2000, the seven small nations that make up this narrow isthmus located between Mexico and Colombia have yielded more than 200 feature films, not to mention numerous shorts and documentaries (Cortés, "Filmmaking" 144). While this may seem like a low number compared to larger, more established Latin American film industries in countries such as Mexico or Argentina, it represents a giant leap considering the state of the region's filmmaking in the late twentieth century. In fact, during the entire 1990s, Central America—which has a population of 51.4 million in an area of just over 200,000 square miles—produced only one feature film, *El silencio de Neto* (Guatemala, 1994), directed by Luis Argueta (Cortés, "Filmmaking" 144; Durón 248).[1] However, between 2000 and 2017, the Isthmus nations already released more films than in the entire twentieth century (Alfaro Córdoba and Harvey-Kattou 137). In her comprehensive book *La pantalla rota: Cien años de cine en Centroamérica* (2004), a pioneering work of Central American film studies, María Lourdes Cortés explains that while the region has been producing films since the 1910s, its audiovisual industry "is perhaps one of the least known and invisible in world cinema" (17). A key factor for this marginal status during the twentieth century was the lack of continuity in the various efforts to develop local film industries (Cortés, *La pantalla rota* 18). However, much has changed in the past twenty years.

Today, most of the countries in the region have active filmmaking scenes, a growing number of professionals dedicated to audiovisual production, local or regional film funds, and international film festivals. The number of films produced in the Isthmus continues to grow and find audiences, both domestic and international. A number of these films have received prestigious international awards and/or broken local viewership records for domestic productions. Internationally, film critics and publications are taking notice of this cinema. In a *Variety* article from 2018, Anna Marie de la Fuente writes about the success that countries like Costa Rica and Panama have had in recent years, citing Hilda Hidalgo, director of the features *Del amor y otros demonios* (Colombia/Costa Rica, 2010) and *Violeta al fin* (Costa Rica, 2017). Referencing the fact that in 2017 Costa Rica saw seventeen films locally produced, Hidalgo explains: "That's equivalent to all the films made in Costa Rica in the twentieth century" (quoted in De la Fuente). De la Fuente also cites the role that the Panama International Film Festival (IFF) has had in showcasing the region's new cinematic production. By all indications, it appears that the continuity and consistency that were sorely missing in the past century have finally become a reality.

The goal of this edited collection—the first in English dedicated to the study of Central American film—is to explore the main trends, genres, and themes that characterize this emerging small cinema. In doing so, we seek to contribute to the incipient but slowly growing scholarship on this subject, which we discuss later in this introduction, and which is overwhelmingly dominated by Spanish-language articles and books. This volume also adds to the field of Central American cultural studies, which has been making important strides in the past few years. Finally, the larger field of Latin American film will benefit from the essays gathered in this collection, as they advance the study of one of the continent's least explored cinemas. The authors who have graciously provided their expertise and insights to this project are film, cultural studies, and/or literary scholars based in Central America, the United States, and Europe. We consider the variety of their backgrounds, perspectives, critical approaches, and countries of origin a valuable asset to this scholarly endeavor.

Continuities and Discontinuities in Twenty-First-Century Central American Film

In writing about the twenty-first-century Central American cinematic production, some film scholars have suggested the idea of a "new" cinema being developed during this period. Hispano Durón (a Honduran researcher and director, among other films, of the 2017 historical feature *Morazán*), uses the term *Nuevo Cine Centroamericano,* concluding his essay by claiming that "New Central American Film is contributing to the consolidation of a regional identity, upon telling stories with local themes and characters" (253). Regarding Costa Rican cinema, María Lourdes Cortés uses the term *El nuevo cine costarricense* to refer to the boom in production in the first fifteen years of the new century (Cortés, *Fabulaciones* 35). While she does not explain the use of the term "new," we might understand it as a signifier that denotes the prolific increase in production between centuries. We have chosen not to employ the concept of a "New Central American Film," concluding that this recent cinematic production might be better characterized as a new phase in the region's path toward consolidation and professionalization of its film industry. The ushering of a "new" cinema involves an obvious break with the previous filmic tradition. One example is the New Latin American Cinema (NLAC) of the 1960s through the 1980s, which challenged the prevailing industrial, Hollywood-inspired mode of filmmaking by advancing a political cinematic movement and distinctive aesthetic "dedicated to the people of the continent and their struggles for cultural, political, and economic autonomy" (López 309). Here, the rupture with the previous cinema was radical.

In the case of Central American film, we see a number of continuities and discontinuities between twentieth-century cinema and the new phase represented by twenty-first-century productions. First, there are important continuities in the way that regional filmmakers have set out to make documentaries and fiction features (the two types of film studied in this book). While documentaries have been produced in the region since 1914 and Guatemalan Marcel Reichenbach won Cannes Festival awards for best documentary in 1957 and 1959 (Cortés, *La pantalla rota* 565, 165), the Central American documentary film came of age during the 1970s and 1980s. Sharing the aesthetics and principles of NLAC, several filmmaking groups and state-sponsored institutions emerged during this period of socialist utopia and war: the Grupo Experimental de Cine Universitario (GECU) in Panama; the Centro Costarricense de Producción Cinematográfica (CCPC) in Costa Rica; Radio Venceremos and the Instituto Cinematográfico de El Salvador Revolucionario in El Salvador; the Instituto Nicaragüense de Cine (INCINE); and the Costa Rica–based, regional, independent film production project Istmo Film. These groups produced a number of documentaries (and in the case of INCINE, also some fiction feature films) that sought to advance social causes, denounce U.S. imperialism, and document and support the revolutionary causes in the region (Cortez and Ortiz Wallner; Fumero and Cortés 2–3; Cortés, *Violencia* 13).

As Cortés indicates, some of these groups contributed to a certain degree of professionalization in countries such as Costa Rica and Nicaragua, which permitted "a relative continuity in cinematographic production" (Cortés, *La pantalla rota* 540). Moreover, the sociopolitical tradition of documentary filmmaking from this transformative period was inherited by a new generation of documentarians. The commitment to making socially conscious documentaries has not changed. However, new historical realities, production modes, and aesthetics have shifted the focus of these films toward new priorities: reconstructing memory, seeking justice, exploring trauma and disenchantment with failed revolutions, denouncing new forms of violence, documenting the phenomena of migration and diasporic communities, fighting for environmental conservation, and visibilizing traditionally underrepresented populations in the region's postwar, neoliberal period. Additionally, narrations about the collective "we" have turned into stories about the filmmaker's intimate "I" (Cabezas Vargas and González de Canales Carcereny 167).

Meanwhile, when it comes to fiction feature films, a common thread that connects the two centuries is the search for a sustained level of production (both in terms of quantity and quality) that would generate local and international recognition as well as adequate funding sources to support additional film projects. Thematically, fiction cinema has strived toward telling stories and crafting images that reflect local realities; that is, to create a distinctively Central American cinema through the generation of "images of our identity, our own reflections on film screens" (Cortés, *La pantalla rota* 18). This has been evident from the first fiction feature film that the region yielded, *El retorno* (A. F. Bertoni, Costa Rica, 1930), which depicts an idyllic coffee-farming way of life being threatened by the city and modernity. Several other features produced in the following decades subscribed to this theme of *costumbrismo* (stories of rural life and traditions), which are still popular in twenty-first-century film as Liz Harvey-Kattou explores in her chapter in this volume. Other features engage with specific historical events in the Isthmus. *Alsino y el condor* (a 1982 Nicaraguan coproduced film directed by Chilean Miguel Littín and the only Central American film nominated for a Best Foreign Film Oscar to date) is a war drama set during the Sandinista revolution. *El silencio de Neto* (1994) is also set during a time of conflict, in this case the 1954 coup against Guatemala's socialist President Jacobo Árbenz. Showing a connection with this legacy, recent films such as *Princesas rojas* (Laura Astorga, Costa Rica, 2013) and *La Llorona* (Jayro Bustamante, Guatemala, 2019) revisit the scars left by twentieth-century conflicts such as the war in Nicaragua in the 1980s and the genocide against Indigenous people during the Guatemalan civil war, respectively. Finally, Bértold Salas has pointed out that about a third of the feature films produced in Costa Rica in this century favor stories that are tied to the past, "establishing a continuity with that discourse of time, preserving it, and adapting it to the twenty-first century, returning their characters—and with them, the public—to a mythical past or lamenting its loss" (7).

On the other hand, there are a number of significant changes or discontinuities that help to explain Central American cinema's distinctive features and tremendous growth in its new, twenty-first-century phase. One key transformation has to do with the models of production and the overarching goals of isthmian film. The cinema of the 1970s and 1980s was dominated by the work of film collectives and state-sponsored film institutes, which sought to advance revolutionary change in the effervescent sociopolitical climate of the time. This film movement's specific goals dictated the themes, content, purpose, and aesthetics of their productions. However, by the 1990s these groups had either disappeared (which was the case with INCINE) or lost state support, meaning a return to independent film production (Cortés, *La pantalla rota* 540–41). This independent film production model has dominated the region's film landscape ever since, leading to a diversity of themes and approaches in regional filmmaking, even as some of its concerns or narrative tropes remain connected to the past (as explained above). While documentaries continue to be a substantial component of Central America's film output, what stands out the most in this new phase is the strong impetus fueling fiction feature film production (Cortés, *La pantalla rota* 541). The new crop of documentaries and fiction features represent a wide array of genres, themes, and goals, which are discussed later in this introduction.

Other changes have to do with the social and economic transformations in the region, new technologies, training, funding, distribution, and exposure. As Amanda Alfaro Córdoba and Liz Harvey-Kattou explain, in the past two decades "political stability and economic prosperity have increased while the costs of filmmaking have decreased, thanks in large part to the digital turn" (138). These new, more accessible technologies have "allowed the younger generations that studied filmmaking abroad or in the more established institutions in the region to tell their stories through images" (Cortés, "Filmmaking" 144). This new cohort of professional filmmakers has been fundamental for the consolidation of isthmian cinema. While some of them have received training at various schools in Europe and the United States, a majority has attended the International Film and Television School (EICTV) in San Antonio de los Baños, Cuba—a NLAC-influenced institution that has been instrumental in promoting filmmaking throughout Latin America and other parts of the Global South (Cortés, *Violencia* xiv). Training opportunities within the region have also arrived with the new century—for instance, in 2003, Costa Rica's Universidad Veritas founded the first film and television school in the Isthmus.

The creation of national and regional film festivals in recent years has also contributed to the circulation and visibilization of Central American cinema. Started as a Guatemalan film-only festival in the late 1990s, Festival Ícaro began showcasing films from throughout the Isthmus in 2000. Meanwhile, the Muestra de Cine y Video Costarricense (founded in 1992) became the Costa Rica International Film Festival in 2012. Launched in 2012, the region's most ambitious and successful festival is IFF Panama. Its artistic director, Diana Sánchez, explains that "We started the festival partly because only English-language films were showing in Panama; we wanted to add more diversity" (quoted in De la Fuente). In other words, the festival became a site of resistance against Hollywood's international dominance and influence in the region. Seeing Hollywood as a legacy of colonialism, Ella Shohat and Robert Stam write that, "[d]espite the imbrication of 'First World' and 'Third' Worlds, the global distribution of power still tends to make the First World countries cultural 'transmitters' and to reduce most Third World countries to the status of 'receivers'" (30). In this regard, festivals such as IFF Panama (and the regional films it shows), help to contest this colonial power structure and even uses its capitalist underpinnings to its advantage.

A number of local, regional, and international funding initiatives have also helped Central American filmmakers turn their ideas into filmic reality. For example, Costa Rica and El Salvador have created funds to support local audiovisual production, of about half a million dollars each annually (Cortés, *Violencia* xvi; Alfaro Córdoba and Harvey-Kattou 138). Panama leads the way in governmental support of its film industry, allocating $2 million a year in funds in addition to enacting film legislation that regulates and incentivizes movie production (Fumero and Cortés 3). Another important funding source during this period was the Cinergia Foundation (2003–2015), created by Cortés with the goal of providing financial assistance to filmmakers and producers in Central America and Cuba. Annually the foundation gave $20,000 to $30,000 in support to filmmakers and, in its first five years, backed sixty projects (Durón 249; Sánchez). In its twelve years, the organization awarded $989,000 in funds and held workshops that convened more than 500 attendees (Sánchez). The funds supported production of some of the region's most successful films, including Julio Hernández Cordón's *Gasolina* (Guatemala, 2008), Ishtar Yasin's *El Camino* (Costa Rica, 2010), Paz Fábrega's *Agua fría de mar* (Costa Rica, 2010), and Jayro Bustamante's *Ixcanul* (Guatemala, 2015). In the new millennium, Central American filmmakers have also found support through the Ibermedia Program (a Spain-led coproduction fund that provides financing to audiovisual projects throughout Latin America) as well as from other outside sponsors. In this regard, the Isthmus's cinematic resurgence has greatly benefited from coproduction and funding from transnational foundations, which has been the case for other Latin American film industries since the 1980s when state support for moviemaking dried up across the continent (King 265; Tierney 4).[2] Additionally, some films (especially comedies and dramas that have a wider appeal) have managed to garner financial backing from local businesses and investors. This proves that a commercial film industry (albeit incipient) may be possible in the Isthmus given the right conditions and the "right" type of films.

While distribution outside the region remains a challenge, more and more local films are finding distributors that share them internationally. Through subscription services or direct purchase, media platforms like Netflix, Amazon Prime, YouTube, Vimeo, and Kanopy have begun to include Central American films as viewing options—challenging the unidirectional flow of images and sequences from the north to the south. For instance, *Ixcanul* and *Presos* (Esteban Ramírez, Costa Rica, 2015) were distributed on Netflix. Movies from the region can also be found on the catalogs of Spanish and Latin American film distributors such as New York City–based Pragda, which allows theaters and schools in the United States to access lesser-known films that would be difficult to procure otherwise. In addition to these channels, international festivals continue to play a significant role in showcasing local productions on the world stage and boost their recognition. However, to simply celebrate the international distribution of Central American films is problematic, given that these media platforms and many of the festivals reproduce another iteration of coloniality where the Global North profits and ultimately controls distribution. Regional films have also found distribution through other channels, including airlines. For example, IFF Panama has strategically partnered with Copa Airlines to reach a wider viewership for the Latin American and Central American films chosen by the festival, reaching hundreds of thousands of viewers (de la Fuente; IFF Panama). Delta Airlines has also offered Central American films on some of its flights.[3]

Another sign of Central American cinema's resurgence is the growing recognition and opportunities some of the region's directors have found abroad. For instance, Hernández Cordón has been able to leverage the positive reception of his early movies—the above-mentioned *Gasolina* (2008) and the hybrid film *Las marimbas del infierno* (2010) among them—into a successful and prolific career in the Mexican film industry. There, he has directed the features *Te prometo anarquía* (Mexico, 2015, which earned him a best director nomination for the prestigious Ariel Awards), *Atrás hay relámpagos* (Mexico-Costa Rica coproduction, 2017), and *Cómprame un revólver* (Mexico, 2018, also nominated for several Ariel Awards). Another filmmaker from the Isthmus who has a budding international career is Hernán Jiménez, writer and director of three feature films in Costa Rica: *A ojos cerrados* (2010), *El regreso* (2012), and *Entonces nosotros* (2016). In 2019, Jiménez made his English-language directorial debut in the United States with the comedy-drama *Elsewhere*, which includes recognized actors such as Beau Bridges, Ken Jeong, and Parker Posey. Jiménez also directed the Netflix romantic comedy *Love Hard* (United States, 2021), whose cast includes Darren Barnet, James Saito, and Costa Rican–born Harry Shum Jr. (*Love Hard*). Year after year in the past two decades, Central America-made films have won awards at some of the most prestigious international festivals. The most successful so far is Bustamante's *Ixcanul* (Guatemala, 2015), which won the Silver Bear at the 2015 Berlin Film Festival and quickly became one of Central America's most decorated films ever. Bustamante followed up his volcanic debut with *Temblores* (Guatemala) and *La Llorona* (both premiering in 2019), which have also drawn critical praise. His reputation was cemented in early 2020, when South Korean filmmaker Bong Joon-Ho (whose film *Parasite* won the 2020 Oscars for Best Picture and Best Director) listed Bustamante as one of twenty emerging directors whose work will define the 2020s—the Guatemalan being the only Latin American on the list (Betancourt).

This volume recognizes and appreciates the change in flows of knowledge and cinematic production within the North-South configuration of power. If Hollywood has been the hegemonic goliath that drives film production, representation and viewership globally, the first two decades of the twenty-first century in Central America are indicative of changing tides. In the Isthmus now, there are hundreds of films produced locally by local directors for a local viewership, giving way to alternative representations, modes of knowing, and interventions in the cinematic landscape. In this sense, questions of post-colonialism, decoloniality, and epistemological democratization all become possibilities as the North-South colonial relations of power are challenged by Central America's film democratization. To use Shohat and Stam's words, Central America's cinematic boom questions the formula of "First World" countries as cultural "transmitters" and "Third World" nations as the cultural "receivers" (30). One of our goals with this book is to show that this colonial relation of power is no longer necessarily the case in Central America, as a healthy dose of domestic film productions and talent now coexist (and it has shown that it can successfully compete) with imported movies. One good example of this trend is Costa Rica. As Durón notes, local films like *Asesinato en el Meneo* (Oscar Castillo, Costa Rica, 2001) and *Gestación* (Esteban Ramírez, Costa Rica, 2010) drew a viewership similar to Hollywood films playing in Costa Rican theaters at the time (250). More recently, the 2014 film *Maikol Yordan de viaje perdido* (Costa Rica, directed by Miguel Gómez, and which Liz Harvey-Kattou studies in chapter 9), became the most viewed in Costa Rican history—attracting 770,000 viewers (17 percent of the country's population) in a six-month period and easily surpassing even popular Hollywood blockbusters.

Cinema in the Context of Central American Realities

Central America's new cinema offerings are diverse in their genres, styles, topics, and issues they address—ranging widely from the treatment of violence to light-hearted comedies, from traditional storytelling to more innovative forms, and from socially conscious documentaries in the NLAC tradition to Hollywood-influenced commercial entertainment. The films discussed in this collection are representative of this variety of offerings and approaches to filmmaking. Regardless of genre or theme, all of these films establish important dialogues with the political, social, economic, and cultural realities that have shaped Central American history—and which distinguish this region from others in the Americas. A few of these historical processes are worth mentioning here to better understand the contexts in and from which these cinematic productions (and their makers) have emerged: U.S. intervention in the Isthmus; civil wars, revolutions, violence, and political unrest; migration and diaspora; and the region's large and diverse Indigenous and Afro-Central American communities that have long suffered from discrimination and violence.

The United States has had a long interventionist history in the Isthmus that goes back at least to the 1850s, when U.S. mercenary William Walker seized control of the Nicaraguan government and was later ousted by a coalition of Central American armies. According to Noam Chomsky, "[n]o region of the world has been more subject to US influence than Central America and the Caribbean" (6). By far, the longest and most pervasive process of U.S. intervention in the Isthmus took place in Panama, which was part of Colombia until 1903. A year later, the United States took over construction of the Panama Canal from France, finishing the strategically and economically relevant project in 1914. The United States controlled the Canal (and the adjacent Canal Zone) until its handover to Panama in 1999. Tensions and even violence between the two countries were common during the twentieth century, culminating with the U.S. invasion of Panama in 1989 and overthrow of

Manuel Noriega's government. Three chapters in this volume analyze films that explore this conflicted history and its aftermath from a variety of perspectives and genres. The United States has also intervened in the affairs of other Central American nations in direct or indirect ways, including support of the long Somoza family dictatorship in Nicaragua (1936–1979) and funding of the Contra army that fought against the leftist Sandinista revolution during the 1980s. Two chapters in this volume analyze documentaries that contend with the legacies of the Sandinista revolution and the Contra war.

Elsewhere in the Isthmus, the United States played a role in the ouster of socialist Guatemalan President Jacobo Árbenz (1954) and in supporting right-wing regimes in Guatemala and El Salvador—which were engulfed in civil war during the second half of the twentieth century as leftist guerrillas clashed with those U.S.-supported governments. In addition to the conflicts in Nicaragua, these civil wars (1960–1996 in Guatemala and 1980–1992 in El Salvador) destabilized the region and reshaped it in long-lasting ways.[4] Despite a period of democratization that began in the 1990s and the implementation of a neoliberal agenda that has boosted local economies, violence in a variety of forms (gangs, femicides, drug and human trafficking, political repression, etc.) and inequality have continued to plague most of the region. Three chapters in this volume analyze how postwar documentaries attempt to reconstruct the past, seek justice, and dialogue with issues of memory and trauma in Guatemala and El Salvador. Another consequence of violence—along with economic adversity and, more recently, also climate change—is the phenomenon of migration, which has marked the lives of millions of Central Americans. The number of migrants from the Isthmus grew from 2.6 million in 2000 to 4.2 million in 2015, most of whom (3.3 million) have migrated to the United States (Orozco 2). In fact, 12 percent of Central Americans now live outside of their countries of birth, which is four times the global migration rate (Sandoval García xvi). Three chapters in this book deal with migration-related films, including one centered on the experiences of Salvadorans living in Los Angeles.

Finally, recent Central American film production has begun taking into account the region's diverse cultural and ethnic landscape and the particular features that emerge from such a configuration. Central America is home to a large Indigenous population, from the Maya in northern Central America to the Guna Dule in southern Panama. In Guatemala alone, there are 6.2 million Maya people, accounting for almost 42 percent of the country's population (Instituto Nacional de Estadística Guatemala). Recent prominent films such as Bustamante's *Ixcanul* and *La Llorona* have featured Maya stories, protagonists, culture, and languages—while also addressing the legacy of discrimination and violence this population has experienced in Guatemala's history. Afro-Central Americans are also present throughout the Isthmus, facing discrimination and cultural violence since colonial times. To that end, this volume includes the analysis of films about the Afro-Indigenous Garifuna people of Honduras and their struggles to preserve their way of life. The preservation of land and natural resources is closely connected with issues of Indigenous and Afro-Central American rights and self-determination in the Isthmus. Films addressing environmental issues and their relationship with native inhabitants have also been an important part of the region's recent filmography. While not included in this volume, studies about these films have appeared in recent ecocriticism scholarship.[5]

Scholarship Meets a Growing Film Scene

The rising production and international exposure of Central American cinema in the twenty-first century has caught the attention of film and cultural studies scholars from the Isthmus and elsewhere. Both Amanda Alfaro Córdoba's dissertation "Archipelagoes and Constellations: Political Economy and Aesthetics in Twenty-First Central American and Hispanic Caribbean Film" and Andrea Cabezas Vargas's dissertation "Cinéma centraméricain contemporain (1970–2014): la construction d'un cinéma régional: mémoires socio-historiques et culturelles," examine Central American films produced in this century. A number of journal articles and book chapters addressing different films and various aspects of isthmian film have appeared since the mid-2000s—including many by this volume's contributors. These articles and chapters also feature prominently as bibliographic sources throughout this book. In addition to individual essays, a small but growing number of journal issues and books dedicated to the region's film industry (partially or entirely dealing with twenty-first-century productions) have appeared in the past fifteen years.

The first journal issue dedicated entirely to Central America cinema appeared in 2006 in the Central American literary and cultural studies journal *Istmo: Revista virtual de estudios literarios y culturales centroamericanos*. The dossier—titled "Producciones audiovisuales en Centroamérica" and edited by Beatriz Cortez and Alexandra Ortiz Wallner—includes essays on films from the twentieth century and a few from the twenty-first century, produced inside the region as well as in the U.S. diaspora. In 2010, *Istmo* published another issue ("Cine, comunicación audiovisual y participación política," edited by Claudia Ferman), which included analyses of a few twenty-first-century films among other contemporary media formats. In 2018, Patricia Fumero and María Lourdes Cortés edited another thematic dossier in *Istmo,* titled "Una mirada al cine centroamericano actual." As local audiovisual production had grown significantly by the time of publication of this issue, the dossier covers mostly films released since 2000 and highlights the unprecedented development and recognition of Central American cinema during this period. Finally, *Studies in Spanish & Latin American Cinemas* published a number on Central American cinema in the twenty-first century (vol. 15, no. 2, 2018), edited by Amanda Alfaro Córdoba and Liz Harvey-Kattou. This is the first journal issue in English dedicated to the region's recent cinematic production, with articles by several of the contributors to this volume.

Regarding books, Cortés devotes the last section of *La pantalla rota* to exploring new Central American film production in the first few years of the twenty-first century, noting how fourteen feature films had already been made by 2004 (when the book was published) while ten others were in the process of production (541–42). Cortés's 2016 monograph *Fabulaciones del nuevo cine costarricense* (which deals with Costa Rican cinema exclusively) is also dedicated to twenty-first-century productions in its entirety. Since the call for proposals for this edited collection went out in late 2018, three books about twenty-first-century Central American cinema have been published in Spanish, which in addition to the journal issues mentioned above show a significant increase in academic attention to this body of work. Ileana Rodríguez's *Modalidades de memoria y archivos afectivos: Cine de mujeres en Centroamérica* (2020) examines six politically themed Central American documentaries by female directors, arguing that they represent an articulation of film and memory that reflects on Central America's political processes of the late twentieth and early twenty-first centuries and creates a poetics of cinema (95). The book *Violencia, marginalidad y memoria en el cine centroamericano,* edited by Cortés and published in 2021, examines some of the most popular Central American films of this century from a variety of approaches, including the role of violence, memory, and popular culture in contemporary Central American society. Meanwhile, Charo García Diego's edited collection *Cine centroamericano y caribeño siglo XXI* (2021), includes a diverse set of essays that analyze Central American films dealing with various topics, including gender. Finally, in 2022, David Inczauskis published *El cine hondureño: Arte, identidad y política,* which focuses on the political and civil rights interventions of contemporary Honduran film.

Screening Central America in the New Century: Key Trends, Genres, and Themes

Taking into account the thematic tendencies present in Central American cinema since the turn of the century, in this book we identify four broad categories that encompass a majority of the movies made in the region since 2000: post-trauma and memory films; films of movement (social and migratory movements); films dealing with portrayals of the nation in the neoliberal era, popular culture, and counter cinema; and films focused on minorities and issues of gender. While some of the films analyzed in the various essays overlap in terms of themes, we have organized the book along these broad categories to better guide readers (especially those unfamiliar with Central America's audiovisual production) in their exploration of this regional cinema. Finally, we have made an effort to be inclusive not just with regards to themes but also in terms of genres and countries represented.

This collection's essays analyze both fiction films and documentaries. We believe that including both types of films helps to paint a more comprehensive picture of the topics, styles, filmmaking approaches, sociopolitical concerns, and production challenges represented in contemporary Central American cinema. While new feature fiction films often receive more attention from the media and the public (especially because their production has been historically scarce in the region), documentaries continue to be a significant and innovative component of Central America's cinematic output. To that end, several of the essays included in this volume deal exclusively with documentaries, reflecting on their diversity of approaches: some more traditional in their use of archival footage and testimonials, others more experimental and even poetic. In other cases, analyzing documentaries alongside fiction films that deal with the same topic allows us to more clearly visualize their different approaches to storytelling and use of historical references. One example is present in Mauricio Espinoza's chapter about Pituka Ortega-Heilbron's documentary *Los puños de una nación* (Panama, 2005) and Jonathan Jakubowicz's biopic *Hands of Stone* (United States/Panama, 2016), both of which deal with Panamanian boxer Roberto Durán and the tense relationship between Panama and the United States. The fiction films studied in this collection also reveal the variety of genres Central American screenwriters and directors are exploring, among them comedy, drama, romance, road movie, science fiction, biopic, historical drama, art house/experimental, and hybrid (mixing documentary and fiction, as in the case of Julio Hernández Cordón's *Hasta el Sol tiene manchas,* Mexico/Guatemala, 2012). Finally, this book studies films from all of the Central American countries except Belize—a nation of fewer than 400,000 inhabitants where local cinema production is just beginning to develop.

Postwar and Memory

In most of the region, conflict, and war marked the second half of the twentieth century. Today, one of the thematic tendencies within Central American film is postwar and memory, yielding films such as Mercedes Moncada's *Palabras mágicas (para romper un encantamiento)* (Nicaragua, 2012), Marcela Zamora's *Los ofendidos* (El Salvador, 2016), Abner Benaim's *Invasión* (Panama, 2014), and Gloria Carrión Fonseca's *Heredera del viento* (Nicaragua, 2017). These and similar films use memory as a vehicle to return to the past and understand it in the present. Guiding questions in this section of the book include: How do Central American films intervene in the present to remember the past? What do the films contribute to the respective social, cultural, and political realities of each country? How do the films address and remember the past and for what purposes? What role does documentary film play in re-membering and re-presenting the past?

In the first chapter, Jared List posits that Benaim's 2014 documentary film *Invasión* provides a counternarrative, a counterhegemonic narrative that challenges the U.S.-imposed official narrative about the 1989 military intervention in Panama. List claims that *Invasión* imbues its political intent and content with affect, creating a sensorial relation between the film and its spectators that becomes another means of *concientización* (raising awareness). Benaim uses embodied, de-hierarchized memories to representationally and sensorially transmit hi/stories silenced by "official" discourses regarding the invasion.

Lilia García Torres also explores the transformative potential of documentary film in chapter 2, claiming that this format serves to denounce, name, record, and overcome the collective trauma of the past. In her essay, Torres examines four Salvadoran films: *La palabra en el bosque*, by Carlos Henríquez Consalvi and Jeffrey Gould (2011); *El Salvador, archivos perdidos del conflicto*, by Gerardo Muyshondt (2014); *Los ofendidos*, by Marcela Zamora (2016); and *La batalla del volcán*, by Julio López (2018)—all of which are framed within the transitional justice process and propose a dialogue between the armed conflict and the present. For the author, these films recount memories that, only with the passage of time and new knowledge, can be understood through the interrogative realities of today.

In chapter 3, Juan Pablo Gómez Lacayo examines four Central American documentary films: Susan Meiselas's *Pictures from a revolution* (United States,

1991), *El lugar más pequeño* (El Salvador, 2011), directed by Tatiana Huezo Mixco, and Moncada's *Palabras mágicas* (2012). He argues that documentary film, including these films, serves as a means to recuperate the past, interrogate it, and participate in the construction of social and collective memories. Furthermore, as in the case of *Granito*, documentary film can right the injustices of the past through its role in seeking justice in the present, while at the same time giving space and voice to surviving victims of Central America's violent civil wars.

Tomás Arce Mairena argues, in chapter 4, that Moncada's *Palabras mágicas* (2012) and Carrión Fonseca's *Heredera del viento* (2018), through their unique documentarian approaches, put before viewers the legacy of the Sandinista government and its failed attempts to achieve the promises of the 1979 Sandinista revolution in Nicaragua. Using a poetic mode of documentary filmmaking, Moncada calls attention to the failed ideals, while Carrión uses her personal and familial story to represent the limits of revolution. Within each approach, both films incorporate historical context to recognize the previous pain and trauma associated with the war and the government's failure to live up to its revolutionary discourse, which can be understood with the recent context of the Ortega-Murillo dictatorship.

Migration, Movement, and Place

Migration and movement have also characterized recent Central American realities, and, accordingly, various films produced in the last two decades examine and reflect upon displacement inside and outside the region. From Ishtar Yasin's *El Camino* that explores Nicaraguan migration to Costa Rica and sexual violence to Marcela Zamora's *María en tierra de nadie* (El Salvador, 2011) that captures the difficulties surrounding migration from Central America to the United States through Mexico, films of movement and migration are an emerging genre in the region. Furthermore, we understand movement here to include movements, or shifts, in social, political, historical, and/or cultural domains; for example, the ways in which diaspora is understood in and outside Central America. In that vein, some of the guiding questions in this section are: How is migration represented in the region and to what end? What knowledge do the films share between the screen and the spectator? How can films within this domain address questions of culture, class, gender, politics, and social justice? And in what ways do the films themselves contribute or promote social, cultural, and political "movements"?

Chapter 5 is María Lourdes Cortés's analysis of three films dealing with Central American migrants: Cary Joji Fukunaga's *Sin nombre* (United States/

Mexico, 2009), Luis Mandoki's *La vida precoz y breve de Sabina Rivas* (Mexico, 2012), and Diego Quemada-Díez's *La jaula de oro* (Mexico, 2013). Her analysis employs Christian León's concept *el cine de la marginalidad* (cinema of marginality) when dealing with the three fictional films. All three features—grounded in historical, social, and political realities—are what Cortés terms films of borders and tensions: between the national borders, between fiction and nonfiction, between hegemony and marginality, and between and within subjects themselves. The films give visibility to those "without image" or "without voice" through the fictionalized stories tied to historical, social, and political referents. While produced in Mexico, all three movies center around the lives of Central American unaccompanied migrants traveling north to the United States and prominently feature the Guatemala-Mexico border in their plots and visual construction.

In chapter 6, Esteban Loustaunau examines Zamora's documentary film *María en tierra de nadie,* paying attention to the ways in which the women migrants interviewed in the film confront precarity and exploitation. He argues that the women's stories and perspectives represented in the film point to what he terms "credence," that is, that their experiences and stories are meaningful and truthful for themselves albeit the precarious conditions in which they find themselves as migrants. Rather than seeing the women as examples of bare life who are subjected to the violence that permeates the migrant's journey, Loustaunau claims that the stories represented in the film are examples of survival—supported by a network of individuals and organizations that reveal various articulations of collective agency.

In chapter 7, Patricia Arroyo Calderón analyzes Jennifer A. Cárcamo's documentary *Children of Diaspora: For Peace and Democracy* (United States/El Salvador, 2013) to explore issues of belonging, displacement, memory, and identity within the context of Central American diasporic communities. When considering the growing number of Central American films of migration, there has yet to be much research over the cinematic subgenre in relation to Central American-Americans. Arroyo Calderón argues that the film captures the ambivalent sense of belonging that U.S.-born Salvadorans may feel as they negotiate their identities while experiencing the intergenerational trauma passed on from their parents who fled El Salvador as a result of the civil war. Using Marianne Hirsch's concept of "postmemory," Arroyo Calderón argues that the documentary film visibilizes the intergenerational transmission of trauma and memory present in the Central American diaspora and offers a glimpse of the issues facing U.S.-born Central American youth.

Re/presenting the Nation, Counter Cinema, and Popular Culture

Furthermore, twenty-first-century Central American directors have yielded a diverse filmography in terms of topics and genres that responds to the region's changing realities in a period marked by neoliberal policies and rapid globalization. Included here are entertainment films or sports biographical dramas that are commercially produced and have experienced box office success. Additionally, other films address preoccupations with hot-button issues of the times, including millennial life, individual disenchantment in an era of post-grand narratives, consumerism, aging, inequality, and the perspectives of underrepresented populations. In this section, the chapters draw upon contested representations of national and cultural identities as well as the aesthetics of counter cinema.

In chapter 8, Carolina Sanabria examines *Historias del Canal* (Panama, 2013), a collaborative production between Central American directors Carolina Borrero, Pinky Mon, Luis Franco Brantley, Abner Benaim, and Pituka Ortega-Heilbron. Sanabria explores the fictionalized account that the film puts forth surrounding the construction of the Panama Canal. Comprised of five shorts, each director chose a year in the hundred-year span, beginning with 1913 and concluding with 2013. In Sanabria's analysis, she reads the canal's construction in parallel with Panama's development as a country and proposes a filmic reading that envisions the canal as an allegory for the nation. She argues that the shorts employ various marginalized perspectives through their main characters who are either women, migrants, or of African ancestry. The fictionalized accounts emerge from what she denotes as the "fringe" rather than the hegemonic subjects who are white and colonizers. Thus, for Sanabria, *Historias del Canal* narrates the story of the canal (and ultimately the nation) from a locus of hybridization.

Liz Harvey-Kattou, in chapter 9, discusses the popularity of the 2014 Costa Rican film *Maikol Yordan de viaje perdido* (Miguel Gómez), exploring the comedy's strategy in using an idealized past that engenders patriotic feelings within the viewers. For Harvey-Kattou, *Maikol Yordan de viaje perdido* employs *costumbrista* practices to produce this sense of patriotism, largely through the trope of the humble, heteropatriarchal, Euro-descendant farmer as a common ancestor for Costa Ricans. This trope plays on the rural-urban dichotomy, valorizing the rural over the moral degradation of the urban as the source of traditional Costa Rican values and nostalgia; and at the same time, the film privileges the countryside and the traditional *tico* farmer over notions of Eurocentrism or contemporary Western civilization.

In chapter 10, Mauricio Espinoza analyzes Central American sport films about soccer and boxing (two of the most popular sports in the region and the two that have garnered the most attention in cinematic production) to uncover the connections between these narratives and issues of nationalism, national and regional identities, reproduction or contestation of gender norms, and race/ethnicity. The chapter focuses on biopics and documentaries that recount the heroic feats of national football teams or internationally renowned athletes such as boxer Roberto Durán: *Los puños de una nación* (Pituka Ortega-Heilbron, Panama, 2005), *Hands of Stone* (Jonathan Jakubowicz, United States/Panama, 2016), *Uno, la historia de un gol* (Gerardo Muyshondt and Carlos Moreno, El Salvador, 2010), and *Italia 90* (Miguel Gómez, Costa Rica, 2014). The relationships between nation-building discourses, memory, nostalgia, and popular culture are further explored in this analysis.

Meanwhile, using a framework of counter cinema, Júlia González de Canales Carcereny analyzes Tatiana Huezo's *El lugar más pequeño* (2011) and Hernández Cordón's *Hasta el Sol tiene manchas* (2012) in chapter 11. She claims that both films experiment with cinematographic narrative techniques that break with dominant filmmaking practices. In doing so, these films challenge hegemonic notions of cinematography through their use of counter-aesthetics, experimental cinematic form, and the international dynamics of the film industry—all while interrogating social and political contexts in Central America. These characteristics have led the movies to receive international recognition among the art house cinema industry.

The Oppositional Lens: Minorities and Gender Issues

Building upon some of the themes and trends explored in the previous section, the final section of the book includes articles and interviews that zero in on the cinematic depictions of Central American racial and sexual minorities; issues of gender and representation; and the experiences and challenges faced by female and queer screenwriters, directors, and producers.

Analyzing the documentary film *Garifuna in Peril*, Jennifer Carolina Gómez Menjívar argues in chapter 12 that the intangible heritage and culture of the Afro-Indigenous Garifuna peoples, as acknowledged by UNESCO, strongly depends on the presence of their tangible heritage—that being the land and the sea along the northern Central American Caribbean coast. She explores the challenges that the Garifuna have faced amid settler colonialism, tourism, and the lack of any recognized title to the land. At the same time, the film draws attention to the role the land and the sea has played in the Garifuna past and present, as well as the importance of its sustainability for the future. The film calls attention to these people's struggles as they defend themselves from outside attempts to dispossess them of the land, sea, and ultimately, their culture.

In chapter 13, Arno Jacob Argueta traces the treatment of masculinity in Guatemalan films from the aforementioned *El silencio de Neto* to a number of twenty-first-century movies from a variety of genres. According to Argueta, films such as *La jaula de oro* (2013) and *Ixcanul* (2016) have strong female characters that challenge hegemonic, patriarchal, and violent masculinity. But this struggle against patriarchal masculinity is also present in a group of Guatemalan movies where male characters fail to ever achieve traditional masculinity—including several films by Hernández Cordón and others that exploit male stereotypes such as the slacker (*Puro mula*, Guatemala, 2011), the geek (*Ovnis en Zacapa*, Guatemala, 2015), or the artist (*Maquillaje*, Guatemala, 2013). Argueta claims that more often than not, the men in these films benefit from their position in the patriarchal structure instead of standing against it.

The book concludes by noting the growing and increasingly central role played by women in Central American film production and direction, as roughly half of the films being made in the region are women-helmed projects (Luna). As readers can observe from the names of the directors whose films are analyzed in this book, the leading scholars of this regional cinema, and the leadership roles in funding and promotional efforts, women have played a crucial role in the development of New Central American film and most likely will continue to do so. This salient feature of the region's film industry (unique among other large and small cinemas of the world) is explored in chapter 14 through interviews with directors Laura Astorga and Ishtar Yasin (Costa Rica), Gloria Carrión Fonseca (Nicaragua), and producer Pamela Guinea (Guatemala). Additionally, this chapter includes an interview with Guatemalan director Luis Fernando Midence over his gay-themed short films.

While diverse in their methodology and theoretical underpinnings, the essays in this edited collection mainly draw from cultural studies and film studies imbued with historical and sociological frameworks to carry out their analyses. Guided by the scholars who have made this book a reality, we now invite readers to embark on a journey across the Central America of the twenty-first century through the stories told in its courageous and innovative cinema.

Notes

1. Numbers based on 2021 data from the United Nations Population Fund, https://www.unfpa.org/world-population-trends. Central America consists of seven countries: Guatemala, El Salvador, Honduras, Nicaragua, Costa Rica, Panama, and Belize. The first five were part of Spain's General Captaincy of Guatemala during colonial times until independence in 1821. Panama was part of the Viceroyalty of New Granada and later belonged to Colombia until independence in 1903. Belize was a British territory and later a colony called British Honduras, until it gained independence in 1981.
2. A Costa Rica-Colombia coproduction, Hilda Hidalgo's *Del amor y otros demonios* (2010) is a good example of how this model has helped to propel Central American filmmaking. Based on the homonymous novel by Colombian Nobel Literature Laureate Gabriel García Márquez (also a cofounder of Los Baños film school), the film had a multimillion-dollar budget—something Central American cinema has seldom achieved during most of its history.
3. Co-editor Jared List flew on Delta from New York City to Omaha in early 2020 and was delightfully surprised that one of the movies available for free viewing was Costa Rican director Laura Astorga's *Princesas rojas* (2013). The recent availability of these additional venues for distribution and exposure of small cinema films challenges another colonial legacy within the film industry, which Shohat and Stam discuss: "While the Third World is inundated with North American films, TV series, popular music, and new programs, the First World receives precious little of the vast cultural production of the Third World" (31). The novelty of Central American films playing on Copa's and Delta's planes addresses this unequal access to viewership, reaching passengers returning home to the United States or Europe.
4. According to The Center for Justice and Accountability, more than 200,000 people were killed or disappeared during the Guatemalan civil war, 83 percent of them being Indigenous Maya ("Guatemala," https://cja.org/where-we-work/guatemala/). In El Salvador, over 75,000 civilians died at the hands of government forces ("El Salvador," https://cja.org/where-we-work/el%20salvador/).
5. See, for instance, Julia Medina's "Refracting Lenses on the Atlantic Coast of Nicaragua: Documenting Social Ecologies and Biospheres in *El ojo del tiburón* and *El canto de Bosawas*" (*Pushing Past the Human in Latin American Cinema*, edited by Carolyn Fornoff and Gisela Heffes, SUNY Press: 2021, pp. 281–304) and Liz Harvey-Kattou's "Performing for Hollywood: Coloniality and the Tourist Image in Esteban Ramírez's *Caribe/Caribbean* (2004)" (*Studies in Spanish & Latin American Cinemas*, vol. 15, no. 2, 2018, pp. 249–66).

Works Cited

A ojos cerrados. Directed by Hernán Jiménez, Miel y Palo Films, Costa Rica, 2010.

Agua fría de mar. Directed by Paz Fábrega, Tic Tac Productions/Temporal Films/Les Films du Requin, Costa Rica, 2010.

Alfaro Córdoba, Amanda. *Archipelagoes and Constellations: Political Economy and Aesthetics in Twenty-First Central American and Hispanic Caribbean Film. Dissertation, University College London, 2020.

Alfaro Córdoba, Amanda and Harvey-Kattou. "Central American cinema in the twenty-first century." *Studies in Spanish and Latin American Cinemas,* vol. 15, no. 2, 2018, pp. 137–141.

Alsino y el condor. Directed by Miguel Littín, INCINE, ICAIC, Productora Cinematográfica Latinoamericana de México, La Cooperativa Cinematográfica Costarricence, Nicaragua/Mexico/Cuba/Costa Rica, 1982.

Asesinato en El Meneo. Directed by Oscar Castillo, Producciones la Mestiza/Producciones OM, Costa Rica, 2001.

Atrás hay relámpagos. Directed by Julio Hernández Cordón, De Raíz Productions/Melindrosa Films, Mexico-Costa Rica, 2017.

Betancourt, Manuel. "'Parasite's Bong Joon Ho's List of Directors Who Will Define the 2020s Includes Guatemala's Jayro Bustamante." *Remezcla,* 26 February 2020, https://remezcla.com/film/bong-joon-ho-list-jayro-bustamante/. Accessed 17 September 2020.

Cabezas Vargas, Andrea. *Cinéma centraméricain contemporain (1970–2014): La construction d'un cinéma regional. Mémoires socio-historiques et culturelles.* Dissertation, Université Bordeaux Montaigne, 2015.

Cabezas Vargas, Andrea and Júlia González de Canales Carcereny. "Central American cinematographic aesthetics and their role in international film festivals." *Studies in Spanish and Latin American Cinemas,* vol. 15, no. 2, 2018, pp. 163–186.

Children of the Diaspora: For Peace and Democracy. Directed by Jennifer A. Cárcamo, United States/El Salvador, 2013.

Chomsky, Noam. *Turning the Tide: US Intervention in Central America and the Struggle for Peace.* Chicago: Haymarket Books, 2015.

Cómprame un revólver. Directed by Julio Hernández Cordón, Woo Films, Burning Blue, Mexico, 2018.

Cortés, María Lourdes. *La pantalla rota: Cien años de cine en Centroamérica.* Ciudad de México: Taurus, 2005.

———. *Fabulaciones del nuevo cine costarricense.* San José: Uruk Editores, 2016.

———. "Filmmaking in Central America: An overview." *Studies in Spanish & Latin American Cinemas,* vol. 15, no. 2, 2018, pp. 143–161.

———, ed. *Violencia, marginalidad y memoria en el cine centroamericano.* San José: Editorial de la U de Costa Rica, 2021.

Cortez, Beatriz and Alexandra Ortiz Wallner. "Producciones audiovisuales en Centroamérica: Introducción." *Istmo: Revista virtual de estudios literarios y culturales centroamericanos,* no. 13, 2006, http://istmo.denison.edu/n13/articulos/intro.html. Accessed 15 February 2020.

De la Fuente, Anna Marie. "Caribbean and Central American Films Flourish Despite Headwind." *Variety,* 7 April 2018, https://variety.com/2018/film/festivals/caribbean-central-american-films-flourish-iff-panama-1202745172/. Accessed 20 February 2020.

Del amor y otros demonios. Directed by Hilda Hidalgo, Alicia Films/CMO Producciones, Colombia/Costa Rica, 2009.

Durón, Hispano. "Rompiendo el silencio: Diez años de nuevo cine centroamericano (2001–2010)." *Revista Reflexiones*, vol. 91, no. 2, 2012, pp. 247–253.

El camino. Directed by Ishtar Yasin, Producciones Astarté/DART/Gedeon Programmes, Costa Rica, 2008.

El lugar más pequeño. Directed by Tatiana Huezo, Centro de Capacitación Cinematográfica/Foprocine, 2011.

El regreso. Directed by Hernán Jiménez, Miel y Palo Films, Costa Rica, 2012.

El retorno. Directed by A. F. Bertoni, Costa Rica, 1930.

El Salvador: Archivos perdidos del conflicto. Directed by Gerardo Muyshondt, El Salvador Films, El Salvador, 2016.

El silencio de Neto. Directed by Luis Argueta, Buenos Días, Guatemala, 1994.

Elsewhere. Directed by Hernán Jiménez, Evoke Productions, United States, 2019.

Entonces nosotros. Directed by Hernán Jiménez, Evoke Productions, LaLaLa Productions, Costa Rica/United States, 2016.

Ferman, Claudia. "Cine, comunicación audiovisual y participación política: Introducción." *Istmo: Revista virtual de estudios literarios y culturales centroamericanos,* no. 20, 2010, pp. 1–7.

Fumero, Patricia and María Lourdes Cortés. "Una mirada al cine centroamericano actual." *Istmo: Revista virtual de estudios literarios y culturales centroamericanos,* no. 36, 2018, pp. 1–4.

García Diego, Charo, editor. *Cine centroamericano y caribeño siglo XXI.* Sevilla: Extravertida Editorial, 2021.

Garifuna in Peril. Directed by Ali Allie and Rubén Reyes. Aban Productions, United States/Honduras, 2012.

Gasolina. Directed by Julio Hernández Cordón, Melindrosa Films/Buena onda América/Mediapro Producción Gabriel, Guatemala, 2007.

Gestación. Directed by Esteban Ramírez, Cinetel, Costa Rica, 2009.

Hands of Stone. Directed by Jonathan Jakubowicz, Fuego Films, United States/Panama, 2016.

Harvey-Kattou, Liz. "Performing for Hollywood: Coloniality and the Tourist Image in Esteban Ramírez's *Caribe/Caribbean* (2004.)" *Studies in Spanish & Latin American Cinemas,* vol. 15, no. 2, 2018, pp. 249–66.

Hasta el Sol tiene manchas. Directed by Julio Hernández Cordón, Melindrosa Films, Mexico/Guatemala, 2012.

Heredera del viento. Directed by Gloria Carrión, Caja de Luz, Nicaragua, 2017.

Historias del canal. Directed by Pinky Mon, Pituka Ortega-Heilbron, Abner Benaim, Luis Franco, Carolina Borrero, Pragda, Panama, 2014.

IFF Panamá. "IFF Panama Channel via Copa Airlines Promotes Latin American Cinema." 25 September 2019, https://www.iffpanama.org/en/iff-panama-channel-copa-airlines-promotes-latin-american-cinema. Accessed 20 February 2020.

Inczauskis, David published. *El cine hondureño: Arte, identidad y política.* Tegucigalpa: Editorial de la U Nacional Autónoma de Honduras, 2022.

Instituto Nacional de Estadística Guatemala. "Resultados del Censo 2018." 15 October 2021, https://www.censopoblacion.gt/. Accessed 27 January 2020.

Invasión. Directed by Abner Benaim, Ajimolido Films/Apertura Films, Panama, 2014.

Italia 90. Directed by Miguel Gómez, Italia 90 La Película S.A., Costa Rica, 2014.

Ixcanul. Directed by Jayro Bustamante, La Casa de Producción/Tu Vas Voir Productions, Guatemala, 2015.

King, John. *Magical Reels. A History of Cinema in Latin America*. New York: Verso, 2000.

La batalla del volcán. Directed by Julio López Fernández, Argos Comunicación/Cine murciélago/Trípode audiovisual, El Salvador, 2017.

La jaula de oro. Directed by Diego Quemada-Díez, Animal de Luz Films, Mexico, 2013.

La Llorona. Directed by Jayro Bustamante, El Ministerio de Cultura y Deportes de Guatemala/La Casa de Producción/Les Films du Volcan, Guatemala, 2019.

La palabra en el bosque. Directed by Carlos Henríquez Consalvi, Museo de la Palabra y la Imagen, El Salvador, 2011.

Las marimbas del infierno. Directed by Julio Hernández Cordón, Les Films du Requin/Melindrosa Films/Axolote Films, Guatemala, 2018.

La vida precoz y breve de Sabina Rivas. Directed by Luis Mandoki, FIDECINE, Mexico, 2012.

López, Ana M. "An 'Other' History: The New Latin American Cinema." *Resisting Images: Essays on Cinema and History*, edited by Robert Sklar and Charles Musser, Temple UP, 1990, pp. 308–330.

Los ofendidos. Directed by Marcela Zamora, Kino Glaz, El Salvador, 2016.

Los puños de una nación. Directed by Pituka Ortega-Heilbron, Hypatia Films, Panama, 2005.

Love Hard. Directed by Hernán Jiménez, Wonderland Sound and Vision, United States, 2021.

Luna, Ilana. "Women Rising: Central American Filmmaking for the 21st Century." 20 November 2017, Invited Lecture, University of Cincinnati.

Maikol Yordan de viaje perdido. Directed by Miguel Gómez, Audiovisuales LMD, 2014.

Maquillaje. Directed by Joel López Muñoz, Guatemala, 2014.

María en tierra de nadie. Directed by Marcela Zamora, Ruido, El Faro, I(dh)eas, El Salvador, 2011.

Medina, Julia. "Refracting Lenses on the Atlantic Coast of Nicaragua: Documenting Social Ecologies and Biospheres in *El ojo del tiburón* and *El canto de Bosawas*." *Pushing Past the Human in Latin American Cinema*, edited by Carolyn Fornoff and Gisela Heffes, SUNY Press: 2021, pp. 281–304.

Morazán. Directed by Hispano Durón, Fundaunpfilms, Honduras, 2017.

Orozco, Manuel. "Recent Trends in Central American Migration." *Inter-American Dialogue*, 14 May 2018, https://www.thedialogue.org/analysis/recent-trends-in-central-american-migration/. Accessed 14 July 2020.

Ovnis en Zacapa. Directed by Marcos Machado, Guatemala, 2015.

Palabras mágicas (para romper un encantamiento). Directed by Mercedes Moncada, Producciones Amaranta/Bambú Audiovisual, Mexico, 2012.

Pictures from a Revolution. Directed by Susan Meiselas, GMR Films, United States, 1991.

Presos. Directed by Esteban Ramírez, Cinetel/Ibermedia, Costa Rica, 2015.

Princesas rojas. Directed by Laura Astorga, Hol y Asociados/La Feria Producciones/Suécinema, Costa Rica, 2013.

Puro mula. Directed by Enrique Pérez Him, Best Picture System, Guatemala, 2011.

Rodríguez, Ileana. *Modalidades de memoria y archivos afectivos: Cine de mujeres en Centroamérica*. San José: Editorial de la U de Costa Rica, 2020.

Salas, Bértold. "Un hoy que se narra a la sombra del ayer. El cine costarricense y la inquietud por el tiempo." *Istmo: Revista virtual de estudios literarios y culturales centroamericanos*, no. 36, 2018, pp. 5–17.

Sánchez, Alexánder. "Falta de fondos obliga a Cinergia a suspender apoyos económicos para el cine regional." *La Nación*, 13 June 2015, https://www.nacion.com/viva/cine/falta-de-fondos-obliga-a-cinergia-a-suspender-apoyos-economicos-para-el-cine-regional/PZEN6CFPHFBOFOYUXQOVBZ3QXI/story/. Accessed 20 February 2020.

Sandoval García, Carlos. *No más muros: Exclusión y migración forzada en Centroamérica*. San José: Editorial de la U de Costa Rica, 2015.

Shohat, Ella, and Robert Stam. *Unthinking Eurocentrism: Multiculturalism and the Media*. London: Routledge, 2000.

Sin nombre. Directed by Cary Joyi Fukumaya, Primary Productions, Canana Films, Creando Films, United States/Mexico, 2009.

Temblores. Directed by Jayro Bustamante, La Casa de Producción/Tu Vas Voir Productions, Guatemala, 2019.

Te prometo anarquía. Directed by Julio Hernández Cordón, Interior13 Cine/FOPROCINE/Rohfilm, Mexico/Guatemala, 2016.

Tierney, Dolores. *New Transnationalisms in Contemporary Latin American Cinemas*. Edinburgh: Edinburgh UP, 2018.

Uno: La historia de un gol. Directed by Gerardo Muyshondt and Carlos Moreno, Antorcha Films, El Salvador/Colombia, 2010.

Violeta al fin. Directed by Hilda Hidalgo, Cacerola Films/Producciones La Tiorba, Costa Rica, 2017.

I

Postwar and Memory

1

"¿How Many Deaths?"

Official Silence, Subversive Memory, and Death's Performativity in Abner Benaim's documentary film *Invasión* (2014)

JARED LIST

> Documentary provides: a source of "counterinformation" for those without access to the hegemonic structures of world news and communications; a means of reconstructing historical events and challenging hegemonic and often elitist interpretations of the past; a mode of eliciting, preserving, and utilizing the testimony of individuals and groups who would otherwise have no means of recording their experience; an instrument for capturing cultural difference and exploring the complex relationship of self to other within as well as between societies; and finally, a means of consolidating cultural identifications, social cleavages, political belief systems, and ideological agendas.
> Julianne Burton, *The Social Documentary in Latin America*, pp. 6–7

Tracing its origins back to the 1950s and 1960s, New Latin American Cinema (NLAC) is a term that encompasses and describes filmic tendencies rooted in a "sociopolitical attitude," as Ana M. López notes in her essay "An 'Other' History: The New Latin American Cinema" (311). "That attitude can be summarized as a desire to change the social function of the cinema, to transform the Latin American cinema into an instrument for change and of consciousness-raising or *concientización*" (311). Other unifying characteristics of the movement include eschewing a Hollywood model of filmmaking and opting for other European models, such as neorealism, a cinematic genre focused on representing the under or unrepresented (López 312). López also explains that rather than being necessarily a pan-Latin American movement, NLAC uses the national as a point of departure and analysis. NLAC became a means to imagine and represent the nation as a collective body. In this sense, cultural renovation vis-á-vis the national was part of the movement's defining characteristics (López 314). López writes:

> That critical consciousness—a new subject position, a national culture in the process of becoming—will be simultaneously national and Latin American because of the many parallels among Latin American nations: Underdevelopment, dependence, colonialism are shared by all even though differentially at work in each society. (314)

As Michael T. Martin details, NLAC was a socially committed national and continental project that sought to counter foreign and capitalist intervention while at the same time support national and popular cultural production and expression (16).

In *La pantalla rota: Cien años de cine en Centroamérica,* María Lourdes Cortés synthesizes the history of Panamanian cinema. Its emergence coincided with NLAC, and as she describes, the first films produced during the 1970s exemplified many of values that NLAC espoused.

> As with almost all of Latin American cinema of the time, the model that was followed was Cuba's. This had caused a large impact on some of the Panamanian intellectuals, since it was the first time they saw an anti-establishment cinema, done with few resources and very distinct from what for all was "cinema," in other words, Hollywood. (Cortés 227; my translation)[1]

Born out of funds from the Torrijos government and an initiative of a group of individuals with little professional film experience (save Enoch Castillero's expertise), the Grupo Experimental de Cine Universitario (GECU) [University Experimental Film Group] first appeared in 1972. The first Panamanian films were documentaries that were political in content, often addressing questions over the canal, U.S. intervention and its presence, and the country's continued struggle toward sovereignty and autonomy. The first film *Canto a la patria que ahora nace* ["Song to the Homeland that Now is Born," (my translation), Panama, 1972] covered the student massacre of January 9, 1964, made nine years later with footage and images from the violent event (King 237; Cortés 226–230). As Cortés notes, "the anti-imperialist struggle was one of the fundamental themes of the GECU's production" (232; my translation).[2] This period of cinematic production in Panama was a push toward a national cinematographic presence that offered an alternative cinema to Hollywood's dominance and hegemony.

Considering the films produced in the new millennium in Panama, NLAC traits continue to appear. For example, Abner Benaim's recent films address sociopolitical topics in the country: films like *Invasión* (Panama, 2014), the focus of this chapter; *Panama Canal Stories* (Panama, 2014), which Carolina Sanabria analyzes in detail in her chapter in this volume; and *Rubén Blades Is Not My Name* (Panama, 2018). The films represent and explore national and cultural artifacts and figures that have given shape to the country's social, political, and cultural histories. To date, Benaim's preferred genre appears to be documentary, the majority of his films being such. This chapter examines one of Benaim's documentaries, *Invasión*, through a framework of (post)hegemony and documentary film. Such a theoretical framework seeks to analyze how Benaim using documentary film to bring to light subjugated histories through *affectivized,* personalized, and embodied memories. In this sense, the chapter aims to highlight how Benaim's film continues to follow the theoretical framework of NLAC to produce a socially committed film that is political in its content and address. Burton explains that "[s]ocially committed filmmakers embraced documentary approaches as their primary tool in the search to discover and define the submerged, denied, devalued realities of an intricate palimpsest of cultures and castes separated and conjoined by an arbitrary network of national boundaries" (6). Paying particular attention to the end of which documentary films are the means, Benaim's documentary 'discovers' and lays bare "the submerged, denied, devalued realities" that U.S. dominance and hegemony negated in its control and influence over the Central American nation. However, *Invasión* also imbues its political intent and content with affect, creating a sensorial relation between the film and its spectators that becomes a form of the content's transmission.

In his essay, "La guerra de los nombres" ["The War of Names"], Juan Carlos Mazariegos employs the testimony of Gilberto Ramírez, a Kaq'chikel Mayan who shares his experience during the Guatemalan civil war, to make the following argument. Mazariegos maintains that Gilberto is "a narration, a text, an enunciation that disseminates in the winding paths of the story; in many ways, Gilberto is a story, a *narrated* life" (15; my translation).[3] What the author underlines here in the quote is the discursivity of the subject. Gilberto has a story, and, at the same time, he is a *historia*. Here I use the term in Spanish given its double meaning: story and history, or, put differently, telling and remembering. He shares, through words and memories, his story. His name, Gilberto, is a means of tying *historia* with a subject. It historizes and defines him. Inevitably, this quote finds a way to come up in the courses I teach. I use it to exemplify the discursivity of the subject, and their positionality, or in other words, location of enunciation. Each name carries its story and makes an intervention at some moment during the history of the world, whether it be a forgotten, ignored, silenced, erased, or documented hi/story.

The name gives body to the hi/story. It is the axis of articulation that organizes hi/story, tying together experiences, memories, thoughts, and identity markers. In other words, the name is the title of a narrative, and, like a book, naming makes possible the hierarchization, subjugation, inclusion, and exclusion of hi/stories. Let's consider documentary films, for example. When we see traditional documentaries, the names of the interviewees accompany their image on the screen. Often, other qualifying information is included as well, conferring to the individual the authority to speak about a certain topic in the film. Including the interviewees' names and titles legitimizes them, locating them in a privileged or hierarchized space. Their words weigh more, as if to say that we as spectators should believe, or at least, pay attention to the interviewee. With their name and title, we can search for more information about the person, verifying the veracity of their claims. What happens then when a filmmaker makes the intentional decision of not including the interviewees' names and titles? In other words, how do we understand a story without a title? Or, does the story still have a title?

Abner Benaim's documentary *Invasión* leaves out the names. The film intentionally does not include the social actors' names and titles. Their image in front of the camera is sufficient. Such a decision is novel given the topic of the documentary. *Invasión* remembers and explores the U.S. invasion of Panama on December 20, 1989. What we as spectators see, hear, and perceive are the personal memories of the event. The film is structured in such a way that the memories are interwoven to give body to a collective hi/story—all recorded without any previous context but under a unifying thread. The articulation of personal memories narrates the event from the invasion until Noriega's surrender. In other words, the fragmented memories come together to form a historical narrative. However, in what ways are the memories framed? How do the social actors remember the invasion? And what intervention does the documentary make in understanding the invasion? In this section, I address these questions using the first part of the film contextualized from a framework of hegemony. I argue that the democratic filmic strategy of the filmmaker recuperates an intentionally silenced and forgotten past for ends of hegemony and dominance and, as such, the documentary articulates a multiplicity of submerged memories that fills a historical void, defying the official silence.

Death as Axis of Articulation

The concept of hegemony finds its roots in Antonio Gramsci's work, and some of the most salient contributions to the exploration of the concept come from Ernesto Laclau and Chantal Mouffe. In their work *Hegemony and Socialist Strategy: Towards a Radical Democratic Politics*, Laclau and Mouffe critique and expand the concept of hegemony. Departing from the notion of social class—a fundamental concept of Marxism—they break with the classificatory paradigm in order to expand the notion of hegemony. In its definition, social class, or to say, social determinism and reductionism, no longer carries the same weight that Gramsci had placed on social class; they go beyond social determinism and reductionism (Laclau and Mouffe 3). For them, they approach the concept from a post-structuralist and anti-essentialist framework that understands hegemony vis-à-vis discursivity. By hegemony we can understand the concept from its Gramscian formulation to refer to social consensus. Laclau and Mouffe expand the concept arguing that hegemony incorporates antagonistic forces that obey and accept an amalgamation of basic articulations. Hegemony predicates itself on an organized system of difference whose constitution emerges from elements and materializes into moments (Laclau and Mouffe 134–135).

This means that there are many ways to construct and maintain hegemony, what Laclau and Mouffe call articulatory practices. According to them, articulations come from relations between elements converted into moments. Before articulation, elements are differences without a discursive articulation; once articulated and converted into moments, they are discursive positions. Hegemony does not exist in a field full of moments because if that were the case, there would not be the possibility for articulatory practices, rather only repetitive acts in a system of fixed and well-defined identity relations (Laclau and Mouffe 136–137).

To give an example that better explains the articulatory practices, we can use the U.S. invasion of Panama, particularly related to the question of the number of deaths caused by the invasion. When we talk of the event, it is important to recognize that we are speaking of dominance, rather than hegemony. In the case of the U.S., the superpower invaded a sovereign nation to carry out its desire to overthrow Noriega and his government. The United States' attempts to exercise power and control through hegemony failed. Noriega ignored the Bush administration's calls to step down, which resulted in the military intervention. While there has been much published and investigated, a fundamental question still remains unanswered. How many deaths were there as a result of the invasion? This question becomes an articulation. To begin to estimate the number of deaths resulting from the invasion is to break with U.S. hegemony.

In his article "The End of Hegemony? Panama and the United States," Peter Sanchez explains that, through political strategies of dominance and hegemony, the United States has attempted to intervene and/or influence Panamanian politics for economic or geopolitical ends for more than a century (85). Sanchez offers that the history of Panama reveals the costs of the United States' presence in the country and notes the contradictions between North American discourses and their actions. He writes that "US foreign policy rhetoric is replete with allusions to democratic and economic development. In reality, US policy is motivated by a desire to acquire power and influence at virtually any cost" (Sanchez 85). What I want to underscore is the discourse of democracy that the United States often used to justify its influence and interventions in Panama. Such an example includes a resolution that the U.S. Senate approved two years before the invasion. In 1987, responding to Noriega's suppression of the opposition, the senate adopted a resolution that, among other points, declared that Panama should fulfill the international treaties on human rights and the restoration of democracy and constitutional guarantees in Panama (Carrier 16).[4]

During the invasion, the U.S. installed 27,000 soldiers in the Panama Canal Zone, and Panamanians saw 422 bombs fall in the first thirteen hours of the invasion (Carrier 26). There were deaths, but the quantity remains unknown because one of the strategies of the invasion was to hide the number. In their book *State Crime, the Media, and the Invasion of Panama*, Christina Jacqueline Johns and P. Ward Johnson share the various intents of the U.S. military and government of obfuscating international and local groups and organizations' attempts in finding out the number of deaths. Depending on the source, it is estimated that from 250 to 3,000 civilians were killed and more than 20,000 displaced Panamanians due to the destruction (Johns and Johnson 88–89). As Johns and Johnson detail, the U.S. military claimed that 250 Panamanian civilians were killed; yet, subsequent evidence and personal testimonies as detailed in the Independent Commission of Inquiry on the Invasion of Panama put the death toll much higher (87–89). Thirty years later, the figure is still unknown. Nonetheless, it is important to mention that the lack of knowledge was part of the U.S. plan. As the former U.S. attorney general Ramsey Clark had affirmed in 1990, not knowing the number of deaths was "a conspiracy of silence" (cited in Johns and Johnson 88). The United States' position was to hide the number of casualties in order to avoid more condemnation of the government's actions. They erased any official discourse, for example, confiscating hospitals' official logs where the dead arrived (John and Johnson 88). The United States wanted to write and control the historical narrative—one that goes something like this: they invaded the country to liberate the Panamanian people from a dictator and return the country to democracy. This narrative aims to uphold U.S. hegemony as opposed to U.S. domination or imperialism.[5]

Despite the attempt to frame the narrative as the U.S. acting benevolently in the interest of freedom and democracy, the U.S. could not erase the memories of Panamanians that said otherwise. In his book *Memoria, olvido, silencio: La producción social de identidades frente a situaciones límite* [Memory, Forgetting, Silence: Social Production of Identities Facing Limit Situations], Michael Pollak coins the term "framing of memory" (40).[6] By this, the term refers to the articulation of memory with national and ideological ends. Memory "can be the motive of dispute between various organizations" (Pollak 40; my translation).[7] In other words, it is an articulatory practice that emerges from antagonistic forces.[8] Using a Gramscian framework, Pollak explains that memory is constituted and organized depending on the work of intellectual and moral leadership. If we consider Laclau and Mouffe, we can say that memories before they are articulated and organized for hegemonic ends are elements, that is, floating differences that lack discursive organization and meaning. Pollak says that "memory is selective. Not everything is registered" (37; my translation).[9] Unregistered, private memories are elements. When memories are appropriated for ideological, national, and/or hegemonic ends, they materialize in moments, forming part of and contributing to the maintenance of an organized discursive system. And it is here where we see the historian's role in organizing memories in a historical narrative concordant with the hegemonic project to which the narrative is interpolated (Pollak 40–41). In Benaim's case, returning to the question "How many deaths?" is to play the role of historian. If silence and forgetting form part of the hegemonic power's plan, asking this question is to subvert such power. It reveals a disagreement between the memories of the event and the official non-discourse. Thus, as Pilar Calveiro argues in her essay "Los usos políticos de la memoria," that "memory is above all, an act . . . ," then in the film's case, it is a subversive act (377; my translation).[10]

Death's Performativity: Acts of Re-Membering

Strewn around the street, bloodied bodies, victims of the invasion, seared in the minds of the survivors—Benaim and his film crew seek to represent one of the scenes of the invasion some twenty years after. In the shot after the initial interviews, the spectators see the staging for the film crew's next scene. The plan is to record a scene that attempts to represent one of the invasion's results: the deaths. Conversing with his team and the social actors, Benaim explains that the actors are going to lie in the middle of the street in a plastic bag, a cadaver bag. The scene's goal is to reimagine the retrieval of the bodies. While the team is preparing the shot, the filmmaker tells his team that they need one more actor. His idea is to enlist the help of a man who he had previously seen in the area, offering him compensation for his effort. Upon talking to him, the man accepts Benaim's offer. As it turns out, the man was living in El Chorrillo at the time of the invasion. The neighborhood suffered extensive damage as a result of the U.S. intervention. Before filming the scene, Benaim asks the man about his experience in the neighborhood. One of the questions inevitably is if he knew the number of deaths in the area as a result of the invasion, to which the man replied that the streets were full of dead bodies, "from 27th street to 21st street" (*Invasión*).[11] After, asking if there were many deaths, the man responds "Uff," or in other words, yes, there were (*Invasión*).[12] The filmmaker continues his line of questioning, this time wanting to know how the dead bodies were collected from the streets. "They threw them," says the man making the movement of tossing a body up into a truck (*Invasión*).[13] And like that, the man's memory informs the re-creation of the scene. The film crew records the social actors inside plastic cadaver bags lying in the street. The scene has its purpose. How do they remember the deaths resulting from the invasion?

The film continues exploring this question. In the following shot, the former famous Panamanian boxer Roberto Durán shares his memory of the invasion and, during the interview, Benaim asks the same question he asked the man in the previous scene: "How many people died in the invasion?" (*Invasión*).[14] Durán's response: "Many, many people, man. There were people shot in the head, big holes like this. A father dead with his son in his arms. A whole family burned in a car" (*Invasión*).[15] Benaim, after his conversation with Durán, speaks with another witness, a former prisoner in the Modelo prison at the time of the invasion. From his cell on the third floor, he could observe the North American offensive from above. He explains that

> At 4:00 a.m. we broke the prison doors and got out. In all the streets we saw dead bodies torn to pieces because the tanks didn't have regular wheels, they were caterpillar tanks, and they passed over the dead bodies. The Americans brought out machines before dawn that would clean the ground and clear away all the flesh . . . I'd say we all presume,

that it was so journalists wouldn't take photos, surely. So there wouldn't be evidence of their butchery. (*Invasión*)[16]

When the filmmaker asks "how many people died in the invasion," the man laughs and responds "Oh, mister! Nobody has ever been able to get an exact number" (*Invasión*).[17]

There is a cut, and the documentary moves on to the next scene, another re-creation of bodies in the street. The actors are from the neighborhood, and their job is to lie down in the street without altering their appearance. This means that there is no use of props or costumes; they simply lie down. While we the spectators see how Benaim directs the scene, the camera captures another voice that attempts to modify the scene according to what he remembers of the event. In this case, for the man, the bodies are too close. They need to be spread out. In order to confirm the representation of the scene and after the bodies are repositioned, Benaim asks if they are now correctly placed, as if he were verifying the witness's memory.

If what we have in the previous examples are personal memories, the following one is as well. Nonetheless, the memory has an empirical aspect to it. As viewers, we listen to the testimony of one of the forensic employees—perhaps a pathologist—in the morgue of an unidentified hospital. The witness shares his experiences during the first two days of the invasion. He had been present in the morgue and in those two days, he counted 480 cadavers. Ultimately, he would calculate that 800 bodies passed through the morgue. He had been keeping track of each cadaver in a notebook, but his efforts were in vain. In the notebook, "[a]ll those pages had been ripped out" from the notebook (*Invasión*).[18] The other unrelated pages were left untouched, he explains.

What we can take from these scenes is the following. Firstly, throughout the film, no name or descriptor introduces any of the social actors. All are in effect nameless and without any official title. Previously, I named the boxer because he is a famous Panamanian, but Benaim does not identify him in the film. People from different social classes, neighborhoods, races, and economic situations are represented. Nonetheless, the film minimizes the differences, as I argue, for democratic ends. This means that memories are not relegated, negated, or disqualified as a result of exterior factors. In the documentary, all voices carry the same weight and validity. This fact is important given the relationship between power and memory. The filmmaker avoids hierarchized historization. In Víctor Hugo Acuña's *Centroamérica: Filibusteros, estados, imperios y memorias*, he writes about "the multiplicity of memory," that is, official memories, dominant memories, subjugated memories, and silenced memories (190; my translation).[19] In other words, Acuña examines the articulation between power and memory. Benaim seeks to avoid such an articulation. As he says in his film, "My film is not really about what happened during the invasion, but how it is remembered" (*Invasión*).[20] The film is careful to avoid privileging certain memories. There are no dominant memories or official memories, and, in this sense, we see a democratization of memory—memories of the *demos*.

The series of interviews with the social actors are relational or intersectional histories. For Acuña, these two types describe approaches to historiography. The relational approach examines the interconnections and interactions between contexts, memories, and histories. Intersectional historiography, a form of relational history, approaches the study of history from its intersections, exploring the "processes of production of historical phenomenon that are only intelligible as a result of the intersections that transcend national spaces" (Acuña 150; my translation).[21] Both relational histories and intersectional histories have the articulations of memories and histories as the object of study. In *Invasión*, the filmmaker and the crew frame interviewees' memories in such a way that we as viewers see and read a narrative that contradicts the United States' one.

However, it is important to note that the film's narrative comes from the intersections between the witnesses' testimonies over the number of dead. Alone, the memory's veracity is difficult to prove, but the iterative character of the documentary through the repetitious inquiry over the number of casualties constructs a believable narrative bolstered by corroboration between the various voices. According to the multiple memories, yes, there were many deaths. Such a declaration reveals a disagreement between the official history and the private, non-official histories. This takes us to my second point.

Secondly, the documentary supports the notion that dominant memories and hegemonic memories do not necessarily correspond. Acuña explains that dominant memories can circulate in the public sphere, such as, in schools and the media, and in these domains, there exists a particular version of history (204). However, in private or informal settings, there are other versions of history. In the testimony of the interviewees there is a consensus over the costs of human life. In place of the official silence imposed by the state, the agreement between the testimonies provides, on one hand, a story; they break a silence. And, on the other hand, they establish an alternative hegemonic history. As Acuña argues, memory is an articulation of memories and forgetting (218). This is where the question of documentary as a means for hegemony enters into the equation through its role in supporting, resisting, and constructing hegemony through performativity. As an "entrepreneur of memory"—a concept developed by Elizabeth Jelin—the filmmaker has the capacity to reveal and combine memories through the filming and editing process (33–34). Benaim recognizes this when he explains in the film that he is participating in the construction of the narrative as a filmmaker. He states: "I'm portraying everyone's truth. Everyone has a truth. Even if that truth is a lie, I accept it anyway. I cannot be completely objective because I'm deciding what to film. I do want to let something of my personal view come through. But my main intention is to let everyone have their say, telling their own little piece of the story" (*Invasión*).[22] Pollak explains that testimonial and documentary film is an important tool in the intervention and disposition of collective and national memory (28).[23] Not only is the documentary a performance of memory in its circulation in the public sphere, but also it is performative through Benaim's objective of the *mise-en-scene* of the witnesses' testimonies. The last scene of the film is the memory-based re-creation of the invasion. Benaim does not attempt to go to the historical archive to re-present the past. The witnesses and their memories are the archive and the raw material for the film.

What Benaim does is capture and then frame their memories, and, in this sense, the filmmaker is an entrepreneur of memory. Pollak explains that "the work of framing memory has its professionalized actors, [its] professionals of history . . ." (26; my translation).[24] We can come to two conclusions from this quote in relation to this chapter's axis of analysis. Firstly, Pollak's quote highlights memory's performativity (and discursivity). The professional actors (for example historians, governments, military officials, history's winners) construct 'official' or dominant histories. However, in the example of *Invasión*, they are not professional actors (in both senses of the word), and, through their memories, we the spectators, come to understand and see another history represented, another articulation that seeks to unearth a silenced history: the number of deaths caused by the U.S. invasion of Panama in 1989.

Beyond Representation: Affect and Embodied Memories

Returning to the concept of hegemony, Nicholas Thoburn argues that hegemony as a concept no longer describes current political realities given its predilection for class as the central organizing axis of the social and its failure to take into account other phenomena that determine or *affect* the social and the political. For him, theorists of hegemony have failed to register the role affect has in the relationship between the self and other in the realm of the social and the cultural. Put simply, economic reductionism and determinism no longer adequately describe the organization of the political. Furthermore, rather than representational discursivity that characterizes communication and human interaction, he argues that communication is characterized "by simultaneity, patterns and pulsions that configure relations directly" (Thoburn 84). By this, he refers to the role that affect plays not only with regards to the self and corporality but also with relationality and power. "Power as the social modulation of affect can also be seen in the field of work . . ." (Thoburn 86). By affect, he defines it (taking into account Brian Massumi's work) as "an experience of intensity" (Thoburn 84).[25] This approach to understanding the political and social operates on a global macroscale, at a level of a population, rather than a micro or individual scale. One of his criticisms of hegemony is that it does not account for the global character of the social, the economic, and the political (Thoburn 88).

Rather, Thoburn argues that, in place of a "single plane of institution of the social" with cultural studies, cultural studies scholars should examine power and its social production with a "mesh—a 'mechanosphere'—of global social arrangements of production" (82). Such a suggestion appears to dovetail with Laclau and Mouffe's proposal of elements converted into moments along nodal points in articulatory practices. They leave open the sources of nodal points, moving beyond economic determinism. For them, hegemonic formations are predicated upon antagonism and, as social and political spaces, these formations hinge on the nodal points edified from elements converted into moments (Laclau and Mouffe 136). What they do here is take Gramsci's concept and extend it beyond class as the master signifier. Within the hegemonic formation, consensus over basic articulations is what holds the group together. In this sense, Laclau and Mouffe's formulation of hegemony allows for what Thoburn proposes within the field of cultural studies, understanding production with the context of power and culture through "rich social, technical, economic and affective relations" (Thoburn 80).

As a cultural artifact, Benaim's film uses the number of deaths as the axis of articulation, or nodal point, upon which the social, affective, and cinematographic relations rest. Unarticulated, the social actors' memories of the deaths lack a hegemonic anchor. Laclau and Mouffe maintain that hegemony is a "*type of political relation*" [their emphasis] (141). It is not foundational, meaning that hegemony does not come first. Rather it emerges through the antagonistic forces—forces whose existence depends on its negative—and coalesces into "an organized system of differences" (Laclau and Mouffe 135). Thus, given what Laclau and Mouffe state, how can we understand the relationship between the social actors themselves and the filmmaker? How is the relationship political and (counter)hegemonic? *Invasión* lays bare antagonistic forces that surround the U.S. invasion, and rather than attempt to address the morality and justification of the invasion head on like *The Panama Deception* does, it uses metonym and affect to construct an organized system of difference articulated upon the number of deaths and memories of the social actors. In this way, Benaim becomes an entrepreneur of hegemony, in this case, counterhegemony, as he, within planes of discursivity and affect, constructs a counternarrative that challenges the United States' version of the death toll from the invasion.

Laclau and Mouffe recognize the metonymical nature of hegemony. For them, "its effects always emerge from a surplus of meaning from an operation of displacement" (Laclau and Mouffe 141). They go on to give examples such as religious organizations and trade unions whose charges do not necessarily include community organization but end up doing so anyway (Laclau and Mouffe 141). Such dislocations, for the political theorists, are "essential to any hegemonic practice . . ." (Laclau and Mouffe 142). We might add cinematography to that list of examples. Cinematic production as a craft does not necessitate forays into the political and the social; however, frequent dislocations occur where film directly addresses the two domains. Such is the example of *Invasión*. In this way, the film exemplifies one of the functions of film and documentary, as we have seen in NLAC.[26]

However, we note two metonymic hegemonic dislocations, one being the former example of cinematography, and the other, found in the content and form, the democratic, repetitive focus on the number of deaths in the film. The deaths are an example of metonymy. They are paradoxically the dislocation from the political and, at the same time, the location of the political. The deaths stand in place for U.S. intervention and dominance. If the U.S. sought to hide the evidence and minimize the reporting of the number of casualties to help justify its "needed" intervention to unseat Noriega, (and in turn, help maintain any semblance of U.S. hegemony that remained in Panama after the intervention), then focusing simply on the deaths and the violent nature of the invasion and giving attention to the number of deaths dislocates into a (counter)hegemonic practice. In this sense, there is a surplus of meaning in the deaths that metonymically represent U.S. dominance and, at the same time, the deaths articulate an axis of counterhegemony. However, how can we understand different theoretical understandings of hegemony within the context of the film and within the cultural studies debate? Examining the documentary's form helps us understand the debate between the two positions.

Rather than employ the expository mode of documentary film where so-called experts and other qualified individuals speak of the details surrounding an issue or an event, much like what *Panama Deception* does, Benaim follows more of participatory, reflexive, and performative modes of documentary. Instead of emphasizing who is telling the story or sharing the memories, it is the embodied memory that is more important. The memories' retellings challenge the official narrative regarding the death toll that the U.S. and Panamanian governments circulated. The participatory, reflexive, and performative modes possibilitate another transmission of sorts, a transdiscursive one of affect. The embodied memories are fundamental in this transmission. The social actors share their stories and share something beyond that. They share a phantasmagorical loss that haunts the viewers.

For example, in a series of scenes, Benaim interviews a mother and her daughter who appear to be owners of the Gran Hotel Soloy. They both recount their experiences with the invasion. Counting dollar bills behind the desk, the employee next to the daughter fell. She had been shot in the head by a bullet from outside. A bullet had passed through the daughter's shoulder. She recounts the scene, seeing the woman next to her alive counting bills and, in an instance, fall dead, experiencing a gunshot wound herself, trying to hide the magnitude of the moment from her mother who was there, trying to keep from her mother that she had been shot herself. For the viewers, the moment of this phantasmagorical loss comes through the hypothetical situation that would have changed the course of events. "We were counting 25 dollars in one-dollar bills. We were on 23. Just two dollars later and we would have been walking towards the bar" (*Invasión*).[27] Such a statement haunts viewers. The meaning goes beyond its discursivity, a surplus that escapes meaning. The hypothetical here addresses the precarity that we all live. Two bills later, Cecilia would have lived. Two bills later, the daughter would not have the scars of the invasion on her shoulder. The scene apprehends the fragility of life and the omnipresent chance of death. The embodied memory and its telling, as opposed to mere discursivity and textuality, opens up the possibility of transmission of affect, despite the lack of liveness and immediacy in the recorded image. As Jon Beasley-Murray explains, "Affect indicates the power of a body (individual or collective) to affect or be affected by other bodies" (*Posthegemony* xi). The intensity of the "what if" moment may be charged with affective flows that affect the viewers.[28]

Perhaps, through this example, this is where we note the limitations of Laclau and Mouffe's formulation of hegemony. While their exploration of the concept moves hegemony beyond its suture to class, their analysis does not appear to take into account that which is beyond discursivity, for example, affect. As I summarized before, one of their main postulates in the formation of hegemonic practices is the conversion of elements into moments. Let's remember that elements lack a discursive articulation that, once articulated discursively, they become moments. Affect always transcends discursivity. It can be summoned, channeled, and modulated, but its essence cannot be put into words.[29] Thus, affect can never converge into moments. It is never discursively articulated. Nonetheless, affect can be channeled for hegemonic ends—the military flyovers at sporting events, the tombs of the unknown soldiers, for example.[30] Hegemonic practices can account for affect as a means of articulation. Affect's articulation is tenuous, fleeting, unpredictable, surprising, and even haphazard; its transmission is never certain.[31] What may be an affective experience for some, may not be for others. Thus, what Laclau and Mouffe appear to miss in their analysis is the role the non-discursive plays in the formation of hegemony. In her book *Coming to Our Senses*, Dierdra Reber coins the term "feeling soma" in relation to knowledge as a process of "coming to our senses" (xiv). By this, she means "a coming into 'reason' by the way of the nonrational, in which feelings and togetherness become the new basis of forming knowledge and political action aligned with fundamentally horizontal—democratic—moral principles of equality and well-being" (Reber xiv). In other words, "coming to our senses" can emerge as an axis of articulation, one that can manifest in films like *Invasión*.

Conclusion

As a continuation of strategies characteristic of New Latin American Cinema, *Invasión* provides a counternarrative, a counterhegemonic narrative to the U.S.-imposed official narrative. It is a socially committed film. However, what the film adds that goes beyond NLAC is its use of affect and embodied memory to channel that message. In that sense, the documentary film captures the articulation between meaning and affect, between the representable and the unrepresentable, between the articulable and the unarticulable, and between the image and its (affective) address. The *concientización* that was present as an objective of NLAC, in *Invasión,* now includes a *concientización* of affect, recognizing and apprehending the gaps in intelligibility and how those intensities impinge upon us as viewers. Benaim's choice of embodied, dehierarchized memories to transmit hi/stories representationally and sensorially to produce or provoke sensorial and discursive articulations between the film and the viewers captures the counterhegemonic intents of NLAC while, at the same time, imbuing the film with an affective content that posthegemony holds important. Thus, to reflect on the title of this book *The Rise of Central American Film in the Twenty-First Century,* part of my argument is that in the twenty-first century, what is new, or novel, is the use of affect as a cinematic strategy in conveying and feeling the film's content.

Notes

1. Original quote: "Como casi todo el cine latinoamericano de la época, el modelo que se siguió fue el de Cuba. Éste había causado un gran impacto en algunos intelectuales panameños, ya que era la primera vez que veían un cine contestario, hecho con pocos recursos y muy distinto de lo que para todos era el 'cine,' es decir, Hollywood" (Cortés 227).
2. "la lucha antiimperialista fue el tema fundamental de la producción del GECU" (232).
3. "una narración, un texto, una enunciación que se disemina en los vericuetos del relato; en muchos sentidos, Gilberto es una historia, *una* vida narrada" (15).
4. It is important to highlight here that the United States, in the aforementioned resolution, worried for Panama's democracy, that is, the idea that the people, *demos*, have the power to elect the person to govern. If the U.S. worried about the lack of civic representation and voice in the Panamanian government, one might deduce that the loss of Panamanian life would be even worse. Thus, an invasion where innocent Panamanians were to lose their lives would not correspond with the perceived resolution and preoccupation of the United States.
5. For an analysis of other Panamanian films that address the long and complex history of U.S. intervention in Panama, from the construction of the Canal to the 1989 invasion, see Mauricio Espinoza's chapter in this volume.
6. "encuadramiento de la memoria" (Pollak 40).
7. "puede ser motivo de disputa entre varias organizaciones" (Pollak 40).
8. Pollak explains that memory national, for being seemingly clearly organized is an "object of dispute" ["objeto de disputa"] and a terrain where conflict over what is remembered and what is not remains constant (37). Pollak's claim illustrates well the antagonism that gives way to hegemony.
9. "la memoria es selectiva. No todo queda registrado" (Pollak 37).
10. "la memoria es sobre todo acto . . ." (377).
11. ". . . casi de la veintisiete, toda la calle, hasta la veintiuna por la calle" (*Invasión*). All of the English translations come directly from the film's English subtitles.
12. The English subtitle translates the "Uff" as yes.
13. "Los tiraban" (*Invasión*).
14. "Cuánta gente murió en la invasión?" (*Invasión*).
15. "Bastante, hermano, bastante. Hay tipo que tenía un tiro en la cabeza aquí . . . Padre con su hijo en mano; muere con su hijo en mano. Una familia entera en un carro quemado" (*Invasión*).
16. "A las cuatro de la mañana rompimos las puertas y salimos. En toda la esquina de límite que llaman del paso para la zona para acá vimos cadáveres despedazados en la calle porque hay unas tanquetas que no son de llantas sino de arruga, pasaban y pasaban así que . . . Los señores norteamericanos antes de amanecer trajeron unas máquinas que lavaban el piso y se tragaban la carne por la máquina . . . Digo yo presumimos nosotros que era con el fin de que los periodistas no tomaran esas fotos, pues, que los periodistas no tomaran de esta carnicería que había allí" (*Invasión*).
17. "cuánta gente murió en la invasión;" "¡Ay, señor! Nunca nadie ha podido hacer un cálculo preciso" (*Invasión*).

18. "Todas esas páginas se habían arrancado" (*Invasión*).
19. "la multiplicidad de la memoria" (Acuña 190).
20. "Como esta película que estoy haciendo no trata realmente de lo que pasó en la invasión sino la memoria de la invasión" (*Invasión*).
21. "procesos de producción de fenómenos históricos que son solamente inteligibles como resultado de entrecruces que trascienden espacios nacionales" (Acuña 150).
22. "Esta es la manera que estoy haciendo. Cada uno está diciendo su verdad y si su verdad es así, una mentira, pues esa es su verdad. Yo la acepto así. No planeo ser objetivo en el sentido de que no puedo ser objetivo en el momento que decido filmar éste y no otro. Y quiero hacer algo que digamos que también tiene mi parte..." (*Invasión*).
23. In the scene where Benaim shares his intentions, he is conversing with Rubén Blades (again, there is no introduction on the screen of the singer as with the other social actors). Blades shares another important aspect that speaks to the affective qualities of the film. The singer states: "I think one of the most important parts of what you're doing is giving voice to the pain that was there" (*Invasión*).
24. "Este trabajo de encuadramiento de la memoria tiene sus actores profesionalizados, profesionales de la historia..." (Pollak 26).
25. For readings over affect, consult Laura Podalsky's excellent overview of the concept in her book *The Politics of Affect and Emotion in Contemporary Latin American Cinema: Argentina, Brazil, Cuba, and Mexico* (2012), Teresa Brennan's groundbreaking work *The Transmission of Affect* (2004), Brian Massumi's *Politics of Affect* (2015), Eugenie Brinkema's *The Forms of the Affects* (2014), and Dierdra Reber's *Coming to Our Senses: Affect and An Order of Things for Global Culture* (2016), or Melissa Gregg and Gregory J. Seigworth's *The Affect Theory Reader* (2010).
26. The epigraph of this chapter—the quote from Burton—speaks to the role that documentary film plays in relation to the political and the social.
27. "Estábamos contando 25 dólares en dólares. Íbamos por el 23. Si hubiese sido dos dólares más, ya habríamos estado caminando hacia el bar" (*Invasión*).
28. In Brian Massumi's essay "The Future Birth of the Affective Fact: The Political Ontology of Threat," he examines the relationship between the double conditional and affect. I use the notion of the hypothetical thinking with Massumi's text on preemptive politics, the double conditional, and affect.
29. Again, here I am thinking with Massumi's essay "The Future Birth of the Affective Fact: The Political Ontology of Threat." He writes about the ways in which affect is modulated through political discourse (868).
30. See Patrick Colm Hogan's text *Understanding Nationalism* (2009) for a further explanation of the role affect, rituals, and performance plays in fomenting nationalism. In his text, he discusses the affective power of standing at the tomb of the unknown soldier or the military flyover.
31. In her book *The Forms of the Affects*, Eugenie Brinkema's definition informs my understanding of affect. She writes this of affect: "what undoes, what unsettles, that thing I cannot name, what remains resistant..." (Brinkema 264).

Works Cited

Acuña, Víctor Hugo. *Centroamérica: Filibusteros, estados, imperios y memorias*. Kindle ed.: Editorial Costa Rica, 2014.
Beasley-Murray, Jon. *Posthegemony*. Minneapolis: U of Minnesota P, 2010.
Brennan, Teresa. *The Transmission of Affect*. Ithaca: Cornell UP, 2004.
Brinkema, Eugenie. *The Forms of Affects*. Kindle ed.: Duke UP, 2014.
Burton, Julianne. "Toward a History of Social Documentary in Latin America." *The Social Documentary in Latin America*, edited by Julianne Burton, U of Pittsburgh P, 1990, pp. 3–30.
Canto a la patria que ahora nace. Directed by Enoch Castillero y Pedro Rivera, Grupo Experimental de Cine Universitario (GECU), Panama, 1972.
Calveiro, Pilar. "Los usos políticos de la memoria." *Sujetos sociales y nuevas formas de protesta en la historia reciente de América Latina*, edited by Gerardo Caetano, CLASCO, 2006.
Carrier, Matthieu. "Ousting Noriega from Power: Setting the Stage for a Crisis." *Global Media Perspectives on the Crisis in Panama*, edited by Howard H. Hensel and Nelson Michaud, Ashgate Publishing, 2011, pp. 13–34.
Cortés, María Lourdes. *La pantalla rota: Cien años de cine en Centroamérica*. Ciudad de México: Taurus, 2005.
Gregg, Melissa, and Gregory J. Seigworth, editors. *The Affect Theory Reader*. Kindle ed.: Duke UP, 2009.
Hogan, Patrick Colm. *Understanding Nationalism: On Narrative, Cognitive Science, and Identity*. Columbus: Ohio State UP, 2009.
Invasión. Directed by Abner Benaim, Apertura Films, Panama, 2014.
Jelin, Elizabeth. *State Repression and the Labors of Memory*. Translated by Judy Rein and Marcial Godoy-Anativia, Minneapolis: U of Minnesota P, 2003.
Johns, Christina Jacqueline, and P. Ward Johnson. *State Crime, the Media, and the Invasion of Panama*. Westport: Praeger, 1994.
King, John. *Magical Reels: A History of Cinema in Latin America*. London: Verso, 2000.
Laclau, Ernesto, and Chantel Mouffe. *Hegemony and Socialist Strategy: Towards a Radical Democratic Politics*. London: Verso, 2001.
López, Ana M. "An 'Other' History: The New Latin American Cinema." *Resisting Images: Essays on Cinema and History*, edited by Robert Sklar and Charles Musser, Philadelphia: Temple UP, 1990, pp. 308–330.
Martin, Michael T. "The Unfinished Social Practice of the New Latin American Cinema: Introductory Notes." *New Latin American Cinema, Volume One, Theory, Practices, and Transcontinental Articulations*, edited by Michael T. Martin, Wayne State UP, 1997, pp. 15–29.
Massumi, Brian. "The Future Birth of the Affective Fact: The Political Ontology of Threat." *The Affect Theory Reader*, edited by Gregory J. Seigworth and Melissa Gregg, Duke UP, 2009.
Mazariegos, Juan Carlos. "La guerra de los nombres: Una historia de la rebelión, el genocidio y el ojo del poder soberano en Guatemala." *Glosas nuevas sobre la misma guerra:*

Rebelión campesina, poder pastoral y genocidio en Guatemala, edited by Clara Arenas Bianchi, AVANCSO, 2009, pp. 1–68.

Panama Canal Stories. Directed by Abner Benaim, Carolina Borrero, Luis Franco Brantley, Pinky Mon, Pituka Ortega-Heilbron, Hypatia Films and Manglar Films, Panama, 2014.

Panama Deception. Directed by Barbara Trent, Docurama, United States, 1992.

Podalsky, Laura. *The Politics of Affect and Emotion in Contemporary Latin American Cinema: Argentina, Brazil, Cuba, and Mexico.* New York: Palgrave Macmillan, 2012.

Pollak, Michael. *Memoria, olvido, silencio: La producción social de identidades frente a situaciones límite.* Translated by Christian Gebauer, Renata Oliveira Rufino and Mariana Tello. Buenos Aires: Ediciones Al Margen, 2006.

Reber, Dierdra. *Coming to Our Senses: Affect and An Order of Things for Global Culture.* New York: Columbia UP, 2016.

Sanchez, Peter M. "The End of Hegemony? Panama and the United States." *International Journal on World Peace,* vol. 19, no. 3, Sept. 2002, pp. 57–89.

Rubén Blades Is Not My Name. Directed by Abner Benaim, Apertura Films, Panama, 2018.

Thoburn, Nicholas. "Patterns of Production: Cultural Studies after Hegemony." *Theory, Culture & Society,* vol. 24, no. 3, 2007, pp. 79–94.

2

Illuminating from the Darkness

Transitional Justice, Testimonies and Archive in Salvadoran Postwar Documentary (2011–2018)

Lilia García Torres

After eleven years (1980–1991) of armed conflict between the Salvadoran government and the Farabundo Martí National Liberation Front (FMLN), and after twenty-two months of dialogue mediated by the United Nations, the conflict came to an end with the signing of the Peace Accords in 1992.[1] Although the Accords contemplated the end of militarism (one of the key demands with which the conflict began), as well as an agrarian reform and the review of credits for the agricultural sector, throughout the conflict, the FMLN went through a process of de-radicalization,[2] which was reflected in the agreements, but did not include structural changes in the political and economic system.[3] The Accords strengthened the judicial and legislative branches of the state, added guarantees for the respect of human rights, established the formation of a Truth Commission, incorporated the FMLN as a political force with the right to participate in elections, created a civilian disarmament agenda, and conceived social reinsertion programs for former combatants.

On March 5, 1993, the Truth Commission, within the framework of the National Reconciliation Law, released the report "De la locura a la esperanza" ["From Craziness to Hope"], in which it pointed out patterns of violence perpetrated by the Salvadoran government (responsible for 91 percent of the war's victims) and the guerrillas. The report highlighted the importance of recognizing the violence perpetrated by those social actors as a fundamental step for reconciliation, and issued immediate recommendations (removal from office, public disqualifications, and some reforms). It also proposed to eradicate the structural causes linked to the acts of violence, to carry out institutional reforms to prevent the recurrence of these events, and to create measures aimed at national reconciliation, including material and moral reparations, as well as the establishment of a Truth and Reconciliation Forum (Comisión de la verdad 244–258). Although initially the National Reconciliation Law contemplated the prosecution of certain crimes given their severity, five days after the report was released, the Legislative Assembly approved the General Amnesty Law. The amnesty allowed for impunity, while creating a blockage to justice and reparations (Moreno 184); it also shaped the way in which justice and knowledge of the past were culturally interpreted as a threat to social peace.

The precarious conditions for the economic reinsertion of ex-combatants, the implementation of neoliberal measures starting in 1993 with the ambiguous acceptance of the FMLN, the non-binding nature of the Truth Commission's report, and the General Amnesty Law proposed by the government generated disappointment with the revolutionary process—which created a fertile ground for migration and postwar violence. Both Esteban Loustaunau's and María Lourdes Cortés's chapters in this volume examine cinematic representations of Central American migration. Loustaunau analyzes one of Marcela Zamora's documentaries, *María en tierra de nadie* (El Salvador, 2011), which addresses migration from El Salvador.

Under the dominant ideology, injustice, historical ignorance, and oblivion were normalized for the greater part of the population, especially those who were not direct victims or were not linked to them; the past was viewed with indifference. Despite this, a sector of the population did not stop fighting for truth and justice and kept it latent. It was not until June 2016, during the second term of the FMLN government that, facing international pressure, the Supreme Court of Justice of El Salvador repealed the General Amnesty Law. It was evident that peace could not be consolidated if the transitional justice process was not completed (Moreno 187–188); it was necessary to guarantee access to truth and justice, to recognize grievances, to generate reparative actions for victims, and to certify mechanisms to avoid the repetition of violence.

In the review process of the state atrocities of the recent past, according to Pilar Calveiro, three moments are constituted while holding trials leads to the establishment of legal truth: that of "testimony as a break in silence, memory as the plot of the stories of resistance and history as a structuring text of some truth, whether official or not" (68). In El Salvador, the testimonies that denounced state violence became relevant at the end of the 1970s and the beginning of the 1980s (embodied in written and audiovisual form) and did not cease to be present in the postwar period. The construction of historical memory has been a constant at least since the founding of the Museo de la Palabra y la Imagen [Museum of the Word and the Image] (MUPI) in 1996. As for the conflict's incorporation into history education, it must be said that there are few references to the conflict in textbooks of primary and secondary education. Furthermore, any trial for crimes against humanity is still a distant horizon. In El Salvador, the dispute over memory is a living process, present in various areas such as the media, some tending to reinforce cultural hegemony and, others, such as the case of the committed documentary, giving space to "testimony as a rupture of the be quiet" (Calveiro 68).

In this sociopolitical context, four documentaries, all framed within the transitional justice process and produced by Salvadorans or people who have lived in that country for decades, emerged, proposing a dialogue between the armed conflict and the present.[4] They are *La palabra en el bosque,* directed by Carlos Henríquez Consalvi and Jeffrey Gould and produced in 2011 (El Salvador/United States), *El Salvador, archivos perdidos del conflicto,* directed by Gerardo Muyshondt in 2014 (El Salvador), *Los ofendidos,* directed by Marcela Zamora, in 2016 (El Salvador), and *La batalla del volcán,* directed by Julio López, in 2018 (El Salvador). What narrative about the conflict and postconflict do these documentaries offer? Who revisits the immediate past—and how and why? What dialogues are established from the present?

The Documentary Corpus

La palabra en el bosque addresses, in almost an hour, the political process of the peasants in the Department (province) of Morazán, who, from the biblical study they carried out on the farm El Castaño during 1973, were linked with liberation theology. This relationship led them to reflect on their political, economic, and social reality, and to organize themselves into Christian Base Communities (CEB), where in addition to living a process of concientización, they experienced collectivity. A year later, Rafael Arce Zablah, a member of the People's Revolutionary Army (ERP), contacted the priest Miguel Ventura, who promoted liberation theology in Morazán, to invite him to structure a political-military movement with the CEBs. Ventura put him in contact with peasants. Some initially accepted; others were later attracted to the movement after their disappointment of the 1977 electoral process and gradually joined the Ligas Populares 28 de Febrero (ERP's mass front) after the 1979 coup d'état and the ensuing increased repression. The documentary ends with images of the commemoration of the nineteenth anniversary of the

Peace Accords, in which attendees lit candles as an offering while a roll call of the fallen was taken.

El Salvador, archivos perdidos del conflicto (*El Salvador, Lost Archives from the Conflict*) is a documentary series divided into three parts which makes a thematic-chronological tour of the conflict, with a total running time of four and a half hours. The first chapter deals with the causes and emergence of political-military organizations, the foundation of the FMLN, as well as the process of radicalization and polarization of society in 1980. The second part is dedicated to the 1981 offensive, the creation of the right-wing Nationalist Republican Alliance (ARENA) party, the heterogeneous relations of the military and business leaders, the constituent assembly process, the 1982 and 1984 elections, the support of the U.S. government to the Salvadoran government, the impact of the strengthening of the air force, some guerrilla strategies, the crisis and reorganization of the Popular Liberation Forces (FPL, member organization of the FMLN) after the events in Managua, and their responsibility in the so-called San Vicente Massacre. The third part is dedicated to the presidential administration of Alfredo Cristiani (ARENA), a period during which the correlation of forces changed in El Salvador after the fall of the socialist bloc. It also deals with the 1989 offensive, the negotiations that led to the signing of the Peace Accords, the main reforms involved, and the tensions between amnesty and the right to know the "truth," as well as the postwar processes aimed at forgiveness and national reconciliation. The documentary concludes with a voice-over whose position claims that there are no valid reasons for violence and that war is madness to be avoided at all costs.

Los ofendidos, with a running time of eighty-five minutes, is an intimate encounter with torture, its victims, and its perpetrators. It starts with the case of Rubén Zamora (member of the Frente Democrático Revolucionario [FDR] and of the FMLN-FDR diplomatic commission), who was kidnapped and tortured by the armed forces of the Salvadoran government during the conflict. The film also includes other similar cases detailing how the victims were selected based on their political activity, as well as the tracing of their capture, the clandestine procedure of detention, interrogation, and torture until their release or death. The documentary shows disappearance, torture, and murder as a systemic practice and not as isolated or exceptional cases. The film also investigates the way in which the tortured and the torturers were able to continue living after the events. *Los ofendidos*'s dedication is crushing: "To all the torturers who have already forgotten, and to the tortured, both women and men, who, like my father, will never forget."

In a little more than an hour and a half, *La batalla del volcán* deals with the FMLN's offensive on San Salvador in November 1989. The first part shows some planning for the offensive, the entrance of the FMLN, and the occupation of the Mexicanos neighborhood by the guerrilla. The second part is a journey through the experiences of the ex-combatants during the first days of the confrontation and of the civilian population who lived the offensive with horror, hunger, and desperation, especially after the bombings by the Salvadoran air force targeted at popular zones of the city where the guerrilla had entered. This segment closes with the assassination (carried out by death squads) of the Jesuits at the Central American University Simeón Cañas and its subsequent political meaning. The film's third part focuses on the capture of the Escalón neighborhood and the Sheraton Hotel, where some U.S. Marines and the Secretary of the Organization of American States (OAS) were staying at the time. It ends with the announcement of the death of Dimas Rodríguez, FPL commander and strategist, and the subsequent retreat of the FMLN. The documentary is dedicated to the 3,000 who died during the thirty days of combat known as the Ofensiva Hasta el Tope [To-the-Top Offensive].

All the filmmakers mentioned in this chapter wanted to better understand reality, to talk to the people who lived through the events, and to ask them to tell their stories—three elements that are essential for the documentary.[5] As the so-called father of documentary film, John Grierson, postulated, the documentary implies a creative treatment of reality; not a reproduction of it, but a representation from a particular vision of the world (Grierson 143; Nichols 33)—that is, of the person who makes it. Both characteristics endow the medium with potentiality, and from it, one can record, observe, interact, question; create memories, assessments, future projections; and, reflect, expose a problem, express ideas, argue against them, persuade, even interpret, and represent the world in a poetic way. Documentaries, like all cinematographic works, have the potential to provoke emotion, as Bahia Pontes pointed out in "Cine y realidad social":

> Cinema, art of relationships, becomes social since it takes human presence as its objective. It is not a matter, purely and simply, of choosing man as a subject. It is about assuming human presence in its totality, that is, the presence of man in what is socially related, insofar as it presents itself as an emotional and rational present whole. It will be this nature of presence that will define the authentic cinematographic language. From the moment that cinema takes man's presence into account, its language will no longer constitute a pure sociology or a study of social concepts, but will become an aesthetic, in the Greek sense of the word, that is to say, a language that includes, alongside the concept, sensation and feeling. (162)

Through the documentary register, the directors of these films question different social actors and the past, in order to give coherence to the turbulence of war and the postwar period. The works bring the viewers closer to the armed conflict, its causes, development, and conclusion, and to the unresolved problems accumulated by decades of indifference. Through the voice and gaze of their protagonists, the filmmakers even provide viewers with modes of communication sustained in narrative, sound, and visual resources, in which they can sense an echo of what the protagonists may have felt in the face of violence, hope, utopia, and so on, so that the viewers, in some way, can perceive and empathize with the Other.

Based on Nichols's statement that "[i]n every documentary there are at least three intertwined stories: that of the documentary filmmaker, that of the film, and that of the audience" (117), it can be inferred that documentary filmmakers' life trajectories, professional training, and audiovisual experience have implications in the choice of their subject matter, their point of view, the way in which they approach reality and represent the social actors involved, as well as the production-dissemination-exhibition context to which they have access. Documentaries, like any creative product and, like history itself, are produced from the present, from current concerns. In that sense, they are themselves historical in that they account for the way in which the producer approaches reality and represents it, even more so when the documentary obtains a voice of its own. In this case, in addition to what has been presented, we can observe how old and new social actors generate documentary discourses in a political moment marked by the process of transitional justice. Their narratives and forms of production form a sort of mosaic full of continuities and ruptures, of tradition and modernity, and of legacies and new proposals.

The Filmmakers

Knowing the place of enunciation and the filmmakers' career path is fundamental to understand what questions they ask of that past. Carlos Henríquez Consalvi was born in Venezuela in 1947. As a child he lived in different countries because his parents were opposed to the government in power. When he was able to return to Venezuela, he decided to study journalism. Later he lived in Nicaragua, where he witnessed the fall of the Somoza dictatorship and supported the revolutionary process (see Tomás Arce Mairena's chapter in this volume to learn about how Nicaraguan documentarians have dealt with the legacy of the Sandinista revolution). At the end of 1980, he joined the guerrilla radio station Radio Venceremos (from ERP), located in Morazán, where he collaborated, under the pseudonym of Santiago, until the end of the conflict.

In 1996 he founded the Museo de la Palabra y la Imagen (MUPI), an institution dedicated to the research, rescue, preservation, and dissemination of the historical and cultural heritage of El Salvador, where he is currently director.[6]

Jeffrey Gould was born in 1950 in New York. When he married a Costa Rican, he moved to that country. After the Sandinista triumph, he visited Nicaragua, a process that impacted him and determined his academic interest in the region. From Indiana University, he currently researches social movements, ethnic conflicts, and political violence in Latin America, especially in Nicaragua and El Salvador.

Gould and Henríquez Consalvi taught themselves how to make documentaries while working on *1932 Cicatriz de la memoria* (El Salvador, 2002), a project that began as academic research and had the additional purpose of becoming an exhibition at the MUPI. Given the richness of the video testimonies and their great historical value, the project turned into a documentary. Years later, when Henríquez Consalvi invited Gould on a tour of Morazán, he was impressed by his initial conversations with the people he met along the way. He wanted to know how and why the people of that place joined the war—a question that Santiago himself, despite his participation in the conflict, could not answer.

Gerardo Muyshondt belongs to a new generation, but with a deep-rooted heritage. He was born in El Salvador in 1977, into one of the main cotton-producing families in El Salvador. His father was close to Roberto D'Aubuisson, who was a military man and far-right politician, leader of the death squads and founder of the far-right political party Alianza Republicana Nacionalista (ARENA). Ernesto (Gerardo's older brother) joined ARENA at a very young age, a party for which he served as deputy of the Legislative Assembly (2015–2018) and as mayor of San Salvador (2018–2021).

Gerardo studied at the Mónica Herrera School of Communication (a private institution) and later in Chile. He has worked as a commercial publicist for major Salvadoran companies such as Almacenes Simán, Tigo, Taca, Súper Selectos, and Banco Agrícola.[7] His first documentary, which dealt with El Salvador's participation in the 1982 World Cup (discussed in Mauricio Espinoza's chapter in this volume), repeatedly took him into the context of the armed conflict. For his second documentary, he sought a national theme that would awaken patriotic sentiment. According to him, his gradual knowledge of the conflict led him to reflect on the importance of understanding the past in order to heal the wounds of the present and reach national forgiveness, which is how he chose the theme. Asking himself in general terms what happened led him to tell the story of the conflict in a broad and linear fashion. For Muyshondt, this documentary represents the possibility of pedagogically telling the recent history of his country, which, by awakening patriotic sentiments, constituted a marketing opportunity in an election year (Muyshondt).

Marcela Zamora and Julio López also belong to the generation of the children of war. Their parents were political participants in the civil movement. Zamora is the daughter of Salvadoran politician Rubén Zamora, who was linked to the CEBs before the conflict and had a long involvement in opposition parties against the Salvadoran government. He was a member of the first Revolutionary Military Junta and the FDR, was exiled for his political participation in 1980, and returned in 1987 to found Convergencia Democrática [Democratic Convergence], a party that ran in the 1989 elections and also put forth a leftist candidate in the 1994 presidential elections (Zamora 1–3 and Krämer 69–70, 132–133, 149–150). This process marked Marcela Zamora's childhood. She was born and grew up in the years of the flourishing Nicaraguan revolution, only to find herself in a country convulsed by the postwar period, facing social rejection at school for being the daughter of Rubén Zamora. "I think that is what has motivated me to work towards historical memory, to understand: to understand what that 11-year-old girl did not understand when they shouted at her that her father was a murderer, right? And she did not understand what was going on, why, if her father was not. [. . .] That is where the need to dig into the past and put pieces together begins, and to understand things that I did not live through" (Zamora 3).[8] At the age of nineteen, Marcela Zamora decided that she needed to forge her own identity outside her home. She studied journalism in Costa Rica and, once she graduated, went to the International School of Film and Television in San Antonio de los Baños, Cuba, to study filmmaking, specializing in documentary film. Since then she has worked for Al Jazeera, Telesur, and *El Faro*, and founded the production company Kino Glaz Films. Among her documentaries dealing with the armed conflict are *Las masacres del Mozote* (2011) and *Las Aradas: Masacre en seis actos* (2014).

When Zamora worked at the Salvadoran digital newspaper *El Faro*, she came across the *Libro Amarillo* [*Yellow Book*], a photographic album produced by the Salvadoran police in 1987 that served as a blacklist to detain people for their political activities. The third photograph corresponded to that of her father, Rubén. In shock, Marcela Zamora took the book home. Her mother told her that, during the war, her father was detained and tortured for thirty days and encouraged her to ask him about the event. It was an issue that her father did not share. At the time she did not succeed, but when her mother died she felt she had a personal need to know what had happened in order to understand her own history, according to the documentary itself, a history "[. . .] of a generation that does not ask questions out of fear."

Julio López's mother worked at Socorro Jurídico, an institution founded by Monsignor Óscar Romero dedicated to supporting persecuted people. After Romero's assassination in March 1980, its members were at risk of being persecuted and murdered, so López's mother fled to Mexico, where she met her partner. Soon after, Julio López was born. References of and solidarity with the Salvadoran struggle were persistent in the López household; they even visited the country a few times. When his family returned to San Salvador, when he was eleven or twelve years old, someone told him that there had been an important battle there, but no one knew how to explain what happened. The lack of knowledge and the lack of answers made him anxious. López later returned to Mexico City to study communication. He also learned still photography and began making documentaries spontaneously. When he moved to El Salvador in 2008, he joined the newly formed company Trípode Audiovisual, where, in addition to participating in various production experiences, he began to take part in international documentary courses and workshops. He then codirected the medium-length film *La semilla y la piedra* (2011), and later, together with Marcela Zamora, founded Kino Glaz, where he established himself as a producer (López 6–7).[9]

Once López had been in the film industry for some time and wanted to make a documentary, he thought he could not portray the Salvadoran reality because it seemed too brutal to him. He needed to understand the origin of violence, and the immediate origin was war. In 2012, he happened to notice that MUPI kept audiovisual materials of the 1989 offensive. That was when he knew this was the subject of his documentary, as well as the subject to understand what the war had been and what it meant for the people.

At the beginning of his research, López observed the lack of written sources and consequently set two objectives: to tell the story of the offensive in chronological order as a historiographic contribution, and also to offer a broad panorama through as many points of view as possible (López 13). The ethical reference that guided his research was that the processes of recovery and healing the past go through talking about what happened (López 22).

In all four cases, the filmmakers asked themselves: what happened here? They wanted and needed to know what took place, to know "the truth," and for this they turned to oral testimonies and documentary footage. Both aspects recall the social dimension of the archive postulated by Michel Foucault, for whom the archive is a system of enunciation, of discursivity, composed of events and things. The existence of what has been said implies the possibility and impossibility of enunciation, of a discursive level or system: "the archive is, first of all, the law of what can be said, the system that governs the appearance of utterances as singular events" (Foucault 219). In his view, the archive implies the possibility of grouping events and things, starting from their multiple relations, attributing them as distinct figures, with a duration of their own, operating as their system of functioning (Foucault 220). Hence, turning to witnesses who have the possibility of stating the facts is not only to resort to living sources, but also to contribute to their creation (Thompson 268).

The filmmakers of these documentaries directly question the conflict's participants. With their voices they constructed polyphonic documentaries, whose different perspectives and filmmaking revealed the way in which each one approached the past: forms of research-production crossed by the situated place, their organizational heritage, and the old and new forms of audiovisual production.

The scarcity of records of Morazán in the 1970s implied a construction of sources through oral history. In this regard, Gould points out: "I believe this is a very important narrative, especially in a country like El Salvador, or any Central American country. It is not really possible to do work on contemporary history without resorting to oral sources" (2).[10] Henríquez Consalvi and Gould sought out men and women who had joined the CEBs. The individual and collective interviews contained a certain eclecticism. Gould was inclined to ask open questions aimed at oral history, while Henríquez Consalvi, having lived through the armed conflict in the department of Morazán and having known the witnesses for several years, had a more journalistic perspective. Subsequently, the testimonies were contextualized in their historical sense and analyzed respecting the nature of individual and collective memory, that is, taking into account the way in which memory operates, its limitations, and its relationship with oblivion. Gould and Henríquez Consalvi's analytical work provided a plausible explanation to their research question and prompted the people involved to take stock of their political participation, as well as to ask themselves what is needed to achieve a dignified life.

Muyshondt summoned political leaders, military, businessmen, and people who had notable contributions during the conflict, as well as direct relatives of some of the deceased (particularly businessmen and former presidents). He summoned them individually in a studio, sat them in the same armchair and conducted controlled interviews on various previously selected topics. The testimonies were presented thematically in chronological order, some coinciding, complementing, and contradicting each other. Memories of the past swirl in the documentary without distinction between assessments of the present, political stances, and opinions.

Oral and Archival Sources in the Aesthetic Proposal of Documentaries

In *Los ofendidos,* Marcela Zamora's voice-over is a guide in multiple senses. One of them is the partial unveiling of documentary's production. In one of the first scenes, Marcela Zamora and her father are sitting in the dining room, and her voice-over confesses the following:

> In that dining room, my mother told me many stories of my family during the twelve years of war in El Salvador. In that dining room, one day she said to me: "Go on, ask your dad what happened during his capture." I told her I didn't know how to do it yet, that I wasn't ready yet. Then, in the middle of this documentary, my mother died and I had the need to know. In that conversation, my father told me that he chose not to take up arms in the conflict and to bet on the political path. At first he said it was not necessary to tell me about his capture and torture, because what he had lived through did not compare to what had been done to other Salvadorans. He asked me to listen to other stories, so I went and looked for other tortured people. (*Los ofendidos*)[11]

Marcela Zamora met Dr. Romagoza and Néri González at a meeting at a rally in El Salvador Airport (at the time when General Vides Casanova was deported), and later with Miguel Ángel Rogel Montenegro during a visit to the library of the Historical Memory Center of the Human Rights Commission of El Salvador. Marcela Zamora also managed to convince a torturer (as long as his identity was not revealed) to agree to the interview. The torturer thought his way of cooperating in revealing what happened during the war was to agree to the interview. The documentary weaves the filmmaker's personal search with fragments of the interviewees' lives, of their permanent pain, of their bodily memory. The testimonies inhabit us viewers, they let us enter the intimacy of the pain of others, and once there, we cannot help but question ourselves (as Susan Sontag did in her famous 2003 book *Regarding the Pain of Others*): what right do I have to listen to Marcela Zamora cry, after watching, listening, and feeling the pain of others that she can no longer contain? What is the commitment we have to assume as spectators in the face of the denunciation of injustice? The interviewees take us to places of clandestine detention and ruins of former prisons. Thus, the documentary invites viewers to reflect on the importance of knowing the truth and the current need for justice and reparations.

For his part, López decided to give space to testimonies of what he calls "people from the trenches:" soldiers, combatants, and civilians. After conducting extensive archival research, he generated a profile of 100 people around their involvement in the offensive, and selected forty, whom he interviewed. From those interviews, he chose the anecdotes he wanted to tell and wrote a fiction screenplay. He designed a *mise-en-scène,* which consisted of taking the people to the place they mentioned and asking them to narrate and represent their testimony, through their voice and body, respectively. The idea was to cinematographically set up the oral testimony and the action of staging the past events in the places they occurred, as a trigger of memory at a narrative, sensory, and emotional level, which, in turn, allowed viewers observe how the witness and the place have been transformed over time, and how its relationship with that past manifests both verbally and corporeally. López's aim was to assist the process of memory, to generate a dialogue between people, places, times, and thus contribute to reconciliation.

Oral testimonies are an expression and representation of culture. Their narration includes the dimensions of memory (memory/forgetfulness), ideology, and desires that demonstrates in such a way that their enunciation derives from subjectivity (Passerini 53–62). Through the testimonies gathered in these documentaries, we gain access to the meaning that the participants give to their lived experiences: they transmit to us viewers their bodily sensations, their emotions, their political and ideological interests of the past, and the relationship they establish with that past from the present time. The testimonies allow us to access a dialectical relationship between the individual and collective dimensions of the conflict and the post-conflict, periods that constitute distinguishable identities in the documentaries. The testimonies also provide us viewers with elements that help us understand the complexity of the facts. Furthermore, as Graciela de Garay writes, the political possibility of enunciation and legitimacy of the word of any "witness of history," by saying "I was there," generates empowerment and is a democratizing exercise (104–105). In these documentaries, the word of a peasant is not subordinate to that of a military commander, a career politician, or a businessman. The diversity of the testimonies gathered, both in their form and in their content, make clear the current political tensions over the past—visions upon which the public will have the task of interpreting and making sense.

In addition to gathering oral testimonies, the filmmakers of these four documentaries obtained still and moving images from MUPI's collection. During the conflict, the organizations that made up the FMLN (despite their clandestine nature) generated documentary archives, mainly for two purposes: to use them as propaganda elements (magazines, audios, posters, photographs, film, and video) and with the understanding that, when they triumphed, these documents would constitute the historical archive, which, in the case of the latter, in Derrida's terms, refers to the anticipation or endorsement of the future

(Derrida 26). Those responsible for the press and propaganda structures of each organization were also in charge of safeguarding and using the archives of such structures. These individuals acted as *archons,* that is, record keepers. After the conflict with the de-structuring of the guerrilla organizations and the rearrangement of the new organizations to which they gave rise, the archives were abandoned, dismantled, or partially or totally forgotten.

Following the organization of an exhibition about Radio Venceremos in 1996, Henríquez Consalvi conducted a search and collected the surviving documents. Over the years, the effort was consolidated in the creation of MUPI, a non-governmental organization that has the largest collection of catalogued and accessible documents (texts, audios, photographs, moving images, and objects) from the conflict. In a country where there is no national history museum, photo library, film library, or sound library, MUPI began to receive pre- and post-conflict archival remains, mainly donated by individuals who had nowhere to deposit them.

Resorting to these records and documentaries made by FMLN groups, and incorporating them as sources for contemporary documentaries, is an archaeological exercise. The vestiges allow us to observe the perspective of these armed groups in terms of their Marxist historical discourse and their power of self-representation.

The encounter of the researcher-filmmaker with the archival image, and its subsequent editing and montage, can enhance the meaning of the images according to their nature or, on the contrary, can be made to say anything, or even subvert.[12] As Carlos Mendoza writes in his *El guión para cine documental,* "[Images do not possess] the property of explaining their own meaning and implications, beyond what they are really capable of explaining" (208).[13] Hence, the exhaustive knowledge on the part of the researchers-filmmakers about the images, the adequate contextualization of them and the dialogue with other sources are decisive to access the historical, informative, interpretive, and aesthetic potential of the images.

Henríquez Consalvi's knowledge of the images housed at MUPI is profound given his participation in the armed conflict. While he was part of Radio Venceremos, in 1981, he was a witness when Guillermo Escalón (from the independent collective Cero a la izquierda [Zero to the Left], formed by Manuel Sorto and him), to film *La decisión de vencer, los primeros frutos* [*The Decision to Win: The First Fruits*]. He also witnessed the birth of the film, video, and photography unit of the so-called Sistema Radio Venceremos (SRV) in 1982, the year in which, with Escalón's participation, *Carta de Morazán* was filmed. From that moment on, Henríquez Consalvi had a certain closeness with the film, video, and photography unit since it was regularly located in the same camp as Radio Venceremos. In some moments of the conflict, it was possible to screen some SRV productions in the guerrilla camps, so that, at the end of the war, Henríquez Consalvi was familiar with part of the SRV oeuvre. This knowledge was complete when he became involved in the work of organizing, archiving, and cataloguing the documents that arrived at MUPI. From the beginning, the archive was a fundamental element for Gould and Henríquez Consalvi:

> The Museum has a gigantic collection, so that the archive is put at the service of the documentary, it was already clear to us: that any fact or witnesses' account we were sure we would have a backup of what life was like in Morazán, of what El Mozote was like. [...] They talk about so and so, right? "Arce Zahbla arrived and met with the first Christian communities," there is the photo of Arce Zahbla. [...] Or the other way around, sometimes we found photos that gave us a clue, right? We found a photo of Agua Blanca in 1981, and we saw a character, and we said, "Oh well, but this character was a catechist," then the photo leads us to the search for a witness. And so on, other types of links. [...] You have the knowledge and in your mind you have these images engraved, you know that he exists. So that gives great strength to the audiovisual project. (Henríquez Consalvi 5–6)[14]

The practice of collective, solidary, and self-managed work during the conflict (and subsequently at MUPI for many years) was replicated in the research process for the documentary. Coincidentally, under that same logic, they obtained very relevant audiovisual material. On one occasion, Gould was a speaker in a conference commemorating the murder of four American nuns, which took place in El Salvador in 1980. At the end, a nun who attended the conference (held in Cleveland, USA), approached him and offered him a video that her organization had recorded in 1973 in El Castaño (Gould 6). In the documentary *Vayamos jubilosos* [*Let Us Go Joyfully*], viewers observe the spiritual formation of the peasants of Morazán, under the vision of the church of the poor, that is, a vision of the possibility of building the kingdom of God on Earth by being good Christians, working in community, and fighting injustice—images that became, together with the hemerography, sources of research, and as such, are shown in the documentary.

In addition to consulting the MUPI collection, Muyshondt, who had the support of businessman Ricardo Simán as producer, had access to the private archives of individuals and organizations such as Simán himself, the D'Aubuisson family, the Dalton family, the television stations Noticias Univisión, Telecorporación Salvadoreña, and Canal 33.[15] As a result, the work presented images that are little known today. These images serve to illustrate the chronological journey, work as bridges to the thematic blocks, and support the interviews, sometimes decontextualized.

In *El Salvador: archivos perdidos del conflicto*, the concept of "archive" was a key element in the image design for the documentary. For example, the background of the set where the interviews took place was decorated with a series of photographs of well-known social actors such as Monsignor Romero, former president José Napoleón Duarte, and Roberto D'Aubuisson, as well as emblematic events of the conflict, such as the sabotage of the Golden Bridge, the signing of the Peace Agreement at Chapultepec Castle in Mexico City, and the celebration on January 16 at Plaza Barrios in San Salvador. The design of Muyshondt's film advertising and posters emphasized archival materials such as videotapes and files. The design of the documentary, supported by the concept of archive, generated the imaginary that it was the product of a serious research process, since it emphasized that "the source was there." Élmer Menjívar in his article "Los archivos perdidos de los otros ofendidos," placed the word "lost" between question marks to indicate that the documentary was not committed to "revealing anything new."

In addition to consulting the MUPI archive, Zamora and López turned to the archive of Mexican journalist and producer Epigmenio Ibarra, who was a correspondent during the conflict and was close to the ERP. Ibarra keeps the recordings he made during the conflict in the archive of his company, Argos Comunicación. After finishing the first cut, Marcela Zamora realized that the documentary would not work without archival footage and requested support from Ibarra, who, just as during the time of the conflict, provided it in solidarity. Zamora selected fifteen hours of digitized images, which she contextualized to use them correctly in historical terms, and did a similar job with the sound part (Zamora 15).

Although López's research contemplated the use of photographs from the beginning, he decided to include only video materials, most of them recorded by Ibarra. In general, they were familiar scenes. In fact, the first cuts were generated with materials downloaded from YouTube. With Ibarra's support, the filmmaker obtained a digital copy of the "raw" materials, contained in eleven cassettes (López 16), which, in addition to providing better-quality images, show scenes in which one can observe the relationship of empathy and trust that Ibarra's team established with the guerrillas, as, for example, in the interview he conducts with Otto and Choco at the Zacamil neighborhood, and later when he meets them again at the Sheraton Hotel.[16] By having Otto and Choco's collaboration in the present, in the same places where the actions witnessed in the archival images take place, they function as both source and audiovisual resource.

Production and Distribution

Before concluding, it should be noted that the form of production in which the documentary filmmakers were inserted determined the circulation of their works, a circuit in which it is possible to observe continuities and changes in Salvadoran cinema. *La palabra en el bosque* had a form of production closer to the self-managed and solidary mode that prevailed during the conflict. Once the documentary was finished, it was screened at MUPI and was promoted in its community workshops, in academic spaces through the participation of Gould, and in some festivals championing social values. On the other hand, *El Salvador, los archivos perdidos del conflicto* (with a business-financed form of production that recalls the figure of the businessman-filmmaker of the early days, and the publicist-filmmaker of mid-twentieth-century Salvadoran cinema), was exhibited directly in the commercial film circuit.[17]

Meanwhile, *Los ofendidos* and *La batalla del volcán* were shown in new Salvadoran communication channels such as Kino Glaz Films, El Faro, Trípode Audiovisual, and Cine Murciélago, which had the support of companies from other countries, such as Argos and Caravana Production Services. The films also received international cooperation that promoted the establishment of a film industry in the region with an aim for recoginition in international film festivals. Film events such as DocsMx, Ambulante, and Ícaro are interested in Central American narratives, focused on the political participation of new social actors, the defense of human rights, and memory processes. After passing through this circuit and generating interest due to the awards obtained and the positive reviews of film critics, these documentaries were able to forge alliances that made their inclusion in the Salvadoran commercial cinema circuit possible.

Conclusion

Through these documentaries we can perceive a developing process of transitional justice, which reveals tensions about the narrative of the past and its use in the present. On the one hand, there is a demand for clarification of the facts and access to justice, as well as knowledge of the past to revalue social organization in order to achieve a dignified life. On the other hand, it is recognized that the sectors antagonized in the conflict have their own narratives according to their political and social framework and can coexist in the present without reaching a consensus on the facts. Rather than worrying about clarifying them and aspiring to justice, it is possible to talk about the past, but without recognizing violence as a legitimate way to achieve change.

In the documentaries whose views align with the first option, the memory of the past is combined with the questions of the present, those that in the heat of the facts could not be asked before, and others that the passage of time allows us to answer now. They are a tool to name, vindicate, denounce and point out. These documentaries address bloody social processes and at the same time are hopeful, because they show that by recognizing the past, the present can be better understood. These works recover and dignify the role played by subaltern social actors and contribute to modeling a new culture of peace with justice and dignity.

Ryszard Kapuściński in "El encuentro con el Otro como reto del siglo XX" concludes that "the good disposition toward another human being is the only basis that can make the cord of humanity vibrate in him" (15).[18] In the "III Conferencia vienesa," he also points out that "Others are the mirror in which we reflect ourselves and which makes us aware of who we are. [. . .] Others shed light on my own history" (Kapuściński 36).[19] For the filmmakers cited here, the encounter with their interlocutors generated a transformation. As a protagonist of the armed conflict, Henríquez Consalvi states that his documentary process gave him the opportunity to reevaluate the past:

> [It was] a school for one, really, to be listening to history. You had a general framework, you knew that the communities had planned to build heaven on earth based on solidarity and words. But when you start to listen to these dense, intense stories, which begin to reveal unexpected things, alterations, impacts on life, changes in the family fabric, the empowerment of women in the macho society [. . .] Then it's a permanent learning process and it changes your perception [. . .] And it also loosens threads that lead you to investigate other situations. (6)[20]

As for the filmmakers who lived through the conflict as children, their documentary work not only gave them the opportunity to know their own history in order to explain themselves from the hidden and silenced pains, but it also gave them new luminous horizons. In this regard, Zamora states:

> Many doubts I cleared up, I understood many things about my past. [. . .] I had managed to finish putting on the puzzle board those pieces that I needed to understand my father, to understand why, how they had treated me, or have done to me, what they did, or the decisions

they made with my life. So, I think that was it, I matured a lot making the documentary, and I am very calm. I have a very different relationship with my dad, I always had a relationship with him, but after the documentary I think he became... vulnerable. Men in war and women in war, they couldn't give themselves the time to be vulnerable, and I think my father, for the first time in this documentary, became vulnerable. (14–15)[21]

It also gave López a chance to understand his identity but in a different way:

In the end I discovered that I had a restlessness to understand the war in order to understand my family, and that was what I totally achieved. That is, talking to soldiers and understanding why they joined the army: because they were recruited. Why they fought that war, and why they went out to kill people in combat. Talking to students [...] who decided to take up arms, and talking to all those politicians. That gave me a real understanding, not only on a political-historical-military level, but also on a personal level, of what that conflict was about. [Now] I can build and understand my identity much better, my personal identity and that of my family, and what I want my children or the generation of the children of our generation to have, and that is incredible. (29)[22]

As a dialectical tide, the past, the present, and the future constitute a ring in the form of a snake that bites its own tail, which gives meaning to those who cross not the presentism of their time, but the historical becoming.

Notes

1 The loss of human lives during the conflict ranged from 80,000 to 94,000, about 1.5 million people were globally displaced, and half a million Salvadorans were internally displaced (Pirker 208). The Peace Accords were reached on the last minute of December 31, 1991, in New York, while the formal peace signing ceremony took place on January 16, 1992, in Mexico City.
2 The agrarian reform took up the limit proposed by the government itself before the beginning of the conflict, which considered a maximum of 245 hectares for a single person (United Nations 7). According to Vázquez: "The political project of the insurrection was gradually blurred after the explicit abandonment of the platform of the Revolutionary Democratic Government by the FMLN in 1984. From then on, it is not possible to speak properly of an insurgent project. There was none. The successive platforms raised by the guerrillas never aimed to synthesize programmatically any coherent project of structural transformation" (225).

3 In structural terms, the major demands with which the armed movement had begun the fight, such as the nationalization of the banks, foreign trade, the electricity distribution system and oil refining, as well as tax and credit reforms, were omitted. However, the idea of non-alignment was replaced by that of mutual respect with the United States and Latin American integration.

4 Tatiana Huezo's 2011 film *El lugar más pequeño* was not considered for this text because its production process is more closely linked to the Mexican industry, the country where she lives.

5 "The documentary talks about situations and events involving real people (social actors) who present themselves to us in stories that convey a plausible proposition about, or perspective on, the lives, situations, and events portrayed. The filmmaker's particular point of view shapes the story so that we see the historical world directly, rather than a fictional allegory" (Nichols 35).

6 For more information on Henríquez Consalvi's connection with Radio Venceremos, please consult López Vigil (43–46) and the memoir that Henríquez Consalvi himself wrote about the station, entitled *La terquedad del izote* (*The Stubbornness of the Izote*). On the history of MUPI, we recommend visiting its website.

7 Some of the advertising pieces can be viewed on Gerardo Muyshondt's YouTube channel.

8 Original quote: "Entonces, yo creo que también eso me llevó mucho a tener un caparazón, ante estas cosas, pero también mucha curiosidad. Porque yo no había vivido la guerra, pero si sentí después, o la viví muy poco, si sentí después la agresividad de la gente, de uno y de otro bando. Yo creo que eso es lo que a mí me ha motivado mucho a trabajar por la memoria histórica, entender, entender lo que no entendió esa niña de 11 años cuando le gritaron que su papá era un asesino, verdad y ella no entendía que es lo que pasaba. Porque si su papá no lo era verdad. Entonces, creo que más o menos por ahí comienza esa necesidad de escarbar en el pasado y juntar piezas, y entender cosas que no viví" (Zamora 3).

9 Trípode Audiovisual is an audiovisual production company based in El Salvador that operates throughout Central America. Its services include video creation, graphic animation, digital campaigns, film and live broadcasts.

10 "Yo creo que esa es una narración muy importante, sobre todo en un país como El Salvador o cualquier país centroamericano. No es posible realmente hacer un trabajo sobre la historia contemporánea sin recurrir a las fuentes orales" (2).

11 "En ese comedor mi madre me contó muchísimas historias de la familia durante los doce años que duró la guerra en El Salvador. En ese comedor un día me dijo: 'Andá, pregúntale a tú papá, cuente que pasó durante su captura.' Yo le dije que aún no sabía cómo hacerlo, que aún no estaba preparada. Luego, en medio de este documental murió mi mamá y tuve la necesidad de saber. En esa plática, mi papá me contó que optó en el conflicto armado, por no tomar las armas y apostarle a la vía política. En un inicio me dijo que no era necesario contar su captura y tortura, pues lo que él había vivido no se comparaba con lo que le habían hecho a otros salvadoreños. Él me pidió que escuchara otras historias, así fui y busqué a otros torturados" (min. 13:40–14:30).

12 Work on the organization of the elements to elaborate the filmic discourse (Mendoza, *Cine documental y montaje* 21).

13 "[...] la propiedad de explicar su propio significado e implicaciones, más allá de lo que realmente son capaces de explicar" (208).

14 "El Museo tiene un acervo gigantesco, entonces ese archivo se pone al servicio del documental, eso ya lo teníamos claro, de que cualquier hecho o relato de los testimoniantes teníamos la seguridad de que nosotros íbamos a tener un respaldo de cómo era la vida en Morazán, de cómo era El Mozote, [...] hablan sobre fulanito de tal, verdad 'Arce Zahbla llegó y se reunió con las primeras comunidades cristianas,' ahí está la foto de Arce Zahbla. [...] O al revés, a veces encontrábamos fotos que nos daban una pista, verdad, por lo menos encontramos una foto de Agua Blanca en 1981, y vimos a un personaje, y dijimos 'ah bueno pero este personaje fue catequista,' entonces la foto nos remite a la búsqueda de un testimóniante. Y así, otro tipo de vinculaciones. [...] Uno tiene el conocimiento y en la mente tienes esas imágenes grabadas, se sabe que existe. Entonces eso le da gran fuerza a las propuestas audiovisuales" (Henríquez Consalvi 5–6).

15 Simán is a member of the board of directors of ALSICORP, the group that owns Almacenes Simán, founded a hundred years ago, and currently owns fifty stores in Central America (Contreras).

16 Otto and Choco were ERP combatants who were recorded by Epigmenio Ibarra and whom López interviewed years later for his documentary.

17 In El Salvador, the first cinema exhibition took place in 1899, at the hands of itinerant German businessmen. Salvadoran film production took shape in 1925, when Italian entrepreneurs Virgilio Crisonino and Alfredo Massi established supply channels for materials and film equipment, and generated their own productions. This group also included the Salvadorans Federico Mejía and José Anibal Salazar Ruíz, although the latter was not an entrepreneur. Independent, social, authorial, and experimental cinema (with its own discourses and aesthetic concerns) emerged with the works of Alejandro Cotto, José David Calderón, and Baltazar Polío; the first two linked to the film, television and literature industries, and all of them linked to publicity, which allowed them to generate their own cinematographic works (Sermeño 24, Martínez 38, 41–42 and 50 and Cortés 29).

18 "la buena disposición hacia otro ser humano es esa única base que puede hacer vibrar en él la cuerda de la humanidad" (15).

19 "Los Otros—repitámoslo una vez más—son el espejo en que nos reflejamos y que nos hace conscientes de quiénes somos. [...] Los Otros proyectan luz sobre mi propia historia" (36).

20 "[Fue] una escuela para uno, verdad, estar escuchando la historia. Uno tenía un marco general, uno sabía que las comunidades se habían planteado construir el cielo en la tierra a partir de la solidaridad y de la palabra. Pero cuando comienzas a escuchar esos relatos densos, intensos, que te empiezan a revelar cosas inesperadas, cambios, impactos en la vida, en los cambios del tejido familiar, del empoderamiento de la mujer en la sociedad machista... Entonces fue un aprendizaje permanente y te cambia la percepción. [...] Y además te va soltando hilos que te llevan a investigar otras situaciones" (6).

21 "Muchas dudas me las aclaré, entendí muchas cosas de mi pasado,... había logrado terminar de poner en el tablero del rompecabezas esas piezas que me hacían falta para

entender a mi padre, por qué, entender cómo me habían tratado, cómo me trataran, o hecho, lo que habían hecho, o las decisiones que tomaron con mi vida. Entonces, creo que eso fue, madure mucho haciendo el documental, y estoy muy tranquila. Tengo otra relación con mi papá muy distinta, siempre tuve una relación con él, pero después del documental creo que él se volvió [. . .] vulnerable. Los hombres en la guerra y las mujeres en la guerra, no se podían dar el tiempo para ser vulnerables, y creo que mi padre, por primera vez, en este documental, se volvió vulnerable" (14–15).

22 "Al final descubrí que yo tenía la inquietud de entender esa guerra para poder entender a mi familia y eso fue lo que logré totalmente. O sea, hablar con soldados y entender por qué ellos se metieron al ejército: porque los reclutaron. Por qué pelearon esa guerra, y por qué salían a matar gente en combate. Hablar con estudiantes [. . .] que decidieron tomar las armas, hablar con todos esos políticos. Eso a mí me hizo tener una comprensión real y no sólo te digo, a nivel político-histórico-militar, pero también personal de lo que fue ese conflicto. [Ahora] yo puedo construir y entender mucho mejor mi identidad, mi identidad personal y de mi familia y de lo que luego yo quiero que tenga mi hijo o la generación de los hijos de nuestra generación, y eso está increíble" (29).

Works Cited

Bahia Pontes, Norma. "Cine y realidad social." *Pensamiento Crítico* 13, February 1968, pp. 161–185, https://www.filosofia.org/rev/pch/1968/pdf/n13p161.pdf. Accessed July 2021.

Calveiro, Pilar. "Testimonio y memoria en el relato histórico." *Acta Poética*, vol. 27, no. 2, 2006, pp. 65–86.

Carta de Morazán La campaña militar Comandante Gonzalo. Produced by Sistema Radio Venceremos, El Salvador, Ejército Revolucionario del Pueblo, 1982, https://archivomesoamericano.org/media_objects/d217qp49t. Accessed July 2021.

Comisión de la verdad. *De la locura a la esperanza. La guerra de 12 años en El Salvador.* San Salvador: Arcoíris, 2007.

Contreras, Claudia. "Ricardo Simán: El gran retailer de Centroamérica." *Estrategia y Negocios.net* 14, July 2019, https://www.estrategiaynegocios.net/especiales/aniversario/ceos/1301507-521/ricardo-sim%C3%A1n-el-gran-retailer-de-centroam%C3%A9rica. Accessed July 2021.

Cortés, María Lourdes. *La pantalla rota: Cien años de cine en Centroamérica.* Ciudad de México: Taurus, 2005.

Derrida, Jacques. *Mal de archivo. Una impresión freudiana.* Madrid: Trotta, 1997.

El Salvador, archivos perdidos del conflicto. Directed by Gerardo Muyshondt, El Salvador Films, El Salvador, 2014.

Foucault, Michel. "El a priori histórico y el archivo," *La arqueología del saber* [1st edition 1977]. Buenos Aires: Siglo XXI, 2002.

Garay de, Graciela. "De la palabra a la escucha. Una reflexión sobre la legitimidad del testimonio en la historia oral." *Entrevistar ¿para qué? Múltiples escuchas desde diversos cuadrantes,* edited by Graciela de Garay and Jorge Eduardo Aceves, Instituto de Investigaciones Dr. José María Luis Mora, 2017, pp. 91–125.

Getino, Octavio and Fernando E. Solanas. "*Hacia un tercer cine.*" *A diez años de hacia un tercer cine.* Ciudad de México: Filmoteca U Nacional Autónoma de México, 1982.

Gould, Jeffrey and Carlos Henríquez Consalvi. Web interview. 8 May 2019.

Grierson, John. "Postulados del documental." *Textos y Manifiestos del Cine,* edited by Romagueira, Joaquim y Homero Alsina Thevenet, Cátedra, 1993.

Henríquez Consalvi, Carlos. *La Terquedad del Izote.* El Salvador: Museo de la Palabra y la Imagen, 2009.

———. Personal interview. 17 January 2019.

Kapuściński, Ryszard, "'El encuentro con el Otro como reto del siglo XX,' acto de investidura de doctor honoris causa por la Universidad Ramon Llull, Barcelona, 17 June 2005." *Encuentro con el otro,* edited by Ryszard Kapuściński, Titivillus, 2016, pp. 6–15.

———. "III Conferencia vienesa, Institut für die Wissenschaften vom Menschen, Viena, 1–3 December 2004," *Encuentro con el otro,* edited by Ryszard Kapuściński, Titivillus, 2016, pp. 32–38.

Krämer, Michael. *El Salvador unicornio de la memoria.* San Salvador: Museo de la Palabra y la Imagen, 2009.

La batalla del volcán. Directed by Julio López Fernández, Trípode Audiovisual, Cine Murciélago, Argos, and Caravana Production Services, El Salvador, 2018.

La decisión de vencer, los primeros frutos. Directed by Guillermo Escalón and Manuel Sorto, Cero a la Izquierda, El Salvador, 1981, https://archivomesoamericano.org/media_objects/kd17cs888. Accessed July 2021.

La palabra en el bosque. Directed by Jeffrey Gould and Carlos Henríquez Consalvi, Museo de la Palabra y la Imagen, El Salvador, 2011, https://www.youtube.com/watch?v=SG-SbV6WzTE. Accessed June 2019.

La semilla y la piedra. Directed by José Luis Sáenz and Julio López, El Salvador/Guatemala, 2011.

Las masacres de El Mozote. Directed by Marcela Zamora Chamorro, El Faro, El Salvador, 2011, https://elfaro.net/es/201112/video/15409/Documental-Las-masacres-de-El-Mozote.htm. Accessed July 2021.

Libro Amarillo (De uso especial) Álbum fotográfico de los delincuentes terroristas (D/T) de las diferentes organizaciones que integran al FMLN/FDR. Seattle: University of Washington, Center for Human Rights, 1987, http://unfinishedsentences.org/es/the-yellow-book/. Accessed 18 June 2019.

López Fernández, Julio. Personal interview. 21 March 2019.

López Vigil, José Ignacio. *Las mil y una historia de Radio Venceremos.* San Salvador: U Centroamericana Editores, 1991.

Los ofendidos. Directed by Marcela Zamora Chamorro, El Faro, Kino Glaz, Argos, and Caravana Production Services, El Salvador, 2016.

Martínez González, José Antonio. *Historia del cine en El Salvador.* Bachelor's thesis, San Salvador: U de El Salvador, 2003.

Mendoza, Carlos. *El guión para cine documental.* Ciudad de México: U Nacional Autónoma de México, 2017.

———. *Cine documental y montaje.* Ciudad de México: Ficticia, 2020.

Menjívar, Élmer. "Los archivos perdidos de los otros ofendidos," *Los blogs de El Faro,* 11 November 2014, https://losblogs.elfaro.net/unhombredebien/2014/11/los-archivos-perdidos

-de-los-otrosofendidos.html?fbclid=IwAR0oS9Aq9yOvszz1E0qr6EwHGWuU0 Ke7Cx8Q5KlBJ15G1KSzgGMptq1j-xU. Accessed 18 June 2019.

Moreno, José David. "Paz, memoria y verdad en El Salvador: Experiencias y lecciones para la Colombia del Pos Acuerdo." *Análisis político* 90, May-August 2017, pp. 175–193.

Museo de la Palabra y la Imagen. *Reseña histórica, visión, misión,* 2017, http://museo.com.sv/2017/05/informacion-sobre-el-museo/. Accessed June 2021.

Muyshondt, Gerardo. *YouTube,* https://www.youtube.com/user/gerrymeison/videos. Accessed July 2021.

———. "El Salvador: Archivos perdidos del conflicto" Entrevista con Gerardo Muyshondt Parte I. El Salvador.com, 25 November 2013, https://youtu.be/3OXr_kZmCpY. Accessed July 2021.

Naciones Unidas. *Acuerdo de Nueva York.* 25 Sept. 1991. https://peacemaker.un.org/sites/peacemaker.un.org/files/SV_910925_NewYorkAgreement%28esp%29.pdf. Accessed July 2021.

Nichols, Bill. *Introducción al documental.* Ciudad de México: U Nacional Autónoma de México, 2013.

1932 Cicatriz de la memoria. Directed by Jeffrey Gould and Carlos Henríquez Consalvi, Museo de la Palabra y la Imagen, 2005, https://www.youtube.com/watch?v=mLZTTxddCZg. Accessed June 2020.

Passerini, Luisa. "Work ideology and Consensus Under Italian Fascism." *The Oral History Reader,* edited by Robert Perks and Alistair Thomson, Routledge, 2016, pp. 53–62.

Pirker, Kristina. *La redefinición de lo posible: Militancia política y movilización en El Salvador.* Dissertation, Universidad Nacional Autónoma de México, 2008.

Sermeño, Héctor Ismael. *La otra mirada: Ensayo y crítica de cine.* San Salvador: ALKimia Libros, 2006.

Sontag, Susan. *Regarding the Pain of Others.* New York: Farrar, Straus, and Giroux, 2003.

Thompson, Paul. *La voz del pasado. La historia oral.* Valencia: Edicions Alfons El Magnánim, 1988.

Trípode Audiovisual, http://www.tripodeaudiovisual.com/servicios/. Accessed June 2020.

United Nations. "New York Agreement." 25 September 1991. https://peacemaker.un.org/sites/peacemaker.un.org/files/SV_910925_NewYorkAgreement%28esp%29.pdf. Accessed January 2023.

Vayamos jubilosos, created by Cleveland Diocesis, 1973.

Vázquez, Mario R. "Del desafío revolucionario a la reforma política en El Salvador, 1970–1992." *Insurrección y democracia en el Circuncaribe,* coordinated by Ignacio Sosa, Centro Coordinador y Difusor de Estudios Latinoamericanos/U Nacional Autónoma de México, 1997, pp. 195–228.

Zamora Chamorro, Marcela. Telephone interview. 5 May 2019.

3

Memories and Critical History

Documenting the Past in Nicaragua and El Salvador

Juan Pablo Gómez Lacayo

This chapter examines the roles of documentary film in the construction of social memories about the recent past of Central American societies, especially those marked by political violence, war, and human rights violations. I focus on a selection of three documentary films about Nicaragua and El Salvador, two countries that had long armed conflicts in the second half of the twentieth century. The three selected films are directed by women: *Pictures from a Revolution*, directed by Susan Meiselas (United States, 1991), *Palabras mágicas para romper un encantamiento*, directed by Mercedes Moncada (Mexico/Guatemala/Nicaragua, 2012), and *El lugar más pequeño*, directed by Tatiana Huezo Mixco (Mexico, 2011).[1]

My principal claim is that documentary film serves as a vehicle for the critical recovery of the past, and, in that task, the genre occupies a central role in the construction of social memories. In addition, documentary film acquires greater importance in contexts in which state justice has not identified or judged those responsible of committing human rights violations during armed conflicts. In despairing scenarios such as these, the labor of documentary film can be conceptualized as poetic justice, a cultural labor in which societies recognize human rights violators and bring visibility to the victims and people who have suffered violence, war, and injustices that, in the case of these countries, adds up to thousands of people.

To support my thesis on the topic of social memories and its connection with cultural production, I follow the significant contributions of three influential Latin American thinkers who, from different perspectives, have contributed to the analysis of memory processes and its relationship with culture in Latin America: Elizabeth Jelin, Josefina Ludmer, and Ileana Rodríguez. Jelin's research focuses on the construction of social memories in response to state violence and human rights violations. From her well-known book *Los trabajos de la memoria* (2002), I borrow her statement of cultural production as a vehicle of memories, an idea I apply to documentary cinema. Regarding Ludmer, I rely in her claim in *Aquí América Latina, una especulación* (2010), that in Latin America, memory is always a cry for justice. The intellectual work of Rodríguez, especially in her latest book *Modalidades de memoria y archivos afectivos* (2020), adds that cultural production establishes a sense of truth and justice in societies that, like the countries I analyze here, seek to find those responsible of state violence and bring them to justice.

In the following pages, I aim to demonstrate that documentary films have been fundamental in inviting Central American societies to adopt a reflexive and critical attitude to the region's recent past. At the same time, documentary film has been a vehicle of great importance in the critical transmission of this past to the postwar generations, within which I include myself.

Heroic Images/Precarious Realities: The Everyday Revolutionary Nicaragua

I begin with Nicaragua to start thinking about how we can understand the role of cinema in the construction of social memories. To work on this question, I examine the documentary work of Susan Meiselas, a well-known American photographer who worked in Nicaragua and El Salvador since the end of the 1970s. In the late 1970s, Meiselas documented the popular insurrection in Nicaragua. The photographic documentation of the popular insurrection in Nicaragua at the end of the 1970s marked the beginning of a documentary itinerary of the revolution that has lasted several decades and extends to the present. Additionally, in 1981 she visited and documented the El Mozote massacre in El Salvador.

Meiselas visited Nicaragua for the first time in 1978–1979, the last year of the dictatorship of the Somoza family, who were in power for almost half a century. *Pictures from a Revolution* begins with Meiselas's voice-over saying: "When I first went to Nicaragua, I never imagined that I will spend ten years or more photographing there. By chance, I arrived just before the insurrection, in June 1978, when everything was about to erupt" (*Pictures from a Revolution*). From that visit came her book of photographs, *Nicaragua, June 1978 to July 1979* (1981), which documents the end of the Somoza dictatorial regime and the popular insurrection that overthrew Somoza in July 1979. According to historian Frances Kinloch, the armed popular insurrection that put an end to forty-two years of the Somoza dictatorship left 35,000 dead, more than 100,000 people injured, and thousands of orphaned children (305).[2] The overthrow of the Somoza dictatorship marked the beginning of a political transition in Nicaragua. With the end of almost half a century of family dictatorship (1936–1979), the opportunity arose to build a new society. The first decrees issued by the Government Board for National Reconstruction indicated the establishment of peace and a democracy with deep popular roots as its objectives. However, a civil war quickly started that lasted until 1990 and again produced thousands of victims.

Meiselas's photographs are a visual archive of a country in social convulsion and of a society that made history through massive political participation articulated as a national resistence against the dictatorship. She says she began to take photos without a plan in mind. Remembering the moment when she just arrived in Nicaragua in June 1978, she argues: "History was being made on the streets [. . .] I felt the necessity to witness and document what they did" (*Pictures from a Revolution*).

As Margarita Vannini, a scholar knowledgeable about Nicaraguan political history, points out: "many photographers captured images of what had happened in Nicaragua. However, it was the photos of Susan Meiselas that preserved the memory of that event and contributed to shaping a social imaginary about the revolution and its emblematic places" (80).[3]

Ten years after taking the photographs, Meiselas returned to Nicaragua with a series of concerns about the revolutionary decade: What happened in Nicaragua during the revolutionary decade? Did the revolution achieve the social liberation it promised? How did the Sandinista revolution change people's daily lives? What happened to the lives of the people she photographed ten years ago?[4] In her documentary film *Pictures from a Revolution*, the photographer returned to the country in search of the people she photographed between 1978 and 1979. The film follows a script structured by the following questions: What do these people think now after ten years, and what do they remember? With both questions, we notice a reflective gesture of memory; in the context of the present, these questions represent an invitation to explore, reflect upon, and interrogate the significance of the past. Through the act of presenting the original photos to the people she had previously photographed before the revolutionary triumph, the viewer finds a reflexive turn to the past that becomes a criterion for judging the realities experienced by the people photographed and, through them, to the Nicaraguan society. The film, as a photographic archive, guides and leads the memory of the photographed subjects during the revolutionary struggles, giving the opportunity for the documentary film to register some ten years later the value (or not) of the revolutionary sacrifice that many gave in the war against the dictatorship.

Pictures from a Revolution is also the construction of Meiselas's personal memories—a return to a place of personal meaning for her. The Nicaraguan revolution was the social change that she herself as a political subject considered necessary at that time.[5] As she says in the introduction of the documentary: "It was a time of hope, and I felt in some way part of it" (*Pictures from a Revolution*). This film, therefore, is not only a gesture of Meiselas's connection with the lives of Nicaraguans who inspired her as a photographer, but also of a representation of those who prompted her to become and act as a political participant.[6]

Pictures from a Revolution is ultimately a film about Meiselas's re-engagement with a wide range of scenes of a revolution she witnessed and captured with her camera. The film revisits the places and people in her iconic photographs of popular insurrection in Nicaragua in the late 1970s. She delves into the lives of guerrillas, Sandinistas, and members of Somoza's National Guard, exploring the stories and people behind the photos and reflecting upon the Nicaraguan social struggle.

In the film, Meiselas's photos taken in 1979 guide her labor of memory, leading her to search for the people and places that she photographed a decade earlier. Regarding the places, the documentary work ten years later makes them "places of memory," a key concept of memory studies. In her article on photography and memory in Argentina, Ludmila da Silva Catela highlights the importance of space in how photographs evoke memory. Space and public places, such as the streets of the cities of Masaya and Managua (as shown in Meiselas's documentary), are part of the cultural archive of the past. The streets of a neighborhood, says Da Silva Catela, "preserve fragments of the past that can be updated and transported to the present" (77).[7] Relying on the work of philosopher and sociologist Maurice Halbwachs, Catela reminds us that there is no collective memory that does not develop in a spatial framework.

Meiselas's work is no exception, as the places in her photographs also have memory: the walls where she took a photograph, the corners where the fight occurred, the roads, the landscapes. An example that illustrates this relationship between memory and space is her image of a landscape in the outskirts of the city of Managua in which we see in the background the lake and the volcanoes. Ten years ago, on this same hill, Meiselas took one of the paradigmatic photographs that denounce the deaths and human rights violations committed by the National Guard. In the photograph we see a body lying on this hill.

The photograph went around the world and served as evidence of what was happening in Nicaragua, while the dictatorship denied that there were human rights violations. The place where the photograph was taken is the so-called Cuesta del plomo, a place known for the multiple murders committed there by the National Guard. In the documentary, Meiselas remembers how she took the photograph ten years ago—Cuesta del plomo now converted into a site of memory. She takes the steering wheel of a vehicle, drives, and then stops the car midway up a hill. Getting out, she then walks to explore a hill overlooking the lake. The camera follows her on this journey. The act of returning to this place with the voice-over remembering the bodies she found when she got out of her car transforms this space into a "place of memory." The camera stops for several seconds allowing us to see, in a contemplative mood, the landscape of death now transformed into a landscape of memory.

From a place of memory, I now turn to oral testimony. In filming her documentary, Meiselas managed to find one of the photographed subjects in her book. Ten years ago, she photographed a child in the municipal market of Diriamba, a municipality located 42 kilometers south of Managua. The photograph shows a boy, approximately ten or eleven years old, who pauses in his transit through the market. The boy carries a sack and gets down on his knees to look for commercial items deposited on the ground. In his photograph, Meiselas captures the moment when the boy looks up from her and focuses on three toy soldiers offered for sale by a market trader. Despite its quotidian quality, the photo ends up becoming emblematic of the control of the Nicaraguan National Guard in daily life and its vigilant presence even over childhood. Ten years later, Meiselas finds him, now an adult, and shows him his photograph in her book, saying to him "En Diriamba todo mundo dice que sos vos" [In Diriamba everyone says it's you] (*Pictures from a Revolution*). In this scene, the photo's subject recognizes himself, and his reaction is one of happiness and joy, remembering that he was nine years old at the time while at the same time confirming he is the child in the photo.

In her film, Meiselas's act of showing the man the photo fosters an attitude of memory for him. When I say attitude of memory, I cite Elizabeth Jelin when she claims that human agency activates the past through cultural products that become vehicles of memory, as is the case of this photo (Jelin 37). When Meiselas shows the man the photo and asks him if he remembers that day, she begins a process of activating the past. As a result, the man begins to remember the fear caused by the National Guard's presence at the market the morning the photograph was taken. The scene ends with a shot in which he smiles at the book containing his photo and recalls an occasion when he encountered a National Guard motorcade and a Guardsman yelling at him to hide before something happened to him. Recalling this memory demonstrates how the photograph triggers the memory of the political violence and the fear that citizens, even children, had of the National Guard as they carried out military and police functions.[8]

In another scene, her voice-over expands on her memories while the photographs on screen provide visual evidence or support of her memories. The camera focuses on Meiselas's photographs on Nicaragua as she recalls the moment in which the popular armed insurrection emerged against the Somoza dictatorship. While looking at her photos, she pauses on one of them and remembers that she took it in a neighborhood in the city of Managua. She remembers that there were children keeping watch and constructing barricades to prevent the entrance of the National Guard. The moment the Guard entered, she remembers that the people scattered and someone grabbed her from behind and put her into a house to protect her. In this scene, photography again serves as the evidence and the visual representation of what the voice of Meiselas recalls. Her viewing of the photos recalls the difficult circumstances in which she took them, many times in the midst of active combat between the National Guard and members of the Sandinista National Liberation Front (FSLN).

Subsequently, in the film, Meiselas travels from Managua to the city of León to continue her search for people she photographed during the insurrection. The camera follows her as she travels through the city's neighborhoods, recording her dialogues with people on the street whom she asks about those photographed. Thanks to the help of residents, through one of these dialogues, she locates one of the photographed subjects. He is a member of the Sandinista Front who in the photo was carrying the coffin of a person killed by the National Guard during the insurrection—a photo that documented the mass burial of the murdered people. When seeing himself in the photograph that Meiselas shows him, the man remembers:

> walking with the FSLN flag was a risk [. . .] But we were carrying the bodies of those companions, and we knew that their bodies were not going to be left lying around. We were willing to die, because that's the way it was, that was the conviction. (*Pictures from a Revolution*)

This example, as the previous one, demonstrates how the photos awaken memories of the past, and in this case, even the rationale behind such actions as walking with a FSLN flag, through the oral testimony that results from the awakened memory.

The labor of memory not only deals with the past but also with how the struggles of the past resonate in the present, that is, how the past provides or diminishes the meaning of the present—something Meiselas is interested in exploring in the documentary. She is particularly interested in exploring the photographed subjects' perceptions of the past now in the present, wondering if the present matches their desire and ideals of the future once articulated in the past at the time of the insurrection. With that purpose, she documents the daily life of those who were part of the insurrection, which can be read as a filmic strategy that gives evidence or visual support to what life was like before and how life is ten years later. In most cases, if not all, life remains precarious, surrounded by poverty, as supported by and articulated in Nicaraguan poet Vidaluz Meneses's reflections on the postrevolutionary decade:

> I had the feeling that nothing had happened in Nicaragua despite the immense human sacrifice of the population and the investment of efforts to move the country and its revolution forward. (266)[9]

Meneses's feeling that nothing had changed in the country is elaborated by Meiselas through her audiovisual project. In her research evaluating the past and present, the oral testimony is crucial. In a particular scene from the film, she interviews a woman who lives in Monimbó, an Indigenous territory in the city of Masaya. Sitting in her house, the woman recalls how the population of Monimbó organized to prevent the National Guard from entering the neighborhood. The barricades, contact bombs, and the use of traditional masks were part of the elements used by the population to prevent the Guard from entering to kill and rob. After giving her testimony, the camera follows the woman as she does housework in her home. There, the film introduces us to a humble, rustic socioeconomic reality, a house where the family not only lives but also has its crafts workshop, its place of work and survival. In this environment, the woman tells Meiselas about her feelings of frustration:

> At the time we did not think about the future. Supposedly we were going to live better than before. But no, the same has come out. Before, there was everything, not anymore. At that time, we did not think about what was going to happen ten years later. Many mothers of the fallen regret that their children have died, and for nothing, a finished Nicaragua that we have right now. (*Pictures from a Revolution*)

Speaking from Monimbó, one of the most symbolic zones of the revolution, the woman's inclusion in the documentary is brief but significant, as she offers a critical attitude: the revolutionary project did not accomplish the emancipatory expectation that it intended to achieve: "the new society," "the new man." In her testimony, the woman expresses that the purpose of the struggle against the dictatorship and the sacrifice of the population at the end of the 1970s was to have a better life. However, she clearly points out that ten years later that goal was never accomplished. Entering the 1990s, she considers that she is in the same situation as ten years ago, or perhaps in an even more difficult situation. Her words leave no room for doubt about it when she expresses: "Before there was everything, not anymore" (*Pictures from a Revolution*). For the viewer, it is possible to perceive sadness and regret in her testimony.

In addition, her testimony alludes to the war in which thousands of young people lost their lives through a reference to the mothers who lost their sons. The woman's testimony leads to the difficult question: Are these young people heroes if their actions did not change daily life? What was the purpose of so much sacrifice? Following the war, the woman from Monimbó and her compatriots expected to live in a society that fostered a life with dignity, a life beyond survival. These expectations ended in disappointment. By describing the reality, in which life is the "same" ten years later, the documentary interrogates revolutionary identities and ideals, in particular the role of the heroic model of their emancipatory discourse. With *Pictures from a Revolution*, Meiselas does not evoke nostalgia for the revolutionary past but rather problematizes the heroic identities configured in this historical process, aiming to record and preserve a critical and reflective testimony about the revolutionary past.[10]

The attitudes of inquiry and interrogation that we find in this documentary are elements of what Michael Renov argues are fundamental rhetorical and aesthetic functions of documentary practice (21). *Pictures from a Revolution* was produced in a sociopolitical context that promoted forgetfulness as the predominant mode to relate to the recent past. As many authors have claimed, such as Margarita Vannini and Anika Oettler for example, in order to achieve peace in Nicaragua, the elites approved amnesty laws and decreed reconciliation and oblivion. In 1987, with the signing of the Esquipulas Agreements, the search for a way to end wars and armed conflicts was consolidated in Central America. Among other results, the Esquipulas Agreements designed a route for the cessation of military actions, the need to hold free and transparent elections, and the definition of Central America as a region of peace. Amnesties had a relevant space as a tool to reach the end of the war. In the case of Nicaragua, the Sandinista government promulgated amnesty in 1988. In addition, it suspended the State of National Emergency and lifted press censorship. A year later, in 1989, the government advanced the elections to early 1990 and called for a national dialogue. Kinloch indicates that by that time the war had claimed the lives of more than thirty thousand people and a similar number of people were wounded or maimed (305).[11]

The promulgation of amnesties continued even after the defeat of the FSLN in the 1990 elections. Both in the late 1980s and in the political transition that began in the 1990s, amnesties were considered a decisive tool for conflict resolution and pacification. Although the amnesties paved the way to peace, the pacification was chained to a pact of silence and oblivion. Amnesties replaced the possibility of justice. Vannini and Oettler have pointed to the elites who agreed to disarmament and signed peace as those largely responsible for the architecture of pacification. In the words of Vannini, "in the negotiation quotas of power were distributed, amnesty laws were approved and reconciliation and oblivion were decreed from above" (30).[12] Salvador García agrees with the previous approach, adding, "from 1990 to the present, the ethical foundation of the State, in relation to the armed conflict, was reconciliation built on oblivion and silence" (76–77).[13] In this social scenario, *Pictures from a Revolution's* documentary approach interrogates against the grain. Instead of embracing reconciliation, its pursuit is to document and to reveal the persistence of poverty and social injustice. Additionally, documentary practices evidence how cultural production points out inequalities in postrevolutionary societies and makes the affected citizenships visible, those who denounced the failed mystic of the revolutions.

From the search for people photographed during the popular insurrection in the city of Masaya, I examine another example, that of Augusto López González, a member of the Sandinista guerrillas photographed by Meiselas in full urban guerrilla action in the offensive that became known as "the liberation of Masaya." In this scene from the film, Meiselas continues moving through the streets of Masaya. The camera follows her in her search for López González, until she finds a woman who provides a possible address for the López González family. At that moment, the camera zooms in on the photo. Taken from inside a house, the photograph captured the moment in which Augusto López advanced with his rifle through the streets of Masaya with the goal of taking control of the National Guard in that city. In the photograph we see López González holding the rifle with his left hand, while with his right he points forward, indicating a place to go, or perhaps the place where the Guard commando was.

Ten years later, with the probable address in hand, Meiselas moves toward the outskirts of the city, near the city cemetery, until she finds the house of the former guerrilla. The camera follows her as she advances to ask about López González in the photograph. We are no longer in a city where the houses are made of bricks and the road is paved. Here, the houses are made of old wooden planks with dirt floors. The domestic animals on the screen are not dogs or cats but rather pigs.

In the scene, Augusto López González happily meets Meiselas in the company of his entire family. González's wife shows Meiselas a copy of the *Barricada* newspaper from 1981 with López González's photograph on the front page. The newspaper headline read: "Popular Combatant." The ex-guerrilla's wife then explains that, in the photo, he was pointing with his hand to the place where the National Guard was, near the city's movie theater. Next, the camera travels through parts of the López González family house, while Meiselas's voice is heard recalling the moment in which she took the photograph.

Subsequently, she begins to interview López González. He describes to her that the photo was taken when he was part of an insurrectionary contingency attempting to overthrow the National Guard in the city of Masaya:

> When you took my picture, we were in full insurrection in 79, we were about to take the command of the guard, we fought with our nails, with contact bombs. (*Pictures from a Revolution*)

Like the woman from Monimbó, López González describes that little has changed since Meiselas took the photograph.

Originally, ten years ago, Meiselas was motivated to photograph the Nicaraguan revolution because of the Sandinista's fight for change. The fact that other people in the world risked their lives for that longing for change was what aroused her interest. Meiselas herself points out how the photo with López González was seen as an image of heroism and became a symbolic image of the struggle. Excited to meet him ten years later, she finds his situation just as precarious, without any substantial change. López González himself tells the viewer:

> From the triumph till now, we think of a different change. But we have reached a critical economic situation, where we have to find out how to survive, on our own, we make a superhuman effort to survive. (*Pictures from a Revolution*)

In the film, Meiselas includes this testimony in order to reveal the unaccomplished promises of the revolution. The absence of substantive change has contributed to one of the most important public discussions in Nicaragua since the 1990s until today. Following the revolution of 1979, Nicaraguans wondered and continue to wonder: Why so much sacrifice? What remains of the revolution? While she raises these questions in her documentary, following Renov, I maintain that Meiselas's voice functions neither as historiographer nor as judge (27). Rather, her use of testimony suggests another gesture: to record the explanatory power of quotidian voices evaluating the historical process, to reveal the struggle for survival as a counterpoint of the national heroic narratives and identities and their political use, and to provide analytical "tools for evaluation," as Renov says (31). By tools for evaluation, Renov understands that information and knowledge does not render judgment but rather provides inputs so that viewers can evaluate on their own the historical, social, and cultural processes that a film documents.

In his research about the labor of memory in Central America, Ralph Sprenkels claims that the fights over memory in Nicaragua are more related to the meaning of revolution and less to the victims of armed conflict. Compared to the cases of Guatemala and El Salvador, Sprenkels says that true and transitional justice is eclipsed by the Nicaraguan political agenda (41). Following his argument, *Pictures from a Revolution* could be considered part of the cultural labor that contributes to the construction of memories of revolution and the analysis of social changes lived during one of the most convulsive decades in the Nicaraguan history, that is, the period between the overthrow of the dictatorship, the revolutionary process, and its electoral defeat in 1990. Furthermore, its labor of revealing discontent with the heroic identities could be understood as a contribution to denounce the persistence of social injustices and to seek a critical recovery of the past connected to the need for a different present and future. Definitively, one of the achievements of this documentary is to stress the past of heroism with the situation of precariousness that Meiselas finds upon returning to the country. Thus, the cinematographic support functions as a vehicle of memories and, at the same time, a critical inquiry of the Nicaraguan sociopolitical process.

Archiving Disenchantment: Documentary Film and Confrontational Memory

Palabras mágicas (para romper un encantamiento) (2012), directed by Mercedes Moncada, is another film that illustrates the role of cinema in the construction of social memories. While Meiselas registered disenchantment through testimony of others, Moncada herself is the subject of disenchantment. The documentary film is, therefore, conceived as a vehicle through which Moncada constructs her memories of the Sandinista revolution and publicly manifests her disenchantment with it and with the return of the Sandinista National Liberation Front (FSLN) to state power beginning in 2006. Although Meiselas and Moncada bet on documentary practice, Meiselas focuses on recording and revealing, while Moncada pushes for an aesthetic potential to evoke an emotional response. In *Palabras mágicas*, the construction of personal and national-collective memory in the film works as a critical interrogation of the revolutionary past. Thus, documentary film continues to tell us about its importance in critical reflection on the recent past and the present itself.[14]

Palabras mágicas (para romper un encantamiento) is a film narrated in the first person that builds off of Moncada's memories of the Sandinista revolution, marking July 19, 1979 (the triumph of the Sandinistas), as day zero of the history of Nicaragua. The film covers some of the main problems of the Sandinista revolution: war, corruption, authoritarianism, and the demagoguery of several of its main leaders. In addition to the above, the film examines the political transition of 1990, the loss of the revolutionary project, and the imposition of neoliberalism. The film ends by providing a critical perspective on the return of the Sandinista Front to power in 2007 and the persistence of violence in the management of power—something I will cover in the subsequent pages.

In *Palabras mágicas,* personal memory tries to intervene in the linear temporality of national history, denying such a linear interpretation and rather establishing a circular one. The circularity of memory argues for a return to the past as a symptomatic manifestation of a society that repeats itself and stagnates. National history is the social framework in which personal memory finds meaning. In the documentary, the recurring allusions to Sandino, the need to re-create a national narrative, the idea of turning July 17, 1979, into the zero point of history, and constantly returning to this date throughout the film illustrate my statement. Although Moncada uses her film as a means to distance herself from national history, and in particular from the Sandinista revolution—what she calls "breaking an enchantment"—the process of remembering that we see in her film forces her to return to the Sandinista revolution as the place of meaning of her own history, even if it is to problematize the revolution. The result is that through her documentary practice, Moncada develops a discourse of disenchantment with the Sandinista revolution. In the words of Valeria Grinberg Pla, Moncada uses documentary as an instrument to elaborate a confrontational memory, from a critical dialogue with the Sandinista discourse, as it was elaborated audiovisually by the Instituto Nicaragüense de Cine (INCINE) in its cinematographic productions (539).

Moncada's work is not to respond to the ethnographic documentary impulse, a documentary mode in which the director observes reality as if they were not part of it. Instead of following this mode, she eschews recording the lives of "others." In this regard, there is a difference with Meiselas and her concern in oral testimony. In Moncada's film, her documentary labor is introspective, and her challenge is to configure a discourse by connecting emotional structures with political knowledge.

Moncada's introspective approach allows for a subjective turn to the past.

Memory re-creates the past not only as the national, homogeneous past, but as a personal past, as a past that belongs to her and gives her meaning as a person.[15] What is most interesting is not the review of national history itself, but how Moncada remembers this past. An example that illustrates how personal memory reorganizes history is that, through the film, Moncada reorders the country's recent past. In her proposal, July 19, 1979—the day of the triumph of the Sandinista revolution—becomes day zero, the beginning of her memory. The past now has another criterion of temporal order: before day zero, after day zero. The documentary is set to go back and forth between before day zero—the time of the Somoza dictatorship—and after day zero—which can be the revolution, the war, the elections in 1990, and the return of the FSLN in 2007.

In Moncada's documentary, memory constitutes an exceptional mechanism to express her disenchantment with the Sandinista revolution due to its legacy of corruption and authoritarianism. As Valeria Grinberg Pla points out, Moncada configures a confrontational memory of the revolutionary past to which she was politically and affectively linked.[16] The gesture of moving between past and present throughout the film is characteristic of an intentional focus on memory because understanding of the past is not only relevant in and of itself, but also fundamental for the present. Moncada's disenchantment with the Sandinista revolution comes from the fact that the revolution was not capable of building a new society, a more just and equitable society, as it promised. Instead, its main leaders became corrupted and fell into authoritarian practice; above all, war and death continued to mark life in the country. If sacrificing one's life for a better future had made sense during the struggle against the dictatorship, it began to lose meaning as the revolution was not capable of bringing peace and progress to the country. As Moncada says: "Soon, the dead were too many for me to be with. They became part of everyday life" (*Palabras mágicas*). Here I identify a connection with oral testimonies registered by Meiselas. As pointed out before, these testimonies propose a critique of heroic identities and the mystique of sacrifice through an aesthetics of everyday life. The next step of Moncada's disenchantment occurs with the loss of elections in the 1990s and the distribution of properties among the Sandinista elite through laws known as *La Piñata*. At that time, she says she felt betrayed by everyone, some for being corrupt and others for being accomplices.

Memories of Life during War in El Salvador

The struggles for survival during and after wars is a crucial element in memory work on Central America. One of the central concerns of Central American documentary cinema is to consider how the war is understood during the postwar period and to capture the new struggles for survival following a war. In the documentary *El lugar más pequeño* (2011), director Tatiana Huezo Mixco follows the survivors of a Salvadoran rural community nearly erased by the National Army during the war in El Salvador (1980–1992).

By the early 1970s there was already a serious social crisis in El Salvador. The higher the level of organization of popular and democratizing demands, the greater the closure of all spaces for dialogue and conflict resolution. The systematic violation of human rights produced an accumulation of frustrations and anger. The 1979 coup formalized the conflict and the country entered the 1980s in civil war. Three years later, in 1983, Ignacio Martín-Baró affirmed that the war had already become the most totalizing reality in the life of El Salvador and that other existing forms of violence could only be adequately understood in reference to the war context and as effect of the loss of viable schemes of coexistence. The war ended with the peace agreements signed in 1992. The number of victims has been calculated at 75,000 dead and 15,000 missing persons.

El lugar más pequeño constructs the memories of five families from the town of Cinquera who survived state violence during the civil war in El Salvador. During the war, the Salvadoran government described the population of Cinquera as communist. This was reason enough to be marked for elimination, and as a result, Cinquera was practically erased from the national map. Part of the population managed to flee to the mountains and survive the violence. The film narrates the process of return and the town's rebuilding and shares the memories of what happened, as well as the scars and lasting trauma for members of the surviving families.

To document the memories of the community, Huezo Mixco establishes a highly intimate connection between herself, as the director, and the survivors. Huezo Mixco's documentary work activates a remembering of the past that is also a politics of place. In addition to contributing to the construction of survivors' memories, the film is an ethical and aesthetic proposal that suggests the importance of human life and nature as constitutive elements of the dignification of life. These points lead back to the idea that memory is not only an understanding of the past but also a discourse about the future.

El lugar más pequeño introduces the viewer to memories of two generations of survivors of the Salvadoran war: the parents who lived through the war and were victims of state violence, and their children, who were very young at the time of the war but still left indelible marks on their lives. Both generations tell of the difficult experiences during the war: the escape from Cinquera as a result of the army's bombing, the municipality's erasure from the national map, and their return to the community once the armed conflict ended.

El lugar más pequeño represents an effort to make a non-traditional documentary film. In Huezo Mixco's work, we do not find the traditional format of the recorded interview. Instead, in this film, the interviewee is not simply an informant who provides information that allows the film director to reconstruct the events of the past. In this documentary approach, the interviewee has value exclusively to the extent that they allow another (that is, the filmmaker) to reconstruct and tell a story. For her part, Huezo Mixco does not try to find the "truth" or the "facts" of what happened through the voice of the key informant. *El lugar más pequeño* is a permanent *voice-over* documentary of survivors of state violence. As Andrea Cabezas and Julia Gonzalez affirm, "Huezo does not direct the camera at people as they narrate their stories, instead she films symbolic images, which she later combines with voice-overs. As a result, she creates intimate and moving films" (176–177). In agreement with Cabezas and Gonzalez, Huezo Mixco invites us to feel as close as possible, symbolically and physically, to the survivors' memories and memoirs.

The centrality of the survivors in the documentary is presented explicitly in the first seconds of the film. It does not seem that it is the camera that captures them; rather, they are the ones who look directly into the camera. As viewers, we are immediately drawn in by the silent faces of the survivors of state violence in El Salvador. Scholar Kaitlin Murphy describes these techniques as unique:

> This is striking and unusual for a documentary film, all the more so for a documentary in the post-conflict, human rights genre—in which subjects are generally filmed looking and speaking directly to the camera as they share their testimonies, likely because this is how testimony is generally structured in courtrooms and other such official settings. (580)

I read the faces of the inhabitants of the town of Cinquera looking in silence at the camera as a vindication of their place in history, as survivors. More than seeing, the camera invites us to contemplate the survivors without haste. Cinema is the vehicle for these voices to be heard and these faces seen. The first voice we hear is that of a woman who survived the army's invasion in the town of Cinquera. Such an action demonstrates the epistemic privilege that the survivors have to document the war's past, simply through the act of survival and being able to share their story. Voice-over is a discourse of its own, a discourse of remembering. This discourse joins that of the image, which operates as evidence.

Huezo Mixco's documentary recovers the traumatic memories that the war had for the people of Cinquera. The survivors' testimonies show the articulation of memories around a past tied to war and that takes us back to the 1970s. The memories reflect the trajectory of a peasant community marked by poverty and agricultural work on land they did not own. In the film, one of the survivors introduces the war's past:

> From the 1970s we began to discover that we were subdued. I remember that the new parish priest who was sent to us, and who was young, since he arrived in my town was totally the difference. (*El lugar más pequeño*)

The narrator sets up two pasts: the distant past and the one that began in the 1970s. The change between the two time periods produced an awareness in the people of Cinquera, triggered by the arrival of a new priest in the municipality. The survivors of Cinquera have a preserved oral history of the community's politicization, beginning with the arrival of liberation theology that motivated the civic and political participation of the members of the community. From that moment on, the community began to see themselves as people with rights, with the ability to change the community's situation, and they began to transmit these messages to the younger members of the community. Following Renov, preservation is a fundamental function of documentary. *El lugar más pequeño* preserves a visual memory of the social process by which the community members were configured as political subjects. In one scene, the camera focuses on a bookshelf full of books in the house of a survivor. The camera's zoom-in allows us to read the titles: *La memoria del pueblo cristiano. Experiencia de Dios y justicia. Serie I*; *No basta la justicia, es necesario el amor*; *Compendio de la catequesis social de Monseñor Romero*, all books linked to liberation theology and the base ecclesial communities that had a leading role in the religious and civic life of Central America in the last decades of the twentieth century. Also, the camera captures a psalm written in cursive handwriting:

> Salmo 1. *Dichoso el hombre que no va a reuniones de malvados, ni sigue el camino de los pecadores.*

Along with these books is a notebook with a white label that has *Coord. Com. Cristianas* written on it. From there, the camera moves toward another box with books, and we viewers can identify several copies of the Bible and a book on top of them with the title: *La herencia colonial de América Latina*, by Stanley and Barbara Stein, whose first edition in Spanish was published by Editorial Siglo XXI in 1970. The camera follows the movement of hands that seems to show more books. This is how we come to notice two more books: *Los obispos latinoamericanos entre Medellín y Puebla. Documentos episcopales de 1968 a 1978*. We have before us a set of texts on ecclesiastical thought and action in Latin America. Perhaps it is important to remember that there are testimonies of several Latin American bishops included in the film, and the second book, *a Catechism of the Catholic Church*. The camera records the largely religious bibliography that not only operated as a legitimator and promoter of a large part of the community social struggles during the 1970s and 1980s in El Salvador but also in many Latin American countries.

The liberation theology priest who came to the village is remembered by a survivor as a man close to the community who pointed out, in the language of the people, that the state was upside down, "patas arriba," using a popular Spanish phrase whose meaning referenced the state's neglect of the nation's common needs. This historical period in the film was a moment of rupture in the municipality. The entrance of liberation theology in the 1970s, represented by the new priest, broke with the depoliticized, monotonous, and linear past of agricultural work. From that moment, as is pointed out by a survivor who was a member of the base ecclesial communities, the division between "those who had consciousness" and "the sleeping ones" was clear, also broken because a new word appeared in its political vocabulary: subversives (*El lugar más pequeño*). From the early 1970s, the inhabitants of Cinquera were classified by the national government as subversives, communists, and internal enemies of the state. Fueled by these accusations, the army settled in the municipality and began a cycle of repression and death: "nobody was aware of what was coming, nobody, nobody, because nobody thought of a war, nor did anyone imagine such a thing" (*El lugar más pequeño*). In the next scene, the camera focuses on the forest of Cinquera, while one of the survivors with voice-over says: "We were shoved with an invasion, there were 14 airplanes, I already felt as if all the bullets would fall on me" (*El lugar más pequeño*). The politicization of the people is quickly followed by the beginning of state violence: a state that eliminates its own citizenship, politics transmuted into violence.

Another survivor remembers that he was a child when the army attacked the town of Cinquera. The community ran to the forest to protect themselves from the attacks of the army. As the camera continues to show the forested landscape of Cinquera, the survivor's voice-over recalls his experience of fleeing into the forest with the following words: "We ran from one place to another; I came to jump over the dead. Then I knew that was what it was about: to survive or die; I remember when the dead fell behind me" (*El lugar más pequeño*). As we can read in this excerpt from a survivor's testimony, state violence produces a precarious life marked by survival, escape, hiding, and resistance against the military machinery of death. That seems to be the logic of life to which we have access through the survivors.

In this film, the voices of the survivors take precedence in the construction of the past. The director is not concerned with investigating the perspective of the state or the military on the war, or with relying on an analytical explanation of the war. Her interest focuses on detailing the past from the victims' voices. In this task, recuperating the past through the survivors' voices is her priority as a documentary filmmaker. Thus, cinema constitutes a vehicle that investigates and audiovisually constructs the extreme experience of fleeing and surviving state violence. The witness and survivor names the past:

> someone wanted to mutilate us, destroy us, make us disappear as a social sector and claim for our rights, and to demand rights is not a war. (*El lugar más pequeño*)

The memory of this survivor shows the state violence and its destructive logic. In particular, the survivors' testimonies denounce how the state, considering them internal enemies, legitimized their deaths. The social psychologist Ignacio Martín-Baró was one of the thinkers who contributed the most to understanding violence and war in El Salvador. Regarding the use of the figure of the internal enemy, he said the following (which makes sense of the stigmatization to which the population of Cinquera was subjected):

> Killing another person ceases to be a crime and becomes a social necessity as soon as that person is defined as enemy of the country and his murder is protected by the authority. (375)[17]

The report of the Truth Commission in El Salvador, entitled *De la locura a la esperanza,* coincides with what was argued by Martín-Baró when it stated, "violence originated in a political conception that had made synonymous the concepts of political opponent, subversive and enemy" (42).[18] The execution of this population was not considered a crime but rather a justified necessity for the "good" of the country. However, the testimony of the survivor belies the state narrative and denounces it for what it is, a state crime. Thus, memory operates as counter history, that is, working against the narrative of official history by revoking the label of political enemy and by placing the issue of citizenship and the struggle for rights in the foreground. The irrationality of the military state offensive and the Salvadoran state as a necropolitical machine is then evident. As Rodríguez points out, memory is not only a witness of historical suffering but also a witness of affect. In her words, memory is a "fever, drive, archive that extrapolates history and political memory to trauma, aesthetic and affect" (59).[19]

The War's Past: Trauma, an Ethics of Collectivity, and a Bond of Solidarity

In *El lugar más pequeño*, the war's past manifests itself as trauma in the present. The memory of war is not only preserved through orality, that is, it is not only socialized through language, but it is also a corporal and psychic manifestation. The past war maintains its presence, becoming apparent in the survivors' bodies through insomnia and nightmares, in still hearing shots and feeling panic in the body, knowing that nothing will be the same again. As the viewers can see in the testimony of one of the survivors, the past also manifests as madness in those who look at the army even after terror—the survivor recounts his hallucinations of those "ugly men, with glasses and gold teeth," some "devils," who say: "We come to kill you!" (*El lugar más pequeño*).

"Even if there is no war I always listen to the bullets;" "The emptiness that I carry is never going to recover" (*El lugar más pequeño*). These phrases, present in the testimonies of the survivors that the documentary reconstructs, are the sensitivities that mark the narration and transmission of the experience of war. One of the survivors who mentions with certainty the statement "Yo ya no me compongo" is the one who best illustrates the lasting durability of terror and incompleteness that constitute the social link (*El lugar más pequeño*). Laia Quílez's reflection over the documentary film and memory in Argentina's post-dictatorship supports my analysis. She mentions that the purpose of these stories "is not only to reclaim the wounds left by state violence, but to measure the exact length of the scars that still persist in social and political life" (Quílez 90). In a similar way, in *El lugar más pequeño* we see how state violence produces mental and physical scars in the people who survived.

Survival is also linked to an ethics of collectivity and a bond of solidarity. In a later scene in *El lugar más pequeño*, the camera shows us a close-up of a survivor's face while he speaks about his father. The survivor narrates, "The first time you could say I became aware, as a child, as a person, was when someone came to the house and told my mom, hey look, they killed Aníbal. Aníbal Avalos was my father. He was killed by troops of the National Guard" (*El lugar más pequeño*). This testimony allows us to analyze how the film constructs the experience of war violence in childhood. As we can see from this quote, the news that the father had been killed constitutes one of the earliest memories of the war. In this sense, violence is an awareness of the past and an element that shapes personality. If, for the surviving parents, the memory of war is a historical break, for the children, the memory of war connects the social/community and generational bond because it constitutes the foundational experience of all memories. This is evident when the viewer hears that "the first time [...] I became aware" is when someone comes to tell your house that your father has been killed (*El lugar más pequeño*). State violence is a double zero point for memory: first eliminating a life, the life of Aníbal, the witness's father; second, creating a new one, the life of the son, who becomes aware of what was happening after knowing that his father was killed by the army. This is also the case for another survivor, a woman who since she was three years old collaborated with the guerrillas by recognizing people killed by the troops of the National Guard. Now, as an adult, she paints skulls on the walls of her house. Referring to her paintings, she shares: "everybody in the family has some trauma related to the war. We have all been hit in some way" (*El lugar más pequeño*). This quote reminds again of Martín-Baró's work. In his introductory text to *Psicología social,* he pointed out how the war spread and continued throughout the 1980s until its impact reached "the entire population, directly or indirectly" (15).[20] He considered that the scope of the war was not limited to the two warring parties—the state army and the guerrilla forces of the Farabundo Martí National Liberation Front (FMLN)—but rather it reached practically the entire society. In his words:

> It is difficult to find a family in El Salvador today that does not have a child in the war, whether on one side or the other, or who has not suffered firsthand the impact of violence, repression or death. (15)[21]

Thus, war became a fundamental frame of reference for social life, an issue that on a day-to-day basis meant the naturalization of war.

On the one hand, state violence marks the stories of children during the war as citizens under siege, children caught up in the politicization and criminalization of the family. For the army, the children meant "future guerrillas," enemies of the state like their parents. The army's imperative was to root out subversion and not leave any seed alive, including children. On the other hand, the family as victim of state violence did everything possible to save their children, not only out of love, but also to preserve that politically besieged life. Although analyzing the consequences of the war on children is beyond the scope of this chapter, it is important to mention that they were one of the social sectors of the country most affected by the war. Martín-Baró called them "Hijos de la Guerra" [Children of war] (35). He also claimed that childhood was the "group that should have our attention the most" (Martín-Baró 35).[22] In accordance with the traces of the war that we can perceive in the survivor's statement that that the war hit all families, Martín-Baró drew attention to the need to think about the consequences of the war on the mental health of childhood.

The survivors who were children during the war are subjects of memory that transmit the past to their children. They represent the tranmission of experience to a third generation who did not live this past—a topic (that is, postmemory) that Patricia Arroyo Calderón discusses in her chapter. In this postwar generation, the possibility of establishing a social bond that is no longer marked by terror can be found between the experience of survival or death in which their parents and grandparents understood that they were risking their lives. Memory and citizenship are articulated in this transmission of experience. For example, a survivor who as a child experienced the murder of his father, today tells his children: "An organized people, a people with memory is more difficult to oppress" (*El lugar más pequeño*). Following this thought, family can be read as a public subject that narrates the historical continuity between the past and the future. As Fernando Chacón points out in his research with postwar youth in El Salvador, the family functions "as an emotional bridge that brings the youth closer to the unlived past" (2).[23] This function as an emotional bridge has an important role in the transition between authoritarianism and democracy, as Josefina Ludmer points out in *Aquí América Latina, una especulación* (73). As a subject of memory, family has the power to construct a memory of the struggle for rights and democracy to generations that did not directly experience those struggles. The possibility of transmitting these experiences can contribute to the non-repetition of authoritarianism and violence, saving subsequent generations from "the exhausting effort of learning everything anew each time," as indicated by Paul Ricoeur (86).[24]

Talking about the family implies asking oneself through whom the past emerges. One of the contributions of this documentary to those interested in the study of political violence in the region's recent history and memory formations is the importance of the family as a transmitting subject of the past. When the experience of violence was transmitted from parents to their children, they often resignified this memory in many ways. Perhaps the best example in this regard is the importance that sons and daughters give to the democratic nature of the civic struggle for rights begun by their parents, much more present in comparison to the process of fleeing from their homes and losing everything—their houses, their belongings, their territory—in order to survive.[25] There is also a channel of remembering when it is the parents who remember their sons and daughters killed during the war. One of the most prominent examples in this regard is that of the mother who, despite the fact that many years have passed since the end of the war, maintains an altar for her murdered daughter and sings to her every night. In addition to the sentimental bond, the mother defends her daughter's decision to become a guerrilla. But in both relationships, from children to parents and vice versa, family is the public subject and the affective bond that brings the violent past of war to the present. Thus, establishing the present-past-present dialogue through family ties, *El lugar más pequeño* constitutes the family's role as a public subject and as a transitive and intermediary subject from the past to the present.

The reflective attitude of the documentary celebrates a poetics of everyday life, a joining of poetics and politics. The long-term shots focused on the cloud forest of Cinquera, as well as the close-up shots of the faces of the survivors while we listen to their voice-overs, have a relevant aesthetic beauty. The stories told in the documentary could correspond to an epic story: a town that is attacked decides to fight and survive and, despite being erased from the map of the country, returns to settle again in its place. However, instead of narrating the history of the town from an epic narrative, the film focuses on daily life, on the scars, feelings and affections of the people of Cinquera and the cloud forest that seems to protect them. Rodríguez identifies this when she reflects about a cinema of "long-lasting shots that lull the spectator's contemplation" (47).[26] The camera always follows the survivors in their daily activities, inviting us to enjoy these activities: walking in the countryside, going to bed, and talking. *El lugar más pequeño* tells us about the resistance and strength of the survivors; their ability to escape death, survive, and reunite with the people who they thought had disappeared. If before we saw that war puts life in an extreme situation of fighting for survival, considering what has been said before, it is necessary to indicate that the fight for survival configures a collective ethics and a bond of solidarity.

El lugar más pequeño is a production positioned in conflict for the meanings of the past, for memory, for the present, for life itself. Although the documentary recalls familial loss, there is no victimization. Affection, politics, and justice converge. The director is not interested in arousing compassion. She cares more about showing the strength and firmness to survive the ultimate experience, and the serenity that can exist when remembering loss and terror. Life rises above pain. I quote Ludmer again when she mentions that in Latin America, "memory is always a cry for justice" (58).

Documentary Film as a Cultural Vehicle for Social Memories

I began this chapter arguing that documentary film on Central America can be considered a vehicle for the critical recovery of the past and, in that task, occupy a central role in the construction and transmission of social memories. I quoted Jelin to propose documentary practice as a vehicle of memory. To conclude, I want to emphasize this connection between documentary film and social memories. In the films analyzed here, the subjects of memory have a significant link to the past of dictatorships, revolutions, wars, and state violence in Central America. Rodríguez, in particular, highlights documentary cinema as a memory-cinema that accompanies political processes in Central America, exercising a critical reflection about them and elaborating a cinematographic poetic (95).

In her book about politics and memory in Nicaragua, Vannini wonders about the social and cultural mechanisms for memory transmission (23). In this chapter, I have tried to demonstrate that documentary is a significant mechanism for the construction and transmission of memory. In the case of *Pictures from a Revolution*, the film documents a social subject with a power to define the value or not of the revolutionary past in Nicaragua. The reflective attitude about the past is activated from the present, the moment when Meiselas, the director of the film, interviewed the people that she photographed ten years ago. The precariousness lived during the 1990s is the place where social subjects interrogate the revolutionary heroism of the past (the 1970s and 1980s). The result is a critique of heroism and sacrifice, because despite the bloodshed everything remains the same. The role of documentary film here is to juxtapose the heroic images of the revolution with the continued precariousness of daily life even after revolution.

The Sandinista revolution continues to represent the past in the case of *Palabras mágicas*. Through the film's questioning, the film proposes a necessary break with any notion of enchantment with the revolutionary past. Therefore, documentary film promotes a social memory that not only interrogates the past but also functions as a cultural vehicle for breaking a political and emotional link with the past. With Rodríguez, I conclude that in Nicaraguan cinematography we find an essential characteristic: cinematography that serves as a critical history beginning with the Somoza dictatorship to the revolution and post-revolution (96).

Regarding *El lugar más pequeño*, documentary film functions as a vehicle through which survivors elaborate their memories of state violence during the war in El Salvador. Here, to document means to encourage a social process: the oral and audiovisual construction of memories. Also, to document is to archive and preserve this social process, bringing it to the public sphere.

There is no doubt that the survivor is the subject of memory, the privileged point of view about the relevant past. However, this film also points to the family as the public subject and the affective bond that brings the violent past of war to the present. The cinematographic production constitutes the family's role as a public subject and as a transitive/intermediary subject from the past to the present. All three documentary films employ memory as a means to recuperate and interrogate the perspectives of the late twentieth-century conflicts in Nicaragua and El Salvador, as well as transmit the past into the present.

Notes

1 About Central American female filmmakers, see: Valeria Grinberg Pla, "Mujeres cineastas de Centroamérica: Continuidad y ruptura." For a recent analysis about Central American film and memory, see: María Lourdes Cortés, "La búsqueda de la memoria en el cine centroamericano actual."
2 In this chapter, all translations from Spanish to English are made by the author. "La guerra de liberación que puso fin a cuarenta y dos años de dictadura somocista dejó un saldo de 35 mil muertos, 110 mil heridos y 40 mil niños huérfanos" (Kinloch 305).
3 "Muchos fotógrafos captaron las imágenes de lo que pasaba en Nicaragua. Sin embargo, fueron las fotos de Susan Meiselas las que preservaron la memoria de ese evento y contribuyeron a conformar un imaginario social sobre la revolución y sus lugares emblemáticos" (Vannini 80).
4 For a more complete overview of the projects of Meiselas about Nicaragua, see: Magdalena Perkowska, "De la historia (narración) a la memoria (fragmento): La Revolución Sandinista en la obra de Susan Meiselas."
5 For a reflection about Susan Meiselas as a traveler in the second half of the twentieth century, the production of visual narratives and the construction of social memories, see: Julia Medina, "Miradas en tránsito: (Dis) utopías y feminotopías en narrativas de viaje a Centroamérica."
6 Medina develops an interesting discussion about aesthetics and social engagement in Meiselas's work. See: "Miradas en tránsito."
7 "preservan fragmentos del pasado que puedan ser actualizados y traídos al presente" (Da Silva Catela 77).
8 Since its creation in the 1930s, the National Guard had military and police attributions. Additionally, the National Guard had several public functions in public health, the national railway administration and many more (Kinloch 258). Michel Gobat shows that the National Guard took military and judicial attributions, removing local leaderships and *caudillos* (360). Also, see Richard Millet, "Guardians of the Dynasty."
9 "volvía a tener la sensación que nada había sucedido en Nicaragua a pesar del inmenso sacrificio humano de la población y de la inversión de esfuerzos por sacar adelante el país y su revolución" (Meneses 266).
10 In this sense, I find a difference with the evocative and nostalgic use of Meiselas that Florence Babb and Julia Medina point out in postrevolutionary Nicaragua. Babb, "Recycled Sandalistas: From Revolution to Resorts in the New Nicaragua;" Medina, "Miradas en tránsito: (Dis) Utopías y Feminotopías en narrativas de viaje a Centroamérica."

11 "En 1989, esta nueva guerra había cobrado 30,865 vidas humanas y 31,019 personas habían sido heridas o mutiladas" (Kinloch 305).
12 "En la negociación se distribuyeron cuotas de poder, se aprobaron leyes de amnistía y se decretó, desde arriba, la reconciliación y el olvido" (Vannini 30).
13 "Desde 1990 hasta el presente, el fundamento ético del Estado, en relación al conflicto armado, fue la reconciliación construida sobre el olvido y el silencio" (García 76–77).
14 Jared List develops an original analysis about *Palabras mágicas,* based on the concepts of precariousness and social ecological contingency, in "Terrenos revolucionarios: Precariedad y contingencia social y ecológica en el documental nicaraguense Palabras mágicas (para romper un encantamiento) (2012) de Mercedes Moncada."
15 Another documentary with a subjective turn to the Nicaraguan recent past is *Heredera del viento* (2017) from Gloria Carrión. During an interview with Jared List about her documentary production, Carrión reflected on how the documentary production of directors Albertina Carri and Nicolás Prividera, well-known authors of the subjective turn to the past, influenced her work. An important aspect of this documentary is its inclusion of the voices of sons and daughters into the process of construction of the memories of the revolution. I quote the following reflections of Carrión as evidence: "With *Heredera del viento* I intend to tell the revolution from the generation of the sons and daughters of the revolutionaries" (310). See: Jared List, "Miradas humanizantes, lazos subjetivos, memorias horizontales: Entrevista a la cineasta nicaraguense Gloria Carrión Fonseca."
16 Valeria Grinberg Pla, "Interpelaciones al sandinismo desde el cine nicaragüense contemporáneo: Palabras mágicas de Mercedes Moncada."
17 "Matar a otra persona deja de ser un delito y se convierte en una necesidad social en cuanto esa persona es definida como enemiga de la patria y su asesinato es amparado por la autoridad" (Martín-Baró 375).
18 "la violencia se originó en una concepción política que había hecho sinónimos los conceptos de opositor político, subversivo y enemigo" (Martín-Baró 42).
19 "fiebre, pulsión, archivo que extrapola la historia y la memoria política al trauma, la estética y el afecto" (Rodríguez 59).
20 "la totalidad de la población, directa o indirectamente" (Martín-Baró 15).
21 "Es difícil encontrar una familia en El Salvador hoy que no tenga un hijo en la guerra, sea de un lado o del otro, o que no haya sufrido en carne propia el impacto de la violencia, la represión o la muerte" (Martín-Baró 15).
22 "grupo que más debe llamar nuestra atención" (Martín-Baró 35).
23 "como puente emocional que acerca al joven al pasado no vivido" (Chacón 2).
24 "el esfuerzo agotador de aprender todo de nuevo cada vez" (Ricoeur 86).
25 Another example that is very present in the film is that of the daughter who builds her memories of violence through art. While other children talk about the importance of political participation, she distances herself from this discourse, but it is clear that art represents a practice in which the past of the war is still present.
26 "planos de duraderos que arrullan la contemplación del espectador" (Rodríguez 47).

Works Cited

Babb, Florence. "Recycled Sandalistas: From Revolution to Resorts in the New Nicaragua." *American Anthropologist*, vol. 106, no. 3, 2004, pp. 541–555.

Cabezas Vargas, Andrea; González, Julia. "Central American cinematographic aesthetics and their role in international film festivals." *Studies in Spanish & Latin American Cinemas*, vol. 15, no. 2, 2018, pp. 163–186.

Chacón, Fernando. "El peso del pasado: Jóvenes en El Salvador, conflicto armado y memorias de sufrimiento." *ILA*, vol. 412, 2018, pp. 23–24.

Comisión de la verdad para El Salvador. *De la locura a la esperanza. La guerra de 12 años en El Salvador. Informe de la comisión de verdad para El Salvador.* San Salvador, Nueva York, 1992–1993.

Cortés, María Lourdes. "La búsqueda de la memoria en el cine centroamericano actual." *Revista de historia No 36, Recordar el pasado para imaginar otro futuro: Artes y políticas de la memoria en Centroamérica*, 2019, pp. 110–131.

Da Silva Catela, Ludmila. "Re-velar el horror. Fotografía, archivos y memoria frente a la desaparición de personas." *Revista de historia*, no. 27, primer semestre, 2012, pp. 45–60.

El lugar más pequeño, Directed by Tatiana Huezo Mixco, Centro de Capacitación Cinematográfica (CCC), FOPROCINE, Mexico, 2011.

García, Salvador. La guerra, el pueblo miskito y la dimensión pedagógica de las memorias. *Serie Memorias*, edited by Gloria Carrión, Salvador García, & Sofía Argeñal, (pp. 65–80), Fundación Nicaragüense para el Desarrollo Económico y Social (FUNIDES), 2020.

Gobat, Michel. *Confronting the American Dream: Nicaragua under U. S. Imperial Rule.* Durham: Duke UP, 2005.

Grinberg Pla, Valeria. "Interpelaciones al sandinismo desde el cine nicaragüense contemporáneo: Palabras mágicas de Mercedes Moncada." *Revista Iberoamericana*, vol. LXXXI, no. 251, 2015, pp. 539–553.

———. "Mujeres cineastas de Centroamérica: continuidad y ruptura." *Mesoamérica* vol. 55, 2013, pp. 103–112.

Heredera del viento. Directed by Gloria Carrión, Caja de Luz, Nicaragua, 2017.

Jelin, Elizabeth. *Los trabajos de la memoria.* Madrid y Buenos Aires: Siglo XXI Editores, 2002.

Kinloch Tijerino, Frances. *Historia de Nicaragua.* Managua: Instituto de Historia de Nicaragua y Centroamérica, Universidad Centroamericana (IHNCA-UCA), 2016.

List, Jared. "Miradas humanizantes, lazos subjetivos, memorias horizontals: Entrevista a la cineasta nicaraguense Gloria Carrión Fonseca." *Imagofagia, Revista de la Asociación Argentina de Estudios de Cine y Audiovisual*, no. 17, 2018, pp. 299–315.

———. "Terrenos revolucionarios: Precariedad y contingencia social y ecológica en el documental nicaraguense *Palabras mágicas (para romper un encantamiento)* (2012) de Mercedes Moncada." *Revista Istmica*, no. 25, 2020, pp. 73–89.

Ludmer, Josefina. *Aquí América Latina, una especulación.* Buenos Aires: Eterna cadencia editorial, 2010.

Martín-Baró, Ignacio. *Acción e ideología. Psicología social desde Centroamérica.* San Salvador: U Centroamericana Editores, 1983.

Medina, Julia. "Miradas en tránsito: (Dis) utopías y Feminotopías en narrativas de viaje a Centroamérica." *Mesoamérica,* no. 55, 2013, Pp. 122-129.

Meiselas, Susan. *Nicaragua June 1978-July 1979.* New York: Pantheon Books, 1981.

Meneses, Vidaluz. *Balada para Adelina. Memorias.* Managua: Anamá Ediciones, 2016.

Millet, Richard. *Guardians of the Dynasty. A History of the U.S. Created Guardia Nacional de Nicaragua and the Somoza Family.* New York: Orbis Books, 1977.

Palabras mágicas (para romper un encantamiento). Directed by Mercedes Moncada. Amaranta Producciones, Mexico, 2012.

Murphy, Kaitlin. "Memory Mapping: Affect, Place, and Testimony in *El lugar más pequeño* (2011)." *Journal of Latin American Cultural Studies,* vol. 25, no. 4, 2016, pp. 571-595.

Oettler, Anika. "Justicia transicional y los significados de la elaboración del pasado nicaragüense." *Encuentro,* vol. 95, 2013, pp. 7-27.

Perkowska, Magdalena. "De la historia (narración) a la memoria (fragmento): La Revolución Sandinista en la obra de Susan Meiselas." *Istmo: Revista virtual de estudios literarios y culturales centroamericanos,* no. 20: Cine, comunicación audiovisual y participación política, 2010, pp 1-20.

Pictures from a Revolution. Directed by Susan Meiselas, GMR Films, New York, 1991.

Quílez, Laia. "El cine documental y la memoria en la argentina posdictadura." *Archivos de la filmoteca,* no. 70, 2012.

Renov, Michael. "Toward a poetics of documentary." *Theorizing documentary,* edited by Michael Renov, Routledge, 1993.

Ricoeur, Paul. *La memoria, la historia, el olvido.* Madrid: Trotta, 2003.

Rodríguez, Ileana. *Modalidades de memoria y archivos afectivos: Cine de mujeres en Centroamérica.* San José: U de Costa Rica, CALAS-Laboratorio Visiones de paz, 2020.

Sprenkles, Ralph. "El trabajo de la memoria en Centroamérica: Cinco propuestas heurísticas en torno a las guerrasen El Salvador, Guatemala y Nicaragua." *Revista de Historia,* no. 76, 2017, pp. 13-46.

Vannini, Margarita. *Política y memoria en Nicaragua. Resignificaciones y borraduras en el espacio público.* Ciudad de Guatemala: F & G Editores, 2020.

4

Palabras mágicas and *Heredera del viento*

Two Diagnoses of the Sandinista Revolution's Decay

Tomás Arce Mairena

The following chapter deals with two Nicaraguan documentary films: *Palabras mágicas (para romper un encantamiento)* (Mercedes Moncada, Mexico, 2012) and *Heredera del viento* (Gloria Carrión, Nicaragua, 2018). These documentaries address the Sandinista revolution's historical process, from its triumph in 1979 to its electoral defeat in 1990 to its resurgence in the 2000s under a progressively authoritarian regime run by former guerrilla leader and president Daniel Ortega. In this essay, I aim to demonstrate how both films question the official narrative of the Sandinista revolution by supplying the audience with a series of lyrical reflections on this relevant historical process. Based on *The Cinema of Poetry* theory proposed by Pier Paolo Pasolini, I will demonstrate how the two Nicaraguan filmmakers interrogate the historical facts by creating poetic sequences that provide an intimate view on the grieving processes experienced by Moncada and Carrión in the aftermath of the last Latin American leftist revolution of the twentieth century, zeroing in on the directors' personal relationship with the revolutionary regime during the 1980s, when Nicaragua also faced a civil war between the Sandinistas and the U.S.-backed Contra rebels.

While the Sandinista revolution was a watershed historical moment in Latin American politics and in U.S.-Central American relations, it did not last long. In February of 1990, Ortega ran for president a second time. However, the Sandinista party (FSLN, or Sandinista National Liberation Front) was massively defeated by a democratic coalition that ran Violeta Barrios de Chamorro as its presidential candidate, in what has gone down in the history books as the first democratic election to ever take place in Nicaragua. The

1990 election ended with more than a decade of *los muchachos* ("the boys," as the revolutionary leaders were called) ruling the affairs of the Nicaraguan nation. However, after sixteen years of a series of neoliberal governments, Ortega regained power in 2007. The documentaries' use of poetic images reflects an intimate reading of these historical events and allows Moncada and Carrión to confront reality in the aftermath of the Sandinista revolution, as the directors recall their respective childhoods during the revolutionary period with the purpose of sharing with their audiences their grief and disillusion as a nation's utopic dream became a nightmare in just a few decades. This utopia was destroyed not only because of U.S. President Reagan's anti-socialist plan for the Central American isthmus during the Cold War era, but also because the Sandinista leaders transformed the revolutionary impetus into a political and economic machine at the service of their own personal gain. In the 1980s, both Mercedes Moncada and Gloria Carrión were children born into families that believed in the new political revolutionary order and participated in the *guerrilla* war against the Somoza right-wing dictatorship—which had ruled Nicaragua with an iron fist since 1936. From the perspective of childhood, both directors were direct witnesses of one of the last revolutions of the twentieth century, which rose to power in 1979 after several years of internal armed conflict. In the following pages, I will prove how both films (by presenting poetic sequences and interrogating the filmmakers' own personal past) diagnose how Nicaragua's *authoritarian condition* destroyed the Sandinista utopia.

To better understand this authoritarian condition, it is necessary to review how the Somoza family updated Nicaragua's governmental system in the past century. Beginning in 1936—when Anastasio Somoza García, the son of a wealthy coffee planter and head of the National Guard, seized power—the Somoza family ruled Nicaragua following the political tradition of *caudillismo*. Under a *caudillo*, or strongman, the government made important national economic decisions that not only benefited the dictator's family and their inner circle, but the private business sector as well, without caring for the impact that the implementation of these policies would have on the majority of the population. The Somoza era was characterized by inequality and political oppression: those who dared to protest and act as citizens of a free republic were punished with exile, beatings, or ultimately execution by the National Army at the service of the ruling family. The Somoza dynasty was at first a government model endorsed by Nicaragua's cultural and political elite—following two decades of U.S. military occupation (1912–1933) and a six-year (1927–1933) armed rebellion against this occupation led by Augusto César Sandino, after whom the Sandinista revolutionaries named themselves.

Juan Pablo Gómez states that the decision to back up Somoza García's coup against President Juan Bautista Sacasa in 1936 "was related to the need to implement a strong and lasting political authority as the only possibility of establishing order in a society that was considered chaotic, disorganized and aimless" (13).[1]

Somoza García managed to rule Nicaragua for two decades until his assassination in 1956, after which his oldest son, Luis Somoza Debayle, seized power. Luis died in 1967 and was succeeded by his younger brother, Anastasio Somoza Debayle, who ruled as president or through figurehead politicians until his ouster twelve years later. During this time, the brothers were supported by the United States, which saw them as important anti-communist allies despite their regime's brutality and corruption (Gilbert 157–160). Meanwhile, popular discontent was brewing in the country, leading to the formation of anti-government groups that coalesced in the FSLN's founding in the 1960s. After years of guerrilla warfare, the revolutionary movement claimed victory on July 19, 1979. After the last member of the Somoza family fled to Miami, a sense of joy and happiness filled not only the triumphant FSLN guerrilla members but also the general population. The overthrow of the dictator Anastasio Somoza Debayle's regime was the result of Nicaraguan class unity against a common enemy: the Somoza regime. However, the deep-seated inequalities (economic, social, ethnic, cultural, geographic, etc.) as well as the decades of violence and poverty that afflicted Nicaraguan society were much more difficult to bridge once the FSLN went from rebel army to ruling party.

This significant political shift is at the heart of what *Palabras mágicas* and *Heredera del viento* attempt to do. For example, Moncada questions the revolution's historical process and the evident deformation of progressive ideas and notions that the FSLN used to represent. Meanwhile, *Heredera del viento* narrates from a private and personal perspective how the revolutionary process marked Carrión's family and her childhood. While remembering her childhood years, the director confronts her nuclear family to discuss personal traumas. Carrión also interviews former members of the Contra-revolutionary army and family members who were affected by the civil war that broke out in the 1980s in Nicaragua, and which divided the country into two antagonist groups: Sandinistas and Contras. I will address this confrontation that takes place in this section of the documentary by establishing a dialogue with the concept of ethics and the *face* proposed by Emmanuel Levinas.

In *Palabras mágicas,* the moment of revolutionary triumph is what Moncada's voice-over calls *Día cero:* a Spanish expression that literally means "Day zero." On that very first day (July 19, 1979), the people believed in the possibility of a *Nueva Nicaragua*. Moncada's film displays the massive joy experienced during that day. By using historical footage and newsreels, the film shows a crowd congregated in front of the ruins of the Cathedral of Managua, in the earthquake-devastated area very close to Lake Xolotlán. Before the catastrophic tremor that tore down the city in 1972, this urban area used to be the downtown of Nicaragua's capital city. In the film, it is noticeable how the crowd celebrates the ending of the ruthless, corrupt system led by the Somoza family—which had been accused of misappropriating relief funds meant to reconstruct the city and help the earthquake's victims. The footage underscores a multitudinous excitement and a naive hope among the general population. Regardless of social class or ideology, the crowd and the *guerrilleros* shared a common hope of building a fairer, more egalitarian society. Finally, the younger generation had defeated the old order. Thus, for many Nicaraguans, this was going to be their first chance of living in a democracy; or, at least, that was the initial hope. This audiovisual archive displays a sense of infinitive possibilities and joy for the country's future. Nevertheless, due to the outcomes of the revolutionary project, for Moncada it was important to contrast this initial expectation with the crude aftermath of the utopic dream. As Adriana Palacios notes, this documentary film is a type of incantation based on the use of historical footage, which provides the ingredients needed to cast a spell against the blindness of nostalgia. Moncada casts this spell with the purpose of confronting the decay of the Sandinista revolution, which she achieves by demystifying this watershed historical movement in which she believed during her youth. She does so by visually making evident the contrast between the transformative cultural and educational activities carried out by the Sandinista Youth movement during the first stage of the revolution (shown through historical footage) and the regime's instrumentalization of younger people to beat up civil protesters during the municipal elections of 2008 (shown with footage shot during the time the film was made).

Filmed almost thirty years apart, the two historical archives come together through careful editing to reveal how a revolutionary movement that in the 1970s suffered from and fought against political repression, had degenerated into the very thing it once denounced and opposed. Moncada utilizes images of young people (which metaphorically signifies renewal and hope for the future) to emphatically display how the tables had turned after Ortega's and the FSLN's return to power in the 2000s. The decay of the Sandinista Youth (shown suppressing peaceful protests and restricting the free circulation of citizens through the capital city) and Nicaragua's young people in general (who speak to the documentarian about the violence, drug use, unemployment and other ills they face every day), is contrasted with one of the most important outcomes of the Sandinista revolution: The literacy campaign implemented in the rural areas of the nation, mainly by young people.

In this regard, it is important to expand on the role that INCINE (the Nicaraguan Film Institute) played as part of the Sandinista cultural project. INCINE—which captured the literacy campaign shown in Moncada's documentary—was created shortly after the revolution's victory, its main objective being to develop "a production and dissemination network, recovering the cinematographic experience developed since the popular uprising of the previous year" (Getino and Vellegia 106).[2] According to scholar Daniel Chávez, even beyond the triumph of *los guerrilleros,* two main ideological attitudes toward audiovisual media coincided with the rise and triumph of the Nicaraguan revolution during the 1980s. These were the "sources that tended to alienate and exploit the viewer under the ideological tenets of late capitalism" and "a resisting and liberating media that presented a critical stance against the penetration of capitalist ideology in developing countries" (Chávez 238). This type of media had an important production peek immediately after the Cuban revolution's victory in 1959, helping to develop a type of independent, ideologically driven cinema that spread throughout the continent and led to what is now known as "New Latin American Cinema." At the moment of the triumph of the Sandinista revolution in 1979, ICAIC (the Cuban Film Art and Industry Institute) was well established. For this reason, it was natural for members of INCINE and the institution itself to receive support from its Cuban counterpart. Chávez points out that this meant both institutes pursued the same objective: "The construction of ideological consciousness was supposed to become an integral part of the overall process of national reconstruction [...] Therefore the New Man's critical consciousness must come from an overtly ideological retraining" (243). And because it was part of revolutionary discourse, when the Sandinista project was over, INCINE was dismantled by the new neoliberal government. It should be noted that this institution was at the service of ideology and the revolutionary project. All of the films and newsreels that were produced by INCINE were under the influence of revolutionary rhetoric and the Sandinistas' revolutionary cultural project. As the Sandinista project encountered external and internal resistance during the 1980s, INCINE's goals shifted from educational to more overtly propagandistic ones:

> The subsequent situation of Nicaraguan cinema and its official projects of production and internal and international distribution were naturally conditioned by the evolution of the country's political circumstanc-

es, the war against the "Contras" and North American interference—which imposed a total embargo on the country in 1985. (Getino and Velleggia 107)[3]

Despite the enormous success and moral victory of the literacy campaign and what that meant for the new revolutionary order and the Nicaraguan people, these policies indeed responded to the "political nature" of the time (Chávez 235). Chávez states that for the new revolutionary regime, cinema was mainly considered as "an important element in the transformation of people's perception of and engagement with the revolution" (236). While Moncada relies on historical footage produced by INCINE to document the early years of the revolution, her film also confronts the official audiovisual narrative created by the Sandinistas through its state film institute. For example, there are several instances when footage of explosions that took place during the revolutionary and Contra war periods is juxtaposed with shots of similar explosions taking place in the country after the FSLN regained power in 2007. This perspective illustrates how, despite the fact that a violent rebellion occurred, there was no real change in Nicaraguan political culture. The political class continued to reinforce a lack of democratic procedures. The same strategies deployed by the authoritarian Somoza regime began to be implemented during the so-called second stage of the Sandinista revolution in the 2000s.

In this regard, Daniel Chávez point outs that "Somoza's views on power and his conception of governance by personal decision making and naming and removing of regional authorities, members of the judiciary, and members of the government at all levels were traits of a conservative central republic" (42). This was established with the approval of the conservative leaders and had the ideological support of the intellectual elites, at least in the early stages of the consolidation process of *el somocismo*. Chávez argues that this group of intellectuals "was looking rather for a modern reconstitution of a Hispanic commonwealth" (42). The young conservative intellectuals "dreamt of an arrangement with certain similarities to what the British Empire was developing at this time in relation to its ex-colonies" (58). Somoza García persuaded the conservative elites. Once the allies defeated the fascist axis powers, it was not convenient for the Somoza regime to be associated with this group under the eyes of any U.S. administration. The project of modernity instituted by Somoza García was a "conservative utopian reconstruction" (Chávez 68). This Eurocentric project had a significant impact on the national economy; nevertheless, progress was achieved by an authoritarian regime on good terms with the U.S. State Department.

This concept of the authoritarian leader or *caudillo* with enough power to do his will without caring about the constitution and the constitutional rights of Nicaraguan citizens, is updated by the last two *caudillos* in Nicaraguan history: former neoliberal president Arnoldo Alemán (1997–2002) and Daniel Ortega (2007–present). In the case of Alemán, he was the second president of the postrevolutionary period after Barrios de Chamorro (1990–1997), who introduced "a new round of reforms to dismantle the economic and social policies of the previous decade giving way to structural adjustment programs and a process of sweeping privatization and liberalization in order to 'reinstate' a market-based economy" (Chávez 267). According to Karen Kampwirth, Alemán "started to use tactics of the first Somoza" and by employing "a flamboyant nationalist rhetoric, he established different ideological or social fields of attack, a very transparent but effective division of us versus them: 'us' being modern and progress [. . .] 'them' being Sandinistas, totalitarian oligarchs" (quoted in Chávez 287). What is new about this update of *el somocismo* is that it was occurring in a neoliberal world. Regarding this particularity, Chávez states the following:

> In contrast to the Somoza dynasty, in the 1990s the resources of the state that were available to choose winners and losers in the march toward development and modernization were tied to the strict austerity agreements signed with the international financial institutions. The diversion of the bulk of those resources would have meant derailing a delicate process that was under constant surveillance by the foreign banks. (287)

When it was over, the Alemán presidency was labeled as one of the most corrupt governments in the history of Nicaragua: "On August 7, 2002, the official announcement was made that the new administration had charged Arnoldo Alemán, and thirteen other persons [. . .] with fraud, embezzlement, criminal conspiracy, and money laundering" (Chávez 292). The neoliberal promise of democracy was deceived by the voracious ambition of the last liberal *caudillo*. This demonstrated that no matter who was in charge, national economic stagnation remained. The authoritarian way of ruling the country and concentrating power around one person and their family seemed like a permanent state in Nicaragua. This is because *caudillismo* has worked as a conservative blueprint for exerting power and achieving economic growth in a country in constant *tabula rasa*.

Against this historical background, Moncada uses film language to propose not only a historical revisionist journey but also to share her own experience with a revolutionary process in which she had faith. In depicting this process, she crafts a panoramic perspective of the Sandinista revolution. She achieves this by creating an equilibrium between cinematic poetry and cinematic prose. The cinematic poetic sequences that relate to her individuality and personal memories implement what the Italian writer and filmmaker Pier Paolo Pasolini theorizes about cinema language in general: irrationality. Pasolini proposes "the deep dream quality of cinema" but also "its absolute and essential concretion" (13).[4] This means that "[t]he linguistic or grammatical institution of the cinematographic author is made up of images: and images are always concrete, never abstract" (Pasolini 18).[5] This is why in *Palabra mágicas,* Moncada composes a series of metaphors to propose an allegory of what she personally and intimately felt about the revolution. The audience experiences how the feeling of joy later became one of disenchantment. Moncada edits her movie—not intending to tell the spectator what to think about the revolutionary process in Nicaragua or to show information that is possible to find in several books on the topic—but rather to reveal her process of disenchantment and grief with the utopic dream she and her country once had.

The series of poetic cinematic sequences that Moncada presents to the audience throughout the documentary constitutes a dialogue with her audience. For example, regarding the multiple shots of water that the director employs in her film, Valeria Grinberg Pla explains that "[t]he lake serves to represent the stagnation that the country is going through [...] but also, as a repository, it functions as an image of memory" (545).[6] These poetic cinematic sequences are effective because they propose a language in direct correspondence with the personal sensitivity of Moncada. As Pasolini points out, "the 'cinema of poetry' is therefore, in reality, deeply based on the exercise of style as inspiration, in most cases, sincerely poetic" (36).[7] *Palabras mágicas* creates a rupture with the previous documentary film production in the Isthmus, given the fact that we find a balance between factual historical events and poetic symbolic sequences in Moncada's work. In the end, the poetic images and the reflection that she proposes to the viewer end up being more honest than the revolutionary promises of the 1980s. And even with this intimate and lyrical approach to history, Moncada managed to create a new cinematic approach with the purpose of examining the aftermath of the Sandinista revolution. For instance, the influence of Moncada's film is evident in *Heredera del viento.*

As a filmmaker, Gloria Carrión cannot elude the influence of Moncada's work because she is also telling her own story of growing up during the war period. Yet, she tells a more intimate and private story because her main subjects of study are her Sandinista parents and their own relationship with the revolution. Similar to what Moncada does, Carrión confronts the idealization of the revolution that inevitably divided the nation into two antagonistic sides: Sandinistas and Contras. Through a series of interviews, the director revisits different places with her parents to activate their memories. In this analysis, I will focus on the insights she provides regarding the treatment of otherness when a nation is engaged in a civil war. Levinas's explorations of the *other* and the *face* are important for understanding how images relate to processes of humanizing or dehumanizing others in situations of violence. For Levinas, the *face* of the *other* become philosophical and ethical categories. This implies seeing the *face* not as a physical object but as the most important feature of humankind—the *face* shows and exposes human nature. As a sign of vulnerability and as an expressive aspect, the *face* is something legible that forces us to be ethical with the *other* as we recognized his or her humanity (348). For example, in *Heredera del viento*, Carrión chooses to engage with her parents' enemies (the Contras) and show their side of the story. By including the perspective (and the face) of a former Contra soldier, the documentarian participates in an act of recognizing the humanity of the people on the other side of the conflict and their right to oppose the Sandinista national project. In this regard, Carrión allows the audience to hear to what the other side had to say regarding the new national project and its exclusionary practices. Viewers then have the opportunity to see how the Contras understood their ideology during this time.

It is in the last section of her documentary when Carrión meets face to face with former members of the Contra army and surviving relatives of soldiers killed in action. Before opening this last and important sequence in the film, the director shares the following reflection: "Years after my uncle Alvaro's death, the fear of the Contras I felt as a child turned slowly into a rage. The Contras became my enemies. Although I had never seen or heard them" (*Heredera del viento*). In this meaningful statement, a key aspect is the fact that she recognizes that she "had never seen or heard [the Contras]." Yet, despite not knowing any Contra during her childhood, she felt strong negative feelings toward the rebel army because of her uncle's death: the perpetrator or perpetrators did not have a specific identity or *face* but hid in the anonymity of war. Irene Agudelo points out that, during the civil war, the propaganda constructed by each side reduced the conflict to an essentialist binarism, therefore denying the right to disagree as a citizen (42). Decades later, Carrión meets with those whom she once considered her worst possible enemies—faceless, nameless enemies that once terrified her. For Levinas, there is something mystical in recognizing and meeting *face to face* with someone else, stating that:

The ethical relation, the face to face, also cuts across every relation one could call mystical, where events other than that of the presentation of the original being come to overwhelm or sublimate the pure sincerity of this presentation, where intoxicating equivocations come to enrich the primordial univocity of expression, where discourse becomes incantation as prayer becomes rites and liturgy. (202)

In the case of the Sandinista revolution, the party became a sort of religion; while the ideology that was defended allowed for only one way of constructing a new society, devouring all other points of view about how to develop the nation after the defeat of *el somocismo*. In other words, it denied otherness by imposing a single political and economic ideology. This is the portion of the documentary that I find innovative in dealing with the topic of the Sandinista revolution. As a child traumatized by the war, Carrión listens to the events that marked two former soldiers of the Contra army. Just like her, these two former soldiers probably were just children or teenagers when the civil war took place. However, I consider that she should have named these former Contras or the mother who lost her young son in the battlefield—because providing their names would contribute to further humanizing those that were vilified by the Sandinistas and their propaganda machine during the civil war. But beyond this issue, Carrión is successful in giving back the *face* to what the Sandinista revolution considered "otherness." By interviewing former members of the Contra army, she is choosing to humanize the other side. The audience can see their facial expressions and hear why they did not align with the Sandinista system back in the 1980s. As part of her voice-over, Carrión states that: "[i]nterviewing these men and women who fought on the Contra's side was not easy. As I filmed them, I could not stop thinking about all the pain they caused. But slowly my camera lens revealed that same pain. War is a spear that wounds us equally" (*Heredera del viento*).[8] She adds that "during those years, we were blinded. We became arrogant and we stopped listening" (*Heredera del viento*).[9]

But who is this "we" to whom she is referring and including herself as part of ? After hearing three testimonies of loss similar to hers, Carrión juxtaposes audio footage of a young commander encouraging even more younger Sandinista troops to defending the revolution even with their lives. The voice is that of Carrión's father, Carlos Carrión Cruz (former head of the Sandinista Youth), who is playing the role of "the revolutionary superhero" according to Carrión's childhood gaze. In the archival footage, Carrión Cruz is giving a speech that encourages young soldiers to defend the revolution at all costs, concluding with the words: "Keep fulfilling your duty" (*Heredera del viento*). Levinas claims that "[l]anguage thus conditions the functioning of rational thought: it gives it a commencement in being a primary identity of signification in the face of him who speaks" (355). After showing the archival footage, the filmmaker now faces her father in the present time. This is one of the most crucial and sensitive moments in the documentary, as the aging man bursts into tears. The historical footage breaks him because he now realizes how power can blind people. Diane Perpich claims that, for Levinas, the face acquires a philosophical notion as "The idea of infinity" (241). The former guerrilla leader sees in his daughter's face what Levinas believes is something infinite and hard to grasp, but meaningful. Carrión's father cries because he no longer recognizes the "other" that he once was during the time of revolution. He is being faced by the image of his own old self. His younger face appears to him all powerful and almighty. He regrets the speech given to the young Sandinistas. While delivering his speech to the crowd, it was impossible to recognize otherness because the crowd is faceless. But now he can see those *faces* through the archival video included in the sequence.

There's a realization that takes place in the film that the revolution was defeated in part because the killings of fellow Nicaraguans did not stop with the end of the Somoza dictatorship. According to Michael L. Morgan, for Levinas the face "puts the self in question or calls it into question; it speaks out of nakedness, destitution, and weakness; it forbids murder; it challenges the self from its humility and height; it summons the self to respond" (80). In this particular scene with Carrión Cruz and the Sandinista Youth, otherness is not represented by the Contra army, but by the regime's failure to recognize the humanity of its own members. The Sandinista revolution failed to include all of the actors conforming Nicaragua's social structure. *Los guerrilleros* too easily forgot that it was unity against a common enemy that had carried them to victory, instead of defending a vertical approach to the implementation of structural reforms that the Nicaraguan society needed, and which had motivated the need for a revolution to begin with. In the end, the same old authoritarian tradition of government was imposed. Even worse, one of the main leaders of the revolution, Daniel Ortega, is now oppressing and limiting the possibilities of a new generation of Nicaraguans with the consolidation of yet another dictatorship following the violent crackdown on protests that began in 2018 and has continued through to today.

In the previous pages, I proposed a reading of how *Palabras mágicas* and *Heredera del viento* address the decay of the Sandinista revolution and how this historical process affected not only Nicaragua's politics, but the lives of entire families in the country and the region. From a personal perspective,

Moncada and Carrión created a series of carefully crafted images and sequences (some poetic, others more expository) with the purpose of presenting a subjective perspective on the same historical process. Thus, the documentaries seek to evoke emotions on their audiences and to share glimpses of how Moncada and Carrión recall the revolutionary cause from their younger gaze and how they now view it as adults. Ironically, many of the historical audiovisual archives that are incorporated in both films were created as political propaganda for the FSLN, which the filmmakers criticize for its role in turning the revolutionary dream into a nightmare. In both films, the historical footage's purpose is to create a contrast between the initial revolutionary euphoria and the revolution's decline and disenchantment, once Ortega and the FSLN returned to power in the 2000s.

Palabras mágicas innovates the documentary film tradition in Central America, presenting the audience with a subjective and poetic perspective of a factual issue, full of symbolic elements created to engage with viewers and to question the current FSLN administration. This questioning helps Moncada (at the personal level) to heal from disenchantment, after she had deposited hope in the failed Nicaraguan revolution. Additionally, it seeks to refresh the memory of a generation that, even at a young age, did witness this crucial moment in Central America's history—a topic that Juan Pablo Gómez's chapter in this volume addresses in detail through the analysis of how *Palabras mágicas* endeavors to construct social memories. Moreover, Moncada shows the enduring symptoms of Nicaragua's *authoritarian condition*—represented in this case by the FSLN's lack of a democratization after losing power in 1990. Since then, the FSLN political leaders, along with right-wing *caudillos*, have been devouring Nicaragua's resources while defending their own personal interests and recycling the old authoritarian system for ruling the country's affairs. This has had a detrimental effect on the impoverished population, as it could no longer count on a single political party that would defend the interests of the proletarian and rural classes.

Meanwhile, Carrión's film is courageous because it shows her difficult relationship with her revolutionary family. Her trauma is a symptom of all the pain and resentment accumulated in the Nicaraguan nation. She dares to share this personal grief with the audience with the purpose of rethinking the nation's violent past by listening to the political radicalism of a nation in constant division. She is brave to break the silence regarding the awful consequences of the last civil war in Nicaragua, between Sandinistas and Contras, during the 1980s. Additionally, both films work as a reminder to the Nicaraguan population that there are still war traumas to deal with and wounds to heal from as a nation. Unfortunately, under the current political situation in

Nicaragua, new wounds and traumas are being created—as the Ortega regime, along with its political allies and government officials, continues to impede a civic solution to the violent political crisis that started in 2018. In 2022, Daniel Ortega and Rosario Murillo (his wife and vice president) won another election, this time after jailing the political opposition. This was the last action that confirmed that Nicaragua is again suffering the consolidation of another dictatorship. In this regard, Ortega and Murillo have proven to be the most outstanding students of the Somoza family and the authoritarian tradition of *caudillismo*. As the Nicaraguan poet Carlos Martínez Rivas predicted in the early stages of the Sandinista revolution, one is left "Wondering if there was ever a Revolution here."[10]

Notes

1 "[. . .] estuvo relacionada a la necesidad de instaurar una autoridad fuerte y duradera como única posibilidad de ordenar una sociedad que consideraban caótica, desordenada y sin rumbo alguno."
2 "Una red de producción y difusión, recuperando la experiencia cinematográfica desarrollada desde la insurrección popular del año anterior."
3 "La situación posterior del cine nicaragüense y de sus proyectos oficiales de producción y distribución interna e internacional estuvo naturalmente condicionada por la evolución de las circunstancias políticas del país, la guerra contra los 'contras' y la injerencia norteamericana—que impuso un embargo total al país en 1985."
4 "La profundad calidad onírica del cine" [. . .] "su absoluta e imprescindible concreción."
5 "La institución lingüística, o gramatical del autor cinematográfico está constituida por imágenes: y las imágenes son siempre concretas, nunca abstractas [. . .]"
6 "El lago sirve para representar el estancamiento que atraviesa el país [. . .] pero también, en tanto repositorio, funciona como imagen de la memoria."
7 "El 'cine de poesía' está en realidad, por consiguiente, profundamente basado en el ejercicio del estilo como inspiración, en la mayor parte de los casos, sinceramente poética."
8 "La guerra es una lanza que nos hirió a ambos" (1:17:48–1:18:12).
9 "Durante esos años, nos enceguecimos. Fuimos arrogantes. Y dejamos de escuchar" (1:18:39–1:18:56).
10 "Preguntándose si hubo aquí Revolución." This verse comes from the poem "Tríptico 15 de Agosto en Granada," published in the official Sandinista newspaper *Barricada* during the early years of the revolutionary government.

Works Cited

Agudelo Builes, Irene. *Contramemorias. Discursos e imágenes sobre / desde la Contra, Nicaragua 1979–1989*. Managua: IHNCA-UCA, 2017.

Chávez, Daniel. *Nicaragua and the Politics of Utopia: Development and Culture in the Modern State*. Nashville: Vanderbilt UP, 2015.

Getino, Octavio and Susana Velleggia. *El cine de las historias de la revolución. Aproximación a las teorías y prácticas del cine político en América Latina (1967–1977)*. Buenos Aires: Grupo Editor Altamira, 2002.

Gilbert, Dennis. *Sandinistas: The Party and the Revolution*. New York: Basil Blackwell, 1988.

Gómez, Juan Pablo. *Autoridad / Cuerpo / Nación: Batallas culturales en Nicaragua (1930–1943)*. Managua: IHNCA-UCA, 2015.

Grinberg Pla, Valeria. "Interpelaciones al sandinismo desde el cine nicaragüense Contemporáneo: Palabras mágicas de Mercedes Moncada." *Revista Iberoamericana*, no. 251, 2015, pp. 539–554.

Heredera del viento. Directed by Gloria Carrión, Caja de Luz, Nicaragua, 2018, https://www.archivosonoro.org/archivos/himno-nacional-de-nicaragua/. Accessed 11 September 2021.

Kampwirth, Karen. "Arnoldo Alemán takes on the NGOs." *Latin American Politics and Society*, no. 45, 2003, pp.133–158.

Levinas, Emmanuel. *Totality and Infinity. An Essay on Exteriority*. Pittsburgh: Duquesne UP, 2000.

Martínez Rivas, Carlos. "Tríptico 15 de agosto en Granada." *Poesía Reunida*, edited by Pablo Centeno-Gómez, Editorial Anamá, 2007.

Morgan, L. Michael. *The Cambridge Introduction to Emmanuel Levinas*. Cambridge: U of Cambridge P, 2011.

Palabras mágicas (para romper un encantamiento). Directed by Mercedes Moncada, Producciones Amaranta S.A de CV, Casa Comal S.A, Miss Paraguay Producciones, TVU-NAM, Mexico, 2012.

Palacios, Adriana. "Memoria e imagen. Palabras mágicas (para romper un encantamiento)." *Revista Carátula*, vol. 53, 2013, https://www.caratula.net/memoria-e-imagen-palabras-magicas-para-romper-un-encantamiento/.

Pasolini, Pier Paolo and Eric Rohmer. *Cine de poesía contra cine de prosa*. Translated by Joaquín Jordá. Barcelona: Anagrama, 1970.

Perpich, Diane. "Levinas and the face of the other." *The Oxford Handbook of Levinas*, edited by Michael L. Morgan, Oxford UP, 2019.

II

Migration, Movement, and Place

5

Borders, Body, and Violence

The Representation of the Central American Migrant in Contemporary Cinema

María Lourdes Cortés

The migration of Central Americans to the United States—and the difficulties they face crossing Mexican territory—is one of the most important themes of Latin American audiovisual production, calling into question the relationship between visual representation and politics in Central America. Who speaks on behalf of Central Americans and why? Who has the legitimacy to tell their stories? During its history, Central America has been a space "between" borders—let's remember that we speak of the narrowest isthmus on the planet between the two largest oceans and joining two large land masses—and this geographic determinism has been seen reflected both in the physical and symbolic borders and in the representation of 'Central Americanness.' In this chapter, I analyze the ways in which Mexican-produced films about Central American migration represent this phenomenon and the subjects they portray, claiming that they all employ the aesthetic of what I call "cinema of marginality." In employing this aesthetic, the migration films analyzed here also engage with key contemporary discussions about dehumanization and neoliberal subjects that become marginal, abject and disposable in an increasingly interconnected global economy that demands large numbers of immigrant workers while lacking the protections or legal frameworks to ensure their well-being.

With the exception of the attention received by its conflicts, Central America has almost always been invisible to the world. Thus, this region exists in and through its potential for conflict, whether it be the so-called banana republics, dictatorships, civil wars, or migration, in a model of representation that political scientists refer to as a "regional agenda." On the other hand, Central America is visible; it exists through the images tied to the mode of hegemonic production due to the fact the region lacks developed cultural industries and a market of audiovisual products. Because it produced very few of its own audiovisual representations, during the twentieth century the Isthmus came to be known through stereotypes that, although they did not show it directly, revealed the physical and symbolic borders that form the imaginary cartography of Central America. The legitimacy of Central American images—who speaks for whom and why?—proposes the space that lies between what is shown and what does not want or should not be shown.

Many Central Americans found themselves forced to migrate during the decade of the 1980s as a consequence of civil wars in the region, and there is a line of continuity between said migrations and more recent ones after peace accords were signed in the 1990s. The flows between Mexico and the United States intensified at the end of the twentieth century and the first decades of the twenty-first century. In Central America, between 10 percent and 12 percent of the population have abandoned their countries of origin as part of intra- or extra-regional migrations. These migrations, a product of an exclusionary political and economic model, have accelerated due to recent neoliberal policies that have furthered social inequality. This is compounded by the absence, in some countries, of the rule of law, and a structural violence dominated by drug-trafficking and gangs, known as "maras" (Sandoval 38).

The recent "migrant caravans" have caught the attention of citizens, governments, human rights organizations, the mass media, etc., as a new form of migrating and even as an act of civil resistance.[1] While this type of movement has been taking place since 2011, it is since 2018 that the migrant caravan phenomenon intensified as a particular form of migration and political visibility. Previously, Central American migrants were practically invisible, despite the fact that they have become the second largest Latinx immigrant group in the United States after Mexicans (O'Connor et al.). In the caravans, a form of self-defense emerges that involves walking in masses, without *coyotes* (smugglers), without legal documentation, and through routes controlled by immigration agents, who in some cases conspire with organized crime. The novel aspect of the 2018 caravans is that they formed in the countries of origin—Honduras and El Salvador. The caravans also call attention to the volume of migrants—with estimates of up to 6,000 people being part of the October 2018 caravan—and its composition, with large participation of women, children, and entire families (Varela and McLean 12).

In Mexican and Central American cinema, the topic of migration has become a priority in the past two decades, even when the movement of people into and out of the region has been a long-standing societal and political issue. It is estimated that more than one hundred movies focusing on Mexico's northern border with the United States have been made since 1990, to the extent that migration-related movies are now considered a subgenre of Mexican film (Maciel 5). It is important to highlight that, in addition to migration from Central America to the United States, important intraregional migration also exists—for example, from Nicaragua to Costa Rica, and from the Caribbean and South America to Central America and Mexico. Also, some Central American-produced films have delved into the topic in recent years—such as Isthar Yasin's *El Camino* (Costa Rica, 2008) and Marcela Zamora's documentary *María en tierra de nadie* (Mexico/El Salvador/Guatemala, 2011), the latter of which Esteban E. Loustaunau analyzes in detail from the perspective of migrant credence in chapter 6 of this volume. However, due to reasons of space and focus, I will concentrate on the representation of Central American migrants in Mexican-made films in this particular text.

"Cinema of Marginality"

For this essay, I have chosen three Mexican fictional full-length films, whose particularity is that their protagonists are Central American migrants. They are Cary Joji Fukunaga's *Sin nombre* (Mexico, 2009), Luis Mandoki's *La vida precoz y breve de Sabina Rivas* (Mexico, 2012), and Diego Quemada-Díez's *La jaula de oro* (Mexico/Spain/Guatemala, 2013). In my previous work, I have not analyzed films made by directors outside of Central America, even if their themes were Central American. Taking hold of the concept of national cinema—or regional cinema—was a form of cultural resistance in my book *La pantalla rota: Cien años de cine en Centroamérica* (2005), which sought to affirm a certain regional autonomy against Hollywood's hegemony. Nonetheless, productions made outside of the Isthmus often create a model of representation of the Central American migrant and acquire legitimacy in the context of Latin American film, which is a phenomenon that is important to analyze. In fact, as I already indicated, Central America exists through exogenous images to a certain extent, and it is fundamental to ask the question: How does Central America become visible through an external view? It is undeniable that, just like the human migration processes from the periphery to the territorial centers, audiovisual communication also implies a renegotiation of borders, whether they are visible or invisible.

The films I will analyze very well could be included in what has been called "cine de la marginalidad" (cinema of marginality). In this type of cinema, there is a constant dialogue between filmic text and social text, between the image and the referent, between fiction and documentary (León). These filmic universes are constructed through an intertextual connection with historical, social, and political discourses that go beyond the disciplinary field of film. As a result, authorship is decentered in different instances in the "social text" (León 33).[2] In other words, these filmic universes break the boundaries of the cinematographic image, as the realities they portray are too strong and overwhelming to be contained by it. For this reason, directors who produce this cinema of marginality often turn to the use of real settings; in some cases, non-professional actors; and, above all, to the dissolution of borders between documentary and fiction film, as is observable in the movies *Sin nombre* and *La jaula de oro*.

While these two films are presented to audiences as works of fiction, they are based on surveys and interviews with real migrants; the directors even partially completed the migratory route from Central America to the United States themselves. While I claim these films are "cine de la marginalidad," I do not mean that their authors are inscribed in the margins of hegemonic cinema. In Latin American cinema, the boundaries between marginal and hegemonic film are not always precise, although one must recognize that none of the movies analyzed here speak on behalf of migrants and usurp their place or agency. Christian León argues that "the Cinema of Marginality and its particular realism is a minor expression insofar as it does not remain in the rejection of dominant culture and commercial cinema but rather uses and re-elaborates them. It is capable of appropriating the narrative genres of hegemonic cinema and putting them to work in showing social, political, and cultural problems that go beyond the autonomy of the creative individual and of the cinematographic practice" (34).[3] In the case of the migration films explored here, the directors employ hegemonic film genres such as the road movie, but go beyond a Hollywood treatment of such genres by revealing the structural violence and poverty that's at the root of Central American migration.

Central American Adolescents on the Road

Just as we see in the titles of films about Central American migration, words such as "nameless" (*sin nombre*) and "belonging to nobody" (*de nadie*) are some of the terms that have been used to name the mass of Central American migrants who are *invisibilized* by hegemonic images or reduced to a statistic or social stereotype. Despite these limitations, the fictional films I will address in this chapter attempt to put a face to them and identify some of these thousands of people who are looking to cross Mexico into the United States in search of a myth: "the American Dream." In the three films, there are Central American adolescents, including children, who are represented on a journey that is always dangerous and difficult to finish. If we follow W.J.T. Mitchell's assertion that "In everything from ornaments to monuments, toys to territorial surveys, images acquire forms of surplus value and excess vitality" (294), we could say regarding these films that the characters' displacement is narrated through images whose mobility itself is a symptom of the indispensable role of human life to try to persist and transcend seemingly insurmountable obstacles and suffering. Mobility seems to be the leitmotif of these films of marginality, as their characters refuse to stay in one place where there's no longer hope—even if the migratory is no guarantee of a better life and things may turn out to be even worse.

La vida precoz y breve de Sabina Rivas is based on the novel *La Mara* (2004) by Mexican writer Rafael Ramírez Heredia, and it narrates the story of a brother and sister, Jovani and Sabina. The movie, anchored in an immutable and insurmountable border—a border made of other borders—condenses a long escape that does not have an exit: an escape from Honduras, from a dysfunctional family, and from sexual abuse. The siblings run into each other in the Guatemalan town of Tecún Umán, near the border with Mexico. Sabina, abused by her father and her brother, is a singer, dancer, and sex worker in a seedy nightclub called El Tijuanita, where she is trapped while hoping to obtain legal documents that would permit her to travel to the United States. Her brother Jovani is part of the gang known as Mara Salvatrucha and, thanks to him, we become acquainted with the symbols, rituals, and practices of the gangs that act under the protection of the Guatemalan, Mexican, and North American authorities. In the strict social stratification of organized crime, the gang occupies a lower level compared to the powerful drug cartels that operate along the migratory route and is dedicated to assault, rape, and (often) the killing of migrants.[4]

In the film *Sin nombre*, two stories converge in a similar fashion: the story of Sayra, who travels to the North in company of her father and her uncle, and the story of Willy, a young gang member—known as Casper—who crosses another boundary that cannot be crossed: he betrays the gang. He flees aboard a cargo train that transits the 5,000 kilometers between the southern border of Mexico and the northern border with the United States, known colloquially as *La Bestia,* and on the journey, he meets Sayra. An emerging and unrealistic love story emerges between them. Benito, nicknamed Smiley (a twelve-year-old child whom Casper had recruited into the gang), is in charge of killing Casper. He follows him along the train's route until finding him on the border; when he is at the point of crossing with Sayra, Smiley kills Casper on the bank of the river. Again, we find ourselves here with a boundary that is not possible to cross. Casper's corpse is thrown into the water, while Sayra makes it to the United States.

In *La jaula de oro,* three Guatemalan adolescents are the ones who depart for the insurmountable border: Juan, Sara, and Samuel. During the trip, they meet Chauk, a Tzotzil Indigenous young man who joins the group, even as Juan, who acts as the group's leader, rejects him due to his ethnicity. Throughout the journey, the adolescents are beaten up by the police and deported back to Guatemala, where Samuel gives up on the trip. During an attack against the migrants, gang members uncover Sara's identity: she is a girl disguised as a boy. What happens to her? We do not know. It is not shown. Her body, like the bodies of many Central American women who are only visible within masculine desire or in the act of rape, disappears from the frame. Juan and Chauk, who despite their ethnic differences and language barriers (Chauk does not speak Spanish) begin to develop a relationship. Another gang kidnaps them, and Juan decides to pay for Chauk's freedom, in the first act of solidarity toward the Indigenous boy, an even more invisible subject in Guatemalan and Mexican societies. Later, they cross the border carrying packages—presumably drugs—for some *coyotes* who abandon them in the desert. When they are at the point of crossing to the other side, a vigilante sharpshooter (not shown on the screen) kills Chauk. Juan continues alone and is the only one who manages to attain the "American Dream"—although this dream is paid with a steep price, as we find out later on.

The Context of Departure

Theorists of migration consider that there are three fundamental moments for the migrant: emigration or the departure from the place of habitual residency, immigration or the entrance and process of reorganization of life in the place of refuge, and the reconstruction of bonds with the place of origin. Alcira Beatriz Bonilla adds another stage, which is presented in detail by the films I am studying here: the stage of transit between borders, whether they be physical or invisible (23). It is important to analyze what the films show us of the first stage, the place of residency. Although it is the context that allows us to understand, within the filmic text, the motives for migration, often that context remains hidden from the audience and absent from the image. It seems to be of relatively little interest to the directors to show the story or background of the protagonists previous to the journey. However, they show the audience just enough visual or narrative clues to point to a reality of violence, poverty, and desperation—with viewers being asked to either know about the region's socioeconomic and political situation or to fill in the blanks from the clues they are given.

In the case of *Sin nombre,* a brief scene presents Sayra's departure from Honduras. We find a young woman with her uncle in front of a hill populated with shacks. "Here there is no future for you, Sayra," the uncle tells her.[5] The film's director does not go in depth over the social and economic background of these countries that "*exportan pobres*" (export poor people, according to a common Latin American saying). However, there's a perverse logic underlying the expulsion of poor people from the Isthmus: these migrants, once they are in the United States, contribute with their remittances to preserving the same economic model that expelled them to begin with. Since no significant structural changes have occurred in Central America in the past few decades to deter migration, this idea of "finding a better future" elsewhere has become a vicious cycle and perhaps even a replacement strategy for national governments to address the issues faced by a large percentage of their local population.

In *La vida precoz y breve de Sabina Rivas,* this context of departure is presented as an escape without an exit at the end of the film. A brief flashback shows us the family context, a dump in which Sabina's family lives and whose overcrowding insinuates incest. The father goes to his daughter's bed while the mother turns her back. The abusive father finds Sabina with her brother Jovani, in another transgression of limits, and reacts by hitting his son. Jovani kills his father with a kitchen knife over the shouts of Sabina, who reminds him of their filial relationship. Jovani also kills his mother, in the repetition of parricide, and sets fire to the shack. Sabina escapes running, although she knows that she will not be able to escape from the borders that she leaves behind.

Although it negates showing the major causes for massive migration in the region (poverty and generalized violence), this scene at least reveals a part of the context of poverty and social inequality that the majority of the population in El Salvador, Honduras, and Guatemala endures. Incest, partially visible on screen, serves to depict a sociology of sexual violence that causes a dissolution of the family bond and tragedy. While showing and denouncing intrafamilial abuse and child sex work is nothing new for Latin American cinema, what this film does remarkably well is focusing on the pattern of sexual exploitation that impacts particularly young women in the region—and which is exacerbated as they migrate through Mexico to the United States.[6]

La jaula de oro develops a more elaborate and precise *mise-en-scène* of the context of departure of the three young adults who leave Guatemala. The film begins with Juan as he walks through the alleys full of cardboard houses and half-naked children who play with their toy guns, an allusion to the violence that took Central America from civil war to organized crime in the past four decades. Although it is not shown on screen, the sound of babies crying, dogs barking, and sirens remind the viewer of an overcrowded environment full of risk. Juan runs into a pair of police officers who apparently pursue *mara* members, whose gang-related tattoos visually places them into categories of social exclusion and constant suspicion. Meanwhile, Sara abandons her gender identity as a girl, cutting her hair, taping her breasts and putting on a baseball cap. She knows the danger to which she is exposed in her double exclusion as a migrant and a woman, as we see her take a birth control pill. According to Amnesty International (2010), six out of ten migrant women are raped during the journey through Mexico. Upon leaving the bathroom she is no longer Sara and transforms into Osvaldo, renouncing an essential part of her subjectivity and perhaps assuming without knowing it that the migrant does not have another possible identity other than being a migrant. In other words, not being anyone, not having a name, being invisible. Juan picks up Samuel at one of the enormous landfills that, like crematoriums of modernity, populate Latin American cities, and the three leave for the Mexico border by bus. Upon leaving the city's outskirts, the camera shows a wall covered with photos of the disappeared. It is the new dirty war against the civil population, the one that becomes visible in its invisibility.

The image on the wall, which shows faces without bodies, not only appeals to an already established imaginary in Latin American representation of extreme violence—but also connects with the political-military crisis of the 1970s and 1980s, which led to the first wave of migration out of the Isthmus. The film's introduction does not contain dialogue. There are no goodbyes, there is no family, there is no one who seems to care about them. This is a constructed context, at a narrative level, in terms of negativity. The point of departure represents something that cannot be articulated, spoken because it is pure lack: absence of feeling and negation of life. Three children abandon a country that does not offer them a future in a context of structural violence and social inequality. From the beginning of the film, we are faced with precarious bodies on the margins of society, on the edges of the representable, merged with an atmosphere of garbage and decay—in other words, as we will see later one, abject bodies. They are the bodies that a restrictive and exclusionary modernity expels from its urban centers, no longer toward the periphery of their own countries but rather beyond the national borders, as part of global migratory flows toward societies of consumption and supposed well-being.

In this regard, the scene showing the protagonists of *La jaula de oro* in a small Mexican town is emblematic. The group decides to have photographs taken in front of different versions of the "American Dream." Sara and Samuel pose in front of a banner with the Statue of Liberty and the U.S. flag; they carry a small Guatemalan flag that turns out crooked in the picture. Chauk, the Tzotzil Indigenous boy, is dressed up as a "Hollywood Indian" against a snowy backdrop. Juan, obsessed with his cowboy boots from the beginning of the film, rides a toy horse and shoots a gun at the camera, reproducing the visuals of Shane, the western's mythical cowboy who, like him, is a nomad of the prairies. This is the imaginary in which the three children seek to insert themselves, shaping an identity that would confer meaning to their voyage. Juan clings to his cowboy boots. Chauk persistently dreams with the unattainable snow he will never see. Snow, a motif used repeatedly throughout the film, is part of the global image of the country these youths are trying to reach—and which contrasts in its material and symbolic purity with the filth and marginality that characterizes the migrants' places of origin.

Borders and "In-Between" Spaces

In the films studied here, the geographic, binational, sovereign borders that separate Latin American states appear as porous; if not easy to cross, they are nonetheless presented as unstable, reconfiguring a "no-man's land" image, where there's either no law or where the law of the strongest is what prevails. In *Sin nombre*, Sayra and her family cross the Guatemala-Mexico border through the Suchiate River on rubber rafts. The same happens in *Sabina Rivas*, where the protagonist constantly crosses from one side of the border to the other by bus or on a rubber raft. In *La jaula de oro*, the protagonists cross Mexico's southern border through a bridge, a trail, or on a boat with other migrants. Even the U.S. border is traversed with relative ease due to the fact that the real borders or divisions that migrants are exposed to are others. In *Sin nombre*, Sayra crosses a narrow section of the Rio Grande on a flotation ring with the help of a *coyote*. In *La jaula de oro*, Juan and Chauk accept the risk of becoming "mules" for drug traffickers so that they can reach the other side, postponing the arrival of the final obstacle—which lies past the physical border (that is, the U.S.-Mexico border wall) they have left behind.

Quemada-Díez's film shows an interesting contrast between the two sides of the border. While on the Mexican side we see barefoot children playing soccer, the United States is portrayed through images saturated by white and gray tones, almost aseptic, and where sound (and not what's shown on screen) is what dominates. The sharp noise of a helicopter's blades, sirens, and other sounds define the cinematic construction of the American side as an apparatus of security and sensory violence that is ready to receive migrants. There are no human beings, we never see the native inhabitants' bodies or races, and the photography prefers long shots that favor natural or artificial landscape over human representation.

In *Sin nombre,* an establishing shot shows Sayra in an anonymous U.S. city. A public telephone, also aseptic, connects her with her family in an ending that seems too good to be true, because during her journey—which is closer to a love story—she hasn't suffered any ill-treatment. On the contrary, in *La jaula de oro,* Juan and Chauk face a brutal realism. Just as they are about to reach their destination (the United States), they cross the desert and a bullet strikes Chauk, who drops dead. In a close-up, we see the telescopic target of a rifle that condenses in one image the permanent surveillance to which migrants are subjected. The sharpshooter's face is out of frame. This is extreme violence, exercised against the migrants' bodies. As stated before, the actual, physical border hides other borders that represent additional obstacles with which migrants must contend. As the militarization of traditional border crossing areas has pushed a growing number of migrants to venture into more isolated border regions, the implacable desert has started to figure more prominently in stories and visual representations of migration into the United States. In this way, the desert has become synonymous with a space of death—another border beyond the border that cuts short the journeys and lives of many migrants. The central role of the desert in recent migration films is evident, for instance, in the film *Desierto* by Jonás Cuarón (Mexico, 2015)—where migrants are stranded in the desert on the U.S. side of the border and are shot by an American hunter.

We must point out that these movies were filmed before the start of the Trump administration (2017) and the implementation of his anti-immigration policies, including demands that Guatemala and Mexico erect a "virtual border" and detain their own migrants at their binational frontier. In the images we have analyzed, territorial lines have been replaced by a "third country" or a "vertical border," which is characterized by invisible divisions dominated by both corrupt government institutions and by de facto powers—organized crime, transnational gangs, and extremist groups.[7]

In addition to borders, these films employ a variety of interstitial spaces to show the complexity of the migratory experience. According to Homi Bhabha, migrants cross an "in-between space" during their journeys. A crossroads adjacent to the railroad tracks, the expanse of the desert as a zone of transit and death, and even atop *La Bestia*—these are the interstitial spaces that the migrants in these three films not only travel through, but also inhabit, and where they try to build a sense of community. The "in-between space" is where identities of cultural difference are negotiated and reconfigured in a conflictive manner. In Bhabha's words, this space opens out "continually, contingently [...] remaking the boundaries, exposing the limits of any claim to a singular or autonomous sign of difference—be it class, gender, or race" (219). The "in-between" space becomes, then, a site where a politics of the margins is constructed (meaning the margins of contemporary society). Here, the center-periphery model of modernity is altered, thus deconstructing the essentialist myth of an identity tied to a place "enclosed" by borders drawn by national states—in turn giving origin to transnational and transborder identities. We are clearly in the midst of a crisis of centrality. New spaces are created that are the result of relations, of identify formation processes, spaces that are always becoming, never fixed (Albet and Benach 158). Along train tracks and inside discarded wagons, in their interstices, migrants travel and live. These are spaces of abandonment, empty spaces full of garbage and excrement to which their bodies fuse and confuse, leading to a representation of migrants as an undifferentiated wave.

The image of the train is emblematic and displays a double tension that crosses the border between fiction and nonfiction. On the one hand, it symbolizes the national State and the idea of progress inherited from positivism. In Central America's reality and in its fiction, railroads were abandoned, their remains dismantled and scattered among the jungles as a metaphor of modernity's failure. On the other hand, the train captures the imaginary of the voyage and movement toward "the north," a hypothetical place located beyond all possible borders. This symbolic space, connected to modernity's utopian identities from the nineteenth and twentieth centuries, is resignified today within the liminal identities of those being pushed out in the twenty-first century. It is a space imposed by the collective imaginary that goes beyond subjective experience (Lamizet 163), as in the case of the image of the Tzotzil Indian Chauk being transformed into a Native American from a western. *La jaula de oro* presents this imaginary space as a metaphor. Mesmerized, Juan and Chauk observe a toy train under falling snow behind a store window. This is the metaphor of everything migrants don't possess and which the "cinema of marginality" does not show as it concentrates on the events of the journey. In the filmic image, the locomotive is at once something that is inhabited, that is crossed, and something that circulates: a train on the run. Multiple images show it from afar, using extreme long shots that reveal the train crossing the horizon over a bridge. Rails are among the most common images we see: rails that are left behind. This is the condensation of space and time that cinema is all about.

Migrant Bodies and Marginality

The aesthetics of the "cinema of marginality" are intrinsically connected with broader discussions about marginal subjects that the films discussed here portray. In this regard, along with the crisis of social bonds in a capitalist society, we also see a weakening of the subject, a crisis of the individual character. This takes us back to our previous reflection regarding the ways of naming those "without a name," those who "belong to nobody," the "invisible" ones. Marginality is the condition of dispersion of the modern subject, originally conceived as self-centered and reflexive. Why? In *Excitable Speech: A Politics of the Performative*, Judith Butler (1997) explains that the modern subject is nothing more than an effect of power. What happens, then, to those individuals excluded from the constructions of power that make up the subject? Butler points out that institutions produce subjects, but at the same time they segregate and exclude those who do not conform to the social order's premises. Writing about marginality and abjection in Latin American cinema, Christian León explains that:

> [p]recisely these abject beings of whom Butler speaks are the marginalized that Latin American film attempts to depict. These characters of the street, excluded from the symbolic systems that configure sociality, are shown dispossessed of the discursive competency that authorizes them to function and speak as subjects. [. . .] The marginality is thus presented as a space where social institutions cannot gain access and, consequently, the process of production of subjects is annulled. (54–55)[8]

Thus, migrants position themselves as abject bodies before the societies that casts them out, and the cinema that represents them shows a reality that has its own existence on the margins of modernity's rationality, including what León has termed "the cinema of marginality," which:

> [. . .] demonstrates a permanent transubstantiation of the topological polarities that compose all narration: the private and the public, home and the street, family and the gang, the citizen and the delinquent, the moral and the immoral. Thus, marginality is represented as the production of a visuality that puts into evidence the mechanisms of exclusion from which the marginal—this indecipherable spot—appears like a symptom of that which is indiscernible to social institutions. (14)[9]

The cinema of marginality is, therefore, a cinema of borders and tensions. In *La jaula de oro,* two subject-bodies are characterized by their double exclusion. Sara surrenders her gender identity, becoming invisible as a female subject, and upon recovering her identity she disappears from the filmic narrative, kidnapped by the drug-trafficking gang. Chauk is the second case. Juan is constructed as a subject by means of alterity, in opposition to Chauk: the mestizo versus the Indigenous individual. Alterity is essential for the enterprise of creating meaning (Guarné Cabello, quoted in Ardèvol and Muntañola 70). This metaphor of total exclusion is expressed through the linguistic incommunicability between the two boys.

It is in *La vida precoz y breve de Sabina Rivas* where we best comprehend the *disposable* nature of migrant bodies. Sabina's body is the territory being disputed by political, sexual, ethnic, and cultural tensions that traverse the movie. The border town where Sabina awaits or the dive where she works are located in an "in-between place," in no man's land. The cabaret El Tijuanita—which recalls Tijuana, the city on the border between Mexico and the United States—is located on the "outside," on the margins, full of undocumented girls who offer themselves to clients. No one cares about migrant bodies, although they carry the slight value of their own marginality. Without papers, money, or family, Sabina defends the only thing she owns, her identity as a subject: "I don't want you to change my name, you understand me. Or do I have to stop the show to say my name?,"[10] she protests to the announcer, adding: "My name is Sabina Rivas and I am well-informed."[11] The *Yo me llamo Sabina Rivas* statement appears to be the only possible affirmation of her identity. In the end, her name names the only thing she possesses, her body, even if it's a space disputed by power constructions. Her body is the only thing she has to survive. It is Sabina's double exclusion as a girl and as Honduran what gives her value, transforming her into a merchandise, into use and exchange value. It is her disputed body that makes her a subject, even if a disposable and abject subject.

"The only thing those people in the train carry are fleas," says Burrona, the corrupt Mexican inspector in *La vida precoz y breve de Sabina Rivas*.[12] Later on, he states he won't travel through Guatemala because "AIDS is in the air, and that's worse than bat rabies."[13] In the same manner that *La jaula de oro*'s female protagonist masks her gender identity, Sabina hides her national identity. Burrona approaches her and smells her: "No, this one is from Honduras, she's a *catracha*," he says. The migrant's body is a political construction that depends on ideological operators that decide its market value.[14] The migrant is weighed, symbolically speaking, is sniffed; his/her skin color is looked at in order to determine whether or not he or she will survive. Sabina Rivas goes from becoming the Mexican consul's trophy to an American agent's object of desire. Once more, Sabina's body is at once an object of repulsion and desire.

The gringo orders her to bathe so he won't be "infected," animalizes her by tying a belt around her neck, rapes her anally, and mutilates her face—which constitutes a new erasure of her identity, a reaffirmation that the migrant has no name and no face.

The migrants' bodies stink, they are dirty, sick, contagious. They are refuse-bodies, or "human waste," as Bauman calls them in *Wasted Lives: Modernity and Its Outcasts*. At the same time, abjection appears to be overcome through the dispute of the female body. The U.S agent makes a political statement regarding the migrant body, the disposable body, abject and yet desired, of Sabina Rivas. As film scholar W.J.T. Mitchell reminds us, "The ocular violence of racism splits its object in two, rending and rendering it simultaneously hypervisible and invisible, an object of, in [Frantz] Fanon's words, 'abomination' and 'adoration'" (34). While she crosses the river separating Guatemala from Mexico, Sabina asks about the semi-naked and unrecognizable bodies she sees: "And why do they kill them?"[15] The boatman answers: "Because they do not matter to anyone and nobody does anything."[16] They are refuse-bodies, waste-bodies, border-bodies that are left in the interstices, "in-between places," among the railroad tracks, in deserted areas, and on the margins of hegemonic film discourse. They are abject bodies before which the image of fiction appears to take a step back or refrain from engaging. As Julia Kristeva indicates, "The corpse, seen without God and outside of science, is the utmost of abjection. It is death infecting life" (4).

Final Image

La jaula de oro is the only film where any of the migrants reach their final objective. At the end of the movie, Juan sweeps the discarded pieces at a meat-processing plant in the U.S. Midwest wearing a spotless white uniform. The waste takes us back to the beginning of the film and the garbage dump from which his friend Samuel seeks sustenance. The plant workers, who are also immigrants, butcher the animals in a mechanical and silent manner. The spectator watches the pieces of discarded carcasses as a metaphor of those "without names" that were left behind. As we have seen, the border is a succession of invisible borders, and Juan is now before yet another border that materializes in the interstices that go from one lost identity to another still to be acquired—that is, a border where identities fluctuate as the migrant becomes an undocumented immigrant that now must negotiate issues of legality and loss of his cultural roots. Is the fragmentation of bodies and the subject's identity the price to pay for migrating? This seems to be the question Juan is asking at the meatpacking plant, which is photographed as if it were a "non-place"—that is, a non-distinctive place of transience where human beings remain anonymous and lonely and where human relations are discouraged (Augé). The meat-processing line is a metaphor for the border line that Central American migrants cross, and which allows them to pick up the scraps of meat that fall from the capitalist system they yearn to join as subjects. Likewise, this also serves as a metaphor for the complex and unequal U.S.-Latin America relations and their representation in contemporary cinema.

The other important metaphor at the end of *La jaula de oro* is snow. At the conclusion of the film, Juan watches snow falling under the flickering light of a streetlamp just outside the meatpacking plant. The young man is alone and simultaneously surrounded by absences of that which has been shown and of what cannot be shown. Let us remember that Juan's murdered fellow traveler, Chauk, dreamed of seeing snow for the first time in his life in the United States. Now, it is Juan who experiences what Chauk had hoped to see with his own eyes, but the abundant presence of snow only functions to reveal the Indigenous boy's absence. The migrant's journey, inscribed in the "cinema of marginality," is constituted by what the voyages negates, by what's lost, by what remains on the edges of the image—on the borders of the image—without ever becoming fully explicit.

While making the borders between Central America and the United States visible, this "cinema of marginality" also crosses borders between fiction and nonfiction. As indicated before, these movies are filmed in real spaces—the desert, the cargo train, the real actual borders—with non-professional actors mingling with migrants, and through *mise-en-scènes* that privilege hand-held cameras and documented plots. We ask ourselves, with Georges Didi-Huberman, "How to do history of the people? Where to find the word of those without a name, the writing of those without papers, the place without a roof, the recognition of those without rights, the dignity of those without images?" (29).[17] The topic of Central American migrants has generated, additionally, many documentaries, both in the region and outside of it. Migration and the audiovisual discourse it generates are made of extremes, making visible the best and the worst of the human condition. And it is in those extremes, in those unspoken borders, still undefined, where the researcher's questions are found, along with the voices and the images of Central Americans "without images" and the ways of naming those "without names."

Notes

1 "... las caravanas son una rebelión, una insurgencia de las víctimas del neoliberalismo en América Central, al mismo tiempo que una insurrección al gobierno fronterizo establecido por los estados de la región" (Varela y McLean 5).
2 "se construyen en una relación intertextual con discursos históricos, sociales y políticos que desbordan el campo disciplinario del cine. Como consecuencia la autoría se encuentra descentrada en las distintas instancias del texto social" (León 33).
3 "El *cine de la marginalidad* y su particular realismo es una expresión menor en tanto no se queda en el rechazo de la cultura dominante y del cine comercial sino que los usa y reelabora. Es capaz de apropiarse de los géneros narrativos del cine hegemónico y ponerlos al servicio de la expresión de problemáticas sociales, políticas y culturales que desbordan la autonomía del individuo creador y de la práctica cinematográfica" (34).
4 The most powerful gangs that operate in Central America are the Mara Salvatrucha (MS-13) and la Pandilla 18, which are both transnational. They were created in the 1980s, in the United States, by Central American migrants who fled the region's civil wars. The Central American immigrants grouped together to be able to defend themselves and survive in the poorest neighborhoods, from other gangs comprised of Mexicans and African Americans. In the 1990s, the United States decided to deport people with criminal offenses and gang members. In this way, the gangs arrived in the region, particularly in the Northern Triangle countries: Guatemala, Honduras and El Salvador, exercising much power and adding significantly to the violence and criminality in these countries (Goubaud).
5 "Aquí no hay futuro para vos, Sayra."
6 According to a 2017 report by the Economic Commission for Latin America and the Caribbean, El Salvador, Honduras, and Guatemala (in that order) have the highest femicide rates in Latin America and the Caribbean and comprise 87 percent of all femicides in the Isthmus (ECLAC).
7 The concept of "vertical border" is further explained by Eduardo Torre-Cantalapiedra and José Carlos Yee-Quintero in "México ¿una frontera vertical? Políticas de control del tránsito migratorio irregular y sus resultados."
8 "Precisamente estos seres abyectos de los que habla Butler son los marginales que pretende retratar el cine latinoamericano. Estos personajes de la calle, excluidos de los sistemas simbólicos que configuran la socialidad, se muestran despojados de la competencia discursiva que los autoriza a obrar y hablar como sujetos. [...] La marginalidad se presenta, entonces, como un espacio donde las instituciones sociales no pueden acceder y, consecuentemente, el proceso de producción de sujetos está anulado" (54–55).
9 "[...] muestra una transustanciación permanente de las polaridades topológicas que componen toda narración: lo privado y lo público, el hogar y la calle, la familia y la pandilla, el ciudadano y el delincuente, lo moral y lo inmoral. De ahí que la marginalidad sea representada como la producción de una visualidad que pone en evidencia los mecanismos de exclusión a partir de los cuales se estructura la interioridad de las

instituciones sociales. La imagen del marginal—esa mancha indescifrable—aparece como un síntoma de aquello que es imperceptible para las instituciones sociales" (14).
10 "No quiero que me cambiés mi nombre, me entendés. ¿O tengo que parar el *show* para decir mi nombre?"
11 "Yo me llamo Sabina Rivas y tengo mucho puesto."
12 "Los del tren lo único que traen son pulgas."
13 "El sida anda en la atmósfera y eso es peor que la rabia de los murciélagos."
14 "No, es de Honduras, ésta es catracha." *Catracha/o* is an expression used to refer to Hondurans.
15 "¿Y por qué los matan?"
16 "Porque no le importan a nadie y nadie hace nada."
17 "¿Cómo hacer la historia de los pueblos? ¿Dónde hallar la palabra de los sin nombre, la escritura de los sin papeles, el lugar de los sintecho, la reivindicación de los sin derechos, la dignidad de los sin imágenes?" (29).

Works Cited

Albet, Abey and Núria Benach. *Doreen Massey. Un sentido global del lugar*. Barcelona: Icaria Editorial S.A., 2012.

Alzate, Natalia. "Infancias migrantes: Fronteras corpóreas en el largometraje *La jaula de oro*." *Polifonía*, vol. 7, no. 1, 2017, pp. 44–57.

Amnesty International. *Invisible victims. Migrants on the move in Mexico*. London: Amnesty International Publications, 2010.

Ardèvol, Elisenda, and Nora Muntañola. *Representación y cultura audiovisual en la sociedad contemporánea*. Barcelona: Editorial U Oberta de Catalunya, 2004.

Augé, Marc. *Non-places: Introduction to an Anthropology of Supermodernity*. London: Verso, 1995.

Bauman, Zygmunt. *Wasted Lives: Modernity and Its Outcasts*. Cambridge: Polity Press, 2004.

Bhabha, Homi. *The Location of Culture*. London: Routledge, 1994.

Bonilla, Alcira Beatriz. "La construcción imaginaria del 'otro migrante.'" *Cuadernos de la Facultad de Humanidades y Ciencias Sociales-Universidad Nacional de Jujuy*, no. 42, 2012, pp. 21–34.

Butler, Judith. *Excitable Speech: A Politics of the Performative*. London: Routledge, 1997.

Cortés, María Lourdes. "La migración centroamericana en el cine, un viaje infinito." *En movimiento*, OIM, ONU migración. Oficina regional para Centroamérica, Norteamérica y el Caribe, 2017, https://rosanjose.iom.int/site/es/blog/la-migracion-centroamericana-en-el-cine-un-viaje-infinito.

———. *La pantalla rota: Cien años de cine en Centroamérica*. Ciudad de México: Taurus, 2005.

Desierto. Directed by Jonás Cuarón, Esperanto Filmoj, Mexico, 2015.

Didi-Huberman, Georges. *Pueblos expuestos. Pueblos figurantes*. Buenos Aires: Ediciones Manantial, 2018.

Economic Commission for Latin America and the Caribbean [ECLAC]. "Atlas of Migration in Northern Central America." 2018, https://repositorio.cepal.org/bitstream/handle/11362/44288/1/S1801071_en.pdf. Accessed 5 August 2019.

Goubaud, Emilio. "Maras y pandillas en Centroamérica." *Urvio, Revista Latinoamericana de Seguridad Ciudadana*, no. 4, 2008, pp. 35-46.

Kristeva, Julia. *Powers of Horror: An Essay on Abjection*. Translated by Leon S. Roudiez. New York: Columbia UP, 1982.

La jaula de oro. Directed by Diego Quemada Díez, Animal de luz Machete Productions, Mexico/Spain/Guatemala, 2013.

La vida precoz y breve de Sabina Rivas. Directed by Luis Mandoki, Laguna Productions, Mexico, 2012.

Lamizet, Bernard. "Semiótica del espacio y mediación." *Tópicos del Seminario*, no. 24, 2010, pp. 153-168.

León, Christian. *El cine de la marginalidad. Realismo urbano y violencia urbana*. Quito: Universidad Andina Simón Bolívar, Ediciones Abya-Yala, and Corporación Editora Nacional, 2005.

Maciel, David R. *El Norte: The U.S.-Mexican Border in Contemporary Cinema*. San Diego: San Diego State UP, 1990.

Mitchell, W.J.T. *What Do Pictures Want? The Lives and Loves of Images*. Chicago: U of Chicago P, 2005.

O'Connor, Allison, et al. "Central American Immigrants in the United States." *Migration Policy Institute*, 15 August 2019, https://www.migrationpolicy.org/article/central-american-immigrants-united-states.

Quemada-Díez, Diego, et al. *Los cuadernos de Cinema 23. La jaula de oro. Guiones Num 1*. México: La Internacional Cinematográfica, Iberocine, 2015.

Ramírez Heredia, Rafael. *La Mara*. Ciudad de México: Alfaguara, 2004.

Sandoval García, Carlos. *No más muros: Exclusión y migración forzada en Centroamérica*. San José: Editorial de la U de Costa Rica, Instituto de Investigaciones Sociales, 2015.

Sin nombre. Directed by Cary Fukunaga, Primary Productions, Mexico, 2009.

Torre-Cantalapiedra, Eduardo and José Carlos Yee-Quintero. "México ¿una frontera vertical? Políticas de control del tránsito migratorio irregular y sus resultados, 2007-2016." *LiminaR*, vol. 16, no. 2, 2018, http://www.scielo.org.mx/scielo.php?script=sci_arttext&pid=S1665-80272018000200087&lng=es&nrm=iso&tlng=es.

Varela, Amarela and Lisa McLean. "Caravanas de migrantes en México: nueva forma de autodefensa y transmigración." *Revista CIDOB d'Afers Internacionals*, no. 122, 2019, pp. 163-185.

6

Migrant Credence in Marcela Zamora's *María en tierra de nadie*

Esteban E. Loustaunau

The 1990s were supposed to mark the beginning of a new era for peace and democracy in Central America. After the brutal devastation and expulsion of human life caused by civil war in Guatemala and El Salvador a decade earlier, the much anticipated return to democracy failed to bring peace and prosperity. Instead, turmoil and inequality remained as the persistence of violence made the implementation of governability in Guatemala and El Salvador almost impossible. Perhaps the main challenge to governability in these societies has been the fact that much of the violence is either caused or sanctioned by the state (Rodríguez 2–3). What caused the state to succumb to violence and what led ordinary citizens to struggle for justice are two perennial questions that need to be continuously addressed from multiple angles. I seek answers to the first question in recent critical theory on precarity, agency, and migration; and to the second question in testimonies by Central American migrant women in Salvadoran-Nicaraguan filmmaker Marcela Zamora's documentary *María en tierra de nadie,* produced in 2011.[1]

To begin to understand the political, economic, and social instability that has led Central American states to fail, we must approach the change from authoritarianism to democracy in the region not as a rupture but as a transition between two power modalities within the same old system. Masao Miyoshi describes the current era of liberalism as the "postmodern modality" of colonialism that remains indifferent to any state that does not belong to the political and economic superpowers of Europe and the United States (Miyoshi 745; Rodríguez 8). Drawing on Naomi Klein's claim regarding Europe and the United States as "megastate fortresses," Ileana Rodríguez considers that, "[t]his indifference amounts to nothing less than an all-out offensive against people outside these two fortresses—although some, considering the multilateral effects of policies such as outsourcing, will argue that the offensive is also internal" (8). Rodríguez finds it ironic that this offensive is being carried out in the name of democracy while it seeks not only the control of natural resources but also the suppression of all forms of multiculturalism and difference across the world (Rodríguez 8). I find it important to consider the megastates' double offensive of indifference to democracy and of control of resources beyond their borders in the context of Guatemala's 2019 presidential elections. The two-round runoff elections, which were tainted with accusations of corruption by a leading presidential candidate and former attorney general Thelma Aldana, and by members of President Jimmy Morales's family that led to the president's decision to eliminate the United Nations-backed anti-corruption and impunity commission (CICIG), not only weakened the legitimacy of democracy in the country but also guaranteed the continuity of the economic status quo that favors free markets (Goldman 2019). This shows that the majority of people living in countries with very little political and economic influence in the global arena suffer severely from exclusion and expulsion by their very governments and market-driven economies.

Saskia Sassen has written extensively on the contemporary logic of expulsion—for example, on the expelling of low-income workers and the unemployed from government and private, assisted social welfare and health programs (Sassen 1). She argues that under present-day liberalism, we are experiencing higher levels of devastation that affect people as well as the environment. Not only do shrinking national economies cut down basic services for the poor, new "innovations" in technology with their aggressive methods of extraction are seriously threatening the biosphere by leaving behind "expanded stretches of dead land and dead water" (Sassen 12). In Central America, a region with a long history of aggressive extractions of agricultural products and natural resources by large multinational corporations, the present-day living conditions of many people have become extremely precarious. By that I mean that more people are increasingly vulnerable to exploitation because of a lack of security and a diminishing sense of belonging (Banki; De Genova).

After the long period of civil war and other recent crises, including the 2009 coup d'état in Honduras, the Northern Triangle countries have been unable to carry out much-needed judicial and financial reforms. Neither have they been able to bring social relief, achieve infrastructure recovery after massive natural disasters, nor generate sufficient integration programs that could help strengthen the national social fabric, especially for women, the young, and the poor. Unfortunately, political activity under democracy in these countries has led to higher degrees of exclusion and expulsion across the region (Carasik).

Arguably, Central American women, children, and Indigenous groups are the most affected by liberal policies of the state and financial markets. Perhaps because of this and also because of the void of governability that was left after the civil war period, women and Indigenous groups are the ones who best carry out "the material and discursive disruptions" that challenge the global and local forces of indifference and violence against them (Rodríguez 3; Loustaunau 91–93). Even when the various mechanisms of social and political exclusion try to keep their voices down, women and Indigenous people find alternative ways to enter the public sphere and thus disrupt the normative rhetoric at the local and national levels. One practice by which subaltern voices break into the public sphere is *testimonio*. When it comes to oral narratives by the dispossessed, John Beverley explains that the key issue in these accounts is not the representation of the marginalized. Instead, "*testimonio* aspires not only to interpret the world but also to change it" (Beverley xvi; quoted in Guerra 190). Following Beverley, Ramón Guerra argues that contemporary documentary filmmaking can contribute to "recognize the act of *testimonio* as doing more than merely depicting stories but instead advancing them" (190). Here, the connection between *testimonio* and documentary film happens when a committed filmmaker like Zamora applies "the film medium to expose and combat the culture of invisibility and inaudibility" (Burton 376).

Despite this connection between *testimonio* and documentary film, there are also differences between the two. Documentary is capable of making a stronger and closer connection between a film's subject and the viewer through audiovisual elements such as image, intonation, gestures, silence, setting, etc. (Aprea). Through the visual exposure to the subjects' bodies, voices, objects, and the environments they inhabit, documentary film enhances the emotional connections and disconnections that the viewer establishes with the film's subjects. Another example of a difference between documentary film and testimonial narrative can be found in Bill Nichols's description of interactive documentary. According to Nichols, the interactive mode of documentary includes two different kinds of images. These are "images of testimony or verbal exchange" and "images of demonstration," which a filmmaker may include in a film to demonstrate the degree of validity of a subject's testimonial account (Nichols 44). In other words, through the application of sound, music, and additional footage, documentary film enhances the textual message of *testimonio* and brings the viewer and the witness or subject closer together.

Finally, contemporary audiovisual modes of production and dissemination, especially through social media and the Internet, help amplify the reach of *testimonio* to audiences that can see on film what they otherwise may not have access to in written form.

In what follows, I will discuss a series of testimonial accounts by Central American women who appear in Zamora's documentary *María en tierra de nadie*.[2] This film introduces the viewer to the life experiences of several migrant women who face expulsion after economic, social, and gender exclusion. In this way, their migration can be interpreted as an embodied action of resistance that reveals the failure of the state's responsibilities to its citizens. Some of the women in the film travel alone, a few share their stories of betrayal and abduction, and others are mothers searching for their disappeared migrant children. This last group of women belongs to the Caravana de Madres de Migrantes Desaparecidos [Caravan of Mothers of Disappeared Migrants], a social movement founded in 2000 by Honduran mother and activist Emetria Martínez, and now coordinated by Martha Sánchez Soler, director of the Movimiento Migrante Mesoamericano [Mesoamerican Migrant Movement].[3] This caravan brings together Central American mothers who, after their children disappeared, became activists traveling along the migrant trail from El Salvador to Mexico in search of their missing migrant children. According to Claudia León, a volunteer at a migrant shelter in Tequisquiapan, Querétaro, most Central American migrant caravans crossing through Mexico on their way to the United States have four common objectives: (a) to raise awareness of the terrible conditions Central American migrants face while crossing through Mexico; (b) to provide safety to migrants; (c) to recognize the services offered by migrant shelters across Mexico; and (d) to promote acts of solidarity by Mexican citizens on behalf of migrants (quoted in Martínez Hernández-Mejía 233). For several years now, scholar and activist Iliana Martínez Hernández-Mejía has been following these caravans across Mexico. She observes how, of the many kinds of mobilizations that migrants have organized over the past ten years, two have received the most attention: the caravan and the *via crucis*. The first kind tends to be large and has the purpose of leading migrants from Central America to the U.S.-Mexico border with the hope of seeking refuge in the United States. The second is based on the Catholic tradition of Holy Week and it covers shorter distances where relatives of missing migrants search for them in shelters affiliated with the Catholic Church. The *via crucis* caravans bring Jesus's way of the cross closer together to the perils of migrants crossing through Mexico (Martínez Hernández-Mejía 233).

Based on these characteristics, the caravan that Zamora follows in the film belongs to the category of the *via crucis*. It took place in 2009 and was known as "Caminata de la esperanza" ["Walk of Hope"]. In the film, the women of the caravan stop in migrant shelters but also in morgues, cemeteries, brothels, and police stations, seeking information that can help them find their lost sons and daughters. Zamora meets the various women migrants across several locations in El Salvador, Guatemala, and Mexico. These locations are not always safe. Yet, by building bonds of trust with shelter volunteers and the filmmaker through storytelling and shared experiences, the migrant women in the film form a collective agency that resists the terror, fear, and exclusion that surrounds them. I argue that it is in these ephemeral moments and remote locations where the migrant women's testimonies disrupt the dominant single story that minimizes their lives as bare life. My aim is to contribute to the ongoing debate on precarity, agency, and migration through the analysis of the collective agency that migrant women and their allies build through their testimonial accounts. These *testimonios* challenge the mischaracterizations and exclusions in dominant discourse enforced on migrants today.

I will now provide an overview of the relationship between precarity, agency, and migration and how these relate to the testimonials in the film. By analyzing some of the experiences of women migrants in the film, I will focus on the dimensions of faith and hope that stem out of the migrants' precariousness. What the migrant women say on camera and what they do with the things they carry produce small but life-saving disruptions against precarity. The migrant women in the film create these disruptions by what I call *credence*, their common confidence and belief that their life stories are truthful and meaningful, that the objects they carry on the road can shield them against violence and death, and that their collective migrant dreams matter to them and to their families despite their precarious conditions.

Precarity, Agency, and Migration

The concept of precarity can be traced back to Pierre Bourdieu's use of the term to differentiate between casual and permanent workers in Algeria (Waite 414; quoted in Paret and Glesson 2). Some critics apply this term today to describe relations of insecurity that go beyond work and livelihood (Paret and Glesson 3). Others, like Judith Butler, consider the idea of precarity as a rubric to better understand "the politically induced condition in which certain populations suffer from failing social and economic networks of support and become differentially exposed to injury, violence, and death" (Butler, "Performativity" ii). At the same time, Butler realizes that not everyone needs to undergo severe suffering to experience precarity. Shared experiences of loss can make different people relate to each other. In her book *Precarious Life: The Powers of Mourning and Violence,* Butler writes:

> [E]ach of us is constituted politically in part by virtue of the social vulnerability of our bodies—as a site of desire and physical vulnerability, as a site of a publicity at once assertive and exposed. Loss and vulnerability seem to follow from our being socially constituted bodies, attached to others, at risk of losing those attachments, exposed to others, at risk of violence by virtue of that exposure. (30)

It is important to point out that Butler does not mean that everybody is equally vulnerable, even if we are all potentially precarious beings. While precarity is a shared condition of many, how each person is exposed to precarious life differs (Kelz 6).

As I have already indicated, precarious life refers to conditions of exclusion and expulsion that many Central American migrant men, women, and children face today. In the particular case of migrant women, precarity can be directly linked to the vulnerability of the body and to gender norms, as these are ways in which power operates (Valencia 140). In particular, migrant women who travel alone are susceptible to higher levels of precarity since their movement defies traditional norms of gender and motherhood that continue to be enforced across the private and the public spheres (Hondagneu-Sotelo and Avila 398). Anyone who does not live by such norms can face the risk of discrimination and violence (Butler, *Frames* 2). Despite the risk, many women on the migrant trail find ways to build networks of solidarity with each other. Rosine Kelz, in her study of the formation of networks of solidarity between citizens and non-citizens claims that for some migrants:

> the spread of insecurity in all aspects of life provides *an impetus to create new connections* that replace lost or weakened societal bonds traditionally provided by social and state institutions. The weakening of the rigidity of former social and work relations can provide an opportunity to challenge inflexible institutional forms of political organization and provide an incentive for social change. The increasing flexibility of social structures can enable unforeseen openings for new social spaces where networks based on an apprehension of shared precariousness and the inadequacy of state institutions are formed. (12, my emphasis)

Similarly to Butler, Kelz sees how shared experiences of precarious life, even if not always the same, lead to the formation of empathetic networks of resistance.

The drama of the hundreds of Central American migrant families being detained, separated, and caged at the U.S.-Mexico Border is the representation of migrant life as "bare life," or the characterization of undocumented migrants as people whose rights of political participation and belonging have been stripped away, and whose "possibilities and potentialities" for a good life have been reduced (De Genova 37; Agamben 35-37). Nicholas De Genova explains how this categorization, historically produced by state power under extreme circumstances, is meant to ban certain groups of people from having any access to political and legal rights. By denying them any juridical validity, the human lives of undocumented migrants are devalued and made invisible to the state. In his critique of Giorgio Agamben's notion of bare life, De Genova argues that even in bare life, the state authority is paradoxically still incorporating undocumented migrants as a vulnerable social entity. De Genova sees how this negative incorporation allows for the abuse and exploitation of, and violence against, undocumented migrants to spread everywhere with impunity (38-39).

Here is where migration as an act of resistance against state power challenges the erasure of all possibility and potential for humanity that characterizes bare life. Migration as an unauthorized free movement is an "incorrigible affront to state sovereignty and the power of the state to manage its social space through law and the violence of law enforcement" (De Genova 39). In other words, undocumented migration is an act of resistance against bare life insofar as bare life as a negative social category denies people the capacity to build sociocultural relations that can lead to collective agency (Wheatley and Gomberg-Muñoz 121). Under the notion of bare life, state authority denies the ability of undocumented migrants to build relations among themselves and their many allies that shape the migrants' sense of collective agency. Still, such agency does not happen independently from state power, but as Abby Wheatley and Ruth Gomberg-Muñoz explain, it "rather constitutes part of a wider dialectic between state governance and resistance among political subjects" (124). As I will show below, the *via crucis* caravan or Caravana de madres is one way in which people can stand in solidarity with migrants and resist the exclusion and violence of bare life. In the film, the various women migrants that Zamora interviews share in common a faith identity that encourages them to move forward despite their conditions of precarity.

Migrant Credence as Relief from Bare Life

María en tierra de nadie opens with a scene in the town of Sensuntepeque, El Salvador, where a fragile, elderly lady named María Inés Méndez, mother

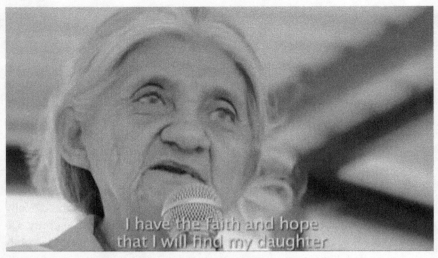

Figure 6.1. Doña Inés speaks with microphone. Still from *María en tierra de nadie*.

of Sandra Mabel Sánchez Méndez, who has disappeared on the migrant trail, walks slowly and pensively along a series of empty streets that give the sense of being in a semi-abandoned village. In this scene, Doña Inés makes her way to the corner store where she greets the storeowner with a blessing. Immediately after, a subtle disruption takes place. Instead of Doña Inés being the one making a purchase at the store, she sells a strip of candy to the storeowner. Gladly, the storeowner buys Doña Inés's candy for a few dollars to help the elderly woman cover the cost of joining the caravan of mothers. During this informal monetary transaction, the viewer can hear the storeowner's voice encouraging Doña Inés to continue to search for Sandra Mabel, her missing daughter and mother of two young girls. This opening scene signals the way in which simple acts of faith and informal transactions help minimize the vulnerability of the women in the film. It alerts the viewer to see undocumented migrants and their families through a different lens; to consider migrant life beyond bare life (Figure 6.1). This moment also serves to make a connection between the filmmaker and the human subjects in the film. It is through Doña Inés that Zamora, the filmmaker, follows the *via crucis* caravan of mothers from Sensuntepeque to Ixtepec, Oaxaca, the place in southern Mexico where Father Alejandro Solalinde, a Catholic priest and human rights activist, runs the migrant shelter Hermanos en el Camino.

As the caravan of mothers sets on its way to Mexico, it becomes clear that faith is the driving force of the women and the few men who accompany them. The film shows how the members of the caravan turn their faith into their common discourse of resistance against precarity and as the source of hope while searching for their missing children. In *María en tierra de nadie*, faith serves as a subversive element against the forces of the state and all other potential abuse within bare life. Once on the road, the mothers who join the caravan make several stops in different towns where they meet with local authorities with the intention of making their demands and gathering information. They also visit shelters where someone could possibly provide information about their missing sons and daughters.

One of Zamora's first stops is at the Casa del Migrante, a migrant shelter in Tecún Umán, Guatemala, where she interviews two Salvadoran migrant women whom she meets at the start of their journey. The first woman is Sandra Campos, who describes how some time after living in the United States, her husband abandoned her and her U.S.-born daughter. Then one day, U.S. Immigration and Customs Enforcement (ICE) agents apprehended her while she was working at a restaurant. Following her arrest, Sandra was deported back to El Salvador without being allowed by immigration officers to bring her young daughter back to El Salvador with her. It is because of this deportation and family separation that Sandra is risking her life again, attempting to return to her daughter in the United States.[4] Suffering abandonment by her husband and expulsion from the state, Sandra's *testimonio* of deportation and family separation reveals the inhumane actions taken against people who have been stripped of protection and safety in both the private and the public spheres.

Sandra is traveling with Marta Muñoz, another migrant mother from El Salvador who has a nineteen-year-old son and a six-year-old daughter. In the film, Marta is migrating for the first time. She shares her story of how the high cost of living in El Salvador pushed her away from her family. She describes how she decided to leave her home without telling her husband, out of fear of being told not to go and of suffering physical abuse by him. The stories by these two migrant mothers are not uncommon; they represent the conditions of precarity that affect hundreds of women on the migrant trail. But at the same time, through their *testimonios*, Sandra and Marta raise the viewers' awareness that something needs to change. As I previously mentioned, the connection that the filmmaker and the two migrant mothers are able to form contributes to exposing and combating the dominant forces that deny women like Sandra and Marta and their children the right to a safe and prosperous life. Zamora's film serves as a medium for undocumented migrant women to bring their life stories into public view. By treating migrant subjects as agents of change through their disruptions of what constitutes bare life, Zamora brings the migrant, the non-citizen, closer to the viewer, the citizen, "a member of civil society, a putative participant in the public sphere" (Chanan vi). Of all the women migrants that Zamora interviews in the film, she appears to develop a stronger bond of affection with Sandra and Marta. For example, at a difficult moment for Sandra and Marta in the film, we see Zamora embracing both of them with a kiss. This brief moment in the film is important as the emotional expressions and body language of the women on camera help draw them and the viewer closer together in their common humanity in ways that a testimonial text cannot always do.

Zamora introduces the testimonies of three other young Central American women whose degree of precarity is so high that not many of these kinds of stories have been documented on film before. These stories are by women forced to interrupt their migration flow, either because they were sold into prostitution or were abducted by Los Zetas, one of Mexico's most dangerous drug cartels until recently. Early in the film, the viewer meets one of the women who was sold for sexual exploitation in Chiapas, and toward the end of the film meets two other young Central American women in northern Mexico who had escaped from captivity by Los Zetas.

As soon as she crosses the Guatemala-Mexico border filming the journey of the caravan of mothers, Zamora makes a stop at El Bambi, a run-down brothel in the border town of Ciudad Hidalgo, Chiapas. Here, the viewer meets Jazmín, a young Nicaraguan mother who left her country in need of work but who, like many other migrant women suffering from expulsion in their home countries, never thought about migrating to the United States in the first place. Jazmín describes the precarious conditions of Central American women caught in the sex-trafficking business along Mexico's southern border. In her *testimonio,* Jazmín tells the horrific story of betrayal when a friend encouraged her to migrate with the false promise of finding a job as a waitress. Little did Jazmín know that her so-called friend was planning on selling her for $50 to the managers of El Bambi. Forced to work as a dancer and prostitute, Jazmín narrates her experience of initial fear and shame, followed by a phase of physical abuse, and alcohol and drug use that led her to attempt suicide. Just after Jazmín describes her failed suicide attempt, the camera cuts to a small table in her room. This table appears to be an altar that holds together a few ordinary and religious objects. The viewer can see a photograph of a pregnant Jazmín, a few lipsticks and cosmetics, and two small statues of the Virgin Mary (Figure 6.2). This camera cut, intended to focus on the makeshift altar, disrupts the narrative of despair and sorrow as Jazmín's story takes a detour where she talks about her hope and desire for a different life. She tells Zamora:

I would like to have a different life, maybe a home where my daughter would be with me. My daughter sometimes says that she doesn't want to be here. And to be honest, I haven't had much peace in my life because I have not experienced it yet. Maybe I will when I have a home or a different life, God willing.[5]

Zamora carefully builds this scene by listening to Jazmín's story and weaving together her *testimonio* of past despair, present sorrow, and hopeful future through the use of camera cuts that first show Jazmín crying, and then the makeshift altar that she keeps in her room. Her daughter's wishes for a different life and the altar serves Jazmín as faithful reminder of a better future. Jazmín's wish for a better life for her and her daughter is another disruption of the normative narrative of dispossession and of the violence that endangers her body at "El Bambi." Jazmín's *testimonio* in which she shares her story of betrayal and false promises underlines the precarious isolation that many migrant women experience in their home country (family abuse and abandonment) and on the migrant trail (the dangers of sexual abuse, being sold into sex work, abducted, and disappeared).

By listening to her young daughter's plea for a change in their lives, Jazmín begins to dream of having a home and of reaching peace, two essential marks of stability that have been denied to her, so far. The camera shot that focuses on the objects on her altar opens up a space of credence that Jazmín manages to fill with her own voice, asserting hope for a new

Figure 6.2. A small altar with photo of Jazmín, cosmetics, and statues of the Virgin Mary. Still from *María en tierra de nadie*.

chance at life. Her trust and belief in her daughter give Jazmín the strength she needs to counter the dominant forces of abuse and violence in her present life. At the film's closing, the viewer learns that Jazmín obtained legal papers for her and her six-year-old daughter in Mexico. After seven years of working at El Bambi, she managed to leave it behind and moved north. Since 2009 she has been working in what she calls, "un trabajo digno" ("a dignified job").

In the film, migrant credence provides relief from the lack of credibility of state authorities and the police. On one of the early stops of the Caravana de madres, the caravan holds a press conference and a meeting with government and police officials in the Mexican state of Chiapas. The meeting took place in 2009 in the city of Tapachula. The women of the caravan set up large posters with the names and photos of their missing children. On film, state officials listen to several mothers tell the stories of their disappeared children. Doña Inés asks the state authorities to help her find her daughter Sandra Mabel. Emetria Martínez describes her daily struggle to fight back the sorrow for her missing daughter. After pleading to the authorities for help, Martínez speaks of the faith that gives her the will to keep on with her search. She states, "[. . .] I have faith in that I will find my daughter. Faith is the last thing that we should lose, because if we lose faith we lose everything."[6] Speaking of faith empowers Martínez. The viewer can witness how, on camera, Martínez's facial expression and tone of voice switch from sadness to self-assurance the moment she mentions the need to keep the faith. Her belief in her commitment to search for her daughter is seen in sharp contrast to the rhetoric of "business as usual" expressed by the authorities in the room, all of whom avoid making eye contact with the women of the caravan.

Frustrated with the empty promises of state officials, Martha Sánchez Soler, director of the Movimiento Migrante Mesoamericano, who accompanies the women of the caravan throughout their journey in Mexico, picks up the microphone to stress the urgent need for a transformational change:

> Forgive me for taking the floor, but I couldn't hold it in. When we started to hear things on television about the crisis, about hope . . . , messages like "if we all work together we'll make it . . ." This is a kind of naïve triumphalism that doesn't allow us to really solve problems. And in some way, I got that same feeling during this meeting. We can't just say "What a nice program we have. Now we've resolved everything," because it is simply not credible. People are going through real humanitarian crises. There are kidnappings every day. So, let's better not go

there and just let me tell you that this requires people, not officials. You as committed people. If not, we will continue to pretend to change the laws for nothing. Because in this country everything changes in order to keep everything the same.[7]

Sánchez Soler's intervention cuts through liberalism's empty rhetoric of democracy and justice for all. Her statement disrupts "the politics as usual" strategy of the powerful and calls for a transformative shift in subject identity. Her urgent appeal to state officials to act as "people, committed people," rather than as functionaries, goes exactly against the current of politicized life (List 41). By showing that the political solutions to the migrant crisis are no longer credible, Sánchez Soler appropriates bare life as desirable, as the only way out of the humanitarian crises that migrants face today. Sánchez Soler's call for an identity transformation of government officials into people resonates with Agamben's notion of *whatever* being, which he interprets from the Latin *quodlibet ens* to describe "being such that it always matters" (Agamben 1). For Agamben, the whatever being is an open singularity that is not indifferent to the particular characteristics of others, but is free "from the false dilemma that obliges knowledge to choose between the ineffability of the individual and the intelligibility of the universal" (1). In this regard, it would be impossible for Mexican state officials to do the work of dismantling the networks of corruption that sustain the system in which they function. This is why Sánchez Soler calls for their detachment from their political identity in order to begin to take action as people, the singularity of "whatever you *want*" to be and to accomplish (Agamben 2).

One of the most transformative moments in the film is when the women of the caravan visit the stretch of the migrant trail known as La Arrocera, in Chiapas, Mexico. La Arrocera, named after an abandoned rice warehouse, is a remote region in Chiapas where migrants climb onto *La Bestia* (The Beast), the freight trains on which they try to cross through Mexico. Journalist Óscar Martínez, who collaborated with Zamora in the production of the film and has written extensively on the precarious conditions of Central American migrants, writes that for most migrants this 262-kilometer region that goes from Tapachula to Arriaga is a "lawless territory," the most dangerous of the entire trek across Mexico (29). Controlled by corrupt police officers in connection with gangs and drug traffickers, La Arrocera is known for its mass graves and many unidentified dead bodies left abandoned.

Zamora's film title, *María en tierra de nadie,* refers to this particular area along the migrant trail. In this "no man's land," the women of the caravan search for any news that could lead them to finding their missing children.

The film shows the women enacting a *via crucis* and converting into a sacred space a site where the body of a missing brother of one of the women had been found dead on July 1, 2000. In this ceremony, the women of the caravan, all dressed in white, sing religious songs and carry memorial crosses that they eventually stick into the ground. This *via crucis* is meaningful in at least three ways. First, by mourning and paying homage to the dead, the women of the caravan resist the insignificance imposed on bare life and claim the lives of their sons, daughters, and siblings as grievable life (Butler, Precarious 20). Here I borrow from Butler's notion of "grievable life" to mean that the lives of migrants who have been lost are lives "that can be regarded as life," and that the caravan itself is a symbol of memory for the missing and disappeared migrants (Butler, *Frames* 15). Second, mourning the dead and the disappeared also implies a deep transformation of the women's lives. Butler suggests that when we lose certain people or when we are dispossessed of a location or community, this change may only be temporary. But when mourning leads us to change what we do, a transformation of who we are can begin to take place (Butler, *Precarious* 22). More than twenty years ago, Emetria Martínez started organizing the women of disappeared migrants. For her and the other women, joining the caravan marks their transformation from biological mothers into pro-migrant activists who resignify their lives and their relationship with each other to form a collective "we" that goes beyond their particular biological family ties. Finally, this act of resistance that both claims disposable bodies as grievable life and re-signifies La Arrocera as sacred ground also watches over the migrants who are currently alive. Once the women of the caravan begin performing their act of memory and mourning, the camera cuts to a scene with Sandra Campos and Marta Muñoz, the two migrant mothers from El Salvador that the viewer meets at the start of the film. Using parallel action, Zamora switches back and forth between the scene of the symbolic act of mourning and of Sandra and Marta walking alone in "no man's land," only following the path marked by the railroad track. Although the women of the caravan never cross paths with Sandra and Marta, Zamora's editing skills draw meaningful connections between them.

As I have already mentioned, another element that serves as a connector between the various migrant women in the film is the objects they carry. Zamora reconnects with Sandra and Marta days after the two women crossed through La Arrocera on their own. On camera, Sandra and Marta tell stories of the violence they experienced while riding on top of *La Bestia*. Sandra describes how they were robbed and sexually abused, and shot by gang members. Sandra regrets losing her backpack with everything that she owned, while Marta tells Zamora the story of how she survived harassment by the gang members:

> Marta: When he searched me, I told him, "Look, this is the only thing I have."
> Zamora: What is it?
> Marta: (Reaches into her pocket to grab a prayer card) I'm carrying the Father of the Immigrants.[8] He watches over the immigrants. This is what I showed him! I told him, "This is what I have. I'm praying." And he didn't try to pull down my pants any lower.[9]

Marta's retelling of the moment when she and Sandra were attacked and robbed on the train is significant as she manages to re-live an experience of vulnerability for both women. At the same time, the viewer becomes aware of the different experiences of the assault for Sandra and Marta. While Sandra suffers the indignity of abuse and loss of all her belongings, Marta survives further humiliation by confronting her captors with imagination and the prayer card she carries with her (Figure 6.3). As a precarious object, this prayer card channels Marta's credence in her actions and final objective, which is to reach the United States and obtain a good job to support her family back in El Salvador. Faith is once again the discourse through which a migrant mother articulates her voice of resistance.

Another moment in the film when the viewer encounters migrant agency under situations of extreme precarity happens at Albergue Belén, Posada del

Figure 6.3. Marta shows the prayer card while walking near train tracks. Still from *María en tierra de nadie*.

Figure 6.4. Janeth and Irma cooking. Still from *María en tierra de nadie*.

Migrante, a migrant shelter directed by Father Pedro Pantoja in northern Mexico, where Zamora meets two young women who had previously been victims of family betrayal and of kidnapping and sexual abuse by members of Los Zetas cartel. Janeth and Irma are two Central American migrant women who narrate how the drug cartel operates. Janeth's *testimonio* shows how Los Zetas carry out mass kidnappings in connection with the federal and local police, railroad machinists, gang members, and local neighbors. As with La Arrocera in the south end of Mexico, the description of the landscape of kidnappings, terror, and violence in the north end of the country informs the title of Zamora's film. The viewer senses that only a few other places in the world can compare to the extreme levels of precarity that undocumented migrants experience along the railroad tracks that cross the Mexican landscape from south to north.

In their testimonies, Janeth and Irma tell stories of gruesome body dismemberment, extortion, kidnapping, and rape. But despite this violence, they also share stories of survival based on a tight bond that they build with each other and that enables them to keep moving forward (Wheatley and Gomberg-Muñoz 127). For example, Janeth explains how she negotiated with her captors to work for a month as a cook in exchange for her ransom. However, Irma could not come to an agreement with her captors since her uncle, with whom she had been traveling and who swore to always protect her, had given her to Los Zetas as ransom for his own release. The two young women explain how they both met in the kitchen of one of the cartel's secret houses. Janeth offered a glass of warm milk to Irma after the kidnappers had physically abused her. This act of compassion, revealed through the sharing of a precarious object in the midst of terror, is what creates a bond of healing, trust, and companionship for the two women. Despite finding themselves confined to the kitchen, their friendship allows them to look beyond traditional bonds of family, to survive and gain freedom from their captors (Figure 6.4). As a final example of credence, this scene where Janeth welcomes Irma into the kitchen with a warm glass of milk symbolizes a maternal gift of new life for the one who had been betrayed by her uncle and abused by her captors. The friendship that these two young women form through mutual credence, despite their conditions of extreme precarity, connects their lives with those of the other women migrants in the film.

Conclusion

As I commented earlier on the connections between *testimonio* and documentary film, the courage of migrant women like Doña Inés, Marta, Sandra, Jazmín, Janeth, and Irma in remembering their painful past is not just meant to represent one more experience of bare life. Instead, the purpose behind their testimonies is to advance their stories of survival, to push forward against the many vulnerabilities that migrant women face on the migrant trail. For their stories to be advanced, they require real people to "take the floor" and intervene on their behalf. The film introduces the viewer to several activists, shelter volunteers, and ordinary people doing extraordinary actions of solidarity on behalf of migrants. Here I have mentioned the intervention by Martha Sánchez Soler, but the film also includes interviews with shelter directors in Guatemala and Mexico such as Ademar Barilli, Fr. Alejandro Solalinde, Fr. Pedro Pantoja, and the women known as *Las Patronas*, who provide food and water to hungry migrants riding on top of *La Bestia*. As previously stated, documentary film can serve as a medium that exposes the hidden stories of expulsion and abuse and, in the process, contributes as an artistic intervention from which to challenge official exclusionary practices that produce precarity—an aim that dovetails with Jared List's argument in his chapter in this volume.

Marcela Zamora's film, with its inclusion of testimonies by various migrant women and the volunteers who build bonds of collective agency with them, provides the viewer with a critical artistic work that goes beyond the single story of precarity as lack, of bare life as exclusion, and instead contributes to the creation of multiple sites of collective agency that can help subvert the configuration of power in our present time.

Notes

1 This chapter was first published as "Collective Disruptions of Bare Life in Marcela Zamora's *María en tierra de nadie*" by Esteban E. Loustaunau, pages 101–112 from *Diálogo*, Volume 23, Number 1, Spring 2020. Copyright © 2020. All rights reserved.
2 Marcela Zamora Chamorro studied journalism in Costa Rica and documentary film at the Escuela Internacional de Cine y Televisión (EICTV) in San Juan de los Baños, Cuba. Her filmography includes a dozen shorts and documentary films including *Xochiquetzal* (Cuba, 2007), *María en tierra de nadie* (2011), *Las masacres de El Mozote* (El Salvador, 2011), *El cuarto de los huesos* (Mexico and El Salvador, 2015), and *Los ofendidos* (El Salvador, 2016). As with some of her other films, *María en tierra de nadie* was coproduced with El Salvador's online newspaper *El Faro*. This film is part of a larger project called, "*En el camino: Migración indocumentada a través de México*," which also produced Óscar Martínez's book *Los migrantes que no importan* (2011), translated as *The Beast: Riding the Rails and Dodging Narcos on the Migrant Trail* (2014). For an analysis of *Los ofendidos*, read Lilia García Torres's chapter in this volume.
3 For over twenty years, Emetria Martínez searched for her missing migrant daughter, Ana Marlén Ortiz, who one day left Honduras in search of work in the United States. Twenty-one years later, first alone and later with the support of others, Martínez found Ana Marlén near Mexico City. A single mother's search for her lost daughter became the spark that encouraged many other mothers in similar situations to gather together and form the *Caravana de Madres de Migrantes Desaparecidos*. Through the assistance of Father Melo of Radio Progreso in Honduras, Martínez disseminated information to help identify missing sons and daughters on the migrant trail. She passed away on January 8, 2013, after having organized eight search caravans from Central America to Mexico (Petrich 1–4).
4 In the film, it remains unknown to the viewer where and with whom Sandra's daughter is staying in the United States.
5 "Quisiera tener una vida diferente. Tal vez un hogar en el que mi hija esté conmigo. Mi hija algunas veces me dice que no quiere estar acá. Y para serte sincera, no mucho he vivido la paz y no tengo mucho conocimiento de eso, porque no la he vivido todavía. Tal vez la viva, si Dios me lo permite y tenga un hogar y una vida diferente." All English translations are quoted from the film's subtitles.
6 "[. . .] Yo tengo fe que a mi hija yo la voy a hallar. La fe es la primera [cosa] que nosotros no debemos de perder. Porque si perdemos la fe, se pierde todo."
7 "Les pido disculpas por tomar la palabra, pero no podía contenerme. Cuando empezamos a oír en la televisión que la crisis y que la esperanza . . . 'que todos dándole vamos a lograr' . . . es una especie de triunfalismo ingenuo que no permite que se resuelvan los problemas. Un poco sentí la misma percepción, 'ya estamos componiendo todo, no pasa nada' . . . [E]so realmente no es creíble. La gente está viviendo verdaderas crisis humanitarias. Los secuestros se están dando todos los días. Sólo quiero decirles, por favor, esto require de personas, no de funcionarios. Ustedes como personas, comprometidos. Porque si no, podemos cambiar leyes pero todo cambia para no cambiar en este país."

8   Marta is referring to Father Giovanni Battista Scalabrini (1839–1905), known for his advocacy of immigrant rights.
9   Marta: "Cuando a mí me revisó yo le dije, 'Mira, esto es todo lo que traigo,' le dije yo."
    Zamora: "¿Qué tenés?"
    Marta: "Tengo al padre de los inmigrantes. El que cuida a los inmigrantes. ¡Esto le enseñé! Le dije, 'Esto es todo lo que traigo. Vengo orando,' le dije. Ahí fue donde no intentó bajarme el pantalón hasta más abajo."

Works Cited

Agamben, Giorgio. *The Coming Community*. Minneapolis: U Minnesota P, 1993.
Aprea, Gustavo. "Testimonios e identidades en documentales argentinos sobre la historia reciente." *XIV Jornadas Interescuelas/Departamentos de Historia. Departamento de Historia de la Facultad de Filosofía y Letras. Universidad Nacional de Cuyo, Mendoza*, 2013, https://www.aacademica.org/000-010/906. Accessed 3 September 2019.
Banki, Susan. "The Paradoxical Power of Precarity: Refugees and Homeland Activism." *Refugee Review*, https://refugeereview.wordpress.com/working-papers/paradoxical-power-and-precarity/. Accessed 10 February 2019.
Biekart, Kees. "Assessing the 'Arrival of Democracy' in Central America." *European Review of Latin American and Caribbean Studies/Revista Europea de Estudios Latinoamericanos y del Caribe*, no. 96, 2014, pp. 117–126, https://www.jstor.org/stable/23722441?seq=1#metadata_info_tab_contents. Accessed 20 June 2019.
Beverley, John. *Testimonio: On the Politics of Truth*. Minneapolis: U Minnesota P, 2004.
Burton, Julianne. "Democratizing Documentary: Modes of Address in Latin American Cinema, 1958–1972." *Show Us Life: Towards a History and Aesthetics of the Committed Documentary*, edited by Thomas Waugh, Landham, Scarecrow Press, 1984, pp. 344–383.
Butler, Judith. *Frames of War. When is Life Grievable?* London: Verso, 2009.
———. "Performativity, Precarity, and Sexual Politics." *Revista de Antropología Iberoamericana*, vol. 4, no. 3, 2009, http://www.aibr.org/antropologia/04v03/criticos/040301b.pdf. Accessed 4 April 2018.
———. *Precarious Life: The Powers of Mourning and Violence*. London: Verso, 2004.
Carasik, Lauren. "Jimmy Morales Can't Fix Guatemala." *Foreign Policy*, vol. 16, 2016, https://foreignpolicy.com/2016/03/16/guatemala-morales-perez-molina/. Accessed 26 June 2019.
Chanan, Michael. *The Politics of Documentary*. London: British Film Institute, 2007.
De Genova, Nicholas. "The Deportation Regime: Sovereignty, Space, and the Freedom of Movement." *The Deportation Regime: Sovereignty, Space and the Freedom of Movement*, edited by Nicholas De Genova and Nathalie Peutz, Duke UP, 2010, pp. 33–65.
El cuarto de los huesos. Directed by Marcela Zamora, La Sandía Digital and Trípode Audiovisual, Mexico/El Salvador, 2015.
Fernandez, Manny, Ilana Panich-Linsman, and Mitchell Ferman. "In South Texas, the First Signs of a Border Swathed with Military Might." *The New York Times*, 1 November 2018, https://www.nytimes.com/2018/11/01/us/border-army-troops-migrant-caravan.html. Accessed 23 June 2019.

Goldman, Francisco. "Trump Enabled an 'Act of Organized Crime' in Guatemala." *The New York Times,* 18 June 2019. www.nytimes.com/2019/06/18/opinion/guatemala-election.html?ref=nyt-es&mcid=nyt-es&subid=article. Accessed 6 September 2019.

Guerra, Ramón. "Testimonial Youth in Flux: Migration, Narrative, and Children in *Which Way Home.*" *Telling Migrant Stories. Latin American Diaspora in Documentary Film,* edited by Esteban E. Loustaunau and Lauren E. Shaw, U of Florida P, 2018, pp. 175–192.

Hondagneu-Sotelo, Pierrette, and Ernestina Avila. "'I'm Here, but I'm There:' The Meaning of Latina Transnational Motherhood." *Women and Migration in the U.S.-Mexico Borderlands. A Reader,* edited by Denise A. Segura and Patricia Zavella, Duke UP, 2007, pp. 388–412.

Kelz, Rosine. "Political Theory and Migration: Concepts of Non-Sovereignty and Solidarity." *Movements. Journal für kritische Migrations- und Grenzregimeforschung,* vol. 1, no. 2, 2015, https://movements-journal.org/issues/02.kaempfe/03.kelz--political-theory-migration-non-sovereignty-solidarity.pdf. Accessed 23 June 2019.

Las masacres de El Mozote. Directed by Marcela Zamora, El Faro, El Salvador, 2011.

List, Jared. "Documenting Deportable Life: Knowledge, Performance and Memory in *abUSed: The Postville Raid* and *Sin país.*" *Telling Migrant Stories. Latin American Diaspora in Documentary Film,* edited by Esteban E. Loustaunau and Lauren E. Shaw, U of Florida P, 2018, pp. 39–66.

Los ofendidos. Directed by Marcela Zamora, Kino Glaz, El Salvador/Mexico, 2016.

Loustaunau, Esteban E. "The Unending Journey of the Migrant Mother in *Los invisibles* and *De nadie.*" *Telling Migrant Stories. Latin American Diaspora in Documentary Film,* edited by Esteban E. Loustaunau and Lauren E. Shaw, U of Florida P, 2018, pp. 88–118.

María en tierra de nadie. Directed by Marcela Zamora. Ruido, El Faro, I(dh)eas, El Salvador, 2011.

Martínez, Óscar. *Los migrantes que no importan.* Ciudad de México: Surplus Ediciones, 2011.

———. *The Beast. Riding the Rails and Dodging the Narcos on the Migrant Trail.* London: Verso, 2013.

Martínez Hernández-Mejía, Iliana. "Reflexiones sobre la caravana migrante." *Análisis Plural,* 2018, pp. 231–248. https://rei.iteso.mx/handle/11117/5616. Accessed 5 September 2019.

Miyoshi, Masao. "A Borderless World? From Colonialism to Transnationalism and the Decline of the Nation-State." *Critical Inquiry,* vol. 19, no. 4, 1993, pp.726–751.

Nichols, Bill. *Representing Reality.* Bloomington: Indiana U P, 1991.

Paret, Marcel and Shannon Gleeson. "Introduction: Precarity and Agency through a Migration Lens." *Building Citizenship from Below: Precarity, Migration, and Agency,* edited by Marcel Paret and Shannon Gleeson, Routledge, 2017, pp.1–18.

Petrich, Blanche. "Fallece Emetria Martínez, pionera de las caravanas en busca de migrantes." *La Jornada,* 9 January 2013, https://www.jornada.com.mx/2013/01/09/politica/011n1pol. Accessed 26 June 2019.

Rodríguez, Ileana. *Liberalism at its Limits. Crime and Terror in the Latin American Cultural Text.* Pittsburgh: U of Pittsburgh P, 2009.

Sassen, Saskia. *Expulsions. Brutality and Complexity in the Global Economy.* Cambridge: Harvard UP, 2014.

Valencia, Sayak. *Capitalismo gore*. Tenerife, Spain: Melusina, 2010.
Wheatley, Abby C. and Ruth Gomberg-Muñoz. "Keep moving: Collective Agency Along the Migrant Trail." *Building Citizenship from Below: Precarity, Migration, and Agency*, edited by Marcel Paret and Shannon Gleeson, Routledge, 2017, pp. 120–134.1.
Xochiquetzales. Directed by Marcela Zamora, Escuela Internacional de Cine y TV, Cuba, 2007.

7

Longing for Missing Memories

Journeys of "Return" and Postmemory in *Children of the Diaspora,* by Jennifer A. Cárcamo (2013)

Patricia Arroyo Calderón

In the past few years, we have seen a steep increase in the filmic representations of Central American migrants in their journey toward Mexico and the United States. From foundational films such as Gregory Nava's *El Norte* (1983) to more recent documentary and fictional depictions of the Central American migrant's plight, the majority of these narratives about Central American displacement has been created by Mexican, Chicanx, or Latinx filmmakers.[1] And yet, cinematic narratives of migration and return have also been produced by U.S.-born Central Americans whose work is rarely taken into account neither by the emerging field of Central American film studies nor by the more consolidated field of Latinx film studies. The purpose of this text is, therefore, to consider some of the ways in which the themes of displacement, identity, memory, and belonging appear in the cinematic production of the Central American diaspora, in the hope of widening the conversations about new Central American film by considering these transnational productions. In this chapter, I am particularly interested in discussing documentary films produced by second-generation Central Americans as a privileged space where we can observe the specific process through which postmemories of the traumatic past of the Isthmus are constituted among its diasporas. Thus, my theoretical entry point is the concept of "postmemory," as discussed by Marianne Hirsch in her book *The Generation of Postmemory* (2012), in which she presents a model where intergenerational traumatic memories—in this case, linked to the Holocaust—are transmitted from the affected generation to the next. While Hirsch's model considers that this process of memory transfer happens first and foremost within the immediate context of the family, in this text I analyze the documentary film *Children of the Diaspora: For Peace and Democracy* (2013) in light of similar notions coined by Central American scholars—such as Ana Patricia Rodríguez's "second-hand identities" and Karina Oliva Alvarado's "cultural memory work"—that stress the preeminence of "affiliative" or horizontal modes of memory transfer within the 1.5 and second generation of the Central American diasporas in the United States. As my analysis of the documentary will show, in this diasporic context the primal scene of memory transfer within the familial setting—always overloaded with narrative excess in Hirsch's account, but characterized by oblique or limited narratives, elusions, and silences in *Children of the Diaspora*—manifests primarily as desire, and more often than not becomes realized only after other "affiliative" processes of postmemory formation are set in motion by the second generation (in this case, via a journey of return to the Isthmus and through the exposition to the public archive of past violence in the region). With this approach to *Children of the Diaspora,* I aim to contribute to the ongoing conversation about the role of cultural production, including film, in the constitution of Central American subjectivities and identities within transnationalized contexts, as well as to discussions regarding the suitability of applying Hirsch's concept of postmemory to the study of diasporic communities with no relation to the Shoah.

Children of the Diaspora: For Peace and Democracy was written, produced, and directed by Jennifer A. Cárcamo in 2013. Cárcamo is a young film director who combines her work as a documentary maker with her doctoral studies in the History Department at UCLA, as well as with an intense activity as local organizer and cultural promoter within the Central American communities of Los Angeles. Film production is for Cárcamo, in this sense, a task that exceeds purely aesthetic or commercial concerns and that, rather, needs to be vigorously connected to broader processes of social mobilization and political intervention. We can find a good example of these connections between filmmaking and community-building in her most recent documentary, *Eternos Indocumentados: Central American Refugees in the U.S.,* a film devised to support the efforts of the Human Rights Alliance for Child Refugees and Families, a Los Angeles–based non-profit organization devoted to the defense of the human rights of migrants and refugees—in particular, the rights of women, children, and members of the LGBTQ+ community—who have been forced to flee toward the North as a consequence of U.S. interventionism in the Central American isthmus.[2] As Cárcamo has publicly affirmed on several occasions, the main goal of her films is to contribute to the visibilization of the experiences of (U.S.) Central Americans through the dissemination of narratives created by diasporic subjects—such as herself—and destined to a transnationalized Central American audience.[3] In particular, this effort to center Central American voices in the diaspora would be the most urgent in the circumstances, when Central American communities are spoken for by the mass media—media that, more often than not, associate Central Americans with terms such as "poverty," "violence," "crisis," and even "invasion"—criminalized by U.S. authorities, and harassed by immigration enforcement agencies.

The will to make the multiplicity of Central American diasporic voices heard can be clearly perceived in *Children of the Diaspora,* a documentary that Cárcamo completed as final project for her MA degree in Film & History at the University of Syracuse in New York.[4] The intention of the film was to document the trip to El Salvador that a group of college students affiliated to different higher education institutions in California completed in February of 2009. This trip was sponsored and organized by USEU (Unión Salvadoreña de Estudiantes Universitarios [Salvadoran Union of University Students]), a now defunct transnational organization founded in 2007 that previously had branches both in El Salvador and in a number of California campuses.[5] The aim of the trip was for the California college students to observe the electoral campaign that was taking place in El Salvador, a process that culminated on March 15, 2009, with the victory of Mauricio Funes, the presidential candidate for the FMLN Party. In total, around twenty students participated in a delegation whose goal was to promote "peace and democracy;" some of these undergraduate students in 2009 are today well-known community activists and leaders of local organizations devoted to the defense of the rights of migrants and asylum seekers, graduate students completing dissertations focused on Central American themes, and university professors on California campuses.

However, and notwithstanding the explicit objectives of the film (that is, the audiovisual recording of the progress of the student delegation), the documentary soon turns into vividly registering the process of transformation of the subjectivities, identities, and politics of the students participating in the journey through El Salvador. For some of the young travelers, such as Kenia (student at the University of California, Riverside), the trip to El Salvador is a "return" in quite a literal sense, as she was born in this Central American country and lived there until she was twelve years old; she has not visited her hometown in nine years and is eager to reunite with her relatives and to see how everything has changed. For some other students, like Ernesto (also affiliated with UC-Riverside), born in the United States but self-identified as "Salvadoran" despite the fact that he has never been to El Salvador, defining this displacement becomes somewhat more complex. In a way, Ernesto's trip is also a "return home" because, similarly to many of his contemporaries, he has grown up in a context dominated by Salvadoran aromas, flavors, accents, and inflections. These cultural memories—absorbed mostly within the affective framework of the family—are almost immediately activated upon his arrival to San Salvador, triggering an initial moment of strong identification. As Ernesto himself expresses it in front of the camera: "I am really excited to be here [. . .] I, really . . . I am around people like me, for the first time, and it's . . . really great" (*Children of the Diaspora*). And yet, an immediate sensation of unfamiliarity appears in the very same fragment of interview—a take that lasts less than fifteen seconds: "For the first time in my life I feel like a foreigner . . . hmmm . . . I am really aware of the way I am talking, 'cause my Spanish ain't that great" (*Children of the Diaspora*).

Different scholars have situated this identity ambivalence at the core of U.S.-born Central Americans, a sector of the United States population that critics such as Karina O. Alvarado, Alicia Ivonne Estrada, and Esther Hernández denominate "U.S. Central Americans," poets like Maya Chinchilla have named "Centralamerican Americans" (without a hyphen), and other scholars, such as Nora Hamilton, Norma Stolz Chinchilla, Arturo Arias, or Maritza Cárdenas prefer to call "Central American-Americans" (hyphenated).[6] As Cárdenas discusses in her book, *Constituting Central American-Americans. Transnational Identities and the Politics of Dislocation* (2018), despite the fact that Central American diasporic subjects rarely use any of the aforementioned terms when identifying themselves, these labels are nevertheless useful sociological categories that allow to delineate and visibilize a specific social group, in particular:

> Central Americans who are part of the second generation or the 1.5 generation and/or someone born in the United States with ancestry from Central America. Defined in this manner, both U.S. Central Americans and Central American-Americans are therefore limited to a particular generation and a very specific geopolitical location (the United States). (9)

At the same time, Cárdenas also remarks that—beyond just being productive sociological categories—these terms aim to acknowledge the existence of a concrete subject position formed at the margins of the margins, a subject position fashioned as the negated excess of other labels with holistic aspirations, such as "Hispanic" or "Latino," which "are often constructed through the abjection and the erasure of the Central American-American. [. . .] For this population [. . .] their invisible status, their non-recognition, generates a sense of non-belonging, of nonbeing, a cruel invisibility" (Arias 186). Within the context of California university campuses, it is not infrequent to find students who express similar feelings as the ones so aptly described by Arturo Arias. College students of Central American descent often lament the invisibility of U.S. Central Americans in the public sphere and within institutional contexts, and it is not rare to hear them expressing mixed feelings in relation to their interactions with members of other ethno-cultural groups perceived as dominant within the context of Latinx populations, Chicanxs in particular.[7] These tensions emerge as well within *Children of the Diaspora* when Ernie (a student at UCLA) explains in front of the camera the emergence of USEU at California campuses:

> We really thought that we had to be careful with everything that we are doing 'cause, it was a space that people were asking for, you know? There were spaces, you know, for all these other students, you know, for African-American students, but a space specifically for Salvadoran students has never been there. It takes time, you know, for a certain Salvadoran . . . a consolidated group of Salvadorans to begin to feel comfortable, to be like, OK, you know? We exist as well.

Despite these frictions, the main source of frustration for the college students who share their thoughts in *Children of the Diaspora* is not so much linked to the complexity of interethnic relations, but to the quality of the intergenerational bonds within their own families—specifically, as related to the quality (or lack thereof) of communication with their parents, who made the decision to flee to the United States during the 1970s and 1980s. Central American scholars such as Leisy Abrego have explored the different layers of "silence" that have marked, and still mark, the lives of Salvadorans in the United States. In her text "On Silences: Salvadoran Refugees Then and Now," Abrego shares her own experience growing up without hearing the stories of state violence that forced her own mother to flee El Salvador, and points to the fact that these narrative absences build a "large void in generations of children of Salvadoran immigrants [who] grow up in the U.S. being denied access to our own stories" (76).[8] In a similar vein, Ana Patricia Rodríguez has developed the concept of "second hand identities" in order to explain the highly mediated ways in which the transmission of memories to the second generation of the diaspora occurs. According to Rodríguez, whereas the elder members of the family may sometimes constitute a source of "knowledge of the *homelands*," cultural materials such as "music, film, the media, and other reliable (and non-reliable) information-generating circuits" are more often the main places where U.S.-born Central Americans acquire their "*second-hand* memories"

("Second hand identities").[9] As such, the "cultural memory work" produced within the second generation of the Central American diaspora becomes, according to Karina Oliva Alvarado, a privileged site where issues of identity and belonging are explored, negotiated, re-created, and/or dramatized, as well as the place where silences, denials, gaps, and "the missing" are addressed in order to "reconstruct, recover, and voice silences maintained by their parents, prior generations, and institutionalized hegemonies" (495).[10]

These absences and voids emerge in the first sequence of the film—a sequence that extends for about six minutes, which opens with an intertitle where a brief explanation about the Salvadoran civil war and its aftereffects is offered, followed by a quote by Bertolt Brecht. Immediately after, we listen to the first notes of Silvio Rodríguez's song, "Sueño con serpientes" ["I dream of snakes"], while images of Los Angeles—mostly shot around Pico Union and Westlake/MacArthur, both areas heavily populated by Central Americans—occupy the screen. The places chosen by Cárcamo include *pupuserías*, buses, big public murals, inner-city playgrounds, transportation and remittances businesses, community pharmacies, street vendors' food-carts and, very significantly, a number of shots of the sculpture "Por qué emigramos / Why we emigrate," a work created by Salvadoran artist Dagoberto Reyes that can be visited in MacArthur Park.[11]

Some visual aspects of this sequence made up of disparate urban shots illustrate particularly well the sense of ambivalence toward self and place that Arturo Arias analyzed in depth in *Taking Their Word. Literature and the Signs of Central America*. The sequence opens at ground level, with an extreme close-up of blades of grass swaying in the wind in sharp focus, against a completely blurry and indeterminate background. A few seconds after, the camera tilts slightly upward, simultaneously pulling the focus. Now the tips of the blades appear fuzzy, but we can clearly see the formerly blurry background: we are situated in a city park, where a mother and her two children are playing and strolling. Thus, the opening of the film already introduces, using exclusively visual cues, some of the main goals and themes that will be pursued and explored throughout the rest of the documentary. As such, the will to center the experiences and voices of the Salvadoran youth growing up in the United States is adroitly symbolized by the sprouting grass shown in sharp focus, while the motifs of intergenerational relationships and unknown family histories are respectively rendered by the images of the mother and her sons, as well as by the initially out-of-focus background of the park. These shots also introduce a noticeable tendency to alternate between focused and unfocused images that will persist throughout the opening sequence. Clear images tend to coincide with identifiable places that mark the Salvadoran experience in

Los Angeles. This is the case with certain street signs, bus lines (such as the one that connects Pico Union and Echo Park), sites of memory and community worship (like the tile mosaic dedicated to St. Óscar Romero at La Placita/ Our Lady Queen of Los Angeles Church), and everyday places, such as the interior of a *pupusería*, that render the experiences of L.A. Salvadorans with a rich texture and reclaim concrete spaces of the city.

Blurry images, on the other hand, include bird's-eye views of the city at dusk and by night, fleeting passersby, and long shots of unidentified streets and businesses. This alternation between focused and out-of-focus images is sometimes delivered through the juxtaposition of different takes, but other times is presented through the abundant use of rack focus and flash pans; in the latter instances, a seemingly unsure camera quickly scans unidentifiable sections of the city until it latches onto clear Central American referents such as a waving flag of El Salvador, or a business named "El Pulgarcito."[12] Some of these stylistic traits—especially the abundance of long shots immediately followed by flash pans and very quick zooms, the profusion of blurry and out-of-focus images, and the numerous shots of faces and places that appear distorted behind glasses or semi-hidden behind vehicles and various elements of urban infrastructure—can be attributed, no doubt, to the scarcity of means with which the documentary was shot, to the fact that the filmmaker did not count on the help of a professional photography director, or to the inherent complications of filming in a big and busy city. However, the combination of the erratic camera movements with the oneiric and melancholic tune of Silvio Rodríguez's song, plus the notable number of images recorded at twilight, transmits a sensation of loss to the spectator, allowing her to glimpse the expression of a subjectivity marked by an ambivalent affective relationship with the spaces it inhabits. Similar to Ernesto's impressions upon his arrival to San Salvador, the initial sequence of *Children of the Diaspora*—fully shot in the filmmaker's hometown, Los Angeles—communicates at the same time familiarity and strangeness, proximity and distance, feelings of belonging and feelings of alienation, thanks to a restless camera that seems to be looking for the signs of Central Americanness in the global metropolis.

The nostalgic mood and sense of loss intensify mid-sequence, when the volume of Silvio Rodríguez's song recedes in order to give entrance to a series of off-screen voices that start expressing the difficulties encountered by the students when trying to inform their parents of their decision to travel to El Salvador as part of the electoral delegation. Cárcamo chooses to disconnect the voices from the speaking subjects, who will only be identifiable via a series of cut-out images snipped off old childhood photographs. Suddenly, the urban landscape that we have been contemplating fades to black and white and becomes the background for a series of new images that will be overlaid on top of it. These are digitized and semitransparent versions of the analog family photos, together with fragments of the testimonies that we are simultaneously listening to, transcribed in bold red and white letters. While the superimposed text appears and disappears from the frame following the rhythm of the voices, the childhood photographs never cease moving across the screen, as if freely floating.

What we read—and what we hear—is a polyphonic narrative made of silences, negations, and concealments:

> Voice #1: So, for me, basically, my mom, does not know, at all. Because, she's always been really anti . . . of me, like, being involved in anything political. Even more so if it is Salvadoran. Like, it's really, really bad.
> Voice #2: My dad was actually very against me doing anything that has to do with history, or politics, in my life.
> Voice #3: So, my mother is the only person that's actually here, that I live with and she is from El Salvador. And, basically, she is very anti anything that has to be with me involved with El Salvador or, even, to this very day, she denies that I am Salvadoran. (*Children of the Diaspora*)

Some aspects present in the testimonies displayed in *Children of the Diaspora* can be illuminated by considering the concept of "postmemory." Marianne Hirsch's book, *The Generation of Postmemory*, presents us with a model for understanding the ways in which traumatic memories get transferred from one generation to the next and, since its publication in 2012, has been vastly influential in the interdisciplinary field of memory studies. In particular, Hirsch's concept of "postmemory" aims to describe—and explain—the subjective effects that these acts of transfer have in the 1.5 and second generation of Holocaust survivors, defining it as "the relationship that the 'generation after' bears to the personal, collective, and cultural trauma of those who came before—to experiences they remember only by means of the stories, images, and behaviors among which they grew up" (5).[13] In the first pages of her book, Hirsch graphically illustrates how "postmemory" functions by showing the opening vignettes of *The First Maus*, the original strip that later inspired Art Spiegelman's comic book *Maus*.[14] The second vignette shows us a scene where a father retells his son about his own experiences in Poland during World Word II and subsequent internment in Auschwitz. This act of storytelling develops within a context of great intimacy: it is bedtime, the bedroom barely lit by a bedside lamp; the child is already in his pajamas, tucked in and warm below the blankets, and is listening to the narration with his head on his father's lap. Right above it, we can observe the first vignette of the comic, an illustrated version of a well-known photograph taken by Margaret Bourke-White in 1945, during the liberation of the Buchenwald concentration camp. In *The First Maus*'s version, the photograph—an image that belongs to the public archive of the Holocaust—shows a small mark, an arrow that points to one of the prisoners, identifying the figure as "poppa" (dad). Besides that, Hirsch directs the attention of the reader toward the four corners of this vignette-photograph, pointing out to the small triangles covering them (30). These four triangular shapes indicate that this particular public image—that is, Bourke-White's original photograph—has been appropriated as part of the private album of *The First Maus*'s family.[15]

This graphic example shows, according to Hirsch, how "postmemory" works: (post)memories are transmitted in a vertical way—i.e., from a first-generation victim of trauma to a second generation of direct descendants—generally during childhood, within the intimate framework of the family and mostly via affective (vs. cognitive) mechanisms (1–6). "Postmemory" then forms a fundamental part of the second generation's subjectivity, to the point that its members are permanently at risk to have their own life stories "evacuated" by the traumatic experiences of their parents (Hirsch 5). In sum, "postmemory" is nothing else than a vicarious memory of somebody else's trauma; nonetheless, it produces very real effects in the affective arrangements, the psychic structures, and the identities of the members of the second generation.[16]

All of the students who participated in *Children of the Diaspora* are indeed the daughters and sons of an older generation of Salvadorans directly impacted by the trauma of civil war, forced displacement, and a prolonged exile oftentimes in precarious circumstances. In this sense, the protagonists of this documentary fit perfectly within the "generation of postmemory" category proposed by Hirsch. However, the students' testimonies recorded in Cárcamo's film allow us to glimpse a different structure of "postmemory" than the one presented in the opening vignettes of *The First Maus*.

In *Children of the Diaspora,* trauma does not manifest through bedtime stories told at night but is made present in the form of elusion and secretiveness, limited narratives, or dramatic silences. Ricardo (student at UC-Berkeley) alludes to this discursive vacuum after visiting the Museum of the Salvadoran Revolution in Perquín; reflecting on his experience at the Museum in front of the camera, he shares that his father—who was part of the Army during the civil war and spent several days in captivity when he was captured by a guerrilla cell: "no habla mucho de su experiencia pues, por el trauma y, no sé, no le gusta mucho recordar" (*Children of the Diaspora*).[17] In a similar manner,

Denny (student at UCSB) points out that "growing up in a family that escaped from the war . . . I remember that actually they never told me anything . . . any critical, like, any facts. They just said: 'Those are the bad guys'" (*Children of the Diaspora*), whereas Kenia (student at UC-Riverside) says, visibly agitated after visiting El Mozote:[18]

> It's such a feeling . . . I was never aware of all of these massacres, or of the history of El Salvador during the civil war. My grandfather was killed during the war, and so did [sic] my uncle but, did I find how they were killed, or why? No. My family never talked about it and most likely it was because of the drama and all the . . . the traumatic things that they went through and they did not want to repeat over and over again to us. (*Children of the Diaspora*)[19]

This very same student, Kenia, will add the following reflections toward the end of the trip:

> I understand my family much better now but I just wished that they had told me, at least, a little bit of it so I could . . . I could understand it better. Because, all of this for me, it's new, and I wish I had, like, a background on it, so I would not be so . . . so confused. (*Children of the Diaspora*)

As we can see, the contents of the students' testimonies, together with Cárcamo's decision of opening up the film with fragments of testimonies accompanied by photographs taken from the family album, suggest that these "children of the diaspora" attribute a great deal of importance to the intimate and affective context of the family as a privileged space where memories are passed from one generation to the next. And, despite this fact, the memories of their parents are so inaccessible to these students as the memories of the Salvadoran migrants deposited, sealed, and buried until 2093 in the Time Capsule at MacArthur Park. In this sense, the excess of parental memory that lies at the core of Hirsch's model of transfer manifests exactly in the inverse way in *Children of the Diaspora*, where it disappears as loss, as lack, as a blank space from which the members of the second generation find difficulties to build up stable subjectivities. Perhaps, as if to show us this lack of anchor, the childhood photographs of the students' float—without ever stopping—over the screen surface while the spectators listen to their adult voices.

During their journey through El Salvador, the USEU students will visit—besides the already mentioned Museum of the Salvadoran Revolution in Perquín and El Mozote—other spatial markers of the traumatic and turbulent past of El Salvador, including the campus of the Universidad Centroamericana José Simeón Cañas (where the students are toured around the Museum of Monseñor Romero and the UCA Martyrs) and its rose garden commemorating the six Jesuits and two housekeepers assassinated by the Army in November of 1989.[20] Some days later, the travelers will visit the Military Museum Cuartel del Zapote, as well as a number of communities founded along the banks of the Bajo Río Lempa during the civil war by forcibly displaced population. Finally, the students will conclude their journey with a series of public appearances on radio and TV programs, and with a number of meetings with other groups of students—such as the one organized at the Universidad Panamericana, as well as with representatives of different political parties. Cárcamo introduces in her documentary abundant footage recorded during these visits, including long sequences where the tour guides in charge of showing these sites of memory recite detailed historical explanations of the Salvadoran recent past. The sequences shot at the museums and other commemorative spaces will alternate almost until the end of the documentary with a series of scenes where the off-screen voice of the filmmaker narrates different episodes of Salvadoran history while the screen fills up with images taken from the public archives. These images—provided by cultural institutions and student organizations such as the Museo de la Palabra y de la Imagen or the Unión de Estudiantes Revolucionarios Salvadoreños 30 de Julio—include photographs and film footage shot during different historical periods, although with a strong emphasis on the wave of social mobilizations that swept the country during the 1970s. This constant appropriation of the visual archive preserved by the former generation finds its aural replica in the soundtrack of the film as the viewers listen to songs such as "Que vivan los estudiantes" (Violeta Parra), "Solo digo compañeros" (Daniel Viglietti), "El Salvador ta' venciendo" (Yolocamba I Ta), "Todo cambia" (Mercedes Sosa), "Fusil contra fusil" and "Hoy mi deber" (Silvio Rodríguez), and other well-known anthems for the revolutionary youth that already belong to the affective memory of several generations of Latin Americans.[21]

Evidently, the physical displacement of the USEU students—that is, the journey of "return" to the places where their parents spent their childhood and youth—becomes, in itself, a powerful incentive for many of them to start filling in the wide gaps of their family's past.[22] This progressive confrontation with their own past sometimes acquires almost comical tones, as in the case of Isaac (student at UC-Merced) who, after visiting the pre-Columbian ruins of El Tazumal, comments:

> Being there ... it was really cool. [...] I called my mom before that and she said ... [he laughs] ... that when she was a girl she was growing

up in Chalchuapa and she would always go play at El Tazumal, and she would climb to the top of it and . . . [laughs again] and . . . like, rip her pants and everything in the process. (*Children of the Diaspora*)

In other occasions, however, these windows to the past can quickly turn rather dramatic. One of these moments occurs when Ricardo (UC-Berkeley) declares that the Museum of the Salvadoran Revolution in Perquín "me impactó personalmente porque vi un pedazo de mi historia"[23] (*Children of the Diaspora*) after finding a photograph of Ana Guadalupe Martínez—one of the members of the guerrilla cell that kidnapped Ricardo's father[24]—exhibited as part of the museum collection. Ultimately, the students will be able to appropriate the materials of the public archive and to resignify them on a personal and familiar level. As one of the students says after watching a documentary about the history of the Asociación General de Estudiantes Universitarios Salvadoreños—an organization created by Farabundo Martí, Mario Zapata, and Alfonso Luna in the 1920s:[25]

Here, learning sobre el movimiento estudiantil [about the student movement], I learned that la lucha [the struggle], it's all in my blood, it's in my history, it's in my culture, is part of who I am. (*Children of the Diaspora*)

Circling back to Marianne Hirsch's conceptualizations, we could say, after this brief review, that the "postmemory" of the second generation of Salvadorans in the diaspora would seem to conform more to the Holocaust scholar's "affiliative" or horizontal model—a structure of "intragenerational horizontal identification that makes the child's position more broadly available to other contemporaries" (36)—than to the already extensively described "familial" or vertical one.[26] In this sense, the journey through El Salvador in the company of other Salvi students, as well as the contact with isthmian-Salvadoran college students of their same generation appears in Cárcamo's documentary as a very powerful tool of identity and political empowerment for everyone involved. And yet, the "familial" or vertical forms of memory transfer—that is, the scene of transfer completed in the intimacy of the child's bedroom—never ceases to manifest in the traveling students as pure desire. As Denny (UCSB) declares toward the end of the film with his eyes full of hope:

Probably, of everything that I've done so far . . . like, it's probably the most . . . the most valuable thing that I've done in my life. Because, everything I've learned so far . . . I mean, I'm going to tell my parents what I've learned and, I mean, I can't wait to see how they take it. (*Children of the Diaspora*)

Cárcamo's documentary reaches its end before we are able to witness the long-awaited parent-child act of transference. When—and if—the transference finally happens, it will hold however a doubly "post" nature. The first "post" element would fully coincide with the sense that Marianne Hirsch attributes to the prefix in her concept of "postmemory," that is, the temporal or vertical nature of the structure that conforms the subjectivity of the direct descendants of a generation affected by a collective trauma. However, and differently to the model proposed by Hirsch, the "postmemory" of these young Salvadorans born in the United States will also be "post" in a second sense. This second sense lies on the fact that the intimate and affective process of memory transmission within the framework of the family only becomes possible "after"—i.e., only will happen in a *post-erior* moment in time—the members of the second generation are exposed to the cultural materials that conform the public archive of the traumatic recent history of the Isthmus. In this sense, we can affirm that *Children of the Diaspora* is, at the same time, a privileged window that allows the spectators to observe the characteristic deferred structure of "postmemory" within the Central American diasporas, and a practical example of cultural activism aiming to encourage and support processes of subjective, identitarian, and political anchoring among the members of the second generation of diasporic Salvadorans. These complex processes do require, no doubt, the construction of new (transnational) affective geographies and the consolidation of community networks at a hemispheric scale—as seen in different context in Esteban Loustaunau's chapter between documentarian subjects and the viewers. If only for this, it should be a sufficiently compelling reason to incorporate the study of the cinematic production created by young Central Americans born and raised in the United States to the debates about how twenty-first-century Central American cinematographies are (re)imagining new configurations of space, identity, and politics for a transnationalized Isthmus.

Notes

1 Without any intention to be exhaustive, recent production includes fiction films such as *Sin nombre* (Cary Joji Fukunaga, 2009), *La jaula de oro* (*The Golden Dream,* Diego Quemada-Díez, 2013) and documentaries like *Which Way Home* (Rebecca Cammisa, 2009), *María en tierra de nadie* (*María in No Man's Land,* Marcela Zamora, 2011), *Eternos Indocumentados: Central American Migrants and Refugees in the United States* (Jennifer A. Cárcamo, 2018), or *Border South* (Raúl Paz Pastrana, 2019).

2 *Eternos Indocumentados* (2018) is a documentary written, directed, and produced by Jennifer A. Cárcamo that examines in depth the root causes of migration from the countries of the Northern Triangle—El Salvador, Honduras, and Guatemala—to the

United States through interviews with Central American migrants, social activists, and scholars.

3 Cárcamo is the daughter of Salvadoran migrants and was born and raised in Los Angeles. The director—in a similar manner as many other local Salvi—self-identifies as "Salvadoran from L.A."

4 This documentary has not received much attention from film scholars, but it is briefly analyzed by Esther E. Hernández (2017), who puts the emphasis on the reception of Cárcamo's documentary by LA-Central American audiences after its screening at local community centers during 2013. *Children of the Diaspora* is also mentioned in passing by Karina Oliva Alvarado (2017) when discussing issues related to "a level of silence or denial [that] continues within transgenerational memory" (482). More recently, two of the chapters included in the edited volume *Teaching Central American Literature in a Global Context* (2022)—Guadalupe Escobar's "Rethinking Refugeeness in Diasporic Documentaries" and Ester N. Trujillo's "Documenting the Salvadoran Diaspora: Countering the Salvadoran Threat Narrative"—engage with Cárcamo's documentary in more depth. In particular, Escobar's chapter engages with discussions around the Salvadoran diaspora and postmemory in a similar manner as this texts does.

5 USEU was a left-leaning, pro-FMLN student organization that promoted Salvadoran identity among the Salvadoran diasporas. The organization had a notable presence in California campuses, in particular within the University of California consortium. During the period in which *Children of the Diaspora* was being shot, other trans-isthmic and transnational organizations created by Central American college students—such as CAUSA (Central American United Student Association, based in Cal State University, Northridge), or CAFE (Central Americans for Empowerment)—were also active in California campuses. These organizations did not necessarily share the same goals, let alone the same politics. To my knowledge, there are not any scholarly texts that have addressed the specific histories and dynamics of these student organizations, nor the relations (or lack thereof) between them. In any case, I am not interested so much in the particular characteristics of the student organization that organized the trip to El Salvador, as in the subjective transformations that the journey itself provoked in the students.

6 Yajaira Padilla (2018) offers, in turn, a Spanish version of the term—"centroamericanos-americanos." It is not my intention to engage here in a discussion about the subtle differences between the terminology created to define the contours and main traits of U.S.-born Central Americans, only to point out that all the students that appear in *Children of the Diaspora* can be grouped within this social category.

7 California has a long history of interethnic solidarity between different Latinx communities. Perhaps the best example of these networks of mutual support can be found during the "sanctuary movement" that—mainly in the 1980s—mobilized Chicanxs and other Latinxs groups in assistance of Salvadoran and Guatemalan asylum seekers who were fleeing from the conflicts in the Isthmus. A good account of these collaborations can be found in Ana Patricia Rodríguez (2009), whereas Steven Osuna (2017) explores the ways in which the narratives of shared activism in the past between Chicanxs and first-generation Mexican and Central American migrants inform the identities and social activism of mixed-heritage, young Salvadoran-Mexicans in the present.

Notwithstanding this history of solidarity, tensions often arise between Chicanx and Central American local communities along different lines; in the context of student organizing, one recent example of these tensions include the turmoil and divisions erupted around the recent change of name of MEChA (Movimiento Estudiantil Chicano de Aztlán).

8 This type of silence—the one that marks the relationship between the Salvadorans who fled the war and other forms of state and gendered violence, and their descendants—is only one of the "deafening silences" (Abrego 75) that the author explores in her text. Other forms of "silence" include the denial of U.S. authorities of their responsibility in fueling the civil war and the commission of atrocities in El Salvador and other Central American nations, as well as in the perpetuation of the conditions that still force Central Americans to flee from their countries at high rates. Additionally, Abrego denounces the silencing of Central American voices, experiences, and stories through stereotypical representations of Salvadorans and Central Americans disseminated by mainstream media, official discourses, and other venues.

9 In addition to the already mentioned sources that contribute to the second generation "second-hand knowledge" of Central America, Rodríguez mentions "parents, relatives, friends, clergy, teachers, newly arrived immigrants (. . .) books and texts of popular culture" ("Second hand identities").

10 Up to here, I have highlighted the works of scholars who put the emphasis on the silences, the gaps, the voids, and the missing narrative pieces that characterize the relationship between the first and the second generation. However, there are other authors who highlight the role of intergenerational communication within the Central American diasporas. This is the case of Steven Osuna, whose model of "obstinate transnational memories" relies heavily on the study of the transmission of memory narratives from parents to children. After completing twenty in-depth interviews with young Salvadoran-Mexicans residing in Los Angeles, Osuna concludes that the role of transmitted memories within the family framework is crucial for the processes of subjective constitution, identity formation, and sociopolitical activism of young Salvadoran-Mexicans. However, Osuna himself acknowledges that only one-third of the participants in his research "did know about their parents' memories of migration and displacement" (89). What happens then with the processes of subjective constitution, identity formation, and sociopolitical activism of those young adults who never had the chance to have direct access to their parents' memories? This is precisely the case of all the students who share their testimonies in *Children of the Diaspora* and, therefore, my analysis of Cárcamo's documentary aims to contribute to the ongoing conversation around the process of conformation of "postmemories" among U.S.-born Central Americans who were never exposed to narratives about their parents' lived experiences while growing up.

11 The work "Por qué emigramos / Why We Emigrate" was created by Dagoberto Reyes in 1993 and consists of a bas-relief with different representations of Central American migrant men, women, and children. The sculpture is completed by a plaque where it can be read: "Why we immigrate / Por qué emigramos / A los que nunca sabe nadie de dónde son / Los eternos indocumentados / Los tristes más tristes del mundo / Mis compatriotas / Mis hermanos. La Festival / El Rescate. Dagoberto Reyes 1993. Time

Capsule containing our memories as immigrants in Los Angeles will be open in the year 2093." The text that appears on the plaque combines some of the verses of Roque Dalton's best-known poem, "Poema de amor," with relevant information about the collective project devised by El Rescate—an LA-based organization founded in 1981 with the goal of empowering Latino immigrants. The project launched by El Rescate in 1993 consisted in creating a multimedia archive of materials—composed of family photos, letters, newspaper clips, audio tapes, etc.—that recorded the experiences of Central American migrants in Los Angeles. This polyphonic memory archive would be sealed and buried in a "Time Capsule" situated by Dagoberto Reyes's sculpture in MacArthur Park, not to be opened until a century after, in 2093.

12 "El Pulgarcito" refers to "El Pulgarcito de América," a moniker for El Salvador that alludes to its small territory.

13 "Postmemory" is not the only concept that aims to account for the transfer of traumatic memories from one generation to the next. Within the field of social psychology, terms such as "intergenerational memory narratives" or "transgenerational trauma"—a concept that has been adapted to the study of cultural production by literary critics such as Gabriele Schwab (2010)—have been also employed to address the issues discussed in this text. However, and despite the fact that Marianne Hirsch's book only refers to the case of memory transmission among Holocaust survivors, the notion of "postmemory" has been profusely employed in the field of Latin American memory studies, in particular to address the haunting legacies of military dictatorships in the Southern Cone (Kaiser 2005; Maguire 2017). In a similar vein, the field of Central American studies has produced concepts such as the already mentioned "second hand identities" (Rodríguez 2003), "cultural memory work" (Alvarado 2017), and "obstinate transnational memories" (Osuna 2017) that try to account for some of the specificities of memory-making among the 1.5 and second generation of the Central American diasporas. Finally, scholars who focus on the literary and cinematic production of the Central American isthmus—such as Magdalena Perkowska (2020) or Valeria Grinberg Pla (2020)—have explored the productivity of the concept of "postmemory" for analyzing recent texts and documentary films.

14 Spiegelman completed *The First Maus* in 1972. Later on, he created the more elaborate graphic novel *Maus* (published between 1980 and 1991), based on his own father's experiences during the Holocaust.

15 For an exploration of how Salvadoran postwar documentaries address the work of memory and justice in the homeland, see Lilia García Torres's chapter in this volume.

16 Marianne Hirsch complements her notion of "postmemory" with the concept of "affiliative memory," an intragenerational form of memory transfer that is completed, mainly, via the access to cultural materials related to the traumatic events of the past. This second concept, according to the Holocaust scholar, allows her to "explore affiliative structures of memory beyond the familial" (21). Different authors have explored in depth the role that literature, film, and other media play as technologies that facilitate the transmission of traumatic memories across family and community lines, developing additional concepts such as "prosthetic memories" or "secondary memories," and adapting them to specific contexts such as contemporary United States or post-dictatorship Argentina (Landsberg 2004; Kaminsky 2014). We will soon see that

the students of *Children of the Diaspora* heavily rely on cultural materials and horizontal relations with peers to reconstruct the missing links of their parents' narratives; however, as I will discuss below, the concept of "affiliative memory" has some limitations when trying to account for the concurrent intimate and familial dimension of the process that the students are undergoing during their journey through El Salvador.

17 "[He] does not talk much about his experience because of his trauma and, I don't know, he does not quite like to remember" (my translation).

18 El Mozote was the site of one of the worst massacres of civilians committed during the Salvadoran conflict. The Batallón Atlacatl—an elite corps of the Salvadoran Army—killed there more than 800 men, women, and children on December 11, 1981.

19 The interpretation offered by Kenia for her family's silences fully coincides with Leisy Abrego's reading of the survivors' reluctance to share testimonies of state terror: "Understandably, survivors and witnesses want to protect loved ones from the haunting memories of such brutally tragic details. My need to learn about our history, therefore, was less pressing than the survivors' need to suppress it" (Abrego 74).

20 Archbishop Óscar Romero was the highest representative of the Catholic Church in El Salvador during the early 1980s. His vocal opposition to the repression of social leaders and political opponents of the Salvadoran military regime eventually led to his assassination, while celebrating mass, on March 24, 1980. Not quite ten years later, another high-profile assassination occurred: six noted Jesuit priests and intellectuals were shot down at the UCA campus on November 16, 1989. They were accompanied by their housekeeper and her daughter, who were also murdered in the attack.

21 With the exception of Yolocamba I Ta—a Salvadoran folk-rock group formed in the 1970s—and Carlos Mejía Godoy—the leader of the Nicaraguan folk band that musicalized the Sandinista revolution—the rest of the bands and singer-songwriters featured in the soundtrack are noted Cuban, Chilean, Argentinean, Uruguayan, etc., artists associated with the revolutionary, anti-dictatorial, and anti-imperialist social movements that swept the Latin American continent during the 1960s and 1970s. This selection highlights the transnational conception of postmemory discussed by the film, as well as the hemispheric nature of the film director's political referents.

22 Whereas much has been written about the dynamics of memory for migrants and within diasporic communities, the role that the "return(s)"—whether a definitive return to the place of birth or a temporary visit to the homeland—play in constructing, reconstructing, or revisiting memories has not received so much attention. Some exceptions include Marianne Hirsch and Nancy K. Miller's *Rites of Return* (2011) and Sabine Marschall's *Tourism and Memories of Home* (2017). And whereas Latin American cultural producers have created a plethora of narratives that explore the impact of return in the subjectivities of the returnees—Central American examples include Horacio Castellanos Moya's novel *El asco* or films such as *El regreso* (Costa Rica, 2011)—there is still a scarcity of works that address this reverse dimension of migration and its psychic effects in those who decide to "come back" (see Ignacio Corona 2017).

23 "[The Museum] personally impacted me, as I could see there a fragment of my own history" (my translation).

24 Ana Guadalupe Martínez was a noted member of the Ejército Revolucionario del Pueblo (ERP), one of the multiple guerrilla groups active in El Salvador during the decade of the 1970s.
25 Martí, Zapata, and Luna were three crucial political leaders during the 1920s and early 1930s. They were all members of the Salvadoran Communist Party and actively contributed to the peasant uprising initiated in the *departamentos* of Western El Salvador in December of 1931. This peasant rebellion was, however, short lived and brutally repressed: Farabundo Martí, Mario Zapata, and Alfonso Luna were executed by the Salvadoran Army during early February of 1932, together with 10,000 to 30,000 Indigenous peasants. The selection of footage related to these historical figures and to the student association they founded clearly puts the emphasis of the film on the process of politicization that the USEU students are undergoing during their trip, as well as visually creates a revolutionary genealogy for their student activism.
26 This second model of "affiliative memory," however, does not account for intergenerational tensions and silences in the transference of traumatic memories and, more importantly, presupposes that the child's subjective position, as well as her identity in relation to the traumatic past has already been conformed within the framework of the family. As I have extensively explored in this text, this is not the case for the Salvi young students who participated in the making of *Children of the Diaspora*.

Works Cited

Abrego, Leisy. "On Silences: Salvadoran Refugees Then and Now." *Latino Studies*, vol. 15, 2017, pp. 73–85.

Alvarado, Karina O. "Cultural Memory and Making by US Central Americans." *Latino Studies*, vol. 15, no. 4, 2017, pp. 476–497.

Alvarado, Karina O., Alicia Ivonne Estrada and Esther E. Hernández. "U.S. Central American (Un)Belongings." *U.S. Central Americans. Reconstructing Memories, Struggles, and Communities of Resistance*, edited by Karina O. Alvarado, Alicia Ivonne Estrada, and Esther E. Hernández, Arizona UP, 2017, pp. 3–37.

Arias, Arturo. *Taking Their Word. Literature and the Signs of Central America*. Minneapolis: U of Minnesota P, 2007.

Border South. Directed by Raúl Pastrana, PBS, San Francisco, 2020.

Cárdenas, Maritza E. *Constituting Central American-Americans. Transnational Identitites and the Politics of Dislocation*. New Brunswick: Rutgers UP, 2018.

Castellanos Moya, Horacio. *El asco: Thomas Bernhard en El Salvador*. Barcelona: Tusquets, 2007.

Children of the Diaspora: For Peace and Democracy. Directed by Jennifer A. Cárcamo, Unión Salvadoreña de Estudiantes Universitarios, United States, 2013.

Corona, Ignacio. "Posfacio. La migración de retorno y la cuestión del capital humano y social." *alter/nativas: revista de estudios culturales latinoamericanos*, vol. 7, 2017. https://alternativas.osu.edu/es/issues/autumn-7-2017/essays4/corona.html

El Norte. Directed by Gregory Nava, American Playhouse, Channel Four Films & PBS, Irvington, N.Y., Criterion Collection, 1983.

El regreso. Directed by Hernán Jiménez, 2011.

Escobar, Guadalupe. "Rethinking Refugeeness in Diasporic Documentaries." *Teaching Central American Literature in a Global Context,* edited by Gloria Elizabeth Chacón and Mónica Albizúrez Gil, The Modern Language Association of America, 2022, pp. 275-285.

Eternos Indocumentados: Central American Refugees in the United States. Directed and produced by Jennifer A. Cárcamo, 2019.

Grinberg Pla, Valeria. "De la memoria afiliativa a la contramemoria en *Heredera del viento* de Gloria Carrión Fonseca." *Las posmemorias. Perspectivas latinoamericanas y europeas / Les post-mémoires. Perspectives latino-américaines et européennes,* edited by Teresa Basile and Cecilia González, U Nacional de la Plata & PU de Bordeaux, 2020, pp. 455-476.

Hamilton, Nora and Norma Stolz Chinchilla: "Identity Formation Among Central American Americans." *Center for the Study of Immigrant Integration,* 2013, pp. 1-33. https://dornsife.usc.edu/csii/identitycentralamericans/

Hernández, Esther E. "Remembering through Cultural Interventions: Mapping Central Americans in L.A. Public Spaces." *U.S. Central Americans. Reconstructing Memories, Struggles, and Communities of Resistance,* edited by Karina O. Alvarado, Alicia Ivonne Estrada, and Esther E. Hernández, Arizona UP, 2017, pp. 144-165.

Hirsch, Marianne. *The Generation of Postmemory. Writing and Visual Culture After the Holocaust.* New York: Columbia UP, 2012.

Hirsch, Marianne, and Nancy K. Miller (eds.). *Rites of Return: Diaspora Poetics and The Politics of Memory.* New York: Columbia UP, 2011.

Kaiser, Susana. *Postmemories of Terror: A New Generation Copes with the Legacy of the Dirty War.* New York: Palgrave, 2005.

Kaminsky, Amy. "Memory, Postmemory, Prosthetic Memory: Reflections on the Holocaust and the Dirty War in Argentine Narrative." *Hispanic Issues Online,* vol. 14, Spring 2014, pp. 104-117.

La Jaula de Oro. Directed by Diego Quemada-Díez, Sol y Luna Films, Mexico and Spain, 2016.

Landsberg, Alison. *Prosthetic Memory. The Transformation of American Remembrance in the Age of Mass Culture.* New York: Columbia UP, 2004.

Maguire, Geoffrey. *The Politics of Postmemory: Violence and Victimhood in Contemporary Argentine Culture.* Cham, Switzerland: Palgrave, 2017.

María en tierra de nadie. Directed by Marcela Zamora Chamorro, El Faro and I(dh)eas Films, El Salvador, 2010.

Marschall, Sabine, editor. *Tourism and Memories of Home: Migrants, Displaced Peoples, Exiles, and Diasporic Communities.* Bristol: Channel View Publications, 2017.

Osuna, Steven. "'Obstinate Transnational Memories': How Oral Histories Shape Salvadoran-Mexican Subjectivities." *U.S. Central Americans. Reconstructing Memories, Struggles, and Communities of Resistance,* edited by Karina O. Alvarado, Alicia Ivonne Estrada, and Esther E. Hernández, Arizona UP, 2017, pp. 77-97.

Padilla, Yajaira. "El pasado vigente: Memoria, historia e identidad en la producción cultural centroamericana-americana." *Literatura y compromiso político. Prácticas político-culturales y estéticas de la revolución. Hacia una historia de las literaturas centroamericanas—IV,* edited by Héctor M. Leyva, Werner Mackenbach, and Claudia Ferman, F&G Editores, 2018.

Perkowska, Magdalena. "Silencios que hieren: La presencia espectral del pasado en la ficción centroamericana de *post*-guerra." *Las posmemorias. Perspectivas latinoamericanas y europeas / Les post-mémoires. Perspectives latino-américaines et européennes,* edited by Teresa Basile and Cecilia González, U Nacional de la Plata & PU de Bordeaux, 2020, pp. 433–454.

Rodríguez, Ana Patricia. "Second Hand Identities: The Autoethnographic Performances of Quique Avilés and Leticia Hernández-Linares." *Istmo: Revista virtual de estudios literarios y culturales centroamericanos,* no. 8, 2003, http://istmo.denison.edu/n08/articulos/second.html.

———. "The War at Home: Latina/o Solidarity and Central American Immigration." *Dividing the Isthmus: Central American Transnational Histories, Literatures & Cultures.* Austin: U of Texas P, 2009, pp. 129–166.

Schwab, Gabriele. *Haunting Legacies. Violent Histories and Transgenerational Trauma.* New York: Columbia UP, 2010.

Sin Nombre. Directed by Cary Fukunaga, Canana Fils; Creando Fils; Primary Productions; Scion Films, United States and Mexico, 2009.

Spiegelman, Art. *Maus I: A Survivor's Tale: My Father Bleeds History.* New York: Pantheon, 1986.

———. *Maus II: A Survivor's Tale: And Here My Troubles Began.* New York: Pantheon, 1991.

Trujillo, Ester N. "Documenting the Salvadoran Diaspora: Countering the Central American Threat Narrative." *Teaching Central American Literature in a Global Context,* edited by Gloria Elizabeth Chacón and Mónica Albizúrez Gil, The Modern Language Association of America, 2022, pp. 286–296.

Which Way Home. Directed by Rebecca Cammisa, HBO Documentary Films, New York, 2009.

III

Re/presenting the Nation, Counter Cinema, and Popular Culture

8

Panamanian Cinema in the Twenty-First Century

Panama Canal Stories

CAROLINA SANABRIA

Translated by Carla Ros

Epic Film

Since their emergence, national cinemas have turned to transcendental historical events to construct national identity. In 1915 the filmmaker D. W. Griffith, in *The Birth of a Nation* (United States), did it in relation to American history and Sergéi Eisenstein also documents Soviet history in his films. In a great deal of emerging film industries, such as many Central American ones, a recurring theme is the recovery of conflicts that revolve around issues associated with their material or symbolic heritage and, ultimately, with their own identities; as we see, for example, with the Indigenous peoples of Guatemala or the Sandinista revolution in Nicaragua. This tendency is clear in films from the beginning and end of the twentieth century which favor subjects that emphasize collective regional traits. By contrast, the young republic of Panama—separated from Colombia in 1903, as opposed to the rest of Central America that became independent from Spain in 1821—is known especially for its geopolitical and historical position and was the backdrop of the construction of the maritime Canal at the end of the nineteenth and beginning of the twentieth centuries. It resulted in one of the longest and most costly construction projects in the history of humanity—even more difficult than the Suez Canal (McCullough 130)—and it favored the development of a different process of colonization from that in other countries of the Isthmus. In Panama's specific case, its distinct geographical position is what has been given most consideration, and through the centuries this has caused different powers to show "interest in the usufruct of this privileged geographical passage" (Castillero Calvo 5). Such attention began with Spain in the sixteenth century, continued with England in the nineteenth century, and around 1880 turned to France with the construction of the interoceanic Canal under the control of Ferdinand De Lesseps. Finally, the enterprise ended up in the hands of the United States at the beginning of the twentieth century—since, as David McCullough puts it, it surpassed the competence of a private initiative and demanded a national effort (215). And thus, as opposed to the rest of the Isthmus countries, Panama's entire development "has been dominated by the historical weight of [. . . its] geographical situation" (Castillero Calvo 22), of which the colonialist process is a component. In this sense, cinema was the ideal mean in order to transmit the narratives projected by nations and empires, as Ella Shohat and Robert Stam said: "National consciousness, generally seen as a precondition of the nation—that is, the beliefs different individuals share about a common origin, status, situation and aspirations—becomes a generally connected set of cinematographic fictions" (117). Without denying the validity of specialists in filmic multiculturalism, the panorama is adequate to describe the twentieth century, when film production implied the control of media in the hands of a minority with the interests that with the film boom—of expanding production, of democratized technologies—in the area, its inhabitants have had the capacity to film their own fictions, with a critical perspective on a centuries-old colonial situation.[1]

Like in the rest of Latin America and especially after the appearance of the Grupo Experimental de Cine Universitario (GECU), Cuban cinema became the model for the Panamanian film industry. It had a powerful impact on many intellectuals mainly because it defended an anti-establishment stance, it was produced with little resources, and it was so different from what movies were expected to be: that is, Hollywood (Cortés 227). After the recrudescence of the economic and political crisis of 1987, before the U.S. invasion, some coproductions were filmed (Del Vasto 58) and now, at the beginning of the twenty-first century, the panorama is quite different.

The film *Historias del Canal* [*Panama Canal Stories*] (Panama) was released in 2013. Both aesthetically and narratively it is closer to the aforementioned dominant film industry, despite the strong anti-imperialist message in its backdrop. The paradox lies precisely in the fact that American presence appears to sneak not only into the story itself, but also into the form. This is the general impression one gets from viewing a film that deviates from the standard model of the Central American region in its production, its support (HD format), and in its impeccable visual manufacture, in contrast to the prevailing atmospheres and textures of the peripheral cinema of the region. Nevertheless, it presents the usual limitations in postproduction and restrictions in distribution, exhibition, and even commercialization.[2] From the global cinematographic point of view led by Hollywood cinema, *Panama Canal Stories* achieves an assertive stance of national sovereignty and is able to become an exemplary piece of what can be referred to as the concept of *hybrid cinema* as well as to its paradoxical repercussions: competitiveness in its lofty aesthetic manufacturing with regards to hegemonic film. And this is because at the turn of the century, an interesting evolution in cinematographic production takes place in many peripheral regions, which appear to leave aside the Cuban model and turn to emulate the aesthetics and narratives of Hollywood.[3] The film in question is also not alien to the national consciousness that connects the stories and revolves around the tremendous work of engineering that is considered world heritage and that, as such, acquires the characteristic of a national symbol.

Bearing in mind the inadequacy of a movie made at the beginning of the active and more formalized cinematographic production of the region (even if it appeared later during this process), *Panama Canal Stories* fictionalizes the construction of the maritime passage which conditioned Panama's history as a country. Therefore, it recovers an epic sense of nation in so far as it assembles the work, the conflicts, and the details of a community around that great feat of engineering. And it does so through fictitious and anonymous situations in different genres (historical cinema, drama, comedy, espionage), interlaced with historical events. Like threads which come together in the storyline, they are all dependent on the feat of construction and maintenance which was fundamental in the constitution of Panama as a country and which its cinematographic industry is interested in keeping alive in its imaginary—as a means of resistance to a medium that is traditionally reserved for the hegemonic circuit, as Shohat and Stam suggest.

Minimal and Anonymous Histories

Panama Canal Stories is a production that, above all, stands as the result of the collaborative work of five directors: Carolina Borrero, Pinky Mon, Luis Franco Brantley, Abner Benaim, and Pituka Ortega-Heilbron. At first glance, one cannot help but to point out the comparison between the joint cinematographic project and the collective coordination that the monumental artificial riverbed required. The coming together of five shorts that last approximately twenty minutes each corresponds to different chronological moments of history that make up the movie.

And thus, while the celebrations for the famous construction's centennial were going on, this fictional feature-length movie comprised of stories that unfold around key moments in history (1913, 1950, 1964, 1977, and 2013) was released on August 15, 2014. The five segments span the construction of the canal from its origins to its development. Each story is told from the perspective of the different characters—anonymous and fictional subjects—who formed part of the life of the Canal along with the leaders, bosses, and more prominent figures that are merely mentioned or referred to as less important parts in the unfolding of events.

The first short, *1913*, directed by Carolina Borrero, opens with a detailed close-up of a bucket of water where a woman of Antillean descent dips her hands; after this, she stands up and the camera provides a spectacular wide-angle shot that frames a group of workers toiling away on the Canal. As the captions inform us, the location is in the area of Corte Culebra, an excavation initiated by the French company belonging to De Lesseps, which ended up collapsing the efforts of the French and which led to sale of the Canal project to the Americans, formalized in 1903 with the signing of the Hay-Bunau Varilla Treaty. The splendid panoramic shot of the imposing canyon is not gratuitous: during the time that work on the Canal was taken up by the Americans, from 1907 to the end of 1913, Corte Culebra became one of the Canal's singular marvels; according to McCullough, its greatest center of attention as it even managed to attract tourists first by the hundreds and later by the thousands (465–466).

The young woman whom we saw with the water bucket is named Clarice Thompson, and this first segment of the film tells the story of her frustrated relationship to Philip Clay. They are both West Indians and work in the construction of the Canal; they are in love and engaged, but due to conflicting relationships with others—first with the white foreman and later with her own family—they find themselves torn apart and forced to escape. The racial factor allows the film to recover an element of marginality (excluded though not invisible) in the configuration of the Panamanian imaginary and narratives: the Black man (Pulido Ritter 36). It is not the only omission that the film claims as it explores the social dynamics of the population of African descent—the general rule that Black workers were affable, educated, temperate, and very religious (McCullough 500), as we can appreciate in the reference to the small community of Corte Culebra.

The second piece, *1950*, is the work of director Pinky Mon, and in contrast to the following two segments, it does not allude to any particular event in history because it centers on showing the daily life of the Zonians once the work on the Canal is underway and the Americans are in charge of its maintenance. The story is told from the point of view of Jake, a boy who suffers the loss of his father, the chief engineer James Charles Wright, in an accident. During the ceremony that the American authorities of the area hold in his honor, they compare him to other historical figures in the construction of the Canal from the first half of the century, such as Major General George Washington Goethals (1858–1928)[4] and William Crawford Gorgas (1854–1920).[5] Historically, Goethals and Gorgas were American soldiers recognized by the community of the colonized who, like the Black workers in the previous short, feel that they are part of the place; like James Charles Wright himself, who had told his son that he was half *gringo* and half Panamanian.

Jake lives with his mother, the young widow Patsy Wright. When she is faced with having to mourn her husband, she goes out drinking and comes home late at night, neglecting her young child. He naturally develops a close relationship with his caretaker, the sympathetic María; they have perfectly fluid conversations in which he speaks to her in English and she answers in Spanish. This is further proof of the film's hybridity, as both dominant languages are equally spoken. And as is befitting of a typical childish curiosity, Jake shows himself to be interested in the neighboring regions to the bubble inhabited by the Zonians, to the point where he manages to escape the latter in order to meet the other half of town that María has spoken to him about. Soon after, he is caught by the police, the Guardia Nacional de Panamá, who take him back to the Canal Zone.

In *1950* we perceive the subtle tension between Zonians and Panamanians which, almost fifteen years later, would lead to direct confrontations. This is the theme Luis Franco Brantley explores in the third segment, *1964*, where he recaptures the incidents of the 9th of January of that year, when between 150 and 200 students of the Secundaria Nacional school faced the American colonizers. What they wanted was to raise the Panamanian flag in one of the local schools, Balboa High School. The event is remembered as the Day of the Martyrs and, according to the final captions, it took the lives of around twenty-four Panamanians. The same historical episode had been the central theme of an anti-imperialist short produced in the GECU called *Canto a la patria que ahora nace* (1972), by Enoch Castillero and Alberto Rivera.

In this context, the political conflict is obvious from the initial, fixed shot of a radio broadcasting an announcement by the governor of the Zone, Robert Fleming, in compliance with the Kennedy-Chiari agreement, issued on December 30, 1963. This agreement regulated the display of the Panamanian flag in the Canal Zone, stipulating that it was to be raised alongside the United

States flag in specific areas of the Zone as of January 1 (Perigault Sánchez 125). Soon after that, the students rallied in protest, marching to Balboa High School while shouting "Yankees go home" and carrying banners that read: "Panamá es soberana en la zona del canal."[6]

The story centers on José, one of the students, and his adolescent love for a Zonian. He follows Lucy in the streets and takes photographs of her furtively. Up to a certain point, *1964* exudes an echo of the relationship between the protagonists of Giuseppe Tornatore's emblematic film *Cinema Paradiso* (Italy/France, 1988) in that it goes back to a similar time past, but especially because the characters of Salvatore and Elena are also students who at first see themselves divided along social classes—a conflict which, in this case, is substituted by the opposing ethnicities and ideologies that separate the protagonists José and Lucy.

In a way, José's story echoes what happened to Lester León Graves. Milton, his father, tells him Graves's story after getting him out of the cell where the American authorities had locked him in for being in the prohibited territory. Something similar had happened to Graves—and also to Jake, but in reverse, since he is found by the Panamanian police but does not suffer the same consequences and is instead merely returned home, where his mother then becomes conscious of having abandoned him. The truth is that the power of the Panamanian police force to which Milton belongs, also called the *Guardia Nacional,* was in a position of inferiority with regards to the American military bases (Méndez 45). Therefore, even though the short is set in 1964, it presents a conflict from a time before that, a conflict that begins with the story Milton tells his son in the bar: it was the mid-1940s, when Graves—who was then nineteen—worked as a gardener in a mansion in the Zone whose landlady fell in love with him. Milton says:

> One night, this man came out of the house very late. And what happened? The police caught him. This poor, frightened guy, confessed everything. The whole thing. The love affair he had with that woman. She denied everything. They gave him twenty years in prison for rape.

Following Louisiana state legislation, the sentence was to be carried out in the prison of the city of Gamboa, in the Zone, and it was reduced to fifteen years by a pardon from the governor of the Zone, William Carter, on January 16, a few days after the incident of the Martyrs. In any case, Graves has become an emblematic figure of national vindication in the history of the Canal Zone.

The backdrop of the following short, *1977*, directed by Abner Benaim, is the gradual process of transference of the Canal to Panama, which was formalized during U.S. President Jimmy Carter's visit to Panama. The tale is set within the framework of the complicated negotiations by the United States for the concession of the Canal, which culminate in the signing of the Torrijos-Carter Treaty. In this volume, Mauricio Espinoza, whose chapter analyzes Ortega-Heilbron's documentary *Los puños de una nación*, and Jared List, in his chapter over Benaim's documentary *Invasión* (Panama, 2014), further examine the complicated relationship between the U.S. and Panama. The Torrijos-Carter Treaty initiated the gradual process of decolonization and would end with the administration's handing over of the Canal on December 31, 1999. Benaim connects these historical events with fictitious events and characters around Silverio Eugenio González, a humble driver hired by the Canal's authorities to transport a couple of American negotiators who arrive in Panama to inform the U.S. president of how the Canal is being managed. He is asked to be discreet, but the main reason he is hired is because of his scarce knowledge of English. What they don't know is that Silverio is actually an undercover agent for the Panamanian national sovereignty movement. The historical context, in fact, corresponds to the second phase of the Torrijos military regime, which produced a civil and military institutionality that was impregnated with nationalist ideology (not necessarily anti-imperialist) and which had great popular support (Beluche). And thus, a topic of profound seriousness—a series of delicate historical events in the relationship between two countries—is told from a humorous point of view whose tone alleviates the severity (especially in regards to the seriousness of the anti-imperialism which was the backdrop of previous movies by the GECU) and simultaneously gives the film a balance between the genres. Laughter implies a different way of viewing reality, interposing a critical distance between things, in this case in equal measure. Thus, the short parodies the spy genre with Silverio as a tropical James Bond who flaunts his *guayabera* as he struts around to the beat of a soundtrack that is characteristic of genre films. In this sense, Benaim achieves a contrast between the professional know-how of the British spy with such unsophisticated means as using masking tape to hold a recorder on the underside of the driver's seat, as well as Silverio's homespun methods of investigation, like when he uses his own daughter, a young schoolgirl, behind her mother's back to translate conversations in English for him in exchange for clandestine chocolate bars.

Silverio's mission is more important than even his immediate superior, whom he calls *Comando,* believes: one night, while he waits in his car for the negotiators who are out partying, he is surprised by none other than the actual Torrijos, the leader of the Panamanian Revolution, according to the Constitution of 1972, although he does not introduce himself as such. He hides his face, so we only get to see his military uniform, his hat and the rest of his silhouette in the darkness of the back seat. It is Silverio who identifies him, because *comando* thinks the story is so unbelievable that he bursts into laughter. The last shot of *1977* shows the signing of the Torrijos-Carter Treaty on a television screen while Silverio is getting his hair cut and speaking to his daughter. One single shot of a mirror allows all of the characters to come together along with the image on the television screen. And while the news is being transmitted, the man, very proud, blurts out to the girl: "Are you watching that? You should know that it was possible because of your father and because of you too." Even despite Silverio's self-delusion, what is most important is that, for him, they both had a decisive role in the historical event.

Finally, *2013* closes with a story by the renowned director Pituka Ortega-Heilbron that connects all the previous segments, though it ended up being "the most difficult one [...] because it is lacking a historical pretext," according to the director (quoted in Domínguez). This short recovers the story directed by Borrero and sets it in a contemporary context. This time it revolves around Clarice Jones, a jazz singer in the United States who is going through a crisis because she has lost her voice. An engineer who is part of the work of expansion of the Canal contacts her because, as we see at the beginning of the short, he had found a skeleton with a stone and two names engraved on it: Clarice Thompson and Philip Clay. This is the point where it takes up the ending of *1913* and sets out to solve the mystery of what had happened to Clarice according to her own written reflections, as she was part of a minority of Black, unqualified workers who were not illiterate (McCullough 414). We know the outcome of her search for her fiancé, whom she had found dead. And, as she was pregnant, she was forced to abandon her family. After fleeing to the Pacific, she finds work in the shop of a businessman whose last name is Tagaropolus. He had been a young Greek entrepreneur who had arrived in Panama around 1908, and who had simultaneously worked in the construction of the Canal and in building a business. In 1911, his company ends up in charge of the distribution of food and drink, and after a few years it opens a division to cater to the boats that transit the area. Tagaropolus shows the young girl's writings to Marcus Garvey, the emblematic figure of the diaspora of people of African descent, who asks her to write in his newspaper. We know that he published papers in many of the regions that he traveled to and that these reported on the conditions of the workers. Even though it is not mentioned, the one in Panama was called *La Prensa*. She accepts, but then immediately questions herself. "Afterwards, I started thinking: who would want to hear my voice?"

The answer appears later, in a journey through the Canal in a small boat—after having traveled to Panama to meet her aunt and her cousins—in which a small homage is paid to the workers who broke the mountain range and faced nature. They were anonymous subjects who made the construction and preservation of the Canal possible. The orator during the journey invites us to pay homage to the forefathers of the Canal, and the various participants come close to pronouncing a name: Harry Gale, Joseph Cumberbatch, Gwendolyn Redgrave ... As in the rest of the film, this material by Ortega-Heilbron does not focus on important or relevant figures that stood out—when these appear at all, they are barely mentioned by name, like Graves or Goethals, or they are represented in passing, like Garvey, or even through archive footage, like Torrijos. These historical characters are falsified, they fade, they are made up of the same fiction-matter than the rest of the cast, so that they all acquire equivalent or at least comparative characteristics. With this, the movie is paying homage to those anonymous workers who contributed to the building of both the Canal and the Panamanian nation.

The Canal Zone, the Contact Zone

As we can see, the film *Panama Canal Stories* is not strictly about Panama, but rather about a specific location that has been historically conflictive: the Canal Zone. That is how it is presented at the beginning in the captions with which the movie starts and offer basic information to situate the spectator in the film, stating the following:

> The Isthmus of Panama was split in two in order to build an interoceanic Canal. Within the areas surrounding it, the US established a territory known as the Canal Zone, which was ruled by its customs and laws between 1903 and 1999. This physical, social and political foreign presence, set in the center of the country, guided the fate and identity of the Panamanian Nation forever. (*Historias del Canal*)

The introduction makes it clear that the movie will essentially revolve around that limited and problematic region that, as of the end of the nineteenth century and beginning of the twentieth century, split the country in two (as María explains) and is known as the Zone. A place colonized by American immigrants and inhabited by immigrant workers, for the most part Black people from the West Indies who interact with the native population; this is why Spanish and English are equally spoken throughout the film. As Pulido Ritter sustains, although this territory was alienated from Panama, it was well embedded in the urban landscape and in the mentality of Panamanians, even if as an 'enclave' constituted "as an element of recovery and foundation of the Panamanian identity and nation" (34). And so the Zone is a space of ethnic and cultural tension, a concept that displaces that of the cultural border in so far as it implies thinking in a space of historical intersection.[7]

The hegemonic and expansionist dominion of the United States manages to provoke changes in the orography, in the geographic map, and it ends up encouraging a revolution for independence in the region in defense of its interests. Due to the overtaking of the region's resources, like the railway—primordial for the transportation of commodities—and other infrastructure, and the subsequent settlement of American colonizers in charge of leading construction and maintenance of the Canal, the Zone ends up working like what Mary Louise Pratt calls the *Contact Zone*. As such, we understand the:

> space between colonial encounters, the space in which people who are historically and geographically divided come in contact with each other and establish lasting relationships, which in general imply conditions of coercion, radical inequity and intolerable conflict. (33)

To be sure, since the beginning of construction work in 1881 under the French, the workers were fundamentally from Barbados and Jamaica and were considered unskilled labor. Because it was an American undertaking, they debated whether construction should use local workforce, but given the comparative inefficiency and technical ignorance of the Caribbean people, the idea was discarded, in so far as skilled workers, like the white foremen, came from the United States (McCullough 413–415). Thus, a great deal of the population of the Canal Zone was constituted by immigrant workers and American colonizers who interacted with the natives, as we can appreciate in the movie. The tension in regard to U.S. military presence is obvious. After the ratification of the 1903 treaty, the apparatus that had been installed was enormous and it showed glimpses of confrontation with the sovereignty of the country: in 1972, 92 percent of the territory was used for military purposes and the existence of the Zone, with the presence of colonizers who had not assimilated, was an obstacle for the urban development of the country's metropolitan sector because of the U.S.-imposed domination strategy (Méndez 45).

By 1913, the vast workforce made up of around 25,000 to 30,000 men and women of African descent, who carried out the most arduous and difficult part of the physical work, was barely visible: "They were not seen as individuals; they were nothing more than part of the work-day landscape. Nobody even considered that they were also starting a new life in a strange land, that they were also raising families, that they felt homesick, fear, sickness or joy because of the success of the construction" (McCullough 495). This is why the movie vindicates this omission as well as others by exploiting the social dynamics of the Afro-descendant population—generally speaking, Black workers in Panama were affable, well-mannered, discreet, and very religious (McCullough 500).[8] It is not a coincidence that the Thompson sisters are the daughters of a pastor who is the community's leader. The presence of the African diaspora converges in the complex ethnic heterogeneity of Black identity in the Central American region. This did not respond to a uniform collective due to the coexistence of two groups: Afro-colonials, the product of miscegenation, who identified with the nation, and Afro-Antilleans, immigrants who followed the cultural model of their native countries (Jamaica, Barbados). Unlike the former, the Afro-Antilleans rejected the three national dogmas—culture, language, and religion—"since they were black, English-speaking and Protestant" (Stephenson Watson 29). Even so, the film does not penetrate further into the differentiation of both cultural groups in conflict—which instead demonstrate analyses such as Pulido Ritter's in literature (2014)—for the sake of an interest in the construction of a national project in a different type of representation: the filmic. This fissure that homogenizes ethnic differences is evidenced, specifically, in the passage in which Philip Clay requests Clarice's hand from her father, Pastor Thompson. In this scene the reverend makes the announcement to the community—in English—in the midst of a joyful outdoor celebration that aims to account for an assimilation that is more idealized than in conflict: "And we will celebrate in this newborn nation we call home, Panama," the reverend says.

The semi-skilled labor force was under the orders of U.S. workers, while those who undertook the more arduous tasks were of different origin, such as the people of African descent who represented a large percentage since the beginning of construction under the French, when segregation imposed by skin color materialized (McCullough 413). In the short, the initial foreman, known for his kind and differentiated treatment, is substituted by the tyrannical Jeremiah. In a clear abuse of power, he snatches the stone that Philip had given Clarice from her hands, and this leads to the confrontation that will later culminate when he attempts to do away with the young man in the middle of an explosion that ends up taking the life of eight Black workers. Not for nothing, in May of 1913, some mechanical shovels had arrived in the Corte Culebra to help in the reduction of the peak and continue the excavations with dynamite explosions. Philip kills Jeremiah in self-defense, and this forces him to flee. When Clarice refuses to marry Jerome, Philip's brother, the response she receives from her inflexible father is: "But the wedding must be! Our people need a hope no more than ever in these sad times," and so she ends up escaping to the forest.

In the other shorts, the concept of the Contact Zone is not solely restricted to the clash. In some cases that contact is one of cordiality, as in *1950*, in the relationship between Jake and María prompted by the boy's curiosity. He asks her about Panama, and she explains to him the ethnic, social, economic, and even aesthetic differences between the two regions of the same country split by the Canal: "We don't have so many pretty things. Cars are uglier, men are uglier. Even dogs are uglier!" but Jake goes to school and tells his friends the exact opposite: "This city is split in two and we get the worst part." As a city, the Zone is certainly more aseptic; it is an enclosed bubble and is close to an idyllic small rural U.S. town nestled in the tropics, with no contact with the rest of the country: that is why it is also a point of conflict.

In fact, the schoolchildren live completely unaware of the rest of the place. They proclaim allegiance to the flag and to the republic of the United States of America as they are captured by a panning shot that travels along in close-ups, but Jake does not share the same convictions as his classmates. That is why he, unlike the rest of them, has absolutely no trouble sympathizing with the Panamanian children whom he catches stealing mangos in the Zonian territory and why he also ends up defending them from the threats made by his own companions—in a dynamic that reproduces the attitude of the armed colonial invaders on a child's scale. He escapes with them to see the city that has so deeply sparked his curiosity, and this gesture reveals a seed of the hybrid identity, a divided sense of belonging planted by his deceased father. Even though he belongs to the ruling class, an asymmetric relationship of power does not ensue, and in a conversation with his mother she even tells him, to his own stupefaction, that he could stay with María and go visit her in the U.S. This emotional closeness is also obvious in the interchanging of charms: María gives him the scapular that protects her from evil spirits, "from the restless souls of the dead that are unhappy to be where they are" and he, in turn, hands over the plaque of Chief Engineer that he received from his father's colleagues.

This explains the youngster's double mourning: once for his deceased father and once for the imminent abandonment of his country, which is expressed in the image of his name carved into the wall of his house before leaving, much like Clarice had carved her own name and Philip's on the stone: "Jake was here." This is why in the final scene, when the chauffer who picks him and his mother up to take them to the airport as they are returning to New Hampshire and he poses the question: "Going home?" we hear an affirmative and a negative response simultaneously. We know which one belongs to whom.[9]

In some of the other shorts, this *Contact Zone* is not marked by curiosity, but rather by the suspicion of each conflicting side. *1964* is more confrontational than the previous short, with the Zonian Lucy who looks down on anything that does not come from the U.S. and who lives in a kind of bubble where she is only interested in music that is in English, in her boyfriend, the cadet, in the roller-skating rink, etc.[10] Lucy and José are adolescents who live in this country that is split in two, as María stated earlier. But at first, not even the language is that decisive, because even though they do not speak the same language, they are able to understand each other (at least minimally) in English, which turns the latter into the contact language. In fact, José, even in his rudimentary English, is able to win her over and in their intimate encounter at the hotel, he tells her with a very basic pronunciation and syntax: "There no two sides. All is Panama, our territory. Don't be colonizers." This is followed by a half-playful, half-childish dialogue between them: "Don't be wild," "Don't be imperialists," "Don't be primitive," "Don't be capitalists." The discussion reproduces the tense relationship maintained between cultural groups, and demonstrates the colonial gaze, the play of oppositions, of attractions and repulsions, between civilization and barbarism (Ardèvol and Muntañola 344). It updates the colonizer's conviction of the natural inferiority of those who are not white. Finally, when she goes toward the door, we hear the question (this time in Spanish), "Lucy, can I see you again?" to which José receives as a sole and very laconic answer: "Yo no hablo español," followed by the slamming of the door. The gesture is conclusive because of what it implies. The young man's interest in a foreign language is not corresponded, and this closes the door on any possibility for communication. That is to say, communication between them is only possible in so far as he is willing to speak the language of the colonizers, because even if she understands some Spanish, she is not, like José, willing to use it.

This sentimental confrontation is transferred to the political realm due to the uprising that José's secondary school organizes in the Zone. The Canal Zone chief of police, Captain Wall—whose name is both symbolic and anticipatory—is opposed to anyone entering the Zone and only agrees to let in six students holding the Panamanian flag; these boys are received by boos and cries from the Zonians, and so the Chief calls his population to sanity: "These students came today to demonstrate in a peaceful manner. You need to treat these Panamanians like people. This is their country," yet the hostility slowly increases. As the film shows (following history), the students who crossed over with the flag were pushed and beaten by Zonian students pressured by their own parents, in a brawl in which the policemen, inexplicably and contrary to orders, decided to join in instead of protecting the Panamanians (Perigault Sánchez 134). The film captures moments of direct confrontation with the faces of José and Lucy in their respective sides. The short ends with a shot of a boy picking up stones, as corresponds to historical events, according to Calzadilla, in which an uneven battle erupted with stones and sticks in the hands of the Panamanians, and tear-gas bombs, firearms, armored cars, and machine guns in the hands of the American troops (155). Neither love nor the passion experienced by the two young people is able to contain the physical confrontation that derived in the deaths of the Panamanians.

The next piece, *1977*, is more subtle in showing these decidedly conflicting relationships, even though it is immersed in the middle of quite energetic political tensions and (unlike the rest of the movie), it develops mainly in the capital, not in the Zone. Bob and James, two U.S. envoys, are neither pretentious nor belligerent; in fact, they prove to be both jovial and friendly in their dealings with the chauffeur. They accept that Silverio take them to discotheques after the meetings and show them how to toast according to local customs, generating complicity. On one occasion Bob even says to the chauffeur in Spanish: "'A mí me están cayendo muy bien los panameños...' Y mira a James [mientras baila entusiasmado con una mujer local], 'parece que a él también.'"[11] Indeed, the mere fact that Bob, a representative of the imperialist country, is predisposed to have fun in the local nightclubs and that he speaks to a subordinate in his own language contains an implicit interest in the other, despite the fact that at the beginning they had referred to the chauffer's performance as 'worrisome.' In any case, these characters stem from a situation that is very different from Lucy's. In the end, the relationship that is generated accounts for a mutual camaraderie which is sealed with the photograph that emerges as an initiative of the Americans, as a farewell, in the Tocumen airport and that optimistically closes with the signing of the treaty.

The last piece also does not accentuate the open wounds of the centenary conflict which, like a river, flow toward a hybrid identity that has crystallized in Clarice Jones, descendant of the Clay-Thompsons and daughter of a white American soldier whom her mother married before moving to the United States. Clarice materializes the ethnic synthesis of the hybridization that José posed as a hypothetical question when, torn between the border conflict and Lucy, he asked himself: "If we had a child, what would it be?" That conciliation is fulfilled in Clarice who, after recognizing her roots and touring the Canal, is motivated to pick up a microphone and speak the names of her ancestors in the homage to the anonymous forebearers and, finally, to sing her song.

The young woman recovers her voice because perhaps there are people who do want to listen to her, as her great-grandmother used to say. The film ends framing a close-up shot of a smiling Clarice while documentary images from that time period pass by (such as images of explosions and of the workers toiling), so that current history is in this way linked to the story of *1913*. Finally, the camera fades to black linking the close-up with the waters of the Canal, recuperating the river as a motif which revitalizes its traits as precious metaphor "to represent both the passing of time as that of History itself" (Salvadó, quoted in Balló and Bergala 346): that of the Canal.

The End

While dominant film industries combine narrative and entertainment in order to tell the history of colonialism from the perspective of the colonizer (Shohat and Stam 126), of Pratt's settled white seer embodied in the Zonian, in the peripheral film *Panama Canal Stories* we are told a story ranging between fiction and reality from the perspective of a subject who is created and interacts in the Zone, who is neither white nor a colonizer: but a hybrid, a half-caste. As a fiction with foundational, romantic pretensions, the film presents colonial and intercultural tensions as facts that form part of the past which have been overcome in the present of the twenty-first century, at least in the film, after the construction—and the possession—of the Canal. Hence, it is not until the last segment that we see a resolution of the conflicts that, unlike preceding ones, imply an authentic recovery in the form of reconciliation. In this case, the confrontation is not with the other (Black Antillean, Zonian, Creole . . .), but with oneself. Hence, Clarice Jones is seen moving through the streets, interacting with her family in spite of the language and cultural differences. None of the five stories are even set out from that mainstream perspective; all the main characters are women, native people, or migrants: a young Black woman, a colonial boy who feels curiosity for the country, a Panamanian adolescent in love with a Yankee, a local chauffeur who interacts with important and kind American envoys, and a Black woman from the United States who returns to Panama to discover her roots. By mixing together anonymous fictions with history, the movie claims the special conditions that mediate the hybridization of the fringe that is literally in the middle; and which has existed in the Central American country from the beginnings of its short history throughout the construction of the Canal—its most obvious national symbol. As for this symbol of nationality of the small Central American country, the film is framed in a project consistent with the interests of the canal fiction novel, to express both the foundation and the recovery of the Panamanian nation in its historical dimension of migration experiences, relations, and conflicts between ethnicities and classes.

Notes

1. This chapter was first published as "El cine de Panamá en el siglo XXI: *Historias del Canal*" (Sanabria).
2. It still hasn't been released in DVD form.
3. There are more recent films—from fictional ones such as *Hands of Stone* (Jonathan Jakubowicz, Panama/United States, 2016) to documentaries such as *Invasión* (Abner Benaim, Panama, 2014) or *Caja 25* (Mercedes Arias and Delfina Vidal, Panama, 2015)—that allow us to outline a cinematographic boom in the region, whose key seems to reside in the fact that local producers and screenwriters have started to connect with the public around central ideas such as the actual construction of the Canal or the 1989 U.S. invasion. "In 2015, ticket offices almost burst because, according to the Asociación de Distribuidores de Películas de Panamá (Panamanian Association of Film Distributors), a total of 5.7 million spectators went to the movies; this is a record amount and unusual in this tiny country with little movie-going tradition" (Mur).
4. Goethals was the highway engineer in charge of bringing down mountains and building the Gatun Dam along with a system of locks which overcame the difference between the sea levels of the Caribbean Sea and the Pacific Ocean.
5. Gorgas stands out for being the doctor who reduced malaria and yellow fever in the area by means of controlling the mosquito population and who, in 1921, participated in the foundation of the Institute of Tropical and Preventive Medicine.
6. "Panama is sovereign in the Canal Zone."
7. Not surprisingly, in her study about Panamanian literature, Miró values it as "*fortunately*, a minimal part of the reality of Panama" (my emphasis) (277).
8. Like that of the other minorities, Jamaican runaway enslaved people, which we see when Clarice interacts with one of them for Philip's escape. They exchange a few words in Kromanti, another English-based Creole language with a strong component of Akan.
9. Pinky Mon goes as far as saying "[in] the end, many Zonians left, but they returned to Panama because that was their home, it wasn't so much a political issue but rather a social one" (Domínguez).
10. This was part of the places of leisure which existed in the Zone for the colonizers since the beginning of the Canal's construction (McCullough 482).
11. "'I like Panamanians…' And as he looks at James [while he enthusiastically dances with a local woman], 'seems like he likes them, too.'"

Works Cited

Ardèvol, Elisenda, and Nora Muntañola, coordinators. *Representación y cultura audiovisual en la sociedad contemporánea*. Barcelona: Editorial U Oberta de Catalunya, 2004.

Balló, Jordi, and Alain Bergala, editors. *Motivos visuales del cine*. Barcelona: Galaxia Gutemberg, 2016.

Beluche, Olmedo. *La verdadera historia de la separación de 1903. Reflexiones en torno al Centenario*. Ciudad de Panamá: Articsa, 2003.

Caja 25. Directed by Delfina Vidal and Mercedes Arias, Betesda Films, Jaguar Producciones, Panama, 2015.

Calzadilla, Carlos. *Historia sincera de la República (siglo XX)*. Ciudad de Panamá: Editorial Universitaria, 2001.

Castillero Calvo, Alfredo. *La historia del enclave panameño frente al Tratado Torrijos-Carter*. Ciudad de Panamá: Ediciones Nueva Universidad, 1977.

Cinema Paradiso. Directed by Giuseppe Tornatore, Les Films/Ariane, RAI, Italy/France, 1988.

Cortés, María Lourdes. *La pantalla rota. Cien años de cine en Centroamérica*. Ciudad de México: Taurus, 2005.

Del Vasto, César, and Edgar Soberón Torchía. *Breve historia del cine panameño 1895–2003*. Ciudad de Panamá: Articsa, 2003.

Domínguez, Daniel. "La película *Historias del canal,* cinco momentos patrios," *La Prensa,* 10 October 2014, http://www.prensa.com/cine_y_mas/pelicula-Historias-Canal-momentos-patrios_7_4046665303.html. Accessed 16 October 2016.

Hands of Stone. Directed by Jonathan Jakubowicz, La Piedra Films, Panama Cinema, Fuego Films, Epicentral Studios, Vertical Media, Large Screen Cinema Productions, Panama/United States, 2016.

Historias del Canal. Directed by Carolina Borrero, Pinky Mon, Luis Franco Brantley, Abner Benaim, and Pituka Ortega-Heilbron, Hypatia Films/Manglar Films, Panama, 2014.

Invasión. Directed by Abner Benaim, Ajimolido Films/Apertura Films, Panama, 2014.

McCullough, David. *Un camino entre dos mares: La creación del canal de Panamá*. Barcelona: Espasa, 2012.

Méndez, Roberto. *Panamá, 9 de enero de 1964*. Ciudad de Panamá: U de Panamá, 1999.

Miró, Rodrigo. *La literatura panameña (origen y proceso)*. Ciudad de Panamá: Editorial Universitaria, 1996.

Mur, María M. "El cine panameño resurge de sus cenizas con un aluvión de estrenos en 2016," *EFE*, 23 January 2016, http://www.efe.com/efe/america/cultura/el-cine-panameno-resurge-de-sus-cenizas-con-un-aluvion-estrenos-en-2016/20000009-2818867. Accessed 18 December 2016.

Nuovo Cinema Paradiso. Directed by Giuseppe Tornatore, Les Films Ariane, Cristaldifilm, TF1 Films Production, RAI 3, Forum Picture, Italy, 1988.

Perigault Sánchez, Bolívar. *Cronología complementada del Canal de Panamá*. Ciudad de Panamá: Editorial Universitaria, 1988.

Pratt, Mary Louise. *Ojos imperiales. Literatura de viajes y transculturación*. Ciudad de México: Fondo de Cultura Económica, 2010.

Pulido Ritter, Luis. "La novela canalera en Carlos Guillermo 'Cubena' Wilson." *Cuadernos Intercambio*, vol. 10, no. 11, 2013, pp. 31–47.

———. "The Panama Canal in the Work of Eric Walrond and Joaquín Beleño: Counterpoint between the Caribbean Diaspora and the Panamanian Nation." *Caribbeing. Comparing Caribbean Literatures and Cultures*, edited by Kristian Van Haesendonck and Theo D'haen, Rodopi, 2014, pp 59–77.

Sanabria, Carolina. "El cine de Panamá en el siglo XXI: *Historias del Canal*." *Violencia, marginalidad y memoria en el cine centroamericano*, edited by María Lourdes Cortés, Editorial de la U de Costa Rica, 2021, pp. 34–151.

Stephenson Watson, Sonja. "La identidad afropanameña en la literatura desde el siglo XX hasta el nuevo milenio," *Revista LiminaR. Estudios Sociales y Humanísticos*, XIII, vol. 13, no. 2, 2015, pp. 27–37.

Shohat, Ella, and Robert Stam. *Multiculturalismo, cine y medios de comunicación: Crítica del pensamiento eurocéntrico*. Barcelona: Paidós, 2002.

The Birth of a Nation. Directed by D. W. Griffith, David W. Griffith Co., United States, 1915.

9

Costa Rican Exceptionalism

Nostalgia, *Costumbrismo*, and Extreme Patriotism in *Maikol Yordan de viaje perdido*

Liz Harvey-Kattou

Costa Rica's movie scene has boomed since the twentieth century when only nine feature-length, fiction productions were released, with every year since 2009 bringing several new cinematic releases. Both the highest-grossing and most-viewed Costa Rican movie to date, *Maikol Yordan de viaje perdido* (Miguel Gómez, Costa Rica, 2014), came out in cinemas in 2014, attracting 770,000 viewers to these screens alone (Cortés 17)—a huge 17 percent of the population of the country—and breaking records along the way. The movie's director, Miguel Gómez, is far from an unknown quantity in the world of Costa Rican filmmaking, having made four movies before the release of *Maikol Yordan*. His works encompass many genres, and while he is the most prolific of Costa Rica's directors, his productions show only a few consistent elements. In *El cielo rojo* (Costa Rica, 2008) and its sequel, *El cielo rojo 2* (Costa Rica, 2015), a group of three young friends consider what they want to do with their adult lives, and a bildungsroman plays out against the backdrop of local humor. *El sanatorio* (Costa Rica, 2010), on the other hand, is a horror movie set in an old sanatorium which is said to be haunted; *El fin* (Costa Rica, 2012) is an apocalyptic comedy; *Italia 90: La película* (Costa Rica, 2014) is a docu-drama which tells the story of the Costa Rican national soccer team's exploits in the 1990 World Cup in Italy (which Mauricio Espinoza analyzes in his sports movies chapter in this volume); while his most recent movie, *Amor viajero* (Costa Rica, 2017), is a romantic comedy. Perhaps what all these have in common is their deep-rooted *tico*[1] characteristics, which can be seen in the actors and backdrops on screen, as well as the language and jokes woven into each narrative. Gómez is clear when he thinks about how he likes to make movies: they must be profitable, and the only way of making a profit in Costa Rica seems to be to make them cheaply, almost exclusively for a local audience, and hope that this patriotic appeal brings in sales. This formula certainly worked for *Maikol Yordan*, and this chapter will consider the roots of its popularity, suggesting that in representing a type of patriotic nostalgia that harks back to the mythical creation story of Costa Rica, the movie uses *costumbrista* techniques to revalorize an idealized past and evoke feelings of patriotism in its audience. Discussing the movie in light of questions around presentations of the past and the interaction between cinema and national identity, this chapter analyzes the extent to which this movie plays on the trope of the Euro-descendant, heteropatriarchal, humble farmer as common ancestor of all *ticos* to make a profit using patriotism as a popularity tool.

Maikol Yordan de viaje perdido

The concept for the movie itself was drawn from an existing, and hugely popular, Costa Rican comedy sketch show and stand-up production company, *La media docena,* as they asked Gómez to use one of its best-loved spoof characters—Maikol Yordan—and make a part of his life into a movie. While he was a traditional country boy, who would be referred to as *polo* locally, making people laugh as he committed several faux pas in the big city of San José while on the small screen, under Gómez's direction, Maikol Yordan Soto Sibaja went international in this feature film.[2] Although the protagonist starts the narrative in the capital city of San José, he quickly states that he comes from the countryside and is in the city looking for a job in order to save his family's farm. When his search is unsuccessful, he returns empty-handed to his family—including his wife, Concepción, and eight children—only to be told that the debts on the farmland have reached $100,000 USD and an evil businessman, known only as Malavassi, is keen to take over the land and make the Soto family homeless. After his various attempts to win money fail, Maikol enters and wins a competition for a holiday in Europe, giving him hope of receiving funds from a long-lost relative who he is connected to by his grandmother. Although he meets well-meaning friends along the way, his time in Europe appears to have been unsuccessful, and he returns to Costa Rica and the farm dejected. Just before he signs the farm away to Malavassi, however, he receives some letters, all of which contain checks from people in Europe grateful for his help and talents, and he is able, along with the final $10 USD given to him by Malavassi's now-repentant sidekick, to save the farm and his family.

The movie borrows from the genres of spoof and slapstick comedy, and actor Mario Chacón, who plays Maikol Yordan, is able to pack in plenty of one-liners and misadventures. While local audiences largely responded to the movie with affection, seen by the number of viewers as well as positive comments on the official Facebook page, critical responses were divided. William Venegas, movie critic for Costa Rican newspaper *La Nación,* stated of *Maikol Yordan* that the "verbosity is detrimental to the flow of the story which, in itself, is anecdotal at best. Thus, the script serves as a filter without taking thematic risks."[3] Moreover, it was not just the screenplay that some viewers disliked, as others expressed distaste for the portrayal of people from the countryside in Costa Rica as stupid and uncultured (Sánchez). To this, Gómez responds that his cinema aims to represent a specific kind of Costa Rican reality and that there are many positive depictions of different *ticos* in the movie too. It is the positive portrayal of the nation itself which is undoubtedly at the very heart of this movie, and although the narrative is set in three locations—the country, the city, and Europe—the patriotic narrative is striking throughout. The stark contrast of the city and the countryside, in which the *campo* emerges victorious, harks back to the roots of the Costa Rican national myth which denotes that, upon arriving in what is now Costa Rica, the European settlers found no Indigenous people in the land and set up small holdings as simple, egalitarian farmers. In this movie, places and people are constructed in binary terms whereby the city remains the protectorate of evil while the *campo* encompasses all that is good. Indeed, the film's ending makes it clear not just which country, but even which town, Maikol would rather be in: he ends the movie unequivocally stating that he will never again leave the *finca.*

Nostalgia and Patriotism: The Evil City

The narrative arc and the movie's conclusion are imbued with a nostalgia which is tied up with an idealized version of Costa Rica's past. According to Diego Muro, nostalgia is both "intrinsic to human experience" (571) and a seemingly "essential feature of modern times, where the pace of social change is intense" (571). He equates the "processes associated with modernity" (Muro 573), which include issues seen in the movie such as the rampant capitalism of San José or the formation of new communities (the punk or the golfers) on display in the capital, with a certain type of patriotic, backward-looking ideal. In Muro's words, "nostalgia posits a present, usually a disastrous one, and an idealized longed-for past: a Golden Age" (574). Although concentrating on the place of nostalgia within Basque nationalism in his article, Muro could certainly be summing up *Maikol Yordan* with these pronouncements:

the monstrous present of the urban metropolis that has become the center of the *tico* world in the twenty-first century is juxtaposed with the simple, rural community at the heart of which sit Maikol Yordan and his family.

Muro's description of a disastrous present is made clear in this movie as the viewer is left in no doubt that although modern life appears to occur in the cities of the Central Valley with their skyscrapers, office blocks, and manicured golf courses, urban Costa Rica is depicted as a site of turmoil for the protagonist of this film. Indeed, the countryside and city are juxtaposed through the narrative and cinematography to continually reinforce the binaries of good (the countryside) and evil (the city). The spatial difference between the two has been noted by María Lourdes Cortés, who points out that, in this movie, "the countryside is the positive space par excellence, while the city is presented as dangerous, confusing, chaotic" (87).[4] Indeed, the city is depicted as a soulless place, where buildings and commerce are replacing community, and where everyone acts according to a set of unwritten, capitalist codes of which Maikol Yordan is unaware. The first shot of the movie shows the protagonist looking down at a motorway through the holes in a chain link fence. As his surroundings are gray, the noise from the cars is deafening, and Maikol assumes a confused expression, the feeling of entrapment is visible and palpable. As he walks up Avenida Central the traffic follows him, and the city is depicted as a hostile environment. Although San José is largely commercial and residential, green parks and open leisure spaces do exist. The decision to show the opposite side of the city by filming in the most overcrowded and traffic-prone areas is therefore a deliberate choice to further the construction of the city as an unwelcoming space. Thus, the capital becomes a place where people work in complex, modern office buildings, continually build even more new office buildings, make money, and speak in incomprehensible corporate jargon. While people are not always unkind, Maikol finds the city to be unfathomable.

Within the narrative these visual depictions are also brought to life. Of the city, Maikol comments that "everyone is always in a rush, and they do not have time to laugh," thus noting not just the spatial but also the lifestyle differences that exist between the city and the countryside.[5] Soon after this proclamation, it is seen that not only have city people lost their capacity to laugh, but that San José is also home to the devil himself. As soon as Maikol's father says to him "I don't understand what happened to the harvest, it's as though the devil has poisoned us," the camera cuts to Malavassi's office block—a movie baddy's lair for the twenty-first century—as one of his henchmen throws away a bottle labeled "poison."[6] It becomes clear that the people of the city, whose only desire is to take the Soto family's land for financial gain, have poisoned their crops in order to bankrupt the farm and repossess it via underhand means, such is the level of capitalist greed prevalent in San José. The use of a thoroughly evil villain who appears to lack morality is a typical Hollywood device, although given the Costa Rican movie's comic nature Malavassi is more akin to Jay Roach's Dr. Evil in *Austin Powers* (1997) than a serious threat to humanity. Indeed, the styling of Malavassi's character is certainly overdone in order to provide a comical element to this narrative: he has women dressed in bikinis bringing him cocktails which he throws in the faces of his henchmen if the paper umbrella is the wrong color; he has a model made of the land he wishes to take from the Soto family and animal heads framed on his walls; while receiving a massage he asks the masseurs to use some liquid from a bottle marked "children's tears."[7] Although this depiction is purposely one-dimensional, the fact that the villain of the piece comes from and, in many ways, represents the city in the movie is no coincidence. While this is a comic take on the confusion caused by rapid change and the modern world for a purposely simplistic hero, Muro's assertion that the feeling of nostalgia can be created through the setting up of the present as overly intense and fast-paced—that is, disastrous—has been employed here.

This feeling is furthered as the spectator sees that it is not just the buildings and people that the city houses which are made out to be disturbing or which reflect an overwhelming process of modernity, but that here the very habitus, or the unwritten codes of social conduct, as coined by Pierre Bourdieu, are also seen to have changed in Costa Rica and are now alien to someone living in the countryside. As Maikol applies for various jobs in the capital, although many of his prospective employers are kind to him, they operate according to a set of rules he cannot understand or adhere to, thus creating a chasm in the narrative between people from these two geographic backgrounds. It becomes clear in this movie that everyday life in the city and in the countryside is performed very differently. Living in the city means adhering to capitalist philosophy by trying to make money, perhaps not just to survive but to be rich or thrive. In doing so, a culture of praise for modern technology, buildings, and inventions has been created and individualist, capitalist aspirations have taken hold. The everyday habits, actions, and conversations open to people in the city are unfamiliar to Maikol just as the unwritten social codes are inaccessible to him. For example, when he tries to use the bathroom in an office building, he cannot understand how the motion sensor-activated taps, soap, and hand dryer work, even after watching another man operate them. When the head of a construction team talks to him about a job as a builder and asks him what he knows about "an electric power plant,"[8] Maikol answers "it's a Christmas tree."[9] When he appears to be working as a gardener on a golf course, Maikol is chased off the green after trying to plant a tree in one of the holes. Even Maikol, who is generally unobservant, notes "it's been so difficult to get used to," about his life in the city.[10] The everyday habits—such as understanding modern technology and contemporary culture—which have been built up in the city therefore present this location as a minefield to someone from the countryside. It would seem that Bourdieu's suggestion that habits form the social codes which then become norms is true of Costa Rica, which has, according to this movie, formed two separate codes which geographically divide people and the parameters of their interactions into countryside and city. In this way, the city is set up as an alien, unwelcoming place whereas the countryside, as will be seen, represents an idealized past.

Costumbrismo and the Revalorization of the *Campo*

The nostalgia that is created in this movie, then, is for an idealized and romanticized idea of Costa Rica's Golden Age, to borrow Muro's term, when humble European farmers settled to create an egalitarian community which would spawn the present-day nation according to the white settler myth. This idea is not a new one, and Víctor Hugo Acuña asserts that Costa Rica invented itself according to this creation story in the two decades following its 1821 independence, while Steven Palmer argues that, by the 1880s, the liberal nationalist project which sought to create peaceful patriotism and national cohesion through a rhetoric of a shared ancestral, agrarian background was complete (4–6). In *Maikol Yordan*, I argue that this form of nostalgia for a Golden Age (however unreal it may be) is steeped in the literary genre of *costumbrismo* which emerged in Spain in the 1830s with the *cuadro de costumbres* (Kirkpatrick) and which was popular in Costa Rican literature in the late nineteenth century (Quesada Soto). Scholars have placed the movement between Realism and Romanticism (Varela; Escobar), and José Escobar makes the point that in mixing these two movements *costumbrismo* works with Modernism rather than problematizing it as Romanticism does—this he terms the "*costumbrista* mimesis" (2–3).[11] He explains this term as denoting a work which is filled with background details of the environment, setting, and ambience, where the surroundings are brought to life and described in detail, and yet at the same time are analogous with "true" history.

This concept of creating a detailed yet unrealistic world are central elements in this movie, and Gómez certainly plays with *costumbrista* tropes to convey a feeling of nostalgia for an unlived past in the audience which, I argue, made the movie so successful. As Dorde Cuvardic García notes, an important part of *costumbrismo* "has as its objective 'to paint' social types," and, furthermore, it also acted to portray a nation and a local identity to the outside world (39).[12] These aspects are certainly visible in *Maikol Yordan:* not only is a very clear stereotype of a *campesino* family and the modern city painted for the audience here, but the juxtaposition between people, attitudes, and values in Europe and Costa Rica, as will be discussed later in this chapter, are also contrasted in order to show the superiority of Costa Rica's warmth and morality.

While the city is seen as intrinsically evil and nothing more than a capitalist playground, the countryside and the *campesino* himself are certainly revalorized in this movie albeit often through the use of provincial stereotypes. This attitude once again takes us to the *costumbrista* folklore of the country's nascent literary scene, and Álvaro Quesada Soto has noted that *costumbrismo* in Costa Rica was always rooted in everyday and popular lifestyles (67). Although written in 1983, Quesada Soto's words about this movement in literature apply to this twenty-first-century movie:

> its focus on popular life forms a certain idealization of the customs and traditions of patriarchy and the countryside, in which tragedies, vices, and social and moral injustices are diluted, absorbed by a picturesque quality or an amusing anecdote. The world of anecdotal *costumbrismo* is a flat, harmonious, seamless world. (67)[13]

It is clear that the "popular life" presented in this movie is the harmonious lifestyle of the *campesino* in his home environment.[14] Before the viewer is offered shots of the countryside, Maikol Yordan's voice-over proclaims: "I was born in the countryside . . . in one of the most beautiful towns, full of trees and rivers."[15] This assertion occurs as the camera follows Maikol in his travails through San José where trees and rivers are in short supply according to this movie. Following him home from the capital, the viewer sees Maikol get off a bus on a dirt and stone road, surrounded by trees and fields. We are shown panoramic shots filled with saturated colors, the sun is shining, and the gray buildings of the city are replaced by Costa Rica's much-famed natural environment. Maikol jumps on the back of an unknown truck, soon sees his cousin, and, later, Maikol celebrates his grandmother's birthday with a huge party of extended family, with traditional dances and music. This scene of community and happiness is certainly a far cry from the individualism of the city. Indeed, the large family, the local population which seems like a family, the feeling of open spaces which do not belong to a corporation, and a land in which Maikol understands the rules around how people live and work together, present a vision of the countryside as a site of hospitality and tradition.

A true rural, *costumbrista* idyll is thus created akin to that celebrated in Costa Rica's creation story, with the feeling of shared community, light, and love that goes with it.

It is also the very people of the countryside who are seen to be traditional, simple, and kind, in contrast with the complex, angry capitalists of the city. When he returns to the countryside everyone knows each other and greets him, welcoming him back. The family party, the warm and loving welcome from his hardworking wife and children, and the support he receives lift him up as a contemporary version of the "simple laborer" from the national anthem.[16] Studied in depth by María Amoretti, she notes that this trope—lauded as the ancestor of all true *ticos*—has two sides to it: "on the one hand, we read in it an attitude seen as a positive quality or virtue: simple is humble, poor, innocent. On the other hand, we translate simplicity as an index of inferiority: ignorant, a synonym of 'polo,' 'maicero,' 'concho,' 'silly' (65)."[17] It is clear that in this movie we, the viewers, are meant to see Maikol in the first sense, as humble and innocent; this, according to Amoretti, is the Christian sense (65). On the other hand, we are encouraged to see the city-dwellers, who we side against, from what Amoretti terms the capitalist point of view—as stupid and ignorant. This chimes with Yazlin Cabezas's evaluation that Maikol Yordan is "a country person who has stolen the heart of the Costa Ricans that identify with him as he has a noble heart, is naïve, even innocent."[18] What this movie creates, then, is an idea of the countryside as still inhabiting the idealized past of Costa Rica, one which when created on screen attempts to instill a feeling of nostalgia for a lost past, a Golden Age, in the national viewer. With the myth that all *ticos* descended from the *campo* used as a unifying image in the nineteenth century according to Acuña and Palmer, and the city as having lost traditional and moral values, this becomes a nostalgic storyline to be cheered throughout the nation. Indeed, as Cortés puts it, "family, Catholicism, and homeland are the pillars that sustain the world of Maikol Yordan" (180), much as they are also the pillars that sustain the traditional concept of Costa Rican national identity (Harvey-Kattou).[19]

As the positive reinforcement of the traditional nature of country life takes center stage, we also see Maikol's home and family as idealized according to national stereotypes. The small house he lives in is white and blue—the way that a typical Costa Rican house is depicted, using the colors of the flag—and stands with a mountain in the background. This is a typical Costa Rican image, one which appears in paintings, books, and on tourist souvenirs, and which demonstrates the national values of patriotism, humble egalitarianism, and family as the center of the nation. It also shows off the importance of the agricultural roots of the country. These patriotic ideals go hand in hand with family life as represented in this movie too: Maikol, as a man, must be the breadwinner, providing the money for his family to keep their land, home, and livelihoods. His wife exists only in the home, in an apron, cooking, cleaning, and looking after—and giving birth to—their eight children (it is no coincidence she is named Concepción).[20] Despite their difficult situation, she is dutiful and supportive throughout the movie, an uncomplicated figure lacking any nuance, even making fresh tortillas and coffee for Malavassi and his henchmen when they come to take the farm away. According to Quesada Soto, this is yet another trait of Costa Rican *costumbrismo* which, he argues, is all about patriarchal customs as well as 'traditional' countryside lifestyles and values (67). This picture-perfect image of an idealized *tico* family and society is perhaps one of the reasons for the movie's success among audiences who are invited to feel that, however comic and exaggerated, there is much truth in the idea that moral degradation lies in the city and that positive, traditional values are maintained in the countryside.

Despite the movie's overwhelming popularity in the Costa Rican box office and among many viewers, however, criticism has been leveled at both *La media docena* and Miguel Gómez for the stereotyped portrayal of people from the countryside as *polos*—or uneducated or uncultured—i.e., the other side of that coin described by Amoretti when discussing the "labriego sencillo" ["simple farmer"] (65) from the national anthem. Indeed, William Venegas states of the movie, "it looks for laughs from the audience on the back of designing a stupid, silly, bland man, capable of speaking more than a windbag."[21] Venegas is not alone in believing that the movie's jokes are often at the expense of all people from the countryside, not just Maikol Yordan, and the politician Ottón Solís's outraged 2016 Facebook post was widely picked up by newspapers in the country. Solís does not just criticize Maikol Yordan, but includes other comedy shows featuring fictional characters from the countryside such as Juan Vainas and Chibolo in his tirade, contending that people in the countryside are seen on TV and in movie as "idiots, ignorant, who live opening their mouths from deformed faces and making nonsense expressions" (Vásquez).[22] He argues that while people living in rural areas do important and profitable work for the country, *Maikol Yordan* "is a movie that shows agricultural people as simpletons, uncultured, superficial, basic, and instinctive" (Vásquez).[23] Gómez has been asked directly about these criticisms and his portrayal of people from the countryside in various interviews but continues to defend the movie. He claims that these stereotypes are not actually present as Maikol Yordan portrays all the positive aspects of the countryside already considered in this chapter—he is hardworking, appreciates his family, and has strong, patriotic values (Sánchez).

While this movie aims to foster a sense of nostalgia through the use of *costumbrismo*, then, it also uses these traits in negative ways, and it is hard to escape the aforementioned stereotypes of *campesinos* as stupid and uncultured that are used for comic value in this movie. For example, despite playing a part in owning and, presumably running, a farm, Maikol has no concept of how businesses work. Having heard that in San José you can find jobs and earn money easily, he goes around from building to building asking if someone will give him a job. When he is asked what he would like to work as, he answers "maybe a manager or boss" for the audience's amusement, given he has shown no knowledge of the industries in which he asks for work.[24] When he comes back from San José, dejected and jobless, he commits a litany of errors in order to make money, all designed to amuse the audience. He begins by correctly predicting the lottery numbers, only for his family to find out that he did not buy a ticket. He enters a children's spelling competition, but he cannot spell. He starts pole dancing but does not remove his clothes. Thus, he is portrayed as more than affectionately silly, and rather comes across as uneducated and uncultured as a direct result of country life. It is this aspect of the movie that may be particularly jarring for a local audience: while a nostalgic view may suggest that in decades and centuries past the *campesino* may not have had access to city life, this is certainly not true of Costa Rica's twenty-first-century rural population who have increasing contact with urban areas, if nothing else through technology and the media (Vásquez). This, however, appears to be another facet of much Costa Rican *costumbrista* writing according to Quesada Soto, who states that "the anecdotal attitude implies, in this sense, an attitude of naive optimism and full confidence—disseminated through tenuous irony and mockery—in moral validity, and the unquestionable need for customs, values, and established social relationships"[25] (67). While these moments of slapstick comedy frequently take place at the expense of Maikol, then, they do drive his narrative arc on and demonstrate the necessity of the customs, values, and social relations mentioned by Quesada Soto in this nostalgic world of the Costa Rican countryside. This again demonstrates how *costumbrismo* is used to revalorize the countryside, depicting it as the location of a Golden Age lost to the city.

Costa Rican Exceptionalism

This nostalgia is not just apparent within the city/countryside dichotomy created in this movie, however, as, when Maikol travels to Europe, Costa Rica's exceptionalism as a nation is also demonstrated. This is a long-standing tendency noted by Acuña, who states that Costa Rica, since its independence, has purposely marked itself out as "different" in a positive sense when compared with other Central American nations (191). Indeed, in this movie although he is told that Europe is "very refined" by his grandmother, and it is clear it is considered a place of high culture, upon arriving, Maikol's character again cannot adapt to the social codes around him.[26] When a taxi driver in the UK shouts at him when he tries to open the driver's door—mistaking it for the passenger door—or when the Parisian tour guide offers to take any money he has in exchange for a dining experience, he does not comprehend what is really going on. Furthermore, when he meets and befriends Carolina, a Latin American waitress who works in London, he cannot understand why she lives in London but can speak Spanish, leaving her to explain she is Latin American, like him. Just like the cities within Costa Rica, then, Europe is similarly confusing to Maikol, and it is also presented as a site of different social norms, habits, and ways of life. This facet of the film reinforces the idea that although the national creation myth states that all Costa Ricans are the descendants of humble European farmers, the Golden Age for which audiences should be nostalgic belongs in Costa Rica's countryside and not in the countries of Europe.

This exceptionalism of the Latin American country when compared with the colonizing continent of Europe in the twenty-first century is an undoing of Enrico Santí's concept of Latinamericanism, which is "never far from the collective notion that identifies Europe . . . as a superior culture in comparison with all other non-European peoples and cultures" (90). Indeed, it is clear that Maikol does not look to the "old continent" as he describes it, for inspiration on how to live, and despite Venegas's criticism to the contrary—the critic states that "the discourse that it is better to live in Lencha Street in San Rafael del Monte than in Europe . . . is no more than a frigid statement"—it is clear that the purpose of the movie is to showcase Costa Rica's countryside as surpassing Europe, just as it has previously been shown to surpass the nation's cities.[27] This is by no means the first time this idea has appeared in Costa Rican popular culture, and the well-known song "Patriótica costarricense" states:

> I do not envy the joys of Europe,
> The greatness that is found within it;
> my land is one thousand times more beautiful
> with its palm, its breeze and its sun. (Mendoza 24)[28]

Initially, this idea of Costa Rica as directly descended from Europe and this being a source of pride is clearly seen in the movie as the whole Soto family speaks with awe about their European relatives. However, the high-culture activities he sees and pursues in Europe are generally seen as pretentious and are, as the viewer eventually finds out, undercut by Maikol's ease of outdoing them. For example, when he is misdirected by one of Malavassi's henchmen onto the stage of London's Royal Opera House during a performance, it turns out he can perform opera better than the lead male whom he has accidently knocked to the floor. When he arrives in France and finds himself in the kitchen of one of the country's best restaurants, he makes a Costa Rican dish—*chifrijo*—which is mistakenly served to the President of France. Just like his operatic performance, the dish is a success, and he is paid for both skills. All these high-culture, artistic talents for which Europe appears to be known are thus actually torn down in the movie, as even the usually incapable figure of Maikol Yordan Soto Sibaja can outdo them without even trying. The Golden Age is therefore reaffirmed as located within Costa Rica's borders, then, and it is clear that while the nostalgia for times past extends to the foundation story of Costa Rica, this is very much a *tico*-centric, backward-looking storyline rather than a Eurocentric one.

This underscores the extreme patriotism of the movie even more and links to Muro's contention that "there may also be nations that, although sovereign, develop admiration for group traits of their ancestors and feel the need to live up to a glorious past" (575). This is seen as movie magazine *Delefoco* asserts of the movie that "*Maikol Yordan de viaje perdido* is a work which showcases Costa Rican and European backdrops, but it does make clear that Costa Rica does not have anything to envy from the old continent" (Anon).[29] While Europe is a poor man's Costa Rica, the *campo* is also the clear ground for the nostalgia that anchors the movie as, when he arrives back at his family's farm, Maikol firmly states "I had to go to the other side of the world to realize that here is where I should have never left."[30] A more patriotic refrain would be hard to find and as Cortés points out, "that Maikol Yordan discovers that the best is in the town he left is a clear defense of nationalism and possibly one of the reasons for the movie's success" (88).[31] This idea that nostalgia for an idealized past is popular is also highlighted by Suzanne Kehde and Jean Pickering, who state that nostalgia and nationalism occur as "at times of change or crisis, nations look to the past and infer a narrative that erases all confusion and contradiction" (3) thus conferring upon themselves "a mythic national identity" (3). This movie, and this closing statement in particular, leave no room for confusion or contradiction: the mythic national identity of Costa Rica is firmly set in the rural idyll of its founding myth, praising the "labriego sencillo" of the national anthem, and decrying the apparent loss of these traditional models and values.

Maikol Yordan de viaje perdido purposely demonstrates what it sees as the harm that has been done in the capital by the loss of certain traditions and traditional ways of life. At the same time, it also contends that the Eurocentrism or perhaps, in the twenty-first century, the Western-centrism of Costa Rica is misplaced, that a humble *tico* farmer—a version of the foundational fathers of the nation—can outdo any foreign talent. Despite also poking fun at country folk, perpetuating negative notions about *polos*, it seems that audiences welcomed this nostalgic outlook on screen. As Dannia Gamboa points out, "beyond the harsh critiques that brand it 'a joke' toward the Costa Rican *campesino*, it is a faithful representation of respect, help, solidarity. Of reminding us of our grandparents and of where we really come from."[32] Perhaps this statement is where we can uncover the continuing hold that myths, an idealized past, and the nation have over movie viewers in Costa Rica, where nostalgia clearly sells.

Notes

1. *Tico* is a common term often used interchangeably with "Costa Rican"; it also carries patriotic overtones (Harvey-Kattou).
2. According to the *Nuevo diccionario de costarriqueñismos*, this term means both "campesino" and "by extension, rude, of poor taste, rustic, someone who likes to dress in bright clothing" (por extensión, mal educado, de mal gusto, rústico, que gusta de vestirse con ropa de colores chillones) (Quesada Pacheco 322).
3. "exceso de palabrería que va en detrimento de la fluidez del relato que, de por sí, es anécdota a lo sumo. Así, el guion se mueve como 'filtro de fácil captación,' sin riesgos temáticos."
4. "el campo es el espacio positivo por excelencia, mientras la ciudad se presenta como peligrosa, confusa, caótica."
5. "todos andan en carrera y no tienen el tiempo para reír."
6. "no entiendo lo que pasó con las cosechas, es como si el diablo nos hubiera envenenado." The bottle reads "veneno."
7. "lágrimas de niños."
8. "una planta eléctrica."
9. "es un árbol de Navidad."
10. "vieras cómo me ha costado acostumbrarme."
11. "mímesis costumbrista."
12. "tuvo por objeto 'pintar' tipos sociales."
13. "su enfoque de la vida popular parte de cierta idealización de las costumbres y tradiciones patriarcales y campesinas, en que la tragedia, los vicios e injusticias sociales y morales, se diluyen, absorbidos por el giro pintoresco o la anécdota divertida. El mundo del costumbrismo anecdótico es un mundo plano, armónico, sin fisuras."
14. "vida popular."
15. "yo nací en el campo . . . un pueblito de lo más lindo, lleno de árboles y ríos."

16 "labriego sencillo."
17 "por un lado, leemos en ella una actitud reputada como cualidad positiva o virtud: sencillo es humilde, pobre, inocente. Por otro lado, traducimos sencillez como un índice de inferioridad: ignorante, sinónimo de 'polo,' 'maicero,' 'concho,' 'tonto.'"
18 "un campesino que se ha robado el corazón de los costarricenses que identifican con él pues tiene un corazón noble, es ingenuo y hasta inocente."
19 "familia, catolicismo y patria son los pilares que sostienen el mundo de Maikol Yordan."
20 Conception.
21 "busca risas de los espectadores a partir de diseñar un campesino estúpido, tontoneco y soso, capaz de hablar más que un heredero inconforme."
22 "idiotas, ignorantes y viven abriendo la boca, cual jeta deforme, y haciendo muecas sin sentido."
23 "es una película que muestra a las personas del agro como simplonas, incultas, superficiales, básicas e instintivas."
24 "puede ser gerente o jefe."
25 "la actitud anecdótica implica, en este sentido, una actitud de ingenuo optimismo y de plena confianza—apenas disimulados por una tenue ironía y cierta burla socarrona—en la validez moral, y la necesidad incuestionable de las costumbres, los valores y las relaciones sociales establecidas."
26 "muy fina."
27 "viejo continente." "el discurso de que es mejor vivir en calle Lencha de San Rafael del Monte que en Europa . . . no pasa de ser frío enunciado."
28 "Yo no envidio los goces de Europa, / la grandeza que en ella se encierra; / es mil veces más bella mi tierra / con su palma, su brisa y su sol."
29 "*Maikol Yordan de viaje perdido* es un trabajo que viene a mostrar escenarios costarricenses y europeos, pero sí deja claro que Costa Rica no tiene nada que envidiarle al viejo continente."
30 "es que tuve que irme al otro lado del mundo para darme cuenta de que aquí es de donde nunca me tuve que ir."
31 "que Maikol Yordan descubra que lo mejor está en el pueblo de donde salió, es una evidente defensa del nacionalismo y posiblemente una de las razones del éxito del movie."
32 "más allá de las duras críticas de tacharla 'una burla' al campesino costarricense, es una fiel representación de respeto, ayuda, solidaridad. De recordarnos a nuestros abuelos y de dónde venimos realmente."

Works Cited

Acuña, Víctor Hugo. "La invención de la diferencia costarricense, 1810–1870." *Antología del pensamiento crítico costarricense contemporáneo*, edited by Montserrat Sagot and David Díaz Arias, CLACSO, 2002, pp. 45–74.

Amoretti, María. *Debajo del canto: Un análisis del himno nacional de Costa Rica*. San José: Editorial de la U of Costa Rica, 1987.

Amor viajero. Directed by Miguel Gómez, Atómica Films, Costa Rica, 2017.

Bourdieu, Philippe. *Outline of a Theory of Practice*. Cambridge: Cambridge UP, 1977.

Cabezas, Yazlin. "Maikol Yordan: 'es tan importante estar bien con la familia sobre todo en esta época.'" *CR Hoy,* 2014, https://archivo.crhoy.com/maikol-yordan-es-tan-importante-estar-bien-con-la-familia-sobre-todo-en-esta-epoca/entretenimiento/ Accessed 18 January 2023.

Cortés, María Lourdes. *Fabulaciones del nuevo cine costarricense.* San José: URUK Editores, 2016.

Cuvardic García, Dorde. "La construcción de tipos sociales en el costumbrismo latinoamericano." *Filología y lingüística,* vol. 34, no. 1, 2008, pp. 37–51.

El cielo rojo. Directed by Miguel Gómez, Ginaluvosi Producciones, Costa Rica, 2008.

El cielo rojo 2. Directed by Miguel Gómez, Al filo de la navaja, Costa Rica, 2015.

El fin. Directed by Miguel Gómez, Atómica Films, Costa Rica, 2012.

El sanatorio. Directed by Miguel Gómez, Ginaluvosi Producciones, Costa Rica, 2010.

Escobar, José. *Costumbrismo entre Realidad y Romanticismo.* Biblioteca Virtual Miguel de Cervantes, 2003. *Biblioteca Virtual Miguel de Cervantes,* https://www.cervantesvirtual.com/obra-visor/costumbrismo-entre-el-romanticismo-y-realismo-0/html/ff87782c-82b1-11df-acc7-002185ce6064_7.html. Accessed 18 January 2023.

Gamboa, Dannia. "El secreto de Maikol Yordan para no perderse en su viaje." *La cuarta CR,* 2015, www.lacuartacr.com/el-secreto-de-maikol-yordan. Accessed 20 June 2019.

Harvey-Kattou, Liz. *Contested Identities in Costa Rica: Constructions of the Tico in Literature and Movie.* Liverpool: Liverpool UP, 2019.

Italia 90: La película. Directed by Miguel Gómez, Atómica Films, Costa Rica, 2014.

Kehde, Suzanne, and Jean Pickering, editors. *Narratives of Nostalgia, Gender, and Nationalism.* London: Macmillan Press, 1997.

Kirkpatrick, Susan. "The Ideology of Costumbrismo." *Ideologies and Literature,* vol. 1, no. 7, 1978, pp.2844.

Maikol Yordan de viaje perdido. Directed by Miguel Gómez, Audiovisuales LMD, 2014.

"Mario Chacón: 'Esta película nació para hacerse.'" *DeleFoco,* 2015, www.revista.delefoco.com/53-mario-chacn-esta-pelcula-naci-para-hacerse.aspx. Accessed 20 June 2019.

Mendoza, José Augusto. "Patriótica costarricense." *Himnos de mi patria,* edited by Bernal Martínez Gutiérrez, Imprenta Nacional, 2016.

Muro, Diego. "Nationalism and Nostalgia: The Case of Radical Basque Nationalism." *Nations and Nationalism,* vol. 11, no. 4, 2005, pp. 571–589.

Palmer, Steven. *A Liberal Discipline: Inventing Nations in Guatemala and Costa Rica, 1870–1900.* Dissertation, Columbia University, 1990.

Quesada Pacheco, Miguel Ángel. *Nuevo diccionario de costarriqueñismos.* San José: Editorial Tecnológica de Costa Rica, 2007.

Quesada Soto, Álvaro. "Actitud crítica en el costumbrismo costarricense." *Filología y lingüística,* vol. 9, no. 1, 1983, pp. 67–74.

Sánchez, Alexánder. "Miguel Gómez: 'Estudié en un lugar donde enseñan a ver el cine como negocio.'" *La nación,* 2015, https://www.nacion.com/viva/cine/miguel-gomez-estudie-en-un-lugar-donde-ensenan-a-ver-el-cine-como-negocio/IGL2JPEE3ZH2PIZK55TNTCYOUU/story/. Accessed 18 January 2023.

Santí, Enrico. "Latin Americanism and Restitution." *Latin American Literary Review,* vol. 20, no. 40, 1992, pp.88–96.

Varela, José Luis. *La palabra y la llama.* Madrid: Editorial Prensa Española, 1967.

Vásquez, Lucía. "Ottón Solís critica a personajes como Maikol Yordan, Chibolo y Juan Vainas." *La nación,* 2016, https://www.nacion.com/viva/otton-solis-critica-a-personajes-como-maikol-yordan-chibolo-y-juan-vainas/GK5KYYHKRJHBDHZOQK5HNI3GXY/story/#:~:text=Asegur%C3%B3%20que%20los%20personajes%20interpretados,realidad%20de%20las%20zonas%20rurales. Accessed 18 January 2023.

Venegas, William. "Crítica de cine: *Maikol Yordan de viaje perdido.*" *La nación,* 21 December 2014, www.nacion.com/viva/cine/critica-de-cine-maikol-yordan/LLBBAF6KMRGUBMQCKIF7DJP2SM/story/. Accessed 18 January 2023.

10

The Games We Play

Forging and Contesting National Identities in Central American Sports Films

MAURICIO ESPINOZA

Sports were one of the first human activities captured by the emerging technology of cinema in its early years, from Thomas Edison's 1895 filming of a boxing match to the Lumiere Brothers' 1897 production of the documentary short *Football* (Jones 2). As David Rowe explains, sports are one of the most filmable of all cultural practices because of "the affinity between narrative (the unfolding story), vision (spectatorship), and time (the framework of action) that lends itself to the big screen" (3). Further, sport is "naturally susceptible to cinematic activity because it is inherently and densely consequential and inherently visual" (Pomerance 311). Finally, sporting practices provide powerful narratives of struggle, overcoming barriers in life, heroic figures, affirmation of national and/or racial/ethnic identities, intense emotional response and identification, and many other themes that fit perfectly into filmic storytelling. Despite this natural affinity between sports and the moving image, a sports movie can never be fully confined to the stadium or the locker room, as it tends "to deal in some way with the relationship between the domain of sport and the greater world of which it is a part, interrogating both the uniqueness of sport that sets it apart from quotidian experience and the way in which it impinges on the social world, and, inevitably, is impinged upon by it" (Rowe 30–31). It is precisely this relationship between sports, sports films, and the social milieu they portray and in which they come into existence that is explored in this chapter.

In Central America, movies about sporting practices or figures were a rare occurrence during the twentieth century, with only a handful of documentaries[1] and one fiction short (marginally dealing with sports) produced in that period: Ramiro Lacayo's *El Centerfielder* (Nicaragua, 1985), based on a story of the same title by Nicaraguan writer Sergio Ramírez about a former baseball player who has been jailed by the Somoza dictatorship.[2] Conversely, the sports films genre has gained a foothold in the current century, as several documentaries and feature-length productions have appeared at a steady pace in the last two decades covering a variety of sports and sub-genres. They include fiction films such as Miguel Salguero's *El trofeo* (Costa Rica, 2004), about a boy from the countryside who dreams of becoming a marathoner; Florence Jaugey's *La Yuma* (Nicaragua, 2009), about a young woman from the Managua slums who trains to become a boxer; Tomás Chi's *11 cipotes* (Honduras, 2014), about a group of mischievous and poor small-town teenagers whose energy is channeled into playing soccer and who end up traveling to the city of San Pedro Sula for a regional tournament; Aldo Rey Valderrama's *Kimura* (Panama, 2017), a Panamanian drama set in the world of mixed martial arts; and Aeden O'Connor's *90 minutos* (Honduras, 2019), in which soccer helps tie together four interlinking stories of violence, romance, suspense, and drama.

Three feature-length biopics have also been produced in the last few years: Miguel Gómez's *Italia 90* (Costa Rica, 2014), about the Los Ticos's remarkable performance in their first World Cup in 1990; Jonathan Jakubowicz's *Hands of Stone* (United States/Panama, 2016), about Panamanian boxing legend Roberto Durán; and Dinga Haines's *Keylor Navas: Hombre de fe* (Costa Rica, 2017), which tells the rags-to-riches story of internationally renowned Costa Rican goalkeeper Keylor Navas. Finally, there are several sports-related documentaries, including Chema Rodríguez's *Estrellas de la línea* (Guatemala/Spain, 2006), about a group of female sex workers who form a soccer team; Gerardo Muyshondt and Carlos Moreno's *Uno, La historia de un gol* (El Salvador/Colombia, 2010), about the Salvadoran national soccer team's only goal at the 1982 World Cup; Pituka Ortega-Heilbron's *Los puños de una nación* (Panama, 2005), also about the career and national symbolism represented by Durán; Alberto Serra's *La fuerza del balón* (Panama, 2016), about the struggles to become a professional soccer player; and more recently Alejandro Irías's *100 horas de furia* (Honduras, 2020), which examines the so-called Football War[3] of 1969 between El Salvador and Honduras from a Honduran perspective.[4]

In this chapter, I have chosen to analyze four of these films: *Los puños de una nación, Hands of Stone, Uno,* and *Italia 90.* There are several reasons for this selection. First, they are about boxing and soccer, which (along with baseball) are the most popular Central American sports and the two that have garnered the most attention in the region's cinematic production. Second, the main events recalled or reenacted in these movies took place mainly during the 1970s and 1980s, a crucial and contentious period in Central America's recent history that saw, among other developments: tense geopolitical relations between the United States and Panama leading up to the 1977 Torrijos-Carter Treaties by which the Panama Canal was eventually handed over to the Panamanians in 1999; the bloody civil war in El Salvador that started in 1979 and lasted 12 years; and the early period of implementation of neoliberal policies in Costa Rica that has profoundly transformed the country's welfare state system and the social contract with its citizens. Third, these films engage not only with the historical events and figures they depict, but in doing so they also expose (purposely or not) dominant discourses of nationalism that shed light on the cultural landscape of contemporary Central American societies. And finally, all these sports films (regardless of subgenre) are constructed around the idea of the *underdog*, a persistent theme of the genre by which individuals who are underprivileged or otherwise handicapped manage to triumph against seemingly impossible odds (Fuller 53–54). My analysis considers how gender, class and race/ethnicity play a significant role in the configuration of national identities around sports and in their filmic depictions.

Sports and National Identities in Central America

A variety of games and sporting practices existed in Indigenous America before the arrival of Europeans over 500 years ago. In Central America, the most popular of these sports was the Mesoamerican ballgame. Played by several cultures such as Aztecs, Zapotecs, and Mayas from as far north as modern-day Arizona to as far south as El Salvador and Honduras, this sport had social, political, economic, mythical, and religious significance for the societies that practiced it (Wittington 17–19; Espinoza).[5]

Central America's most popular sports today (soccer, baseball, and boxing) arrived as imports beginning in the second half of the nineteenth century. As was the case with the rest of Latin America and the Caribbean, these games were brought mainly by the British as part of the expansion of European capitalism and modernity across the globe, or by the Americans as they sought to expand their geopolitical and economic influence in the continent (Arbena and LaFrance xii). Soccer gained traction early on in Costa Rica and northern Central America, while baseball took hold in Nicaragua and Panama due to heavy U.S. economic and military intervention in these two countries during the late 1800s and early 1900s (McGehee 176–78; Thorn). In the 1920s, boxing began challenging the popularity of baseball in Nicaragua (McGehee 192), while in Panama pugilism became extremely popular during and after the construction of the Panama Canal in the early 1900s (Corpas).

During their initial introduction to Latin America, modern sports were novelties practiced by foreigners or local elites. That would soon change, however, as these practices became more widespread and accessible to the masses. For example, by 1930 soccer had "socially and racially democratized, developed a popular base, moved toward professionalization, and become a foundation of emerging national identities" (Arbena and LaFrance xiii). As the twentieth century progressed, sport became a deep-rooted tradition and a source of both loyal and often crazed fandom (in the case of domestic leagues) and national pride (as individual athletes and teams began representing their countries in regional or international events). Even though sports such as soccer were at first an 'imported' cultural practice, they have become a useful tool for promoting symbolic integration, which is crucial for developing the identities that sustain the nation as an imagined community (Villena Fiengo, "Gol-balización" 259). For example, active following of soccer events is regarded as a civic duty, whether a person enjoys the sport or not. In particular, supporting one's national team (regardless of its quality) is a heartfelt and often exalted public declaration of belonging and loyalty to the nation (Villena Fiengo, "Gol-balización" 259). As a result, sports acquired symbolic importance with profound geopolitical implications, being regarded as a form of "ritual war between nations"[6] as it has reached the point of triggering actual international conflicts such as the above-mentioned "Football War" between El Salvador and Honduras (Villena Fiengo, "Gol-balización" 258).

How did sports manage to activate such strong nationalist responses and identification? As Michael Billig argues, one reason may be that modern sports have a social and political significance that:

> extend[s] through the media beyond the player and the spectator by providing luminous moments of national engagement and national heroes whom citizens can emulate and adore. (120)

In this regard, we can see an immediate connection between sports narratives (whether they be moments of triumphant celebration or instances of agonizing defeat) and their telling and retelling through mass media, for which film and television have been fundamental throughout the years. Nation-building and nation-sustaining narratives have always relied on heroes and heroic feats, and sports can certainly supply plenty of those—replacing (or at least supplementing) the figure of the soldier or the founding father in contemporary discourses of patriotism. As Joshua Nadel explains with regards to the development of soccer in Latin America, "not only did players become national heroes, but sporting victories were also seen as victories for the nation's way of life" (9).

Heroism narratives also require adversaries, further making sports and sports stories a ripe terrain for symbolically reenacting nationalist discourses since in sports the construction of a sense of national belonging runs concurrently with the representation of certain adversaries as "others" (Sandoval García 31). Additionally, sports have become a successful modern form of habitualizing nationalism because "they are practiced, lived experience as opposed to nationalism's ideologically explicit inculcations in more formal settings such as the school system" (Fernández L'Hoeste et al. 1). This does not mean that the nationalist discourses created and reproduced through sports and sports narratives (film included) are somehow innocent, spontaneous, or free of ideological maneuvering since "sports have been more often than not a key arena for official forms of nationalism aimed at integrating a given society in the face of internal differences or for schemes aimed at taking advantage of sports' deep popularity to obtain political gains and legitimation" (Fernández L'Hoeste et al. 1). And while sports have long been maligned for their manipulative use as a distraction from political discussion and involvement by the masses, it is also true that at times sports have also served as a form of popular resistance in the face of social or political repression (Villena Fiengo, "El fútbol" 23).

Finally, it is essential to point out that nationalism and the formation of national identities around sports "often intersect with social identities such as those grounded in ethnicity, race, class, and gender" (Bonzel 2). Here I want to recall the quote by Joseph Arbena and David LaFrance included earlier, where they stated that for soccer to become such as an influential phenomenon in the formation of Latin American national identities, it first had to be "socially and racially democratized" (xiii). In other words, a majority of members of the nation across various strata and backgrounds had first to be brought into the fold of sport participation, spectatorship, and fandom for collective identities and narratives to begin forming and, crucially, developing "community ties filled with affective intensity" (Villena Fiengo, "El fútbol" 21).[7] In the case of Costa Rica, the lower classes quickly appropriated soccer from foreigners and local elites and made it a more "plebeian" sport, which helps to explain the fact that in the early twentieth century the country's most popular teams were made up of both aristocrats and working-class youth (Urbina 95). Likewise, in Panama boxing quickly began to be practiced by men from the poorest sectors of society, including Black people. This cross-class, cross-racial appeal of boxing helps to explain why an Afro-Panamanian, Alfonso Téofilo Brown (known as Panama Al Brown), became the first Latin American (and the first gay Afro-Latino) boxer to ever win a world title in the late 1920s (Corpas).

While sports as a cultural practice has proven to be welcoming enough to include a variety of individuals, its profoundly contradictory nature also means that at times it has also led to the formation and consolidation of social barriers (Villena Fiengo, "El fútbol" 21–22), including racial discrimination, homophobia, xenophobia, and misogyny. Gender is perhaps the category in which sports lag behind the most in terms of inclusion. While many Central American female athletes have excelled in the realm of sports and achieved a great deal of notoriety (especially in individual sports), they have seldom—if ever—managed to capture the national imagination in the powerful ways in which their male counterparts have. This, of course, has nothing to do with athletic prowess and everything to do with deep-seated patriarchal structures—after all, in Latin America the nation is *la patria,* and patria comes from the same word as "father." Additionally, when women compete in traditional "male" sports such as soccer and boxing, the media tend to trivialize and feminize their performances (van Sterkenburg and Spaaij 3). In this regard, it is important to remember that both the nation and sport have been "historically male-centered as practice and spectacle" (Fernández L'Hoeste et al. 14) and that for males the practice and mediated consumption of sport "serves as a signifier of their [dominant] masculinity" (van Sterkenburg and Spaaij 3).

Sports films are an ideal genre to explore how narratives about the nation and national identities are constructed and reproduced through audiovisual media, since they multiply "the affective potential of film with that of the sports contest to great effect, creating an emotionally charged experience that can help turn any number of social, political, and cultural issues into a persuasive narrative" and "reflect the ways in which ideas about the nation and national belonging change over time and are always implicated in larger historical developments" (Bonzel 2). While features vary across sub-genres or even sports, Séan Crosson has identified several key characteristics shared by popular sports films: they often manifest dual protagonists and dualistic structures due to the competitive nature of sports; they have a propensity to overemploy many clichés and sentimental endings; they are fairly predictable as they rely on the cumulative effect of the film's often repeated situations, themes, and icons—such as the fight or game sequences or the rise and fall of the hero, often an underdog or outsider; they make heavy use of intertextual references; they maintain a strong connection to the culture that produced them; and, finally, they are functional for their society, allowing viewers to consider or resolve (poetically at least) contradictions that exist in their particular societies or cultures (61–65). In the following pages, I analyze how Central American sports films engage with particularly Central American historical events and ideas about the small nations of the Isthmus, incorporating or challenging any number of conventions of the genre.

The Fists of a Nation: Durán, Masculinity, and U.S.-Panama Relations

The two boxing films studied here have some basic differences in the cinematic strategies they employ from their respective genres and the time period covered in the narrative—*Los puños de una nación* goes as far back as the construction of the Panama Canal by the United States in the early 1900s and ends in 2000 when Durán won his final world title; *Hands of Stone* focuses on the rise, fall, and redemption of the boxer's career from his childhood in the late 1950s to his light middleweight title victory against American Davey Moore in 1983. Despite these differences, both films focus on the Panamanian nation's struggle to find a sense of identity in the second half of the twentieth century in the context of U.S. commercial and military occupation of the Canal Zone. During this period, General Omar Torrijos (Panama's de facto leader from 1968 until his death in 1981) sought to broker a deal with the United States that would hand the Canal over to Panamanian control—and with it a sense of national autonomy for the first time in the country's colonial and later neocolonial history. Against this political background, young and cocky fighter Roberto Durán (1951)—better known as Mano de Piedra, or Hands of Stone, because of his devastating punching power—was quickly rising among boxing's international elite and became the perfect hero for his country's quest to reclaim national pride. It is this combination of nationalism and hypermasculine heroic achievement that is at the heart of both *Los puños de una nación* and *Hands of Stone*. While Panama has had thirty world titleholders in its illustrious boxing history, none has elicited such widespread admiration at home and abroad as Durán—who won world titles in four different weight divisions during a long career that spanned from 1967 through 2002, and is considered one of the best lightweight pugilists of all time (Gems 183), and whom *Ring* magazine named the fifth greatest fighter of the last eighty years shortly after his retirement (Iber et al. 264). But Durán's significance for the Panamanian people and his national-idol status go well beyond his illustrious boxing accomplishments; in fact, they have more to do with what his victories against American boxers (especially the great Sugar Ray Leonard) meant for his homeland during the transformational decade of the 1970s.

More than any other sport, boxing has had a particularly close relationship with film since the infancy of the seventh art (Grindon 3). This connection between boxing and cinema is expressed through certain narrative and visual conventions that have developed over time and which mold our understanding and expectations of pugilist-themed movies. While boxing films share most of the basic characteristics of sports films outlined by Crosson, these conventions provide certain specificity to the boxing movie as compared to films about other sports. For this analysis, I will concentrate on three of these conventions, which both *Los puños de la nación* and *Hands of Stone* employ. First, the basic plot of the boxing film (biographical or not) is usually organized around the rise and fall of the fighter's career (Cook 42), during which clearly defined adversaries and threats play an essential role. Second, the boxing movie thrives on a principle of "intensified realism," which reaches its apex in the narrative and visual power of the fight scenes—integrating "the development of the fight with the dramatic conflicts propelling the plot" (Grindon 23). In the two films that concern us here, these "dramatic conflicts" are intimately tied to the U.S.-Panama geopolitical confrontation that frames the movies' dramatic arches. Finally, boxing films reproduce the common myth of the "hungry fighter," which is closely tied to the figure of the underdog (Wacquant 221). A hungry fighter is an unlikely hero who hails from the very bottom of the sociodemographic and/or racial pyramid and who is hungry in the literal, bodily sense but also hungry for social recognition, economic well-being, justice, and/or freedom from oppression.

Los puños de una nación and *Hands of Stone* are structured along a continuum of ups and lows that traverses Panama's history during the twentieth century, and which at some point during the films begin corresponding with Durán's moments of triumph or defeat. The documentary sets the stage of Panama's historical struggles by highlighting visually and narratively the subordination caused by the Americans' decades-long occupation of the Canal Zone and military presence throughout the country. To this end, Ortega-Heilbron employs cartography and archival footage (two common elements found in documentaries) to make evident this deplorable condition and national frustration with it. For example, a map of Panama is shown with a U.S. flag over the Canal, flanked by Panamanian flags—depicting a sort of fault or open wound that literally divides the country in two. This is followed by clips from an old documentary about the occupied Canal Zone, in which the narrator proudly announces that residents have managed to "recreate a tiny slice of America" in the tropics where everything is "100% American" and goods are much cheaper than for the Panamanians. Immediately after, the film shows footage of a Black female activist complaining about "this bad neighbor we have here."[8]

This historical lesson reaches its apex with the emotional recounting of one of the bloodiest and most controversial episodes of the first six decades of U.S. occupation: the January 9, 1964, anti-American protests in which high school students who tried to raise the Panamanian flag inside the Canal Zone were killed. Following the deadly incident, the documentary's voice-over narrator recalls that relations between the two countries would never be the same again, and that Panamanians "saw the United States as an unbeatable giant that no one could defeat. Except for one man . . ." At this very moment, a young boy is shown on the beach throwing punches—foreshadowing Durán's entrance into the narrative. This is the point at which *Hands of Stone* picks up the story. It does so by inserting a very young Durán into the heroic account of the 1964 protests, showing him stealing mangos from the Canal Zone to feed his starving family and managing to escape American soldiers as riots rage over the city. Later, as he begins his training under American manager Ray Arcel (Robert De Niro) in the early 1970s, Durán (Édgar Ramírez) stares down an armed U.S. guard from the other side of the fence that divides Panama City from the Canal Zone. Now, the stage is set for transition from national defeat to the ascendancy of two men who would simultaneously and symbiotically challenge the status quo of the aggrieved nation in the political arena and in the boxing ring. (To learn more about how conflict in the Panama Canal Zone has been represented in other documentaries, read Carolina Sanabria's chapter in this volume).

The next (and most consequential) segments of both films establish the association between Torrijos and Durán as national heroes whose defiance against the United States led to arguably the proudest moments in the country's history. At the core of this nationalist project is masculinity. According to Michael Donoghue, both Durán and General Torrijos—ambitious, strong men who rose to prominence in traditionally male-dominated activities—embodied the powerful machos who changed the paradigm in U.S.-Panama relations back in the 1970s (18). A nation feminized by the U.S. occupation of the Canal Zone through military and economic dominance, Panama found in Torrijos's intransigence and in Durán's vicious knockouts against 'gringos' the means to reinstate the powerful male at the center of its national identity, which Donoghue calls "Isthmian machismo" (21). The titles of both films also reaffirm the value placed on physical strength associated with a particular kind of violent masculinity, as the Panamanian nation becomes metonymically embodied by Durán's punishing fists. It's no surprise, then, that in *Hands of Stone*'s premonitory opening sequence we hear the extradiegetic sound of a Panamanian broadcaster stating that Torrijos has guaranteed Durán's victory against Leonard (Usher). Though brief, this snippet of sound helps frame the entire biopic as a long nationalist bout and foreshadows its climactic, triumphant fight scene. Meanwhile, the documentary makes it clear that the Panamanian leader considered Durán a popular hero that could be recruited into the struggle to both unify the nation under a political cause and to achieve a symbolic victory against the imperialist enemy. As a photograph of Torrijos and Durán standing together is shown, the narrator relates: "Torrijos sees in Durán a priceless icon that can help him build this sense of nation," as a win over Leonard would represent "a triumph of high symbolic value." Earlier in *Los puños de una nación*, we see a mural that depicts the two men, this time with a Panamanian flag in front of them that visually seems to join them as if they were two sides of the same man. The flag as a signifier of national pride is used abundantly during both films, not so much for its generic patriotic symbolism but because it points to the 1964 massacre in which the Panamanian flag was torn by American "Zonians" just as they also cut short the lives of Panamanian youth.

Hands of Stone depicts the masculine/nationalist discourse through several key scenes. For example, the scene depicting the signing of the agreement between Torrijos and President Carter to hand over the Canal to Panama (which generates excitement for Durán and his fellow Panamanians), is punctuated by several subsequent scenes that culminate with Durán's historic 1980 victory over Leonard for the welterweight title—all of which show Durán in his prime macho public persona, mocking and questioning (through sexually charged insults aimed at his wife) Leonard's (and by extension, the United States') masculinity and legitimacy. The extent to which the two fighters are depicted as symbols of their respective countries is summarized in the way Durán's wife Felicidad (Ana de Armas) speaks to her husband: "If you want your people to be proud of being Panamanian, this is the one you need to beat [pointing to a picture of Leonard in *Ring* magazine]. That clown[9] is the symbol of American sports. If you want the treaty to mean something for Panama before 1999, destroy their idol and make them respect us."[10]

While the biopic does an excellent job of generating the "intensified realism" of boxing films through a careful and beautifully photographed reenactment of the historical fight in Montreal, the documentary does a much better job of merging the purely pugilistic with the political overtones of the match. Ortega-Heilbron achieves this through the use of newspaper clippings, extradiegetic music, and TV footage—techniques that she relies on quite effectively throughout the documentary.[11] In the buildup to the fight we see a promotional poster with Leonard's face that reads: "It will be a war," confirming the political implications of the bout. As the fight unfolds, we hear Panamanian salsa star Rubén Blades singing "Tiburón," whose lyrics address Americans by telling them to "Respect my flag!" and warning them that "A good beating will teach you that there's honor to reckon with" because "in unity there's strength, and also our salvation." Additionally, broadcast of the fight is edited with archival footage of contemporary revolutionary armed struggles in Central America and the Caribbean (El Salvador, Nicaragua, Grenada), creating a regional discourse of resistance in a Cold War context characterized by sustained U.S. interventionist policies throughout Latin America and the Caribbean.

The national "unity" highlighted in the song by Blades (who plays the role of boxing impresario Carlos Eleta in *Hands of Stone*) is visually celebrated in both films, as elated crowds of Panamanians are shown welcoming their hero after his (and their) victory. The documentary chooses footage that highlights the country's ethnic, racial, and class diversity, portraying a moment of national jubilation when internal divisions and distinctions are erased. By contrast, Durán's humiliating defeat in the rematch against Leonard—the infamous "No Más" fight, which also took place in 1980—is followed (in the biopic) by shots that show Durán drunk, lying on a couch; news footage of a defiant President Reagan vowing that the United States will keep the Canal; and the announcement that Torrijos has died. In other words, national redemption (and defeat) is conditioned by the boxer-hero's ring performance and also the state of his masculinity. This sequence—and the documentary's scene showing Durán sobbing next to Torrijos's casket—represents not just the personal and professional fall of the national sporting idol and the untimely death of the country's charismatic leader (which happened within the span of eight months), but also serves as a metaphor of Panama's descent into a new historical low. In the documentary, this dark period is depicted via footage showing General Manuel Noriega's ascent to power and the resulting U.S. military invasion of 1989, which revived the ghosts of past occupation and carnage—a topic that Jared List's chapter details in his analysis of Abner Benaim's documentary *Invasión* (Panama, 2014).

Furthermore, the two films are heavily influenced by (and reproduce) the myth of the hungry fighter. Durán grew up in El Chorrillo, a notorious Panama City slum, fatherless and in extreme poverty. As mentioned before, the first time we see Durán in the biopic, he is risking his life to bring food to his family and friends. Life in the poor barrio is tough, and young Durán quickly learns to use his fists and nurture his intimidating macho personality to make money and survive. Consequently, class is inextricably tied with gender and nationalism in the movie, as Durán's disadvantaged socioeconomic origin conditions to a great extent his hypermasculinity and his relentless desire to avenge his "feminized" and subordinated country. In the documentary, Durán's Panamanian coach Néstor Quiñones says that "He was a boy with hunger. A need to be someone," while boxing commentators recall that he was "ferocious." Hunger (both literal and figurative) is employed throughout the entire narrative of *Hands of Stone*. As an adult, Durán is shown eating one of every flavor of ice cream he can find, because as a child he was denied such simple pleasures. He is also hungry for happiness, pursuing the beautiful and aptly named Felicidad even though she comes from a privileged background. When Arcel announces Durán to the U.S. boxing world, he describes him as "a true hungry fighter, like in the old days." Finally, after his victory over Leonard, he begs Arcel to leave him alone: "I don't want to fight [...] I'm hungry. I just want to eat. I want to enjoy what I have." But Durán is not selfish when it comes to indulging in the abundant fruits of his labor—both films underscore his generosity and deep identification with the poor people of Panama, showing him back in El Chorrillo and giving money away, especially to children.

Durán's humble origins are as much about class as they are about ethnicity, a factor that is explored in the documentary but ignored in the biopic. The fighter's other nickname was "El Cholo," a pejorative term used throughout Latin America's history to describe individuals of Indigenous ancestry or looks, often from the countryside. However, in the case of Durán, the term is appropriated to reflect a sense of collective pride in the nation's multicultural and popular-class constitution. As Panamanian poet Consuelo Tomás explains in *Los puños de una nación*, "Cholo [...] it can be an insult, or it can be the crowning of an identity," that "he is ours, he's very much like ourselves." This convergence of class and ethnic identification is crucial for the appeal of Durán as a popular and unifying hero and his construction as such in the films. Panama was not only "feminized" by U.S. imposition; it was starved and impoverished of both resources and a sense of identity. Durán, Tomás reasons, helped to bring all those scattered pieces of Panamanian identity together: "He didn't know the feelings he was going to generate in the Panamanian people, in terms of emotions. We've always been the little ones, the ugly ones, the ones that are not taken into account [...] So Durán carries with him all our hopes."

"Tom Thumb," "Cinderella," and the Soccer Nation's Collective Heroes

According to Carlos Sandoval García, soccer is both a popular cultural practice and a media spectacle that has been turned into a powerful ritual and symbol "around which broad sectors of society can identify with the nation" (93).[12] In this manner, soccer allows people in modern societies to build a *communitas*, that is, a ritual space where structural differences between individuals (in terms of role and status) can be set aside as these individuals come together with a shared sense of community (Villena Fiengo, "El fútbol" 29).[13] While the connection between sports and nationalism is present and central in the narratives about Durán and Panama, team sports (and soccer in particular) tend to generate a different type of nationalist engagement that develops over a long period and is thus less dependent on specific athletes or historical events—sporting or otherwise. In the case of individual sports such as boxing, an athlete's career is finite; additionally, whatever he or she may come to represent for a group of people or even for an entire nation or region (as in the case of Durán) is circumscribed to his or her accomplishments during a relatively short time and what those accomplishments come to symbolize at a given historical, political, and cultural moment. For instance, Panama has had over twenty world boxing champions after Durán, but none of them have achieved the same degree of collective identification and patriotic association because (1) they are not Durán the athlete and man and (2) their sporting feats did not take place and become interlinked with such a transformational (and highly unlikely to be repeated) period in the nation's history. Conversely, soccer is organized around team dynamics, with fans developing an emotional attachment to the team for which they root. While exceptional players do receive individual adoration at various times, their participation in a team comes and goes and other idols eventually replace them. What remains—some Central American soccer clubs have been around for more than a century now—is the *team* as a unique institution and what it has come to symbolize for generations of followers, whose identification is so strong they may feel they are as much a part of the team as the players.

When it comes to national soccer teams, this powerful sense of identification and *communitas* goes beyond clubs in domestic leagues (where both players and fans develop often-fierce rivalries against other teams and fellow compatriots) to generate national unity around a team that represents all of them despite other affiliations that divide them.[14] Of course, competition also exists among national teams at regional and international tournaments, which provide the perfect arena for the (mostly peaceful) reenactment of national rivalries or for the affirmation of national pride through memorable performances. The most celebrated and meaningful of these international tournaments is the men's FIFA (International Federation of Association Football) World Cup.[15] This competition began in 1930 and has become the planet's most popular single-sport event, barely lagging the Summer Olympics in worldwide viewership.[16] Any soccer-crazed nation dreams of winning or at the very least qualifying to the World Cup, which takes place every four years and gathers the best teams from each region (or confederation) of the world as established by FIFA rules. For the small nations of Central America, making it to this tournament has been historically difficult, as they would often be foiled in their efforts by Mexico—the traditional powerhouse team of the Confederation of North, Central American, and Caribbean Association Football (CONCACAF).[17] Both *Uno* and *Italia 90* revolve around historical firsts for El Salvador (scoring its first and so far only goal at a World Cup in 1982) and Costa Rica (qualifying for its first World Cup in 1990 and making it past the competition's group stage in a first for all of Central America). The documentary and the biopic center on those momentous occasions and the different meanings they had for each nation beyond the realm of sport.

Uno follows simple, chronological storytelling and employs techniques of the traditional documentary (archival footage; interviews with players, team staff, and sports journalists; and stills of newspaper clippings) to reconstruct the events leading up to the historic goal: the CONCACAF qualification process of 1981 and preparations for the tournament in Spain the following summer. However, it also exhibits characteristics of the sports film such as dualistic structures (to highlight regional rivalries and internal divisions), the use of key matches to punctuate important and dramatic moments in the plot, and a structure that revolves around the rise and fall of the (in this case collective) hero. Most importantly—as is the case in the films about Durán and also in *Italia 90*—the documentary exploits the theme of the underdog to generate affective engagement with its audience and to underscore the significance of this soccer feat in the particular context of El Salvador of the early 1980s.

Narratively speaking, *Uno* is a story of ups and downs and how the fate of a team can become intertwined with that of the country it represents. Hence, the documentary suggests that the recent history of El Salvador can also be read as a rollercoaster ride, with soccer functioning as a metaphor for the nation. After the initial sequences that provide context about the tumultuous late 1970s and 1980s in Central America (when civil wars and revolutions swept through the region), the film turns to sport and highlights the rise of Salvadoran soccer within CONCACAF. El Salvador was the first Isthmus country to qualify for a World Cup (Mexico 1970) but failed to score a single goal on that occasion as it was swept in the group stage's three games by a combined score of 9–0. In 1981, El Salvador had one of the best squads in its history, led by Jorge "El Mágico" González—who is regarded as the country's most talented player ever. The directors chose to focus on the November 6 game against Mexico, which "La Selecta" (as the national team is affectionately known) won 1–0 early on during the CONCACAF "Hexagonal" knock-off tournament played in Honduras. This was not the game that helped clinched qualification, but it's the one most remembered by Salvadorans because of the symbolic value of defeating CONCACAF's giant and helping to eventually eliminate it from the World Cup. After the euphoria of qualification, the documentary turns to the difficulties faced by the squad to properly prepare to compete in Spain (a sort of mini-low that has foreshadowing significance). Next comes the first game at the World Cup against Hungary, which El Salvador infamously lost 10–1—the widest-margin loss by any team in the men's tournament's history, even till today. While that game yielded the historic goal scored by "Pelé" Zapata, the lopsided loss was demoralizing and represented the lowest point for the players (who felt they had betrayed their compatriots back home), as well as national disappointment and shame. As forward Guillermo Lorenzana recalls, holding back tears: "I just kept thinking that what had just happened was not only going to affect us, but the country as well [. . .] We didn't deserve that."[18]

Uno presents two confrontations, on and off the pitch, that exploit the powerful dualistic nature of sports films and help to link sport with nation. The first confrontation is with an external rival and has geopolitical implications. Mexico has long overshadowed Central America like a big brother, as the former Aztec Empire and Viceroyalty of New Spain developed into one of the most populated and influential Latin American nations. This dominance translated into negative stereotyping, racism, and mutual animosity between the neighbors—eventually also spilling into soccer dynamics. That's why the victory over Mexico is so central to the documentary. Previous to the game, we see a Mexican newspaper clipping that mocks Salvadorans by joking "they play with a square ball." As TV footage of the game is shown, players recall how Salvadoran war refugees fleeing to the United States were mistreated and even raped as they crossed Mexico—a situation that still occurs today. Beating Mexico is thus celebrated as a form of poetic justice. The second confrontation is internal, as the documentary recalls how the civil war divided the country into two camps: the right-wing government and the leftist revolutionary movement. In the midst of this conflict, soccer becomes a refuge from daily violence and, according to coach Mauricio Rodríguez, "one of the few unifying agents in this country."[19] Journalists and players remember how not even the war could stop the team from playing at home during pre-Hexagonal elimination games and fans belonging to "both sides" from peacefully flocking to the national stadium. Defender Pancho Osorto also explains how the team understood the value of what they were doing for the aggrieved nation: "Our commitment was with the people who suffered day after day."[20]

Finally, *Uno* portrays the struggle to qualify for the World Cup and score that one precious goal through the underdog trope, where again athletes and the nation are presented as indistinguishable from each other. The opening scene already establishes this theme, showing (in the twenty-first-century present) barefoot children playing soccer in a poor community. The precarious condition of these shoeless players foreshadows (from the future) what would happen later on in the story to the national team—effectively criticizing how corruption from government and businesses elites continues to affect one of the countries with the highest levels of inequality in the continent at the time the documentary was produced.[21] El Salvador is also clearly treated as an underdog before their match against Mexico, where the team's strategy was to kick and frustrate Mexican "golden boy" forward Hugo Sánchez. As Osorto recalls, Sánchez (who had recently joined the Spanish league on his way to a highly successful professional career there) tried to insult him: "What you make in a year I make in a day."[22] Despite such stark difference, Osorto played in the World Cup; Sánchez did not.

While qualification to the World Cup was a great accomplishment within CONCACAF—one of FIFA's weakest confederations—El Salvador was far behind the level of the teams it would face in Spain (Hungary, Belgium, and Argentina). Still, their 10–1 loss in no way reflected the actual abilities of La Selecta. As players denounce, soccer federation leaders took money meant for preparing and equipping the team and spent it on themselves—to the point that players were forced to raise funds for their expenses. El Salvador was the last squad to arrive in Spain only three days before their first game, were housed in deplorable conditions, and did not even have balls or cleats to train. Adding insult to injury, the Spanish press mocked the raggedy athletes—shots of newspaper clippings show headlines calling El Salvador the tournament's "Cenicienta" (Cinderella) and asking, "Are these guerrilla fighters or footballers?"[23] In spite of such adversity, the team ended up showing resilience: in their next two games they played well, narrowly losing to Belgium (one of the tournament's best teams) and defending world champion Argentina. As team physician Juan Cálix proudly and optimistically states at the end of the documentary, "This tiny country, this 'Tom Thumb,' will always find a way forward."[24]

Italia 90 depicts a heroic tale similar to the one from *Uno* in many respects and also uses techniques from documentaries in addition to those more commonly associated with fiction films. For example, the opening sequence reenacts the game that booked Costa Rica its first trip to a World Cup—a 1–0 win at home against (coincidentally) El Salvador in 1989. The plot also follows a chronological trajectory and is structured around a series of victories and defeats that heighten the story's dramatism. Furthermore, Gómez constructs the biopic with a visual patchwork of fictionalized reenactments of moments shown on television plus more private situations from the players' lives as they prepared to compete in the World Cup; stock footage from TV broadcasts of games; and video shot by one of the players, which provides a unique first-person account. This use of historical footage and the careful reconstruction with actors of events known to Costa Ricans (including me) old enough to remember the 1990 tournament, lends the biopic a great deal of historical authenticity—while still leaving enough room for artistic freedom with the introduction of lesser-known twists and subplots. This search for authenticity may be explained by the fact that, as Costa Rican film scholar María Lourdes Cortés indicates, *Italia 90* "appeals to memory—the importance of remembering our past through an audiovisual medium—[and to] nostalgia" ("Fabulaciones" 174).[25]

However, the biopic seeks to elicit much more than nostalgia, and in this manner it differs significantly from *Uno* and even *Hands of Stone* (which does not use any archival footage). I argue that *Italia 90* also manages to create an historical and affective bridge between past (late 1980s and early 1990s) and present (2014, when the film was released shortly before Costa Rica debuted at the World Cup in Brazil). This seeks to activate multigenerational engagement and to relive the triumphs of the past in a contemporary setting when the country was going through a drought of any significant sporting accomplishments that most of the nation could be proud of. Following the soccer heroics of 1990 and the Olympic gold medal won by swimmer Claudia Poll in 1996, Costa Rica had not been able to outdo itself—and both older generations and those born after those years longed for such a feat. At the very least, the film could help older Costa Ricans revive the excitement they felt in the past through a highly emotional narrative full of nostalgia and show younger generations that, if it was done before, it could be done again. The film employs three main devices to connect past and present. First, there's the old TV set—which functions as a time machine of sorts. There, a family watches footage of the actual 1989–1990 games pieced together with shots of the actors who portray the players; the difference in stock, image, and color quality are so stark that it creates the sense that what we are seeing are images from two completely different historical times.

Second, the director cleverly cast some of the actual national team players to portray actors in the film—such as defender Mauricio Montero who, in a nod to *Back to the Future*, "travels" back in time to play his own father. In this manner, the historical present and the fictionalized past of the players are made to coexist in the diegesis of the biopic. Third, Gómez includes a scene in which actors play left back Enrique Díaz (who was cut from the team after qualification) and his son Júnior (who was six at the time). This foreshadowing is meaningful because Júnior Díaz—also a left back with similar looks and skills—vicariously fulfilled his father's dream of playing in a World Cup in 2014. Finally, these cinematic techniques were perfectly complemented by an extra-filmic event. As the biopic was playing in local theaters to great success, the 2014 national team surprised the soccer world once again and outperformed the 1990 team—finishing first in the tournament's "group of death" after defeating former world champions Uruguay and Italy, beating Greece in the round of 16, and finishing among the top eight teams after being eliminated by the Netherlands in a dramatic penalty shootout. Costa Ricans who watched the movie and the squad's performance that summer were able to consume the glories of the past and the present at the same time.[26]

Similar to the ways in which Durán and the Salvadoran team became inextricably associated with their respective nations during times of need, 'La Sele' (nickname for the Costa Rican national squad) consolidated itself as a national symbol thanks to its exploits leading up to and in Italy (Sandoval García 80). In the absence of foreign occupation or war, the team's success meant different things for this nation. Since soccer both unifies a country internally and legitimizes it externally (Sandoval García 83), the global buzz generated by Costa Rica's heroic performance helped the country enhance its international image as it sought to develop its now world-famous ecotourism industry and attract foreign investment. On a less positive note, La Sele's morale-boosting victories also coincided with the deterioration of state institutions and other imaginaries of the Costa Rican nation that started in the 1980s as a result of the economic crisis and neoliberal policies whose implementation began back then—and which mostly benefited the banking and exporting sectors while slowly dismantling the welfare state, increasing inequality, and generating pessimism about the future (Sandoval García 74–77). As sports journalist Arnoldo Rivera has noted, "Soccer is the last remaining activity of which Costa Ricans feel proud" (quoted in Sandoval García 75).[27]

Italia 90 re-creates this sense of pride and identification by portraying the national soccer squad as an underdog and as a collective hero (Cortés, "Fabulaciones" 174) that represents individuals from various backgrounds, races, and regions of the country. In this way, the characters who get the most screen time include Juan Cayasso (an Afro-Costa Rican who scored the team's first goal at the World Cup), Claudio Jara (who assisted in that first goal and who comes from a working-class family in the city), Mauricio Montero (a "polo" or hick from the country known for his linguistic gaffes), and future national team coach Alexandre Guimaraes (who is white, immigrated from Brazil as a child, and is the only player of the group to own a camcorder). This collective hero not only carries the hopes and dreams of the nation, but also represents its diversity. Additionally, Gómez chooses to employ a family as a narrative tool to entwine the fate of the players with the fate of everyday Costa Ricans who experienced the team's triumphs mainly through television—thus further strengthening the links between team and nation. In the qualification game scene, a wide shot reveals several members of the Jara family in their living room getting ready to watch Claudio play. Among them is younger brother and also player Geovanny, who later on is unexpectedly called up by the national team and travels to the World Cup along with Claudio. The aspirational message is clear: the national team is all of us, and we all are the national team—so much so that one day we are at home watching La Sele play as any other fan, while the next day we may literally join the team.

While class, race, and background are successfully incorporated into a narrative of national equality, the biopic reveals the preponderance of masculinity as the dominant discourse around which the Costa Rica nation is organized. As men play the role of heroes as coaches and players, most of the women shown in the film perform traditional roles of domesticity and emotional labor that allow men to go out and do their heroic stuff: a lady who washes the national team's uniforms prior to the game versus El Salvador, the wives who dutifully support their husbands and take care of their children while they are away competing, the homemaker who prepares and serves snacks to her family as they watch the game, and the Jaras' religious mother who prays to another woman (the Virgin Mary) for intervention in favor of her children.

Lastly, the film overemphasizes the Costa Rican national team's status as an underdog in order to maximize the heroic nature of its accomplishments. Most of the players are shown as coming from humble backgrounds, especially Montero—who upon receiving the news that he made the World Cup roster, runs (machete at his side) to the sugarcane field where his father is working. After delivering the news, the soon-to-be national idol joins his father and other workers in the harvest. (In her chapter in this volume about another of Gómez's films, *Maikol Yordan de viaje perdido,* Liz Harvey-Kattou explores in detail the prevalence of the campesino trope in Costa Rican popular culture.) The fact that the Costa Rican soccer league back then was amateur or semi-professional at best, is reflected in the fact that the players don't make a lot of money and many work other jobs to support their families. As Serbian coach Velibor "Bora" Milutinović was hired to take over the helm just ninety days before the World Cup, he met his new players and asked them to introduce themselves. When it was midfielder Róger Gómez's turn, Bora added: "You are the policeman," further reminding viewers about the players' working-class status. Milutinović was recruited because he had World Cup experience, having coached Mexico in 1986 to great success. Also, he was known for being a stickler for discipline and physical conditioning (things La Sele was sorely lacking) and for using psychological tools such as visualization and motivational talks to get the best out of his players.

In an almost-comical scene where fictional sports films prove their value by helping real-life underdog athletes believe in themselves, Bora discusses the *Rocky* movies with his pupils: "Do you understand? You are Rocky. And people don't value what you do. When someone says, 'it can't be done,' I say 'yes we can do it' [. . .] You are going to cause a stir at the World Cup."[28] The final part of the film focuses on Costa Rica's disappointing performances and scorelines during warm-up games, constant criticism from the local press, lack of adequate equipment and uniforms, and predictions from the Italian media that the team would lose all games 5–0. In the end, the Central American "Rocky" went on to defeat Scotland 1–0, narrowly lose to former world champion Brazil by one goal, and eliminate Sweden by a score of 2–1. The tournament's "Cinderella" (as Costa Rica was dubbed by the press) had just crashed the party of its supposedly superior European rivals. Interestingly enough, the film does not re-create Costa Rica's games in the World Cup (which in a typical sports film would have represented the moment of climax), but ends instead in a foreshadowing of the events about to take place: inside the tunnel before entering the pitch to take on Scotland, the Tico players overcome their nerves by jumping, screaming, and otherwise trying to intimidate their rivals. Since the film was created for a local audience that knows well how the story ends, perhaps the director felt there was no need for reenacting the actual games. What Gómez does include as the credits roll is TV footage of the team's most memorable moments at the World Cup, which adds an element of historical accuracy and a documentary feel to the film as it ends.

Concluding Remarks

The study of Central American sports films shows us that while this genre was practically non-existent in the 1900s, it is becoming an important component of the region's cinematic production in the current century. This body of work encompasses the major sub-genres of this type of cinema, including documentaries, biopics, and feature-length fictional movies ranging from dramas to comedies. They also reflect the production and distribution trends that characterize Central American film in the twenty-first century: popular films financed locally and for the domestic market (such as *Italia 90*), international coproductions for the Hollywood market (such as *Hands of Stone*), and international coproductions for the festival circuit (such as *La Yuma*). This chapter focused on four boxing and soccer films (documentaries and biopics) that deal with historical events and figures. Their analysis reveals that both sport and the narratives about sport told in these movies are intimately connected with the construction of imaginaries that rely on discourses of national unity and masculinity. Furthermore, these films portray sporting victories or defeats as metaphors for the victories or defeats of their respective nations during times of political turbulence or uncertainty. Because only two of the sports films made in Central America during this century tell the story of female athletes (*Estrellas de la línea* and *La Yuma*), it is important to consider why directors and producers have chosen to ignore the growing participation of Central American women in sport and their achievements—which readers can learn more about in Brenda Elsey and Joshua Nadel's *Futbolera: A History of Women and Sports in Latin America* (2019). In her research about female boxing in Mexico, Hortensia Moreno asks, "Can a female athlete embody the spirit of a nation?" She seems to answer her own question: "The study of sports teaches us that the essence of the practice traditionally lies in the construction and consolidation of masculinity" (182). Will Central American directors step up to the plate and change this representational and power dynamics? Will the next biopic recognize, for example, the as-of-yet unparalleled achievement of Olympic gold medalist Claudia Poll? This story is a film still awaiting its spoiler alert.

Notes

1. These documentaries include *Terceros Juegos de Centroamérica y el Caribe* (Alfredo Massi, El Salvador, 1935) and *VI Juegos Centroamericanos* (Marcel Reichenbach, Guatemala, 1950), about regional sporting competitions; *Pasaporte al Mundial* (José David Calderón, El Salvador, 1968), about the Salvadoran national soccer team's qualification to the 1970 World Cup; and *María del Milagro* (Guillermo Munguía, Costa Rica, 1983), about Costa Rican swimmer María del Milagro París, the first athlete in the country's history who made it to a final round at the Olympics, in Moscow 1980.
2. Assertion based on an analysis of twentieth-century filmography compiled by María Lourdes Cortés in *La pantalla rota: Cien años de cine en Centroamérica* (565–589).
3. I have chosen to use "soccer" instead of "football," as it is the most commonly used name for this sport in the United States. However, I have employed "football" in a few occasions when it is part of an official name (FIFA, for example) or when it refers to historical events such as the "Football War" where its use is standard.
4. Also known as the "100 Hour War," the conflict occurred in 1969, three weeks after El Salvador defeated Honduras in a June 27 decisive match in which the winner would qualify to the 1970 World Cup in Mexico. While the game has been overhyped as the reason for the short-lived but deadly war, it was a merely a trigger as tensions over land disputes and migration between the neighboring nations finally boiled over (Luckhurst).
5. The Mesoamerican ballgame has been the subject of several cinematic depictions, such as the documentary *Ulama* (Roberto Rochín, Mexico, 1986). The game is also played in scenes from the animated films *Popol Vuh: The Creation Myth of the Maya* (Patricia

Amlin, United States, 1989) and *The Road to El Dorado* (Bibo Bergeron, Don Paul, and Jeffrey Katzenber, United States, 2000).
6. "Guerra ritual entre naciones."
7. "Vínculos comunitarios cargados de intensidad afectiva."
8. For all quotes from *Los puños de una nación* that are originally in Spanish, I use the English subtitles provided by the film.
9. Durán repeatedly called Leonard a "clown" and a "ballerina," mocking and feminizing the boxer's signature dancing style in the ring. He also resented Leonard's "privileged" upbringing and the attention media paid to his made-for-TV appearance: "I didn't like Leonard because he was the pretty boy for the Americans and I didn't care less about him. I used to tell myself that I was going to beat the shit out of that American so he will respect us Latin Americans" (quoted in Giudice 181).
10. Here I use the English subtitles provided in the DVD version of the film. The main characters speak Spanish or English, depending on the context.
11. The documentary includes a wide variety of musical genres (calypso, bolero, salsa, hip-hop) that highlight Panama's racial and cultural hybridity and help to quickly identify specific historical times addressed in the film.
12. "desde el que amplios sectores sociales se identifican con la nación."
13. *Communitas* is a concept developed by anthropologist Victor Turner.
14. Because of the intrinsic ambivalence of how soccer operates, this sport becomes a ritual of affirmation of identities that "unites at the same time that it divides" ["que al tiempo que une, también divide"] (Sandoval García 32).
15. This reflects the historical association between soccer, ideas about the nation, and masculinity. As the sport became more popular among women later in the twentieth century, FIFA added a Women's World Cup starting in 1991. It also organized youth world cups (U-17 and U-20) in 1977, which now include both men and women.
16. See Jackman, https://the18.com/en/soccer-learning/world-cup-vs-olympics-tv-ratings.
17. Of the Central American countries where soccer is the main national pastime, Guatemala is the only one that has never qualified to a World Cup. This fact has become demoralizing for the Isthmus's most populous nation and is reflected in films such as *Hasta el Sol tiene manchas* (Julio Hernández Cordón, Mexico/Guatemala, 2012), where populist politician Manuel Baldizón pledges to take Guatemala to the elusive tournament if he's elected president. This film is analyzed in Júlia González de Canales Carcereny's chapter in this volume.
18. "Pensando que todo lo que habíamos hecho no solo nos iba a afectar a nosotros, sino al país [...] No merecíamos eso."
19. "Uno de los pocos factores unificadores en este país."
20. "Nuestro compromiso era con la gente que sufría día a día."
21. See "El Salvador," https://www.oxfam.org/en/what-we-do/countries/el-salvador.
22. "Lo que tú ganas en un año yo gano en un día."
23. "¿Son guerrilleros o futbolistas?"
24. "Este paisito, este Pulgarcito, va a salir a flote siempre." As the smallest country in continental America, El Salvador is affectionately called 'El Pulgarcito de America'—a reference to the diminutive character Tom Thumb from English folklore.

25 "El filme apela a la memoria—la importancia de recordar nuestro pasado por medio del audiovisual—, a la nostalgia."
26 Costa Rica's unexpected performance helped the film's success at the box office, attracting 100,000 people (Cortés, "Fabulaciones" 175).
27 "El fútbol es la última actividad en que el costarricense se siente orgulloso."
28 Spoken with a Serbian accent and some incorrect Spanish grammar: "¿Entienden? Rocky es ustedes. Y gente no valora que ustedes hacen. Cuando alguien dice 'no se puede,' yo digo 'se puede' [. . .] Ustedes van a ser sensación del Mundial."

Works Cited

Arbena, Joseph L. and David G. LaFrance. "Introduction." *Sport in Latin America and the Caribbean*, edited by Joseph L. Arbena and David G. LaFrance, Scholarly Resources Inc., 2002, pp. xi-xxxi.

Billig, Michael. *Banal Nationalism*. London: Sage Publications, 1995.

Bonzel, Katharina. *National Pastimes: Cinema, Sports, and Nation*. Lincoln: U of Nebraska P, 2020.

Cook, Pam. "Masculinity in Crisis?" *Screen*, vol. 23, no 3-4, 1982, pp. 39-46.

Corpas, Jose. "The Secret Story of the Groundbreaking Boxing Champ Who Lost His Title—Because He Was Gay." *Narratively*, 15 June 2017, https://narratively.com/the-secret-story-of-the-groundbreaking-boxing-champ-who-lost-his-title-because-he-was-gay/. Accessed 20 October 2020.

Cortés, María Lourdes. *Fabulaciones del nuevo cine costarricense*. San José: Uruk, 2016.

———. *La pantalla rota: Cien años de cine en Centroamérica*. Ciudad de México: Taurus, 2005.

Crosson, Séan. *Sport and Film*. New York: Routledge, 2013.

Donoghue, Michael. "Roberto Durán, Omar Torrijos, and the Rise of Isthmian Machismo." *Sports Culture in Latin American History*, edited by David M. K. Sheinin, U of Pittsburgh P, 2015, pp. 17-38.

El Centerfielder. Directed by Ramiro Lacayo, INCINE, Nicaragua, 1985.

"El Salvador." *OxFam International*, https://www.oxfam.org/en/what-we-do/countries/el-salvador. Accessed 3 November 2020.

Elsey, Brenda and Joshua Nadel. *Futbolera: A History of Women and Sports in Latin America*. Austin: U of Texas P, 2019.

El trofeo. Directed by Miguel Salguero, Costa Rica, 2004.

Espinoza, Mauricio. "El Corazón del Juego: El Juego de Pelota Mesoamericano como Texto Cultura en la Narrativa y el Cine Contemporáneo." *Istmo: Revista virtual de estudios literarios y culturales centroamericanos*, no. 3, 2002, http://istmo.denison.edu/n04/proyectos/corazon.html. Accessed 11 November 2020.

Estrellas de la línea. Directed by Chema Rodríguez, Producciones Sin un duro/Telespan, Guatemala/Spain, 2006.

Fernández L'Hoeste, Héctor et al. "Introduction." *Sport and Nationalism in Latin/o America*, edited by Héctor Fernández L'Hoeste et al., Palgrave MacMillan, 2015, pp. 1-26.

Fuller, Linda K. "'The Triumph of the Underdog' in Baseball Films." *Beyond the Stars: Studies in American Popular Film*, vol. 2, edited by Paul Loukides and Linda K. Fuller, Bowling Green State UP, 1991, pp. 53–60.

Gems, Gerald R. *Boxing: A Concise History of the Sweet Science*. Lanham: Rowman & Littlefield, 2014.

Giudice, Christian. *Hands of Stone: The Life and Legend of Roberto Durán*. Lancashire: Milo Books, 2006.

Grindon, Leger. *Knockout: The Boxer and Boxing in American Cinema*. Jackson: U of Mississippi P, 2011.

Hands of Stone. Directed by Jonathan Jakubowicz, Fuego Films, United States/Panama, 2016.

Hasta el Sol tiene manchas. Directed by Julio Hernández Cordón, Melindrosa Films, Mexico/Guatemala, 2012.

Iber, Jorge et al. *Latinos in U.S. Sport: A History of Isolation, Cultural Identity, and Acceptance*. Champaign: Human Kinetics, 2011.

Invasión. Directed by Abner Benaim, Ajimolido Films/Apertura Films, Panama, 2014.

Italia 90. Directed by Miguel Gómez, Italia 90 La Película S.A., Costa Rica, 2014.

Jackman, Spencer. "The World Cup and Olympics Are In A League of their Own When It Comes to TV Ratings." *The 18*, 12 June 2018, https://the18.com/en/soccer-learning/world-cup-vs-olympics-tv-ratings. Accessed 12 September 2020.

Jones, Glen. "In praise of an 'invisible genre'? An ambivalent look at the fictional sports feature film." *Sport in Films*, edited by Emma Poulton and Martin Roderick, Routledge, 2008, pp. 1–13.

Keylor Navas: Hombre de fe. Directed by Dinga Haines, PCP Productora, Costa Rica, 2017.

Kimura. Directed by Aldo Rey Valderrama, Tiempo Real, Panama, 2017.

La fuerza del balón. Directed by Alberto Serra, WP Films, Panama, 2016.

La Yuma. Directed by Florence Jaugey, Camila Films/Ivania Films/Wanda Visión, Mexico/Nicaragua/Spain, 2009.

Los puños de una nación. Directed by Pituka Ortega-Heilbron, Hypatia Films, Panama, 2005.

Luckhurst, Toby. "Honduras v El Salvador: The football match that kicked off a war." *BBC News*, 26 June 2019, https://www.bbc.com/news/world-latin-america-48673853. Accessed 2 November 2020.

María del Milagro. Directed by Guillermo Munguía, CCPC, Costa Rica, 1983.

McGehee, Richard V. "Sport in Nicaragua, 1889–1926." *Sport in Latin America and the Caribbean*, edited by Joseph L. Arbena and David G. LaFrance, Scholarly Resources Inc., 2002, pp. 175–205.

Moreno, Hortensia: "Women Boxers and Nationalism in Mexico." *Sports and Nationalism in Latin/o America*, edited by Héctor Fernández L'Hoeste et al., Palgrave MacMillan, 2015, pp. 181–200.

Nadel, Joshua H. *Fútbol! Why Soccer Matters in Latin America*. Gainesville: UP of Florida, 2014.

Pasaporte al Mundial. Directed by José David Calderón, El Salvador, 1968.

Pomerance, Murray. "The Dramaturgy of Action and Involvement in Sports Film." *Quarterly Review of Film and Video*, vol. 23, no. 4, 2006, pp. 311–29.

Popol Vuh: The Creation Myth of the Maya. Directed by Patricia Amlin, Berkeley Media LLC, United States, 1989.

Rowe, David. "Time and timelessness in sport film." *Sport in Films,* edited by Emma Poulton and Martin Roderick, Routledge, 2008, pp. 30-42.

Sandoval García, Carlos. *Fuera de juego: Fútbol, identidades nacionales y masculinidades en Costa Rica.* San José: Editorial de la U de Costa Rica, 2007.

Terceros Juegos de Centroamérica y el Caribe. Directed by Alfredo Massi, El Salvador, 1935.

The Road to El Dorado. Directed by Bibo Bergeron, Don Paul, and Jeffrey Katzenber, DreamWorks, United States, 2000.

Thorn, John. "Panama Baseball: A Brief History." *Our Game,* 10 March 2104, https://ourgame.mlblogs.com/panama-baseball-a-brief-history-e601281f1c8d. Accessed 10 November 2019.

Ulama. Directed by Roberto Rochín, MEJIKA, Mexico, 1986.

Uno: La historia de un gol. Directed by Gerardo Muyshondt and Carlos Moreno, Antorcha Films, El Salvador/Colombia, 2010.

Urbina, Chester. *Costa Rica y el deporte (1873-1921). Un estudio acerca del origen del fútbol y la construcción de un deporte nacional.* Heredia: EUNA, 2001.

Van Sterkenburg, Jacco and Ramón Spaaij. "Introduction." *Mediated Football: Representations and audience receptions of race/ethnicity, nation and gender,* edited by Jacco van Sterkenburg and Ramón Spaaij, Routledge, 2016, pp. 1-11.

VI Juegos Centroamericanos. Directed by Marcel Reichenbach, Guatemala, 1950.

Villena Fiengo, Sergio. "El fútbol y las identidades: Prólogo a los estudios latinoamericanos." *Futbologías: Fútbol, identidad y violencia en América Latina,* edited by Pablo Alabarces, CLACSO, 2003, pp. 21-35.

———. "Gol-balización, identidades nacionales y fútbol." *Futbologías: Fútbol, identidad y violencia en América Latina,* edited by Pablo Alabarces, CLACSO, 2003, pp. 257-271.

Wacquant, Loïc J.D. "The Social Logic of Boxing in Black Chicago: Toward a Sociology of Pugilism." *Sociology of Sport Journal,* vol. 9, no. 3, 1992, pp. 221-254.

Whittingon, E. Michael, editor. *The Sport of Life and Death: The Mesoamerican Ballgame.* New York: Thames and Hudson, 2001.

11 cipotes. Directed by Tomás Chi, Enserio Producciones, Honduras, 2014.

90 minutos. Directed by Aeden O'Connor, Pulsar, Honduras, 2019.

100 horas de furia. Directed by Alejandro Irías, B'alam Entertainment, Honduras, 2020.

11

Toward a Central American Counter Cinema

The Films of Tatiana Huezo and Julio Hernández Cordón

Júlia González de Canales Carcereny

Tatiana Huezo's and Julio Hernández Cordón's films have contributed to take Central American cinema center stage in the international art house filmic scene. Their films have become a cinematic benchmark worldwide, shaping present-day Central American and Latin American art house cinema. However, how do Huezo's and Hernández Cordón's film aesthetics belong in terms of global art house filmmaking? Drawing on Peter Wollen's study on Jean-Luc Godard's counter films and Thomas Elsaesser's claims regarding Third World's counter cinema, as well as on Ruby B. Rich's examination of Third Cinema's goal to decolonize cinematic language (272), this chapter examines the aesthetic characteristics of Huezo's *El lugar más pequeño* (El Salvador, 2011) and Hernández Cordón's *Hasta el Sol tiene manchas* (Guatemala, 2012) to demonstrate how these directors' film aesthetics have led to some of the currently most groundbreaking Central American film productions. More specifically, I first examine the multiple meanings that the notion of counter cinema has historically had. I then explore how contemporary Central American counter cinema critically reassesses its legacy from both the aesthetic modes of Third Cinema and Central American political cinema from the 1980s. In light of this historic-critical cinematographic framework, I argue that Huezo's *El lugar más pequeño* and Hernández Cordón's *Hasta el Sol tiene manchas* employ experimental visualization and differentiation procedures in order to perform counter cinematographic strategies that subvert the cinematographic narrative normativity.[1]

On Counter Cinema

What is counter cinema? Richard Rushton understands it as a filmmaking that, being inspired by the Marxist theories of Bertolt Brecht and Louis Althusser, "opposes the dominance of the commercial cinema associated with Hollywood" (117). This definition clearly draws on Peter Wollen's previous claims on the matter. Wollen understands counter cinema as a filmmaking practice that opposes commercial film productions and presents seven main aesthetic traits:

> (1) narrative intransitivity—created by interrupting and breaking the diegesis of a film;[2] (2) estrangement—provoked either by directly addressing spectators or by employing the same voice for different characters, making it difficult for spectators to identify with them; (3) foregrounding—produced by emphasizing the film's mechanisms of composition (such as camera movements or editing);[3] (4) multiple diegesis—created by portraying a heterogeneous and incoherent world that blends in characters coming from a different time and space;[4] (5) aperture—observed both in films that have an open-endedness and in intertextual films, as intertextuality offers multiple levels of comprehension; (6) unpleasure—provoked in films that avoid entertainment, as they may disturb spectators' expectations; and (7) reality—forged in films that avoid representing an imaginary world, unrelated to our factual environment. ("Godard and Counter Cinema" 500–509)

Not by coincidence, these films often include non-actors who, rather that acting, portray their own living circumstances.

As pointed out by Thomas Elsaesser, Peter Wollen's claims on counter cinema are neither exclusive of a single filmmaker nor of a specific film era. They rather correspond to all counter normative films that involve "a film-politics that would challenge the economic supremacy of Hollywood, its monopolistic distribution and exhibition system not only in the countries of Europe but also in the Third World" (Elsaesser 120). Thus, counter cinema needs to be understood as transversal filmmaking that embraces both Third Cinema's condemnation and protests, which occurred in France in May of 1968, as well as present-day Latin American sociocultural demands.[5] As Ruby B. Rich claimed:

> [Third Cinema] was an oppositional cinema at every level, self-consciously searching out new forms for the new sentiments of a Latin American reality just being recovered. It was a cinema dedicated to

decolonialization at every level including, frequently, that of cinematic language. A cinema of necessity, it was different things in different countries: in Cuba, an "imperfect cinema"; in Brazil, an "aesthetics of hunger"; in Argentina, a "third cinema." (227)

This citation is in line with Fernando Solanas's and Octavio Getino's demand to decolonize cultural audiovisual works.[6] Godard, Solanas, Getino, and Rich asserted that to decolonize the film language means to understand art as a social transformation agent—particularly in nonconformist societies that struggle with their economic classes—but also to examine what intrafilmic strategies contribute to develop spectators' critical mechanisms toward the world they are living in. Two common methods were employed by both counter cinema and Third Cinema to develop the audience's critical gaze: the use of both non-Aristotelian theatrical schemes and queer strategies of representation.

Drawing on Bertolt Brecht's claims on non-Aristotelian theater, counter cinema aims to create a *Verfremdungseffekt* (distancing effect) on audiences. That is to say, by avoiding any sense of belonging between spectators and characters,[7] counter cinema eludes the spectator's thoughtless gaze and compels the audience to see and rethink the everyday oddness of their lives. Moreover, counter cinema is closely related to queer fluid structures. Following Rosalind Galt and Karl Schoonover:

> to assert a queer structure of feeling is to valorise non-linear models of influence, to nourish discursively unstable categories of being, to allow that which is "in solution" to matter, and to resist efforts to banish the more dynamic and disruptive modes of experience as "incompressible," "over styled" or "decadent." (352)

In other words, counter cinema understands counter normative films as queer films that question alleged fixed identities and gender structures and propose a fluid understanding of the world.[8] Accordingly, counter normative films employ a heterogeneous range of formal stylistic strategies. Drawing on Nick Davis's claims, queer films result from Gilles Deleuze's and Félix Guattari's understanding of minor literature as both queer films and minor literature master the same triple challenge: "*deterritorializing* sense and syntax from their usual frameworks; *politicizing* these renegotiated structures; and endowing them with a *collective* value, less on behalf of existing minorities than for new coalitions they catalyze among the oppressed and invisible, along previous unrecognizable lines" (Davis 5). Thus, counter cinematic filmmakers experiment with film form, averting the more common narrative commercial styles. By showing their minority films in international film festivals their works are, on the one hand, institutionalized by the same public bodies that aim to promote alternative narrative strategies. On the other hand, the social-political and cultural demands portrayed in their films are amplified and acknowledged by viewers around the world.

In the following sections, some selected examples of contemporary Central American independent art house cinema will be examined as a case example of counter cinema. I will focus on Huezo's and Hernández Cordón's films as representatives of self-reflective works that experiment with modes of representation, employing Brecht's postulates to artistically reflect on both the present-day Central American sociopolitical context and its artistic characteristics.

From Third Cinema to Contemporary Central American Counter Cinema

Contemporary Central American counter cinema is to be understood as a critical reassessment from the aesthetic modes of Third Cinema and the Central American political film productions from the 1980s. Discussing Third Cinema well into the twenty-first century may seem anachronistic. However, I understand Third Cinema from a non-reductionist perspective, as a result of a variety of filmmaking practices (neorealism, didactic cinema, essay-films) created in the 1950s—in countries such as Argentina, Cuba, Brazil, or Chile—and later displayed in the well-known artistic-theoretical manifests of Glauber Rocha, Fernando Solanas, Octavio Getino, and Julio García Espinosa. Although each Central American country has found its way to cinematographically mirror its own historic-sociopolitical and cultural features, contemporary Central American counter cinema has taken an aesthetically similar path to present-day Latin American counter cinema. As explored elsewhere, the development of both national and regional filmmaking practices in Central America worked, in the 1970s, through the appropriation of the heritage of New Latin American cinema. Over the 1970s and 1980s, Central American cinema mostly produced nationalist anti-imperialist and revolutionary films that expressed the diverse national identities of the region. These films addressed themes such as social discrimination, violence, and Indigenous struggles. The period 1972–1986 was especially prolific for production of sociopolitical documentaries in the Isthmus (Cortés, *La pantalla rota* 208) but, in the postwar period, disenchantment prevailed. According to Beatriz Cortez, filmmakers and national film institutes lost their convictions in drastically eradicating the prevalent neo-colonialist system. Instead, they critically rethought the diverse Central American local and regional realities by employing fictional narrative strategies that mirrored social injustice as a way to reform the system. Due to the emergence of video, the loss of support to film institutions, the rise of independent productions, and the professionalization of young filmmakers abroad, the audiovisual scene of the region was transformed (Cortés, *La pantalla rota* 540). In the present day, Central American cinema has continued to expose sociopolitical inequalities, albeit narrations about the collective "we" have turned into stories about the filmmaker's intimate "I" (Cabezas Vargas and González de Canales Carcereny 167). Moreover, these films continue to present themselves against dominant mainstream commercial dynamics imposed by Hollywood.[9] However, what historical transformations led to present-day critical reassessment of the aesthetic modes of Third Cinema?

Italian neorealism and militant cinema shaped Third Cinema both in Central and Latin America. Yet, as pointed out by John Hess, in contrast to Italian neorealist films, Third Cinema films "are about people in a specific present context and not about their evolving relation to that context" (115). That is to say, such films aimed to be an active part of a sociopolitical revolution in the Latin American continent rather than to only portray its social dynamics of injustice and misfortune. Both *La Hora de Los Hornos* (Solanas and Getino, Argentina, 1968) and *La tierra prometida* (Miguel Littín, Chile/Cuba, 1973) are well-known examples of Third Cinema. According to Robert Stam, these films portray the main Third Cinema features "(1) their constitutive hybridity; (2) their chronotopic multiplicity; and (3) their common motif of redemption detritus" ("Beyond Third Cinema" 32). Moreover, some years later, Robert Stam himself further reflected on the conceptual issues related to Third Cinema, claiming that:

> (1) Three-worlds theory not only flattens heterogeneities, masks and contradictions, and elides differences, but also obscures similarities; (2) Third-worldism might even hinder Third World cinema's chances in the world; (3) The concept of Third World Cinema elides the presence of a "Fourth World." (*Film Theory* 282–283)

Following this line of argument, Ella Shohat asserted the need to rethink the category of Third Cinema after its most militant years (56). After the military dictatorships that occurred in the continent in the 1970s, filmmakers gradually abandoned a militant rhetoric and embraced a conception of Third Cinema as an open category. Moreover, in the 1980s, filmmakers such as Tomás Gutiérrez Alea and Fernando Solanas embraced authorial aesthetics, focusing on their personal artistic expression. As Marvin D'Lugo pointed out, they became:

> authorial icons representing their national culture within the global market [and] their well-established reputations as oppositional, anti-status quo, resistance figures had become refigured as national auteurs, principally through international film festivals which privileged the authorial as an expression of the national. (110)

In light of these words, I claim that three main characteristics resemble filmmakers of the 1980s and those of the present-day art house Central American cinema: (a) the renouncement of revolutionary manifests; (b) the blending of local and global contexts; and (c) the acknowledgment of their works by international film festivals. Thus, present-day art house Central American cinema has turned revolutionary demands into less propagandist, yet socially critical works. They do not have the socialist shape suggested by Getino and Solanas but show a local awareness: the place where these films are created, which resources filmmakers have available, and who belongs to the film crew. That is to say, present-day art house Central American cinema is located in what Teshome Gabriel referred to as a *gray area*: the ambiguous sphere that blends authorial cinema's and Third Cinema's interests.

Central American counter cinema draws on this line of argument and portrays Deleuze's ideas on how to break with colonial discourses: it shows characters that do not act but rather see and feel.[10] Thus, by employing non-actors, Central American counter films distance themselves from impersonal imaginaries and discourses of truth imposed by a dominant North visually explaining the Latin American continent. In that way, Central American counter cinema created its own "local narrative voice" (Moretti 65). This local voice is however framed by global financial, commercial, and exhibition conditions. Following María Lourdes Cortés, the boost experienced in the twenty-first century by Central American cinema and its increased visibility on the international scene results from the international cooperation and financial contributions made by European and North American film industries in order to foster auteur independent films in the region ("Filmmaking in Central America. An Overview" 151–154). The resulting local-global dialectic, however, does not homogenize Central American counter cinematic productions but rather "produces compromise film forms that are often as hybrid and ambivalent as the subjects that such movies represent" (Andrew 13). Finally, these Central American counter cinematic works blend these postulates with new queer cinema claims. As pointed out by Helen Hok-Sze Leung:

many new queer cinemas are emerging, from the margins and interstices of the global power. These films are queer . . . because they unsettle current notions of history and politics while going against conventional paradigms of filmmaking. Most of all, they answer to the legacies of Third Cinema by remaining on the side of the disaffected and disenfranchised. (166)

As will be explored in the following section, Huezo's and Hernández Cordón's films portray these arguments.

Huezo's and Hernández Cordón's Films

Huezo and Hernández Cordón lead present-day Central American counter cinema because their locally based films have taken center stage in the international film scene and critics around the world have praised their counter-aesthetics. Their films portray the above-mentioned three main characteristics that connect the revised Third Cinema's aesthetics from the 1980s with present-day art house Latin American cinema, as well as Peter Wollen's claims on counter cinema. All their films report sociopolitical injustice and war crimes, blend both local and global contexts, and have gained international acknowledgment.[11] Moreover, their films present a narrative intransitivity, produce estrangement and displeasure to the audience, employ foregrounding strategies, a multiple diegesis, have an open ending, and reject an illusionary representation of reality. For the purposes of this study, this section will focus on Huezo's and Hernández Cordón's most experimental Central American film productions—being their latterly produced Mexican films only occasionally mentioned to support the main line of argument.

El lugar más pequeño is Huezo's first feature film and reassesses Third Cinema's claims, rejecting the postrevolutionary filmic modes that in the 1980s were in vogue while it portrays the life story of survivors of the Cinquera massacre, who years after the end of the Salvadoran civil war, returned to the devastated village of Cinquera in order to rebuild it. According to Kaitlin M. Murphy, the film aims to "represent the unrepresentable," that is to say, it gives voice to those who have suffered from the extermination against their communities (588). Rather than employing militant aesthetics, Huezo creates a film based on "the aesthetic process of mapping the affective, polyvocal, temporally layered relationship between past and present as experienced by individuals and the communities in which they live" (Murphy 571). This process draws on the audiovisual composition and the central role that image and sound play. Hand in hand with the memories of Cinquera's citizens,

Huezo introduces the testimonies of the war's brutality, placing them halfway between the past traumatic memories and the joyful feeling of living. According to Yansi Pérez, by doing so Huezo follows Jorge Semprún's ability to go beyond the representation of grief, coming into being (122). This approach is clearly observed in *El lugar más pequeño*'s opening scene. In it, the spectator hears a voice-over that recalls the hard return journey of five families to the village (Cinquera) that some decades earlier they had abandoned to survive the carnage. Further, the voice-over relates the strong impression they had when they finally reached the old Cinquera: they saw nothing, the village did not exist anymore; they only found crumbling houses, the church bell, dead bodies, and many snakes. Huezo combines this heartbreaking narration with images of dawn, a rich blue-violet sky, as well as with images of dim treetops.

As the film progresses, the director shows the faces of the main characters, which never speak to the camera and perform everyday tasks. By doing so, the Salvadoran filmmaker disassociates image from sound. In Huezo's terms:

With one fleeting exception all the stories [in *The Tiniest Place*] were only recorded with audio because of a formal decision made beforehand not to put a camera in front of people. I had a strong desire to experiment, to find a less conventional aesthetic approach to the subject. Form in a movie is half the movie. I wanted to film from the point of view of a ghost, because they live among ghosts. (Cardenas)

Huezo also employs direct sound to capture the jungle's noises (birds, wind, rain, etc.), as well as the noises of the village's daily activities (children playing, stores opening, women doing laundry, etc.). These jungle images perfectly reflect the haptic condition of *El lugar más pequeño*. For instance, the close-ups of ants moving forward through the foliage are combined with background sounds of strident crickets chirping, and the aerial shot that reflects the fog's thickness stagnant in the valley. Such images also contribute to create the story's sensorial background: the jungle's sounds set the spectators in wait for the unknown dangers that might unexpectedly occur in the wild environment, and the apparently motionless fog projects the painful sphere of past death and struggle. Thus, by blending her personal reassessment of the documentary film form with a slow narrative time, and developing an unproductive cinematic time, Huezo places *El lugar más pequeño* in the slow cinema framework. Following on from Karl Schoonover's claim on slow cinema, the film aims to "encourage us to consider how watching wasted screen time differs from wasting time in real life" (65). Thus, Huezo's unproductive use of time, experimental audiovisual compositions, and uneasy war testimonial story mirror Wollen's counter cinematic features. Moreover, her film evokes

Brecht's *Verfremdungseffekt,* with its unconventional aesthetics and critically political plot forcing viewers to adopt an active reflective gaze.

In turn, Hernández Cordón's *Hasta el Sol tiene manchas* portrays similar counter cinematic features. The film offers a triple criticism: it challenges the normative cinematic form, the sociopolitical Guatemalan context, and the international film industry dynamics. The Guatemalan filmmaker develops the first challenge by experimenting with the cinematic form. He blends the documental and fictional filmmaking modes into a strong political context. *Hasta el Sol tiene manchas* opens with some archival images from Guatemala's historical archive. Hernández Cordón combines them with newly filmed fictional scenes that, in turn, are intermittently combined with self-conscious making-of scenes of the same film the spectator is viewing. This variety of image types is unified by a yellow color that tinges the entire film and confers it a symbolic message: the sun does not rise for everybody.

In that way, Hernández Cordón develops the second challenge and criticizes the sociopolitical Guatemalan context. Valeria Grinberg Pla understands Julio Hernández Cordón's films as a cinematographic project that rethinks Guatemalan history and inspires "considerations of the meaning of life or the lack thereof in a Guatemala affected by the continuation of violence from the war" (205). This is also to be seen in *Hasta el Sol tiene manchas*. The film challenges the dominant violent situations that rule in Guatemala but also its political establishment. The film portrays Guatemalan political leaders as patriotic and populists, leaders who have lost the ideals of social justice that characterized the times of the revolution. Thus, the film portrays the character with an intellectual disability, Pepe Moco, who campaigns for the candidate Manuel Baldizón. Baldizón has promised to bring Guatemala to the soccer World Cup if he happens to win the presidential election. Another character, Beto, represents the socially marginalized people in Guatemala. He plays with a plastic ball in order to symbolically denounce the criminal use of firearms in Guatemala City. Finally, *Hasta el Sol tiene manchas* develops the third challenge by criticizing the international film industry. The film questions a healthy budget—a precondition to produce a good film. In Hernández Cordón's words, *Hasta el Sol tiene manchas:*

> is not a commercial film. It is not a problem if the acting's texture is cheap. I aimed to provoke because my Guatemalan colleagues seek to make Hollywood-like films, but they end up doing bad films. I wanted to make this film, as I had never studied filmmaking, which bothers my Guatemalan colleagues. Anyway, to create a 10 million-budget film

does not guarantee that it will be well-received. (Olivares; my translation)[12]

Hernández Cordón's claim to make films that subvert Hollywood's artistic standards has previously been theorized by Lúcia Nagib. She calls for a decentralization of international film networks:

> I would favour a method in which Hollywood and the West would cease to be the centre of film history, and this would be seen as a process with no single beginning ... Against the exclusive method based on Hollywood, be it pro or anti, I propose ... the inclusive method of a world made of interconnected cinemas. (34)

This well-intentioned claim clashes with immutable global geopolitical interests that, according to Tamara L. Falicov, favor "persistent cultural politics stemming from colonial legacies" (3). Despite these global economic and funding dynamics, filmmakers such as Huezo and Hernández Cordón have found a way to both maintain their local counter narrative voices and gain international acknowledgment. Being aware of the North-South economic hierarchies and taking advantage of the existing international funding sources, they have encountered a global audience that praises their counter cinematic, slow, and politically engaged *oeuvre*. Following Ana M. López, their cinematic strategies and global success demonstrate that Third Cinema is not dead, but it has rather adapted to present-day conditions (153). In light of these words, I claim that Huezo's and Hernández Cordón's films reassess Third Cinema artistic postulates in order to create counter normative films that explore alternative modes of personal artistic expression and denounce political injustice without being militant or propagandist.

Conclusion

Tatiana Huezo and Julio Hernández Cordón have contributed to the cinematographic transformation of the Isthmus. They have found a personal filmmaking mode of expression that draws on a reassessed understanding of both Third Cinema's and counter cinema's principals. Thus, they have created locally based and experimentally oriented films, which challenge the commercial modes of movie entertainment and reject normative narratives in order to promote the critical gaze of the audience. Moreover, their films draw on counter cinematic features (as asserted by Peter Wollen) and denounce some of the sociopolitical injustices existing in present-day Central America.

In turn, their artistic films portray features commonly related to slow cinema: a carefully planned photography—long takes, a slow unproductive time, and a contemplative viewing experience. Thus, by focusing on unconventional visual aesthetics, Huezo's and Hernández Cordón's emphasis on film form is as relevant as the political context of their films. Their *oeuvre* blends both local and global contexts. Both filmmakers work together with regional Central American crews, portray local life's circumstances, and work with non-actors from the regions where they shot their films, fomenting their bond with the Central American territory and mirroring their own local narrative voices. This counter cinematic aesthetic has been funded and awarded by major international film festivals, taking Huezo's and Hernández Cordón's counter cinematic films center stage in the international art house filmic scene.

Notes

1. For an analysis of *El lugar más pequeño* that focuses on the construction of social memories, see Juan Pablo Gómez's chapter in this volume.
2. As asserted by Peter Wollen, "[Godard] borrowed the idea of separate chapters, which enabled him to introduce interruptions into the narrative, and he borrowed from the picaresque novel" ("Godard and Counter Cinema" 501).
3. "The whole project of writing in images must involve a high degree of foregrounding, because the construction of an adequate code can only take place if it is glossed and commented upon in the process of construction" (Wollen, "Godard and Counter Cinema" 503).
4. "The first radical break with single diegesis, however, comes with *Weekend,* when characters from different epochs and from different fiction are interpolated into the main narrative: Saint Just, Balsamo, Emily Brontë" (Wollen, "Godard and Counter Cinema" 504).
5. For further information about the alignment of Third Cinema's with the French May's demands see: Godard, Jean-Luc and Fernando Solanas. "Godard by Solanas. Solanas by Godard" *DOCUMENTS. Cinema Comparat/ive Cinema*, vol. IV, no. 9, 2016, pp. 15–19.
6. "Third cinema is [. . .] the decolonization of culture" (Solanas, Getino 37).
7. "The efforts in question were directed to playing in such a way that the audience was hindered from simply identifying itself with the characters in the play. Acceptance or rejection of their actions and utterances was meant to take place on a conscious plane, instead of, as hitherto, in the audience's subconscious" (Brecht 93).
8. Queer cinema is a broad term. As Galt and Karl Schoonover have pointed out, "queer theory has always asked what counts as a queer text. Is a queer film one made by a filmmaker who is queer, or featuring queer characters, or does queerness rather inhere in a film's political commitment or its affective registers? Is queerness a matter of form?" (347).

9   As asserted by Julio García Espinosa, "Neorealism they saw as the model for an appropriate cinema—a humanist and progressive aesthetic that offered a real alternative to the dominant modes of Hollywood and Latin American commercial production. [...] It was a style that placed people on the screen as historical actors but without being too explicit about it" (quoted in Chanan 163).
10 Gilles Deleuze claimed that "the author must not, then, make himself into the ethnologist of his people, nor himself invent a fiction which would be one more private story: for every personal fiction, like every impersonal myth, is on the side of the masters" (222).
11 Tatiana Huezo's first feature film, *El lugar más pequeño,* was screened at the San Sebastian Film Festival and received awards at several international festivals, such as Visions du Reel (Best Feature Film 2011) and the International Film Festival of Monterrey (Best Mexican Feature Film and Audience Award 2011). Five years later, her second feature film *Tempestad* (2016) was premiered at the Berlinale and received multiple Fenix Film Awards. In turn, Julio Hernández Cordón's first feature film, *Gasolina,* competed in 2007 in the section "Films in Progress" at the San Sebastian Film Festival where it landed three awards: the Industry Award, the Casa de América Award and the Confédération Internationale des Cinémas d'art et d'essai (CICAE) Award. His second feature film, *Las marimbas del infierno* (2010), was made with support from the HBF and won the best Central American Film Award at the Ícaro International Film Festival. In turn, his other films have been screened and nominated for awards at the foremost international film festivals, such as Locarno (*Polvo,* 2012a), BAFICI (*Hasta el Sol tiene manchas,* 2012), San Sebastian (*Te prometo anarquía,* 2015), and Rotterdam (*Atrás hay relámpagos,* 2017).
12 "no es una cinta comercial, no pasa nada si la textura de la actuación es chafa. Mi intención fue provocar, porque en Guatemala mis colegas quieren hacer cine como en Hollywood y son copias malas. Quería hacer esto como si nunca hubiera estudiado cine, lo que molesta a mis colegas de allá. De todos modos, si hago una de 10 millones no significa que gustará" (Olivares).

Works Cited

Andrew, Dudley. "An Atlas of World Cinema." *Framework: The Journal of Cinema and Media,* vol. 45, no. 2, 2004, pp. 9–23.

Atrás hay relámpagos. Directed by Julio Hernández Cordón, Melindrosa Films, De Raíz Productions, Rey Poeta, 2017.

Brecht, Bertolt. *Brecht on Theatre. The Development of an Aesthetic,* edited and translated by John Willett. 1957. New Delhi: Hill and Wang, 1964.

Cabezas Vargas, Andrea and Júlia González de Canales Carcereny. "Central American cinematographic aesthetics and their role in international film festivals." *Studies in Spanish and Latin American Cinemas,* vol. 15, no. 2, 2018, pp. 163–186.

Cardenas, Mauro Javier. "The strength to endure the worst: A Q&A with filmmaker Tatiana Huezo." *ZYZZYVA. A San Francisco Journal of Arts & Letters,* 5 May 2011, https://www.zyzzyva.org/2011/05/05/the-strength-to-endure-the-worst-a-qa-with-filmmaker-tatiana-huezo/. Accessed 4 May 2019.

Chanan, Michael. *The Cuban Image*. Minneapolis: U of Minnesota P, 2004.
Cortés, María Lourdes. "Filmmaking in Central America. An Overview." *Studies in Spanish and Latin American Cinemas*, vol. 15, no. 2, 2018, pp. 143–161.
———. *La pantalla rota: Cien años de cine en Centroamérica*. Ciudad de México: Taurus, 2005.
Cortez, Beatriz. "Ficciones contemporáneas: Ixcán y la producción cinematográfica centroamericana de posguerra." *Istmo*, no. 13, 2006, http://istmo.denison.edu/n13/articulos/ficciones.html. Accessed 4 August 2021.
D'Lugo, Marvin. "Authorship, globalization, and the new identity of Latin American cinema." *Rethinking Third Cinema*, edited by Guneratne, Anthony R. and Wismal Dissanayake, Routledge, 2003, pp. 103–125.
Davis, Nick. *The Desiring-Image: Gilles Deleuze and Contemporary Queer Cinema*. New York: Oxford UP, 2013.
Deleuze, Gilles. *Cinema 2. The Time-Image*. Minneapolis: U of Minnesota P, 1989.
El lugar más pequeño. Directed by Tatiana Huezo, FOPROCINE, El Salvador, 2011.
Elsaesser, Thomas. "Hyper-, Retro- or Counter Cinema. European Cinema and Third Cinema between Hollywood and Art Cinema." *Mediating Two Worlds. Cinematic Encounters in the Americas*, edited by John King, Ana M. López, and Manuel Alvarado, British Film Institute, 1993, pp. 119–135.
Falicov, Tamara. "Migrating from South to North: The Role of Film Festivals in Funding and Shaping Global South Film and Video." *Locating Migrating Media*, edited by Greg Elmer, Charles H. Davis, Janine Marchessault, and John McCullogh, Rowman & Littlefield Publishers, 2010, pp. 3–22.
Gabriel, Thesome. "Towards a Critical Theory of Third World Films." *Thesome Gabriel. Articles & Other Works*, http://teshomegabriel.net/towards-a-critical-theory-of-third-world-films. Accessed 6 May 2019.
Galt, Rosalind and Karl Schoonover. "Provincialising Heterosexuality. Queer style, World Cinema." *The Routledge Companion to World Cinema*, edited by Stone, Rob, Paul Cooke, Stephanie Dennison, and Alex Marlow-Mann, Routledge, 2018, pp. 347–358.
Gasolina. Directed by Julio Hernández Cordón, Melindrosa Films, Guatemala, 2008.
Godard, Jean-Luc and Fernando Solanas. "Godard by Solanas. Solanas by Godard." *DOCUMENTS. Cinema Comparat/ive Cinema*, vol. IV, no. 9, 2016, pp. 15–19.
Grinberg Pla, Valeria. "Against Anomie: Julio Hernández Cordón's Post-war Trilogy—*Gasolina/Gasoline* (2008), *Las marimbas del infierno/The Marimbas of Hell* (2010) and *Polvo/Dust* (2012)." *Studies in Spanish and Latin American Cinemas*, vol. 15, no. 2, 2018, pp. 203–216.
Hess, John. "Neo-realism and New Latin American Cinema. *Bicycle Thieves* and *Bood of the Condor*." *Mediating Two Worlds. Cinematic Encounters in the Americas*, edited by John King, Ana M. López, and Manuel Alvarado, British Film Institute, 1993, pp. 104–118.
Hasta el Sol tiene manchas. Directed by Julio Hernández Cordón, Melindrosa Films, Guatemala, 2012.
Hok-Sze Leung, Helen. "New Queer Cinema and Third Cinema." *New Queer Cinema: A Critical Reader*, edited by Michele Aaron, U of Edinburgh P, 2004, pp. 155–167.

La Hora de Los Hornos. Directed by Fernando Solanas and Octavio Getino, Grupo Cine Liberación, Argentina, 1968.

Las marimbas del infierno. Directed by Julio Hernández Cordón, Le Films du Requin, Melindrosa Films, Axolote Cine, Codice Cinema, Guatemala, 2010.

La tierra prometida. Directed by Miguel Littín, Focus Features, Chile/Cuba, 1973.

López, Ana M. "An 'Other' History. The New Latin American Cinema." *New Latin American Cinema*, edited by Michael T. Martin, Wayne State UP, 1997, pp. 135–156.

Moretti, Franco. "Conjectures on World Literature." *New Left Review*, no. 1, 2000, pp. 54–68.

Murphy, Kaitlin M. "Memory Mapping: Affect, Place, and Testimony in *El lugar más pequeño*." *Journal of Latin American Cultural Studies*, vol. 25, no. 4, 2016, pp. 571–595.

Nagib, Lúcia. "Towards a positive definition of world cinema." *Remapping World Cinema. Identity, culture and politics in film*, edited by Stephanie Dennison, and Hwee Lim Song, Wallflower Press, 2006, pp. 30–37.

Olivares, Juan José. "Entrevista a Julio Hernández Cordón." *La Jornada*, 16 April 2013, http://www.jornada.unam.mx/2013/04/26/espectaculos/a14n1esp. Accessed 6 May 2019.

Pérez, Yansi. *Más allá del duelo: Otras formas de imaginar, sentir y pensar la memoria en Centroamérica*. San José: UCA Editores, 2019.

Polvo. Directed by Julio Hernández Cordón, Melindrosa Films, Tic Tac Producciones, Autentika Films, Guatemala, 2012.

Rich, Ruby B. "An/Other View of New Latin American Cinema." *New Latin American Cinema*, edited by Michael T. Martin, Wayne State UP, 1997, pp. 273–297.

Rushton, Richard. "Counter-Cinema." *The Routledge Encyclopedia of Film Theory*, edited by Edward Branigan, and Warren Buckland, Routledge, 2014, pp. 117–121.

Schoonover, Karl. "Wastrels of Time: Slow Cinema's Laboring Body, the Political Spectator, and the Queer." *Framework: The Journal of Cinema and Media*, vol. 53, no. 1, 2012, pp. 65–78.

Shohat, Ella. "Post-Third-Worldist culture. Gender, nation, and the cinema." *Rethinking Third Cinema*, edited by Guneratne, Anthony R. and Wismal Dissanayake, Routledge, 2003, pp. 51–78.

Solanas, Fernando and Octavio Getino. "Towards a Third Cinema. Notes and Experiences for the Development of a Cinema of Liberation in the Third World." *New Latin American Cinema*, edited by Michael T. Martin, Wayne State UP, 1997, p. 33–58.

Stam, Robert. "Beyond Third Cinema. The aesthetics of hybridity." *Rethinking Third Cinema*, edited by Guneratne, Anthony R. and Wismal Dissanayake, Routledge, 2003, pp. 31–48.

———. *Film Theory. An Introduction*. Blackwell Publishers, 2000.

Te prometo anarquía. Directed by Julio Hernández Cordón, Interior13 Cine, FOPROCINE, Mexico, 2015.

Tempestad. Directed by Tatiana Huezo, Pimienta Films, Cactus Film&Video, Terminal, Mexico, 2016.

Wollen, Peter. "Godard and Counter Cinema: Vent d'Est." *Movies and Methods. Vol. II*, edited by Bill Nichols, Los Angeles: U of California P, 1985, pp. 500–509.

IV

The Oppositional Lens
Minorities and Gender Issues

12

Tangible Afro-Indigenous Heritage

Land and Sea in *Garifuna in Peril*

Jennifer Carolina Gómez Menjívar

Scholarly attention to Indigenous peoples in Central America has been largely focused on highland Maya cultures, leading to fewer studies on the coastal Indigenous communities of the Isthmus. This is largely due to a focus on the Spanish invasion of the K'iche' kingdom of Q'umarkaj in many scholarly studies that has led research to omit the cultural trajectories of the Caribbean coastal Indigenous communities of Central America (for example, Mayans in Belize, Garifuna communities in Honduras, Miskitu peoples in Nicaragua).[1] These communities had a distinct relationship to the Spanish empire (and, later, to the British empire) than that of th.e Mayan peoples in the highlands of Iximulew/Guatemala more frequently examined by Central Americanists. Although the Spanish and the British empires vied for control over the Caribbean coastal strip of the Isthmus, few of their settlers chose to establish themselves or their cities there. The heat, humidity, and lushness of the landscape kept settlers off the "rimlands," to echo the name given to this coastal geographic strip by Ian Smart (1984). It remained, well into the twentieth century, home to seafaring Indigenous peoples.[2]

The greater degree of isolation experienced by these communities was of great cultural and political consequence. The reduced presence of settlers on their coastal homelands enabled the Indigenous peoples of the rimlands to possess a greater degree of autonomy and self-determination than Indigenous communities in the Pacific or highland areas. Furthermore, the quarantine they experienced over the course of multiple centuries also prevented linguistic colonization, solidifying the rimlands as a cradle for three principal thriving language families: Mayan languages, Chibchan languages, and Misulpan languages.[3] While elsewhere in the Isthmus many Indigenous languages were steadily extinguished by settler colonial institutions, the peoples of the rimlands continued to transmit their languages to younger generations unencumbered by colonial or even national public education policies developed after 1821. This was the context to which Garifuna peoples—forcibly deported from their Indigenous homeland of Yurumein/St. Vincent by the British in 1797—arrived. This is a history that has been well documented by anthropologist-outsiders like Nancie González in her often-cited work *Sojourners of the Caribbean* (1988) as well as Garifuna anthropologists like Joseph O. Palacio in his landmark volume *The Garifuna Nation Across Borders* (2013). William Noel Salmon and I explain in *Tropical Tongues* (2018) that the Garifuna language spoken in the rimlands is not original to Mesoamerica; it belongs to the Amazonian-origin Arawak language family. However, the high degree of cultural autonomy and the lack of linguistic competition in the isolated rimlands allowed the Garifuna language and culture to thrive in Central America, even as it experienced endangerment and death in the sites from whence it originated. The marked vitality of Garifuna language, music, and dance led them all to be declared Masterpieces of the Oral and Intangible Heritage of Humanity by UNESCO in 2001.[4]

Indigenous mother tongues were a cultural mainstay in rimland communities where daily life was inseparable from the stewardship of these coastal ancestral lands and the life-giving tradition of harvesting from land and sea. *Garifuna in Peril* (2012) poignantly brings together these key cultural issues. As I argue in this chapter, the film demonstrates that the protection of Garifuna language and culture depends on the protection of their life-giving *tangible* heritage, to wit: the land and sea Garifuna peoples have lived with in harmony since their ancestors' arrival on the Central American Caribbean coast. The film thus illuminates the status and rights of this Indigenous community, while also amplifying the concept of "settler colonialism" to include Garifuna peoples.[5] As Chickasaw scholar Shannon Speed observes, this concept has been too narrowly applied, despite its relevance to the entire hemisphere:

> In Latin America, as elsewhere on the continent, white European settlers invaded, occupied, and stayed. They deployed racial logics that worked to construct indigenous peoples as uncivilized, unfit, and inevitably bound to disappear in the face of modern civilization. While national racial discourses differed in significant ways, throughout the hemisphere they worked to eliminate the Native from the present, locate Native people in history in particular ways, and manage the pres-

ent population through ongoing exploitation and dispossession. Here, there, and everywhere, states of the Americas also resorted to violence periodically to further the work of elimination and continued control. (788)

Garifuna in Peril, as the analysis in this chapter illustrates, is a powerful statement on settler colonialism and its old trappings (land dispossession and repopulation by non-Indigenous peoples) as well as its new outfits (neoliberal development rhetoric and tourist resorts). While other studies have used the concept of coloniality to address the epistemic and direct violence in the Central American region, the present chapter's emphasis on settler colonialism highlights the violence (epistemic and otherwise) inflicted upon Garifuna people through the usurpation of their ancestral lands and natural resources.[6] This chapter thus asserts that the film delivers a powerful message about the Garifuna resistance to settler colonialism through the community's ongoing protection of land and water—natural resource stewardship that has continued without interruption for over three centuries.

Water Is Life

Garifuna in Peril is codirected by Rubén Reyes (Garifuna/Honduras) and Ali Allie (United States). It involves a direct discussion of Garifuna history, focusing primarily on the deportation of Garifuna ancestors from Yurumein/ St. Vincent in order to squelch Garifuna insurrection in what historians have come to call the Carib Wars (1769–1797).[7] While it is not a documentary film, it preserves a pedagogical angle with respect to the 5,000 men, women, and children who were deported, and the number of ancestors who survived the trans-Caribbean voyage: approximately 2,500 souls. Along with these important historical facts, audiences also discover that the communities that these Garifuna ancestors established in present-day Honduras, Belize, and Guatemala are now over three hundred years old. As such, the film is an important contribution to the study of Garifuna heritage. It cements its analysis of Garifuna Indigenous *ethnogenesis* and *ethnohistory*, following the terms used by Nancie González, on these historical facts. Yet, the film also attends to the future of Garifuna heritage at a time in which the government-sanctioned land and water speculation activities of tourist developers are putting Garifuna people, language, and culture in an acute crisis.

Like the earlier film by Allie, *El espíritu de mi mamá* (United States, 1999), the film that concerns us here, *Garifuna in Peril*, is a feature-length film produced on a reduced budget that concentrates on the importance of cultural preservation and relational bonds within the transnational Garifuna community. As revealed in both films, even those Garifuna who have left Central America and made their homes in California consider the Isthmus a spiritual and material home. The central conflict in each of the films compels the principal protagonist to return to ancestral land in the rimlands to right a wrong: *El espíritu de mi mamá* follows a young single mother who returns to her homeland to fulfill the wishes of her mother before she can reestablish her own spiritual health, while *Garifuna in Peril* follows an older married man who returns to Honduras in order to fight against the threat of non-Indigenous encroachment in Garifuna ancestral lands. Since Garifuna towns are disconnected from Tegucigalpa and other urban sites due to the lack of transit infrastructure, travel over waterways remains the principal navigational means to Garifuna coastal areas. The landscape of the Garifuna ancestral rimlands thus figures prominently in both films.

Garifuna in Peril makes it patently manifest that this tangible heritage is endangered. The keen insight into the danger that Garifuna water, land, and culture face is possible because the film is not just one director's project or even that of two codirectors, but that of an entire community. Allie and Reyes took their idea for the film to Reyes's community of origin: Triunfo de la Cruz, Honduras (Goett 292).[8] They consulted with the Triunfo de la Cruz Patronato (Council) and partnered with two Honduran Garifuna organizations that focus on defending rights to land, natural resources, and self-determination: the Land Defense Committee of Triunfo de la Cruz (CODETT) and the Black Fraternal Organization of Honduras (OFRANEH) (Goett 292).[9] The centrality of water and land to life and Indigenous experience is a joint concern to all of these Garifuna entities, and it is narrativized in the cinematographic choices the codirectors make throughout the film. To illustrate, the very first sequence of *Garifuna in Peril* begins with a still shot of four Garifuna homes on the shores of the Caribbean Sea that rests for twenty seconds as Garifuna *punta* music plays and wind rustles the palm trees. A low moving shot of two Garifuna boys running over the sand is overlapped onto the first shot until they gradually come into focus. They run to their mother, and she holds her youngest boy, smiling and caressing his head. The shot dissolves into one in which the children face her, their backs to the camera, while she remains centered and in full view with the Caribbean Sea behind her as she tells her children in the Garifuna language:

> Speak your language wherever you are. You are Garifuna. I ask you to guide your younger brother. Encourage him in good things. Speak

your language and you shouldn't be ashamed. Understand, my children? I love you both so much. I love you both very much. That's why I want you to speak your language wherever you go. Do you understand, Miguel? Do you understand, Ricardo?

As she speaks, a man in a canoe passes behind her and the peaceful memory sequence comes to an end as she gives each of her boys a kiss. The next sequence brings the film to the present as two men—the brothers, who have now grown up—speak to each other over the phone in Garifuna. The younger brother, Miguel, stands on the beach against a blue sky as the waves crash around him and he informs his older brother, who wears a hardhat and is at a construction site in Los Angeles: "They stole our pigs. They only left one." It is unknown who "they" are, but it is clear from the juxtaposition of the sequences that more has changed than the transformation of the boys into men. The very conditions of living on Garifuna land seem to have shifted, leading "them" to openly steal from the brothers' family's land.

At 11:15 minutes, the extent of the alterations come into focus as the brothers talk about tourist economy and the large resort that is now in operation adjacent to their family's land. The sequence alternates between shots of Miguel walking through their hometown and Ricardo in the car on his way to work as they formulate a plan while conversing in Garifuna.[10] The two brothers agree to team up: Ricardo will recruit tourists and Miguel will host them in their Garifuna hometown. With the profits, they will build a Garifuna language school on their land. It quickly becomes clear, however, that they cannot compete with the extravagance of neighboring tourist resorts. Despite Ricardo's marketing and Miguel's willingness to meet travelers at the airport and take them to their Garifuna village, tourists flock to the adjacent, and contrastingly glamorous, Copán del Mar complex upon their arrival in Honduras. The brothers' plan is further thwarted when Miguel's car breaks down following a futile airport run and Vera, the mestiza who manages Copán del Mar, drives up to him. Flirting with Miguel, she entices him to leave what she derides as a non-lucrative venture and invites him to work for her at Copán del Mar. The internal conflict that Miguel experiences is manifest in his facial expression in the subsequent scene, as four tourists meander lazily in the background while he navigates the waters of doubt weighing Vera's offer. The cinematographic use of ocean water that was used to evoke a Garifuna connection to the coast is interrupted when Miguel strolls into Copán del Mar and declares that he will accept Vera's proposition. The symbolic use of water as life and ancestral gift will not return until Ricardo arrives in their homeland to right the wrongs faced by the Garifuna community. In between, the unnaturalness of Miguel's sorroundings is powerfully manifested in the treated water that flows through the pipes of Copán del Mar.

The camera follows Miguel for an entire fifty seconds as he walks past a construction site, pillars, a large pool with fountain jets at the center, guests on floatables, mowed lawns, and manicured gardens, and thatched roofs that, instead of serving as part of Garifuna homesteads, are used as umbrellas over white plastic tables and chairs. The sequence is paired with easy jazz music, marking a sharp distinction between the Garifuna *punta* that has played in the first thirty minutes of the film. It is not just the opulence of Copán del Mar that is displayed in these scenes, it is also the distinct use of water by the tourists and the tourist resort. Until Miguel's pact with Vera, the ocean was in the foreground of the boys' conversation with their mother and in the foreground of the brothers' transnational phone calls. As such, the Caribbean Sea holds a strong visual, audible, and spiritual presence until Miguel's decision ushers in sequences featuring chlorinated water in its place. His walk through the grounds of Copán del Mar illustrates that tourists are not interested in learning about Garifuna heritage; they prefer to lounge next to treated water and get suntans while Garifuna workers cater to their needs. They prefer, in fact, the pungent odor of sodium hypochlorite over the salty aroma of the sea. Copán del Mar—and other tourist hotspots like it—are sites of artificiality that are changing the quiet seascape tended to by Garifuna peoples for over three centuries. As viewers perceive how the smell of chlorine permeates the pool sequences on the grounds of Copán del Mar, so too do they intuit the tourist industry's concept of "development" at the cost of Garifuna heritage, tradition, and future.

The film thus manifests the Garifuna Indigenous conception of sea as part and parcel of ancestral territory. This point of departure links the Garifuna community's future to a type of natural resource stewardship that will not leave the same carbon footprint as that left by the tourist industry. In this regard, *Garifuna in Peril* can be understood within the definition of "ecocinema," a genre that overtly engages with environmental justice concerns and puts nature at the center of the film narrative.[11] Importantly, the film answers the philosophical question of what it means for a Garifuna subject to be a member of his/her ecosphere and to tend to the seascape in a sustainable manner for the spiritual benefit of the entire Garifuna community. The contrasting portrayals of water—from ocean water to treated pool water—in this first part of the film anchors the biocentric perspective wherein the ocean in its unadulterated form is presented as intertwined with Garifuna heritage. As the second half of the film turns to the question of Garifuna land rights as cultural rights and the unlawful dissolution of Indigenous peoples' ancestral land holdings, the film's biocentric crux is further underscored.

Consequently, more than with "eco-cinema," *Garifuna in Peril* is aligned with what Brazilian critic Aline Freire de Carvalho Frey calls "eco-fourth cinema," a genre that examines ecological crises in tandem with Indigenous rights to cultural determination. *Garifuna in Peril* shows us that Garifuna peoples believe that nature is not and should not be considered a commodity. Following Freire de Carvalho Frey:

> There is a trend in Indigenous media texts to foreground environmental policies and sustainable lives. These texts situate Indigenous discourses and actors in a central position with respect to the human vulnerability to climate change. This is not only because their traditional knowledges and discourses favour sustainability but also because they are survivors of another type of violent eco-territorial displacement, namely, the process of colonisation. (13)

To the Garifuna community in the film, the financial benefit of water does not outweigh the benefit of sustaining and protecting it for future generations. Specifically, it presents the township of Triunfo de la Cruz as a site threatened by businesses that see it not as a resource but as a commodity. It simultaneously emphasizes the coastal strip as an unspoiled, desirable location today precisely because of Garifuna ancestral land stewardship practices to protect the sea. This perception is also manifest in several other Garifuna-focused eco-fourth cinema productions of the past two decades, including *The Garifuna Journey* (1998), *Garifunas Holding Ground/Lucha garífuna* (2002), *Cuando el río y el mar se unieron* (2004), *Lubaraun* (2014), and *Yurumein* (2014).[12] Like *Garifuna in Peril*, these films align themselves with the "eco-fourth cinema" genre that has been cultivated in Indigenous contexts worldwide, including *Terra Vermelha* (2008, Brazil) and *Mabo* (2012, Australia). As this trans-Indigenous global genre manifests, nature is an Indigenous community's connection to its past and its future, and to its very life and prosperity.

Land as Tangible Heritage

Cassava, otherwise known as manioc, or *yuca*, was the food that Garifuna deportees took aboard ships with them when they were forced out of Yurumein/St. Vincent. The crop was first domesticated and cultivated for nourishment approximately 10,000 years ago in west-central Brazil (Olsen and Schaal 5586). More precisely, oral histories, soil analyses, and anthropological evidence all confirm that its use was widespread in pre-Columbian contexts across the

Americas (Sheets et al. 260). Along with corn, it was one of the most important carbohydrates in Indigenous peoples' diets prior to Spanish invasion. To date, its cultivation remains an important cultural activity in the communities that Garifuna peoples founded along the rimlands of Central America. Cassava/yuca's importance is likewise linked to Garifuna spirituality, particularly to dügu ceremonies, in which living descendants communicate with ancestors and other members of their families who have passed away (Flores 147–152). So important is manioc/yuca in ancestral rites that one of the Garifuna men in the documentary *The Garifuna Journey* states: "Ancestors will not accept fried chicken or bread, has to be cassava." Furthermore, in Garifuna communities, both men and women participate in sowing, harvesting, and storing the crop (Thorne 23).[13] Thus, in the film *Garifuna in Peril*, as Miguel weighs the question of betraying his brother and the rest of his community, he has a conversation with Vera in which he discusses manioc/yuca:

Vera: And what do you do with the yuca?
Miguel: You know, making cassava is hard.
Vera: You went and sold it in the street?
Miguel: No, I sold the yuca.
Vera: Oh, yuca.
Miguel: But that doesn't generate anything. I worked like a mule all day. And for what? Fifty cents profit? No way! That life is too hard.

The close-up scene of the two in bed as they discuss the crop cuts to a shot of stacked white plastic chairs that lingers for three seconds, juxtaposing the materiality of a crop that has profound connections to both physical and spiritual sustenance with the expendable nature of man-made goods made in excess. The scene then abruptly cuts to Ricardo's son, Miguel's own nephew, auditioning for a role in a play about Chatoyer, the Garifuna leader who was killed by the British for his role in the Carib Wars just before his people were forced to surrender and were subsequently deported. With the same abruptness that took the viewer from Miguel and Vera's bed in Honduras to Garifuna ancestral memory in the United States, the camera cuts back to Vera and Miguel in bed. Capitalizing on what he has just said about his ancestral crop and the difficulty of making a living from an agricultural economy as well as the growing discord between the two brothers, Vera suggests that Miguel sell the school that Ricardo is planning to build in their Garifuna village. The medium shot keeps the couple in view, a light sheet covering their bodies, and closes-up on Vera as she lightly taps Miguel's bicep with one finger, smiling, and telling him that he should sell the entirety of the family plot of land itself. When he responds that he will consider the idea very seriously, she taps his arm again three times and adds with a smile that it could turn a good profit.

The scene ends and chlorinated water appears again in the next shot, this time with the pool at Copán del Mar taking up three-fourths of the frame as Miguel walks into the shot from the right. Both his furrowed brow and his body language capture his troubled thoughts. Garifuna music plays in the background and a moving camera follows him into the center of the frame in slow motion. The following scene is fraught with clashing values over land, posited in an even more overt way than the contrasting Indigenous ontologies versus settler ontologies of water that have been rendered earlier in the film. It is a powerful scene in which Miguel sits with Vera and a mestizo lawyer as he reads the document that will lead to his family's land dispossession. The lawyer, who is initially unable or unwilling to make eye contact with Miguel, responds irately to the Indigenous man's hesitation at signing the document:

Lawyer: Well, Miguel, please sign here.
Miguel: No, sir.
Vera: What's wrong, Miguel?
Miguel: (Pointing at the document) I believe this is wrong! I said it was $50,000, not $5,000. (Turning to Vera) Didn't you tell him it was $50,000?
Vera: Of course! That's what we agreed. (Smiles at the lawyer)
Miguel: Then this is a mistake. Correct it, please.
Lawyer: No way.
Miguel: Why?
Lawyer: See all of these signatures? You know them? I had to pay a lot of money for them. These are the signatures of the community authorities.
Miguel: But it's my land.
Lawyer: Yes. And at the same time, it is not. Because you can't sell it to anyone else. (Pause) Ok! I have other options.

The tension of the scene grows as the lawyer finally looks at Miguel squarely in the eyes and, together with Vera, convinces Miguel to sign the document.[14] The lawyer's aggressiveness increases, particularly when he forces Miguel to sign a crucial clause. When Miguel—who, in fact, as well as in the eyes of the law, is an Indigenous landholder—manifests reluctance, the mestizo lawyer's tone changes from forceful to acrid:

In the year 1992, the International Labor Organization Convention 169 established that you can't sell this land to anyone who isn't Indigenous.

Nobody is going to buy your land. Nobody! Only me! So please put your two initials here.

Feeling the pressure from Vera to his right, the lawyer to his left, and the already once-signed document before him, Miguel assents a second signature. The penstrokes have garnered him only 10 percent of his initial asking price and, in tandem with the tangible loss of money, he has also lost his land rights as an Indigenous proprietor.

The outdoor sequences that follow capture a community perspective on Miguel's sale. Miguel—having presumably exchanged his older black Jeep for a new white KIA sedan—arrives in the neighborhood to recruit a young Garifuna woman to work at Copán del Mar. However, his stylish transformation doesn't move her, or her brother, who exits the home and punches Miguel. The brother manifests what they are all thinking when he yells at Miguel in front of all their neighbors: "You can't sell this land, Bro!" and "Bro, you can't sell family land!" Miguel flees and a moving camera captures the dusty dirt paths between the homes and the cement homes with tin roofing and barbed wire fencing as Miguel's pursuer advances. The camera fixes on the two men, and in a surprising turn of events, a grandmother rushes to the scene and punches Miguel, saying, "You sold it! You sold it! You sold our place!" The scene cuts to a frame of Miguel slowly sipping a beer as he looks out to the sea for a full thirteen seconds. His decision to sell has resulted in his being shunned from the community, which now bears the burden of losing more ancestral acreage and the further transformation of their community by yet another tourist resort and its accompanying pollutants. In highlighting this conflict, *Garifuna in Peril* establishes a parallel with scholarly discussions about the effects of tourism on Indigenous communities in the Central American rimlands (Gómez Menjívar and Salmon 2018).[15] In Honduras, the film makes poignantly clear that the vitality of Garifuna culture—its language and culture, all declared Intangible Cultural Heritage of Humanity by UNESCO—is in peril because of the tangible loss of land and access to the sea.

The concept of land rights is central in the scene where Vera and her coworker drive up in a white sedan to a lot where construction for the Garifuna language school proposed by Ricardo early in the film has already begun. They close a barbed wire fence and hang over it a sign that states, "No Trespassing. Property of Copán del Mar," before returning to their vehicle and driving away. The green fields of the village appear in the next scene as Ricardo drives back into his ancestral land. A gentle wind moves through the green brush as he stands outside his old home and learns from a young woman that Miguel is gone (Figure 12.1). The same soft wind moves the tall

Figure 12.1. Ricardo at Miguel's door (*Garifuna in Peril*).

grass as he stands with the young woman and two elders, gazing into the old construction site now behind a sign barring his entrance (Figure 12.2). It is likewise present as a group of children walk into the frame from the left and, one second later, Ricardo and the young woman walk into the frame from the right (Figure 12.3).

The green field and bright blue sky are the background for Ricardo's conversation with the children, in which he reminds them that they must remember that theirs is a Garifuna village and that the Garifuna language is to be spoken when they are in their village. And there they are again, the green field

Figure 12.2. Facing the no trespassing sign (*Garifuna in Peril*).

Figure 12.3. A conversation with the next generation (*Garifuna in Peril*).

and blue sky, in another scene as Ricardo faces down two mestizo men who arrive in a green pickup truck at the school construction site with the intent of asserting the propriety rights of the tourist resort:

> Man 1: You know this land belongs to Copán del Mar?
> Ricardo: Definitely not. It is ours, it belongs to the community.
> Man 1: Why don't you build your school 50 meters that way?
> Ricardo: How am I going to build over there?
> Man 1: Don't you live in the United States?
> Ricardo: I don't have to live here. This is the community's fight, not just mine. I can be here today and there tomorrow, and this will still be defended.
> Man 2: But you don't have the papers.
> Ricardo (pointing at the men): You should be the ones showing me papers. Our ancestors have lived on this land for more than two-hundred years.
> Man 1: Well, you've been warned.
> Ricardo: That sounds like a threat to me.

Ricardo remains standing as the men turn back and leave in their vehicle. A moving camera follows him in the next sequence as he walks along the shore to meet with an elder and obtain advice about the next steps he should take. In the same way that the youth in the preceding scenes waited for him to impart his wisdom to them, Ricardo readies himself to listen to *his* elders in the next. In effect, Ricardo's walk toward wisdom emphasizes Garifuna cultural practices in which elders exercise the roles and responsibilities of knowledge keepers, guiding others in matters that concern the survivance of the entire community.

Settler Colonialism and the Peril of Tourism

Garifuna in Peril captures the importance of land and sea for cultural survival, while arguing that the dispossession of land and sea might very well lead to the disappearance of a people. Sherene Razack meditates on the relationship between law, disappearance, and Indigenous peoples in *Dying from Improvement*:

> As a transitive verb, "to disappear" Indians means to commit an act that results in disappearance. For Indians to disappear, law must actively produce their disappearance as independent sovereign nations. (10)

In Canada and the United States—and readers can apply this observation to the Honduran rimlands—property law depends on Indigenous peoples only as acted upon-human beings; they do not exist in settler law as sovereign subjects (Razack 12). As John Borrows, an Anishinaabe legal scholar, observes in his analysis of the *Delgamuukw v. British Columbia* case, settler colonialism endeavors to disappear a people in order to then disappear their claim to ancestral lands, and vice versa (568). For that reason, the eco-fourth film genre allows *Garifuna in Peril* to transmit the message that the threat to Garifuna ancestral land claim posed by the Honduran tourist industry is a direct threat to its existence as an Indigenous people. In its focus on linking the community's future to the land and water that they inherited from their ancestors, the film highlights the easy coastal breeze, trees, and soil, and juxtaposes them to the cement and concrete of tourist resorts whose ecological impact must be questioned. Importantly, the film puts at center the defense of Garifuna land rights, pointing to both the legal instruments that serve as provisions for it as well as the role of the tourist industry in chipping away at those rights.

An hour into the film, Ricardo consults with an elder *buyei* who, following Garifuna tradition, is both healer and counselor to those in the community in need of her clairvoyance. After arriving at the understanding that he must bring the town together to talk about Miguel's sale of the land, a scene opens with Ricardo walking through the thatched roof huts by the sea. A strong wind causes the sway of palm trees and through Ricardo's clothing as he slowly walks past, out of the shot. During this scene, the image of him and his brother sitting next to each other facing the sea fades in for just two seconds—a mere memory—before slowly fading out once more. The water returns to the frame in a poignant way after his meeting with the community, at which elders express their anger and their commitment to demanding that the land be returned to their community. At 1:09:10, a sequence begins with Ricardo's back to the camera as he looks out at the horizon at dusk. Seven seconds later, the shot widens to include the sun setting over the sea and Ricardo at the center of the frame sitting with water up to his chest, the sequence finally ending at 1:09:28 after he has bathed in the ocean water. As the next sequence reveals, he has gone to the sea to cleanse himself spiritually, for fortitude is what he will need in order to confront the tourist company responsible for the illicit purchase of his ancestral land.

Keri Vacanti Brondo states that:

> the primary economic development strategies [in Honduras] from the 1990s forward have been agro-industrial production, the expansion of export processing zones (maquiladoras), and tourism. Tourism grew 18.3 percent between 1998 and 2001 and is now the third-largest source of income after remittances and maquiladoras. (48)

The principal zone for tourist development is Garifuna ancestral land—the north coast, the Bay Islands, and the Cayos Cochinos—under the premise of tourist enjoyment of the nation's "living cultures," eco-adventure, and "Fun-n-Sun" excursions (Brondo 48). Copán del Mar, the hotel in the film, advertises itself as "Relaxation, Fun, and Adventure: Your Pyramid of Luxury," according to a sign hanging in the developer's office when Ricardo arrives to meet with a man called Richard. Unbeknownst to Ricardo until he looks over and finds himself face to face with a British flag, the developer is neither from Honduras, nor the United States, but from England. Seconds pass as he faces the flag, slowly nodding and understanding that the British are once again at the head of displacing the Garifuna people. The point is emphasized in the overlapping sequence of Garifuna youth performing a play based on their ancestral leader, Satuye, who led the resistance against the British during the Black Carib Wars on the island of Yurumein/St. Vincent. They left a powerful legacy that continues to move Garifuna peoples today. As Chris Taylor explains:

> Elsewhere in the Caribbean only a few families held on at the margins of the new colonial societies. St. Vincent was the last battle of people living a traditional lifestyle against the European colonists anywhere in the islands. It was here that the Caribbean saw its Little Big Horn and its Wounded Knee (5).

Starved, forced to surrender, taken captive, and deported from their homeland, Garifuna ancestors were forced to begin a new life in Central America, but they did so with their keen fight for self-determination. Time stands still as images of Ricardo coming to this understanding phase in and out of images of the youth's performance. Ricardo exits and returns, ever more resolved to confront Richard. He walks into the developer's office and speaks clearly about his purpose there: "I believe you know why I am here. Whatever papers or documents you have related to my family's land that you took. I want all those papers. We're taking our land back." The tension of the scene builds as the two men face each other off, Richard using a variety of rhetorical techniques, including condescension before launching into an angry rant while standing over Ricardo:

Richard: The Ministry of Tourism has objectives. The World Bank has plans. Garifuna want something else. Everything is a tangled mess! You've got the APL, OAS, IMF, INA, 2004 Property Law, PATH, ILO 169, and so on, so on. You can't reconcile it all. Any action a developer takes violates something. You try to do things by the book: hold public hearings, some show up, others boycott. You can't please everyone. [. . .] You people are the last holdouts! What do you want to do? Choke off the only industry Honduras has left? Tourism is Honduras' lifeline. Or should I say, credit line? (Stands by the British flag and looks out the window) Golf courses, hotels. That's just to keep the money rolling into the country. If you end mega-projects and the money from the World Bank and IADB stops, it's over! We're all finished! What am I supposed to do? So I build this place to give your people some jobs and you come here complaining that we used some of your land! Land you weren't even using!

Ricardo: We were building . . .

Richard: (Interrupts) There was nothing there, for Christ's sake! Garifuna people could benefit more from tourism if those Patronatos weren't so patronizingly stubborn. (Pause) Don't you think, Ricardo, that if a piece of land belongs to a person, they have the right to do with it what they want?

Ricardo: (Shakes his head) No. No, not in our lands. Our land is part of who we are. It's part of our family. I don't have the right to sell a member of my family. What do you call it when you sell a human being? What do you call that?

Richard: (Looking at his desk) Slavery.

Ricardo: Right. And I will never sell my land into slavery. Not for any price. Do you know why? Two-hundred years ago on the island of St. Vincent . . .

Richard: (Interrupts) Yes, I know the whole story.

Ricardo: Then you know we were never slaves! Our ancestors fought to the death for their freedom! We would rather die than be dominated![16]

The film thus allows the spectator to understand that the question of land is one in which "development" is used as an argument to dispossess Indigenous peoples of the land that they care for sustainably.[17] The concept of settler colonialism, in the sense put forth by Patrick Wolfe in his seminal article "Settler Colonialism and the Elimination of the Native" (2006), is applicable here.[18] Today, as has been the case since Columbus's 1502 arrival in Honduras, the intent has been to use income-generating activities for a non-Indigenous majority as grounds for land usurpation. That this then leads to displacement and loss of culture for Indigenous people is not a concern for the settler entities interested in using the land to create and accrue capital.

As Kroshus Medina notes regarding legal pluralism, the coexistence and interaction of multiple systems of law has become increasingly transnational.[19] She observes what she calls "the vernacularization of human rights," manifested in their incorporation into grassroots movements across Latin America.[20] This framework serves grassroots movements, as the invocation of rights law drawn from nonlocal sources lifts conflicts out of their local contexts and inserts them into broader contexts.[21] The two competing ideologies about nature at play in the film have made their way into transnational legal and economic frameworks: on the one hand is the commodification of nature begun through settler colonialism and today spurred by agencies like the IMF and the IADB, and on the other hand are the discourses of human rights invoked by Indigenous peoples worldwide, including the Garifuna themselves. Land rights acknowledgment under international bodies like the ILO support Indigenous ontologies of land as a living being, clearly a part of one's family and immediate circle. The extraction of resources from the Honduran coast—as documented by many scholars, including Darío Euraque in his book *Reinterpreting the Banana Republic,* has continued through banana industries, mining, and dam projects that have gained notoriety. While ecotourism was once proposed as a solution that permitted economic development and preservation, the last couple of decades have given rise to discussions about how ecotourism takes decision-making power away from Indigenous communities. It has likewise led to discussions about the environmental impact of hundreds if not thousands of individuals traversing through Indigenous homelands.

The inherited land, the field at the center of the debate, reappears when Ricardo returns home, a machete in hand, to destroy the *No Trespassing* sign left by Copán del Mar after Miguel's sale to the mestizo in the earlier scene. Ricardo looks out to the field and, leaving all foreigners outside of the frame, the film concludes with a sequence that only involves Garifuna people. Standing before the members of the community who have gathered to collectively build the Garifuna language school on Garifuna communal lands, Ricardo declares: "Will the megaproject benefit us? We are not going to sell our lands for a few miserable jobs. We are Garinagu no matter where we are, and we help each other, no matter where we are. We will always fight to ensure our freedom." The words bring to life what connects Garifuna people: the common objective to resist settler colonialism in order to ensure autonomy and self-determination. Despite this being a transnational Indigenous community—like those along the border of the United States and Mexico or those along the border of Guatemala and Belize who have been divided by imposed international borders—the Garifuna community along the rimlands of Central America fighting together for ancestral lands. When the school is inaugurated in the last sequence of the film, Ricardo reminds the community:

We must pray for our ancestors, we must transfer everything to our children, we cannot be stingy with it. This is the type of mindset that must be taught at this school: "Garifuna are unwavering."

Garifuna in Peril thus ends on a poignant note: that the Caribbean coast is where Garifuna people have lived for centuries. The emphasis on the duration of land tenure is significant, as the Garifuna community clearly knows its history and this same grounded knowledge of a historical trajectory enables them to fight for their land rights through the channels opened by international agreements, like the ILO 169.[22] As a result, Garifuna people can legally and successfully challenge the sale of their ancestral lands. It also opens the conversation within this transnational community about the dangers of obtaining individual titles to land, which would enable a single individual to sell his family's (and ancestors' property). As Rubén Reyes explains with relation to the elders from the village of Triunfo de la Cruz that appear in the film: "A lot of them are members of the CODETT group. So they are familiar with the land struggle there. Those are the people that recovered the twenty-two manzanas [~37.8 acres]. Those are the people who stopped the Marbella project. Those are the people that took the Honduran government to the Inter-American Court. So they are very familiar with the land struggle" (quoted in Goett 296).[23] Land allotments are insidious, this film reports to both non-Indigenous and Indigenous spectators alike, and their purpose is to dissolve Indigenous homelands. *Garifuna in Peril* thus brings the question of contemporary settler colonialism into the discussion of Garifuna water/land loss and cultural death—a matter that concerns Indigenous peoples from north to south of this hemisphere.

Inseparable: Tangible and Intangible Heritage

Garifuna in Peril highlights the cultural elements declared by UNESCO as Intangible Cultural Heritage of Humanity, since from the first shot to the last, Garifuna language and music are central to the cinematographic choices featured. This music is often in the background, but it also appears in the foreground in the many different instances where Garifuna people are in action, literally and metaphorically. The auditory and sensory effect of this music, both leisurely as well as ceremonial, highlight the sense of community between the Garifuna community, whether the scenes correspond to struggle in Los Angeles or Honduras. Yet, it also provides a framework from which to examine land itself as a precondition for Garifuna cultural survival. The film calls attention to the international legal instruments that protect this right—like the Indigenous and Tribal People's Convention, 1989 (ILO 169) or the UN Declaration on the Rights of Indigenous Peoples, 2007—while at the same time cementing the idea of ancestral legacies, stewardship, and tenancy as signs of rightful ownership. Overall, the film imparts a clear message about Garifuna land rights in the context of similar Indigenous land rights struggles that have been fought in Central America. The assassinations of Indigenous environmental activists, most notably that of Lenca leader Berta Cáceres in March 2016, and the attempted murder of her daughter in October 2021, highlights the dangers that Indigenous water and land defenders face when they challenge state-sponsored projects of encroachment, extraction, and tourism. Defending the rimlands converts Garifuna activists into targets of state violence—as evidenced by the forced disappearance of five land defenders from Triunfo de la Cruz (the very location featured in *Garifuna in Peril*) in July 2020 ("We are in Danger," 2020). Yet, the alternative is for the tangible and intangible culture of Indigenous peoples to be destroyed. After all, as Shannon Speed observes: "In settler regimes concerned with occupying the land, the impetus is to dispossess and eliminate. Destroy to replace" (786). Garifuna peoples join Indigenous peoples throughout the Americas who see the protection of their water and land as a means to ensure their very own survival as a people with a spiritual—and tangible—ancestral home.

Notes

1 For more on the Quiché civilization and on the Spanish invasion, see Carmack's classic *Quichean Civilization: The Ethnohistoric, Ethnographic, and Archaeological Sources*, which was first published in 1973 and revised in 2018.
2 See the groundbreaking studies by McKillop (2005, 2011), Guderjan (2007), Glover, Rissolo, and Mathews (2011) for more on the Indigenous communities that lived and traded across the Caribbean coastal strip of Central America prior to Spanish invasion.
3 Speakers of Chibchan languages include the BriBri peoples of Costa Rica and the Guna peoples of Panama. Miskitu peoples, whose language belongs to the Misulpan language family, are featured in records from Columbus's invasion of Nicaragua on his fourth voyage.
4 For further information see UNESCO's website: https://ich.unesco.org/en/RL/language-dance-and-music-of-the-garifuna-00001.
5 For more on settler colonialism in what we have come to know as "Latin America," see Speed (2017).
6 Critiques of "coloniality" as a framework have emerged most recently from the subfield of Critical Latinx Indigeneities. As M. Bianet Castellanos argues, one of the problems with the theory of coloniality is that "this approach understands indigeneity in Latin America today as continually shaped by a colonial legacy rooted in racial mixing, rather than indigenous elimination and white settlement [settler colonialism]" (778). To Castellanos's observation, I will add that Quijano's concept is even less clearly applicable to Caribbean coastal Indigenous communities of Central America (for example, Mayans in Belize, Garifuna communities in Honduras, Miskitu peoples in Nicaragua), as it fails to explain the centuries of autonomy experienced by these Indigenous communities and their complex relationships to Spanish, French, and Dutch empires.
7 See Douglas Taylor (1951), Nancie González (1988), and Garifuna anthropologist Joseph Palacio (2005) for in-depth critical discussion of the various histories and hypotheses about the origins of Garifuna community as well as their deportation from St. Vincent.
8 Mr. Rubén Reyes founded the *Clamor Garifuna*, "*Lamumehan Garifuna*" radio program broadcast on Radio Impacto, Tela, Honduras in 1984, which transmitted the Garifuna language on the air for the first time in the region. He became the first president of the OFRANEH (Fraternal Organization of Blacks in Honduras) branch of Triunfo de la Cruz, and was later elected president of SONHOCA (Society of Black Hondurans in California). He translated the Honduran National Anthem, the Guatemalan National Anthem, and the United States national anthem into Garifuna, and designed a Garifuna flag emblem. His trilingual dictionary, *Garudia: Garifuna Trilingual Dictionary (Garifuna-English-Spanish)* (2012) is the culmination of over twenty years of research on the Garifuna language.
9 More information about the landmark *Triunfo de la Cruz vs. Honduras* case can be found in my book chapter, "*Triunfo de la Cruz vs. Honduras:* Garifuna Land under International Law."

10 The majority of the conversations in the film are in Garifuna, though there are also conversations in Spanish and in English. All of the quotes from the film that appear in this chapter use the translations to English and are from the official subtitles of the film released in the United States and to date, available for streaming through Amazon Prime.
11 Two excellent resources for further study of the "eco-cinema" genre are Scott MacDonald's article, "Toward an Eco-Cinema" in *Interdisciplinary Studies in Literature and Environment* and the volume, *Ecocinema Theory and Practice,* edited by Stephen Rust, Salma Monani, and Sean Cubitt.
12 Garifuna-focused cinema is on the rise, and films like *Garifuna in Peril* (2012) *Lubaraun* (2014), *and Wayunagu* (2017) are taking on an increasingly important role in Garifuna cultural revitalization. They contribute to the deconstruction of stereotypes, like that of "Caribbean cannibals," that has been perpetuated against Indigenous communities of Carib ancestry for centuries. See Poluha (2018).
13 Thorne adds that Garifuna peoples are distinguished by their subsistence activities and related gendered division of labor. Garifuna men typically fish, hunt, and are responsible for soil preparation, while women generally assume responsibility for the sale of surplus fish, agricultural products, and making cassava bread. See Thorne (2004).
14 The tension building scene continues:

Miguel (To Vera) I thought you told him that . . .
Vera: Hey, calm down.
Miguel: I said it was $50,000. I don't want to do this. I'm leaving. I won't go through with this.
Lawyer: No, please sit down.
Vera: We already agreed. Don't worry about it! Don't worry!
Lawyer: Sign!
Vera: Remember everything you promised me. We'll go to Roatán and many places.
Miguel: But this money wouldn't last us.
Vera: Don't worry about that.
Lawyer: (Holds up a pen in front of Miguel) Are you going to sign or not?
Vera: Sign it Miguel.
Miguel: (Takes the pen from the lawyer. Hesitates. Signs.)
Lawyer: Put your initials here, please.
Miguel: Why did you cross that out?
Lawyer: Look what it says right here, among other things. In the year 1992, the International Labor Organization Convention 169 established that you can't sell this land to anyone who isn't indigenous. Nobody is going to buy your land. Nobody! Only me! So please put your two initials here.
Miguel: No! No initials. Nothing!
Vera (at the same time as Miguel): Miguel! Do it!
Miguel: My signature is enough! What more!?
Vera: Just do what he says.
Miguel: No!
Lawyer: No?! You don't want to? Fine! I am not going to waste my time here.
Vera (softly, at the same time as the lawyer): You promised me.

> Lawyer: I have tons of things to do right now and I am not going to lose my time over this. (With his hand on Miguel's arm) And another thing . . . I have thousands of options to buy better land than yours.
> Vera (moving the contract back over to Miguel): Do it. Your money is about to leave.
> Miguel (signs and shoos the paper over to the lawyer): Ok, get out of here and give me my money.
> Lawyer (taking a stuffed envelope out of his pocket and slamming it on the table): Here's your money. Count it if you want.
> Miguel (stands abruptly): I'm out of here!

15 The growing tourist industry in Central America's Atlantic coast has also led to the endangerment of the Garifuna language in Belize. See Gómez Menjívar and Salmon (2018).

16 Richard begins the conversation with a paternalistic tone toward Ricardo, to which the Garifuna man does not submit:

> Ricardo: The law is, Garifuna lands cannot be sold outside the community. The land is for the school.
> Richard: I know. The land is for the school. I know. We'll build the school there for you. There will be a school on the edge of the property. This is not a problem!
> Ricardo: The land belongs to us. We'll construct our own school.
> Richard: (Shakes his head) You know, Ricardo, tourism isn't going away. Never mind your school. People want jobs. They want development. Even if we gave you a portion of that land back, (laughs) how many jobs is that tiny school going to create? Copán del Mar will bring jobs, business, more traffic here. With the IADB financing a four-lane highway all the way from San Pedro Sula . . . Do you realize how much tourism will increase? This is just the beginning!
> Ricardo: We won't be an attraction for your benefit. We want to control it. We want to be in charge.

17 For more on "accumulation by dispossession [of public and communal property]" outside of the framework of Indigenous studies, see Harvey (2003), Hart and Negri (2009), and Butler and Athanasiou (2013). I am grateful to the coeditors for signaling the ways that these analyses intersect with the Indigenous theoretical currents I highlight in this chapter.

18 The concept has been widely applied to the United States, Canada, Australia, and New Zealand. Debates exist with regard to its applicability to Abiayala, the name increasingly used by scholars of Indigenous studies for the area consisting of North, Central, and South America. See Wolfe (2006).

19 For more on the subject, see the articles "The Production of Indigenous Land Rights: Judicial Decisions across National, Regional, and Global Scales" by Laurie Krushus Medina and "The Transnational Dimension of the Judicialization of Politics in Latin America" by Kathryn Sikkink, as well as the excellent volume, *Law and Globalization From Below: Towards a Cosmopolitan Legality* by Boaventura de Sousa Santos.

20 See Kroshus Medina's (2016) discussion of trailblazing studies on the subject: Goodale (2007), Speed (2008), and Speed and Leyva Solano (2008).

21 See Richard A. Wilson's discussion of the topic in his conclusion to the trailblazing volume, *The Practice of Human Rights: Tracking Law Between the Local and the Global*: "Tyrannosaurus Lex: The Anthropology of Human Rights and Transnational Law."
22 For the full text of the International Labor Organization's 169 Convention document, see: https://www.ilo.org/dyn/normlex/en/f?p=NORMLEXPUB:12100:0::NO::P12100_INSTRUMENT_ID:312314.
23 Reyes is referring to a case involving the Municipality of Tela's decision to transfer 22 *manzanas* of Garifuna ancestral land to its trade union in lieu of wages; the union then proceeded to grant deeds entitling its members to full ownerships of lots within that area—all without Garifuna consultation or consent. The Triunfo de la Cruz community filed administrative and judicial actions aimed at recovering the land and demanding an investigation. For more information about this case, see Jennifer Carolina Gómez Menjívar (2022) and the Garifuna Community of Triunfo De La Cruz v. Honduras, Report, Report No. 76/12, Case 12.548 (IACmHR, Nov. 07, 2012).

Works Cited

Borrows, John. "Sovereignty's Alchemy: An Analysis of *Delgamuukw v. British Columbia*." *Osgoode Hall Law Journal*, vol. 37, no. 3, 1999, 537–596.

Brondo, Keri Vacanti. *Land Grab: Green Neoliberalism, Gender, and Garifuna Resistance in Honduras*. Tucson: U of Arizona P, 2013.

Butler, Judith, and Athena Athanasiou. *Dispossession: The Performative in the Political*. New York: Wiley, 2013.

Carmack, Robert. *Quichean Civilization: The Ethnohistoric, Ethnographic, and Archaeological Sources*. Berkeley: U of California P, 2018.

Castellanos, M. Bianet. "Introduction: Settler Colonialism in Latin America." *American Quarterly* 69.4 (2017): 777–781.

de Sousa Santos, Boaventura. *Law and Globalization From Below: Towards a Cosmopolitan Legality*. Cambridge: Cambridge UP, 2005.

El espíritu de mi mamá. Directed by Ali Allie, Los Gatos Productions, United States, 1999.

Euraque, Darío. *Reinterpreting the Banana Republic: Region and State in Honduras, 1870–1972*. Chapel Hill: U of North Carolina P, 1997.

Flores, Barbara. "The Garifuna Dugu Ritual in Belize: A Celebration of Relationships." *Gender, Ethnicity, and Religion: Views from the Other Side*, edited by Rosemary Radford Ruether, Minneapolis: Fortress Press, 2002.

Freire de Carvalho Frey, Aline. *Eco-Fourth Cinema: Indigenous Rights and Environmental Crises*. Dissertation, University of Queensland, 2019.

Garifuna Community of Triunfo De La Cruz v. Honduras, Report, Report No. 76/12, Case 12.548 (IACmHR, Nov. 07, 2012).

Garifuna in Peril. Directed by Ali Allie and Rubén Reyes, Aban Productions, United States, 2012.

Glover, Jeffrey B., Dominique Rissolo, and Jennifer P. Mathews. "The Hidden World of the Maritime Maya: Lost Landscapes Along the North Coast of Quintana Roo, Mexico." *The Archaeology of Maritime Landscapes*, edited by Ben Ford, Springer, 2011. 195–216.

Goett, Jennifer. "*Garifuna in Peril:* Film as Critical Pedagogy in the Garifuna Diaspora." *New Frontiers in the Study of the Global African Diaspora: Between Uncharted Themes and Alternative Representations,* edited by Rita Kiki Edozie et al., Michigan State UP, 2018. 289–298.

Gómez Menjívar, Jennifer Carolina. "*Triunfo de la Cruz vs. Honduras:* Garifuna Land under International Law." *Hemispheric Blackness and the Exigencies of Accountability,* edited by Jennifer Carolina Gómez Menjívar and Héctor Nicolás Ramos Flores, Pittsburgh UP, 2022. 116–133.

Gómez Menjívar, Jennifer Carolina, and William Noel Salmon. *Tropical Tongues: Language Ideologies, Endangerment, and Minority Languages in Belize.* Chapel Hill: U of North Carolina P, 2018.

González, Nancie. *Sojourners of the Caribbean: Ethnogenesis and Ethnohistory of the Garifuna.* Champaign: U of Illinois P, 1988.

Goodale, Mark. "The Power of Right(s): Tracking Empires of Law and New Modes of Social Resistance in Bolivia (and Elsewhere)." *The Practice of Human Rights: Tracking Law between the Global and the Local,* edited by Mark Goodale and Sally Engle Merry, Cambridge UP, 2007, 130–62.

Guderjan, Thomas H. *Ancient Maya Traders of Ambergris Caye.* Tuscaloosa: U of Alabama P, 2007.

Hardt, Michael and Antonio Negri. *Commonwealth.* New York: Belknap, 2009.

Harvey, David. *The New Imperialism.* New York: Oxford UP, 2003.

International Labor Organization (ILO). "Indigenous and Tribal People's Convention, 1989 (No. 169)." Geneva, 76th ILC session (27 Jun 1989) Entry into force: 05 Sep 1991.

Kroshus Medina, Laurie. "The Production of Indigenous Land Rights: Judicial Decisions across National, Regional, and Global Scales." *PoLAR: Political and Legal Anthropology Review,* vol. 39, no.1, 2016, 139–153.

MacDonald, Scott. "Toward an Eco-Cinema." *Interdisciplinary Studies in Literature and Environment,* vol. 11, no. 2, 2004, 107–132.

Lubaraun. Directed by Maria José Alvarez and Martha Clarissa Hernández. Managua, Nicaragua: Luna Films, 2012.

McKillop, Heather. "Ancient Maya Canoe Navigation and its Implications for Classic to Postclassic Maya Economy and Sea Trade: A View from the South Coast of Belize." *Journal of Caribbean Archaeology,* vol. 3, 2010, 93–105.

———. *In Search of Maya Sea Traders.* Lubbock: Texas A&M UP, 2005.

Olsen, Kenneth M., and Barbara A. Schaal. "Evidence on the Origin of Cassava: Phylogeography of Manihot Esculenta." *Proceedings of the National Academy of Sciences,* vol. 96, no. 10, 1999, 5586–5591.

Palacio, Joseph. *The Garifuna: A Nation Across Borders.* Belize: Cubola Productions, 2005.

Poluha, Lauren Madrid. "Cannibals in Paradise: Perpetuating and Contesting Caribbean Island Stereotypes in Film." *Post Script,* vol. 37, no.2/3, 2018, 96–116.

Razack, Sherene. *Dying from Improvement: Inquests and Inquiries into Indigenous Deaths in Custody.* Toronto: U of Toronto P, 2015.

Reyes, Rubén. *Garudia: Garifuna Trilingual Dictionary (Garifuna-English-Spanish).* Scotts Valley: Creative Space Publishing Platform, 2012.

Rust, Stephen, Salma Monani, and Sean Cubitt. *Ecocinema Theory and Practice*. New York: Routledge, 2012.

Sheets, Payson, et al. "Manioc Cultivation at Ceren, El Salvador: Occasional Kitchen Garden Plant or Staple Crop?" *Ancient Mesoamerica*, vol. 22, no.1, 2011, 1–11.

Sikkink, Kathryn. "The Transnational Dimension of the Judicialization of Politics in Latin America." *The Judicialization of Politics in Latin America*, edited by Rachel Sieder, Line Schjolden, and Alan Angell, Palgrave MacMillan, 2005, 263–92.

Smart, Ian. *Central American Writers of West Indian Origin: A New Hispanic Literature*. Washington, D.C.: Three Continents, 1984.

Speed, Shannon. *Rights in Rebellion: Indigenous Struggles and Human Rights in Chiapas*. Redwood: Stanford UP, 2008.

———. "Structures of Settler Capitalism in Abiayala." *American Quarterly*, vol. 69, no. 4, 2017, 783–790.

Speed, Shannon, and Xochitl Leyva Solano. "Introduction: Human Rights in the Maya Region." *Human Rights in the Maya Region*, edited by Pedro Pitarch, Shannon Speed, and Xochitl Leyva Solano, Duke UP, 2008. 1–23.

Taylor, Christopher. *The Black Carib Wars: Freedom, Survival and the Making of the Garifuna*. Jackson: UP of Mississippi, 2012.

Taylor, Douglas. *The Black Carib of British Honduras*. New York: Wenner-Gren Foundation, 1951.

Thorne, Eva. "Land Rights and Garífuna Identity." *NACLA Report on the Americas*, vol. 38, no. 2, 2004, 21–25.

Wayunagu. Directed by Christopher Miles, Lake Street Films, United States, 2017.

"We are in Danger: Honduran Afro-Indigenous Garifuna Demand Return of Kidnapped Land Defenders." *Democracy Now*. 17 August 2020. https://www.democracynow.org/2020/8/17/garifuna_land_defenders_honduras. Accessed 5 August 2021.

Wilson, Richard A. "Tyrannosaurus Lex: The Anthropology of Human Rights and Transnational Law." *The Practice of Human Rights: Tracking Law between the Global and the Local*, edited by Mark Goodale and Sally Merry, Cambridge UP, 2007, 342–69.

Wolfe, Patrick. 2006. "Settler Colonialism and the Elimination of the Native." *Journal of Genocide Research*, vol. 8, no. 4, 387–401.

13

¿No que muy machito pues?

Alternate Masculinities in Twenty-First-Century Guatemalan Cinema

Arno Jacob Argueta

In *La pantalla rota: Cien años de cine en Centroamérica* (2005) María Lourdes Cortés notes that Luis Argueta's *El silencio de Neto* (Guatemala, 1994) was the only Central American film in the first half of the 1990s to have a true international presence and as such, became an emblem that proved that quality cinema could be made in the region (541). Nearly sixty years earlier, Miguel Ángel Asturias published what some consider the crown jewel of dictator novels, *El señor presidente* (1946), based around the figure of dictator Estrada Cabrera (1898–1920). Meanwhile, *El silencio de Neto* is set in 1954 Guatemala during the military coup that overthrew President Jacobo Árbenz Guzmán (1951–1954). Argueta's film is foundational to the cinemas of the Isthmus as the first fiction film to enter the independent film festival circuit in the 1990s. Both this novel and this film have been studied as historicizing instances of violence in the Central American country, as such critique has typically focused on the president (in Asturias's novel) and on Neto (in Argueta's film).

From this, the patriarchal and allegorical aspects that underpin both the film and the novel have been studied and explored, although much less critical attention has been given to analyzing the other facets of masculinity that do not conform to patriarchal ideals. This chapter has three goals. First, it explores how from novel to film there appears an "other"—an alternate masculinity that seemingly serves as counterpoint to both challenge patriarchal power and provide a nonviolent future for the country. Second, the paper analyzes a series of twenty-first-century Guatemalan films to look at how these films articulate alternate masculinities in the face of a patriarchal masculinity. And third, this essay shows how these masculinities are, for the most part, continuing the work of patriarchal control and strict gender roles, even if newer films appear to challenge that structure and its violence. Even in Jayro Bustamante's *Temblores* (Guatemala, 2019), where the main character is a gay man, the main character is unable to break from these patriarchal modes of control pushing his own self through conversion therapy.

In "El Mundo de Neto en *El silencio de Neto,*" Edgar Barillas provides a quick study of the masculine cultural symbols that shape the main character's, Neto's, media consumption. While Barillas does not address masculinity directly, he does note that Ernesto, Neto's uncle, provides an alternate model of being male, countering the toxic masculinity of Neto's controlling father. This parallels Asturias's text where Miguel Cara de Ángel is similarly depicted as an affective male as a response to the dictator and his violence. Certainly, some of the best-known contemporary independent Guatemalan films—like Diego Quemada-Díez's *La jaula de oro* (Mexico, 2013) and Jayro Bustamanate's *Ixcanul* (Guatemala, 2016) and *La Llorona* (Guatemala, 2019)—have strong female characters that challenge a hegemonic, patriarchal, and violent masculinity, which points to a concerted effort to challenge patriarchal standards and stereotypes of femininity.[1] The question at hand, then, is whether these seemingly nonviolent male characters truly challenge the structures of gendered violence and can provide non-patriarchal modes of masculinity. Asturias's novel and Argueta's film point to these alternate masculinities as possible responses to masculinity and violence, yet in challenging the patriarchal structure, they also repeat it and strengthen it. In other words, these alternate masculinities fail to provide a resolution to the struggle against patriarchal masculinity since they seem to be structured as fail-safes that abstract traditionally feminine qualities to further alienate women and allow these men to retain their positions of power, turning themselves fundamental to the maintenance of the status quo.

After exploring how *El señor presidente* and *El silencio de Neto* set up this apparent dichotomy, I will provide an overview of films that explore and introduce different male stereotypes and how these fit within the aforementioned patriarchal structure. Some of these character archetypes to explore include: the slacker (*Puro mula,* Guatemala, 2011), the geek (*Ovnis en Zacapa* [Guatemala, 2015]); *Pol,* (2014), the artist (*Maquillaje* [Guatemala, 2014]); *El regreso de Lencho* [Guatemala, 2010]), and other failed masculinities (Julio Hernández Cordón's Guatemalan filmography or Rodolfo Espinosa's *Aquí me quedo* [Guatemala, 2010]) that find men having to deal with their inability to reach masculine standards.

Coloniality and Masculinity: Structures of Power

The most expansive of contemporary Guatemalan studies tend to focus strongly on the colonial legacies and the structures that maintain power in place. They point out how these enable and maintain the monopoly on power that is based on intersectional racist and gendered notions of violence. The work of scholars like Aura Cumes, Charles Hale, Carlos Guzmán Böckler, Marta Casaús Arzú, and others is concerned with this intersectional critique of power and tends to come from the more traditional fields of sociology, anthropology, and literature and, as such, provide key insights into power and representation. This essay attempts to add to this conversation by turning its head to the colonial racialized masculinity that holds and maintains the power and its structures to which Indigenous and gender critique discourses respond. The goal, then, is to expose how it is that those men who seem to be exploited by that system (because they do not perform the empowered patriarchal macho) still maintain it and benefit from it.

In the seminal essay "The History of Masculinity," R.W. Connell points to the simultaneous birth of colonial-modern ideals and modern masculinity. Connell points to four historical events that set modern-colonial masculinity quickly summarized in:

(1) the exchange of valuating the monastic ideal of masculinity to one of marital heterosexuality and the displacement of a relationship with God to an individualism—relationship with the self; (2) the acceptance and synchronization of violence and masculinity at the colonial frontier; (3) the creation of the urban space and its masculinization as spaces of capitalism, thus gendering work, modernity and space; (4) the feminization of religion and the masculinization of the secular nation.

From this, Connell indicates the rise of a classed hegemonic masculinity—gentry masculinity. This is a modern, colonial, racialized, and classed masculinity that, as hegemonic, exists by defining anti-hegemonic genders around it. Connell notes that "the history of European/American masculinity over the last two hundred years can broadly be understood as the splitting of gentry masculinity, its gradual displacement by new hegemonic forms, and the emergence of an array of subordinated and marginalized masculinities" (249). Connell looks at these marginalized masculinities mostly in sociocultural terms (specifically pointing out the lumpenproletariat) as those males from whom the gentry male creates distance. In other words, the gentry males actively distance themselves from the lumpenproletariat.

When talking about Guatemalan masculinities, the patriarchal males are complicated and enabled by these "sensitive," "nerdy," or "slacker" masculinities—or alternate masculinities. In *An Introduction to Female Masculinity*, Judith Halberstam alludes to a "project of producing alternative masculinities"—that is, masculinities that work beyond the limits of maleness, men, and patriarchy (19). To alert the reader to her ideas, Halberstam highlights the presence and performance of M, James Bond's boss in *Golden Eye* (2005), who "is a noticeably butch older woman who calls Bond a dinosaur and chastises him for being a misogynist and a sexist" (3). In addition, Halberstam notes that agent Q, the queer and nerd character in the film enables Mr. Bond to perform his traditional form of masculinity through the gadgets Bond receives. Agents M and Q, then, represent other forms of masculinity that criticize Bond and his sexism (while enabling it). We venture at exploring this seeming contradiction to critique how these alternate masculinities enable the continuation of the patriarchal structure. Halberstam points to the lack of research in this field saying that "much work still remains to be done on the socialization (or lack thereof) of young men in high schools, on domestic abusers, on the new sexism embodied by 'sensitive men'" (19), and this is precisely what this piece tasks itself with doing.

The Dictators, the Military, and the State of Terror

With the failure of the Central American Federation, Guatemala came to be ruled by Rafael Carrera y Turcios from 1851 to 1865. Carrera had been key in the disbanding of the United Provinces of Central America by mobilizing conservative oligarchies as to not lose their power, money, and the structures that supported them, but, for those fourteen years, he ruled the country as a dictator. The year 1871 would see the rise of liberalism under the leadership of Rufino Barrios and Miguel García Granados. Barrios not only led the liberal revolution but also established a system of indentured servitude over Indigenous people.[2] Eventually, in the political history of Guatemala, others like Manuel Cabrera, Jorge Ubico, Miguel Ydígoras Fuentes, and Efraín Ríos Montt would all establish similar strongman, dictatorial governments.

Carlos Figueroa Ibarra notes that these strongmen have recurrently risen and maintained power in Guatemala through the structural and symbolic creation of terror. And while Figueroa Ibarra does note and highlight the central part that economic and capitalist development play in the establishment and maintenance of state politics of state terror, he focuses on exploring how in the 1980s a counterinsurgency impetus pushed the Guatemalan military to enact politics of terror never before seen (Figueroa Ibarra 3–4). Figueroa Ibarra reminds us that this type of terror is structural to the formation of the Guatemalan state; it is not until we turn to the work of Carlos Guzmán Böckler where the racial aspect of terror is explored. In *Colonialismo y revolución* (1975) Guzmán Böckler traces a genealogy of the construction of the racial characteristics and limitations placed on Indigenous peoples in Guatemala. First, he denotes 1524 as an arbitrary date but one when the Spanish government delimits the Captaincy of Guatemala as itself. From here, the relationship between colonizer and colonized grows ever more complicated.

However, it is through his analysis of the colonial mode of production that we can see how, to maintain this structure, those in power fall back on racism and its discourses: "as a profound and largely generalized justification, racism is recalled [. . .]" (Böckler, *Colonialismo y revolución* 54).[3] In other words, racism is not simply a discourse but a historic reality that delimits the subjectification of all subjects to the state: "Thus, in colonized Guatemala, racism and racial differences are as important as the separations built upon economic factors" (Böckler, *Colonialismo y Revolucion* 66).[4] However, this racial configuration is further complicated as whiteness and its full power are unavailable to either of the predominant groups—Ladinos (mestizos and sometimes westernized Indigenous people) and Indigenous peoples—that is, neither truly embodies the whiteness reserved to the first-world, white man.

Indeed, *ladinidad* is a term that within the Guatemalan context recalls a politics of *mestizaje* summarized in the "bettering of the race" or the mixing of white and Indigenous in order to erase the Indigenous population. In this way, like Jean-Loup Herbert notes, *ladinidad* recalls the ideas of superiority (white supremacy) that contrast "primitive-superior, barbarian-civilized, prelogical-logical, magical-rational, etc. in its technocratic version: underdeveloped-developed, traditional-modern [. . .]" (Böckler, *Guatemala* 156).[5] Herbert develops these contrasts to point out, however, that these supposed differences do not actually allow Ladinos to embody whiteness. Instead, *ladinidad* produces the Ladino as a dialectical being, split among these dichotomies—thus paralleling the process of becoming proletariat.[6] In his essay titled "El ladino un ser ficticio," Guzmán Böckler further explores this character. The sixth point that he makes in his essay alludes to the recurrence of the need for a "strongman"—an ever-present tendency to *caudillismo* (as it is sometimes called): "This man is not enlightened by attributes of virility nor does he identify with the father figure; rather, his image is confused with the subject he humiliates, hits, tortures, lacking power and arbitrarily so. In reality, this is no man, but rather a sub-human" (Böckler, *Guatemala* 122).[7] In other words, the *caudillo,* the strongman, the dictator embodies the Ladino male's inability to attain the whiteness that eludes him. In recalling R.W. Connell from the previous section, one could say that because the Ladino is unable to embody the racialized masculinity of the colonizer, he follows a *caudillo* who will perform the white-supremacist colonial violence. In fact, we can see this reflected in Daniel Boyarin's analysis of Fanon and Freud as colonized subjects who are unable to perform the masculinity and whiteness demanded of them. Rachel Adams and David Savarn note in the introduction of their edited book's fourth section that Boyarin argues that Freud and Fanon denigrated "women and homosexuals in their work as a compensatory strategy to regain masculine authority" (Adams and Savran 228). Similarly, the Ladino male as a dialectical being is in the middle, not on either side of the colonial order.[8] This subject may only look up to the colonizer, never truly becoming it. This is precisely where these alternate masculinities appear as modes that enable the violent patriarchal masculinity that contrasts with the Indigenous male, or at the truly opposite extreme, the Indigenous female. Thus, the Ladino male is only allowed a feminized masculinity, a supporting role to the violence of the patriarchy. As such, the Ladino may only enact violence at the behest of the strongman.

Foundational Fictions

In *El señor presidente,* Miguel Ángel Asturias writes the archetypical dictator novel. The dictator, the hypermasculine strongman figure, however, is not the main character. This position is attributed to Miguel Cara de Ángel. Indeed, as scholars like Arturo Arias, Lois Marie Jaeck, and Patricia Lapolla Swier have noticed, both Asturias's larger work and *El señor presidente* provide a blueprint of masculinity for the formation of the national Ladino subject. Miguel Cara de Ángel personifies this national Ladino masculinity. Nearly sixty years later, Luis Argueta releases *El silencio de Neto,* set in 1954 Guatemala during the military coup that overthrew President Jacobo Árbenz Guzmán. In the film Neto is offered two seemingly opposing archetypes of masculinity: that of his oppressive father and his nurturing uncle, Tío Ernesto. The film points to the seemingly opposing standards for masculinity that *El señor presidente* proposes: the powerful and dictatorial macho or an affective not-so-tyrannical masculinity.

Without the complexity of Asturias's questioning of the racialized character of those masculinities in his later *Indigenista* work, *El señor presidente* and *El silencio de Neto,* have, notwithstanding, key foundational positions in the national narratives of literature and cinema respectively. They may both be perceived as critiques of violence in Guatemala. In wanting to find an escape from the violence of nation-building, these texts expose the dialectical and effeminate character of this Ladino masculinity.

Effeminacy—Or the Maintenance of the Patriarchal Structure

Both characters under analysis, Miguel Cara de Ángel and Tío Ernesto, are framed as effeminate beings who do not perform traditional masculine violence, yet this allows the traditional and more violent male characters, the president (in the novel) and Neto's father (in the film) to "deploy gender hegemony more effectively" (Reeser 120). That is, they allow for the permanence of the state of fear. Affection, then, when performed, allows the masculine character to develop a masculinity that might seem less threatening, but in doing so only reinforces the patriarchal dynamics that reproduce the disposability and objectification of the feminine because they themselves are discarded while they ignore the possibility of anti-patriarchal existence that is embodied in the female characters in the stories. Neither Tío Ernesto's nor Miguel Cara de Ángel's revolutions are successful in defeating the structure of violence. In fact, both narratives create a mythical effeminate male martyr while ignoring the female characters that survive them.[9]

Central American filmmakers reference Argueta's film as foundational to the cinemas of the Isthmus, as María Lourdes Cortés notes: "this is the film that first showed Central Americans that quality independent films could be made in the region" (Rocha and Seminet 64). In this film, Neto is beginning his teenage years as Guatemalan President Jacobo Árbenz Guzmán is taken out of power by a U.S.-backed military coup in 1954. It is through the relations of the Yepes family that "we are shown the atmosphere of fear and repression of the period, as well as some sentimental ties outside the norm" (Argueta, *El silencio de Neto* 253). The story revolves around Neto, a restless ten-year-old boy in search of himself. Framed as a bildungsroman, the film sandwiches Neto's identity between his uncle Ernesto and his father, Eduardo, who is at the same time a paternal and patriarchal figure. Meanwhile, Tío Ernesto represents the anti-authoritarian efforts in the country and is a caring and calm character who, like some of the male characters we discuss later, avoids certain types of responsibility. Nonetheless, in his standing up for Neto, Tío Ernesto emulates the characteristics of Miguel Cara de Ángel who, after falling in love, is portrayed as effeminate. Both characters are disinterested in reproducing that violent masculinity, and for Miguel Cara de Ángel this means that he is unable to perform sexually and his lack of malice causes his death.

Luis Argueta, the author and director of *El silencio de Neto*, explores two forms of masculinity as representative of the politics of the time. These, in turn, also recall the models of masculinity established by Asturias in *El señor presidente*. The patriarchal male, Eduardo, Neto's father, is similar to the president in the novel. Importantly, both the president and Eduardo's selves are defined in relation to the state. Moreover, it seems that Eduardo embodies, performs, and enforces terror. At one point, Tío Ernesto criticizes Eduardo saying: "what you want is for them to be robots just like you." If the enactment of agency is what made Cara de Ángel subject to state violence, the film presents Eduardo as stern and strong, following suit, embodying the strongman politics of the state.

Cara de Ángel and Tío Ernesto dress similarly. Cara de Ángel is described as "dressed in gray. His clothes, in the light of twilight, looked like a cloud. He wore in his thin hands a very thin bamboo cane and a Panama hat that looked like a pigeon" (Asturias 16). Tío Ernesto often wears a Panama hat, is dressed in white, and uses a bamboo cane. The lumberjack who first introduces Cara de Ángel describes him as an angel and reacts as if seeing one. Tío Ernesto also has these angelic qualities. After dying, his spirit looks over Neto, very much like a guardian angel. Furthermore, both characters face untimely deaths. One last similarity is that, as Arias reminds us, when leaving the patriarchal hierarchy, Cara de Ángel seems to have also left his malice and in an act of complete gullability falls again and again into the traps the president sets for him. Similarly, Tío Ernesto returns to Guatemala to die in an instance of innocence and purity. Tío Ernesto's death differs from Cara de Ángel, but both are framed within their affectivity. Their affectionate revolution effeminizes them and neither is able to challenge the violence of Ladino masculinity.

Neto's male role models, however, are not only his father and his uncle. In forging the world that Neto inhabits, writers Augusto Chang and Luis Argueta introduce other role models beyond those incarnated in the male character. Guatemalan scholar Edgar Barillas notes this perspicaciously when speaking of mass culture in Neto's world. Unlike previous films made in Guatemala, Barillas notes, this is the first film that mobilized the cultural landscape of the country not simply as background but as a lived world, with its own different and unique history (17–24). This history and culture, however, are framed by transmissions of baseball games over the radio, Neto's collection of baseball cards cut-off from Kellogg's Corn Flakes cereal boxes, and most importantly, the superheroes of Neto's childhood: Los Tres Villalobos, Tamakún, and Tarzan. Los Tres Villalobos was a cowboy radio-novel made in Cuba and reprised in Mexico, then in Guatemala. Tamakún was an Orientalized superhero that served as inspiration to Kalimán and the entire gamut of Middle

Eastern-inspired magic-and-strength-enhanced beings. Lastly, Tarzan (unlike the last two) reached Guatemala as a comic strip. Thus, Tarzan was the forbearer to later comic superheroes like Superman, Batman, and the entire Justice League (Barillas 21–23). The world that Barillas describes perfectly is one where neither his effeminate uncle nor his stern and overpowering father can participate. In fact, Argueta captures the introduction of other masculinities that seem to provide an escape to the tyranny or death binomial presented in Asturias's novel.

In drawing out anti-violent ideals, these foundational texts suggest an effeminate masculine national identity framed within and for the Ladino male, a colonized and dialectical masculinity that sees itself as morally superior to the patriarchal masculinity of the colonizer and more modern than any Indigenous masculinity. In defining a national identity, these two cultural objects also expose the shortcomings of Ladino masculinity as defined by its effeminacy. They thus establish patterns that, as we will see, frame the modes of masculinity possible in contemporary Guatemalan film in the twenty-first century. As we analyze contemporary Guatemalan film, we find that many male characters draw from the paradigms of masculinity that Asturias's novel and Argueta's film delineate.

A New Century, and Alternate Masculinities

After Otto Pérez Molina resigned from his presidency in 2015, Jimmy Morales won the presidential elections, defeating Manuel Baldizón. Morales became famous in the mid-1990s for a comedy skit show that was broadcast on local television: "Moralejas." In the show, Jimmy Morales and his brother Sammy performed as different caricatures or characters that spanned from the offensive Black Pitaya (a blackface character) to the expected Los Gallegos (Galicians are often the center of jokes in Guatemalan comedy). However, it was the skit Nito y Neto, where they play two brothers from the semi-arid department of Zacapa that won them acclaim. The success of Nito y Neto was such that the brother duo, who self-produced the TV show, produced a widely successful play and a series of films based on the characters—including *Un presidente de a sombrero* (2007). In fact, hacercineenguate.com, a website kept by some of the leading producers of Guatemalan cinema, namely Pamela Guinea, counts ten feature-length fiction films from 2000 to 2005, five of these produced and directed by the Morales brothers. Their style of comedy, based on stereotypes and infused with highly localized lexicon as well as with everyday events very much reinforces national discourses. Also, in this vein of comedy, there are other films like *El tamalón navideño* (Guatemala, 2018), by Rafa Tres, or *La vaca* (Guatemala, 2010), by Mendel Samayoa. Masculinity in this type of comedy is either comedic relief or limited to emasculated and effeminate flat male characters. In *El tamalón navideño,* for example, the male secondary characters Arturo and Fernando (compared to the primary female characters) are, respectively, a failed taxi driver whose goal is to drive for Uber, and the other, the director of a TV channel in danger of closing and at the behest of an investor's constant harassment.

Another set of films that seek to portray a national masculinity, notwithstanding sometimes being at odds with the national discourse are (a) the films produced by Casa Comal, the Guatemalan film school, and (b) the films produced in and for consumption outside the capital. Casa Comal films are often produced or directed by Elías Jiménez, one of the founders and a long tenure director of the center. Among them are *La casa de enfrente* (2004), *V.I.P.: La otra casa* (2007), *La bodega* (2010), *Las Cruces: Poblado próximo* (2006), *Toque de queda* (2011), and *Donde nace el Sol* (2013), but also include *Fe* (2010), by Alejo Crisóstomo, and more recently *Los gigantes no existen* (2018), by Chema Rodríguez. Most of their films tend to reflect and depict what they understand as the paradigms of a type of *Guatemalanness,* and as such they tend to be less personal and have larger casts. Similar to Casa Comal, we find films produced for national consumption and not for the film festival circuit, such as *El capitán Orellana y la aldea endemoniada* (2012), *En sentido opuesto* (2008), and the trilogy of *El Profe Omar* (2009) films. Overall, these stories range from comedy to historical fiction including inspirational stories and even political corruption thrillers. It could be said that these films deal with historical constructs and tend to be based on male characters who are fighting for respect and power, thus portraying that central narrative of nation-building—establishing and exposing the pattern of violent masculinity versus effeminacy. Perhaps one of the films to best exemplify this is Ray Figueroa's *La bodega* (2010). In it, Antonio and Jacobo abduct a person they consider to be a member of Mara 18 (a transnational gang) to avenge Jacobo's sister after she has been raped and left in a coma by unknown gang members. Antonio, who is well off, comes up with the idea and spends the film convincing Jacobo to kill the gang member. At the end of the film, neither of them is able to kill the gangster. It is up to Antonio's bodyguard, Chun, who was trained by the military, who kills and gets rid of the body at Antonio's request. Jacobo, even in his anger, is not considered masculine enough because he cannot enforce violence. Rather, Antonio takes him away, hiding him from the violence that Chun will and does enact. Even if these films approach the topic critically, they repeat and establish the national discourse on masculinity: one can either be effeminate or masculine, and this defines the characters' relations to violence.

Possibly the first Guatemalan film to have mass appeal among the local population and cinema attendance was *Puro mula* (2010). Directed by Enrique Pérez Him, the film was produced by the Best Picture System, a collective of recently graduated students from the EICTV, the International School of Cinema and Television in San Antonio de Los Baños, Cuba. The main character, Joel, is a characteristic slacker who begins the story with a bottle of beer in his hand and, after learning his lesson, ends the day with a bottle of beer in his hand—nothing changed. Another slacker film that premiered that same year was *Aquí me quedo* (2010), directed by Rodolfo Espinosa. Espinosa's main character in this film, Paco, takes a bus to Quetzaltenango (Xela), the second largest city in the country. Willy, a psychotic Quetzalteco, finds Paco on a public phone and holds him at gunpoint for nearly the entire film. Their interactions repeatedly show not only Paco's but also Willy's inability to feel empowered and to face up to their respective realities or to enforce violence to gain some semblance of masculinity. Espinosa's other films, even when having more characters, repeat the formula. Even the film *Pol* (2014), titled after Polina, a school-aged nearly teenage girl, and her best friend El Flaco, finds their attempts to make a photocopy of Pol's passport recurrently thwarted often because of El Flaco's effeminate masculinity. Two other important films to highlight here are *Historias absurdamente cortas para tardes desesperadamente largas* (Guatemala, 2012), codirected by Joel López Muñoz and Ivannoe Fajardo Andrade, and *Maquillaje* (2014), by Joel López Muñoz. It should suffice it to say that both films begin with their male characters so drunk and useless that they need others' help to simply get up. In *Maquillaje,* Rosario, the main character, breaks up with her drunkard boyfriend and eventually falls for Julio, a vagabond and hippie musician. Although she was abandoned by her father (who is being chased by gangsters to whom he owes money), she tells him that she doesn't need him. After Rosario returns from a two-year trip with a Russian dance group, she finds out that Julio was killed after becoming a political organizer.

The slacker, as in the stereotypical American sense, points to a masculinity in deficit. We can infer that the figure of the slacker appears as a symbol of the national because he embodies the dialectical male's inability to perform the empowered masculinity of the violent caudillo and, being a slacker, his failures are his fault. Julio Hernández Cordón's first film, *Gasolina* (Guatemala, 2008), follows the same general stereotypes of the slacker. The characters in *Gasolina,* however, are also teenagers who are facing the necessity to behave like men. In the opening scene, Gerardo, one of the main characters, is siphoning gasoline from a neighbor when he is found out. Dressed in army-print khakis, Gerardo tells his neighbor that he will do fifty bench presses in exchange for secrecy. Not only does he skip from twelve to eighteen to thirty, but his asthma also kicks in, forcing him to go home and use a nebulizer. Gerardo's attempt to steal gasoline fails until he returns with rocks in his hand, throwing them at his neighbor. Only after becoming violent can he take the containers filled with gasoline with him. Recurrently, the interactions between Ray, Nano, and Gerardo, including those with other men in the film, are mediated by violence as these sixteen-year-olds attempt to find ways to define themselves, to feel empowered, even if it is just a desire to randomly end up at the beach.

Hernández Cordón's Guatemalan films, including *Las marimbas del infierno* (2010) and *Hasta el Sol tiene manchas* (2012), all deal with the same illusory desire to be empowered and the inability to achieve anything (*Hasta el Sol tiene manchas* is discussed in Julia González de Canales Carcereny's chapter in this volume). In *Las marimbas del Infierno,* the main characters Blacko, Don Alfonso, and Chiqui put together a band that mixes rock with marimba, but after practicing for some time, they are ignored at their scheduled show and have to cancel the project. The film begins in highly personal situations: Don Alfonso's story of running away from extortion (hearing even the director's voice off screen); Blacko is introduced inside a friend's medical office. Two clients complain loudly saying he is dirty and undesirable as the camera shows the audience a close-up of his face: and Chiqui first appears telling a story of how he ran away from gang members as he lies on top of a car in a relaxed and vulnerable position. However, by the end of the film, all three are sitting in a restaurant, after having a few beers, the camera in a wide shot remains static as they flee off screen without paying. The characters are broke and alienated, all show one of the key qualities of the slacker: not being accountable for his actions. The slackers' common sense of defeat turns into comedic relief. Guatemalan Ladino masculinity again seems impossible, but this is not the only masculinity in Guatemalan cinema. Hernández Cordón's *Polvo* (Guatemala, 2012) is one of a few films that glance at a new type of masculinity—Indigenous masculinity.

Other Masculinities

María Lourdes Cortés analyzes the representation of Indigenous peoples in Guatemalan cinema in an article titled "Vacío, silencio y representación: El indígena en el cine guatemalteco." In it she traces a very similar genealogy to what I have traced here, however, focused solely on the ethno-racial character of those represented in Guatemalan cinema. Although the book that contains the essay was published in 2017, the article stops its analysis in 2012. Since then, other films have added to the corpus of Indigenous representation in Guatemalan fiction cinema. Cortés focuses on the first films to open up a space for Indigenous representation in Guatemala: the above-mentioned *Polvo* and *Distancia* (2011), by Sergio Ramírez. In the end, Cortés proposes that these films are different from one another because *Polvo* is disenchanted with the idea of a reconciliation, whereas *Distancia* finds reconciliation as the main character, don Tomás, finds his long-estranged daughter. Yet Cortés reminds us that these two films are similar in that they refuse to establish a dominant gaze, a colonial gaze, if you will, over the characters. For Cortés, this exposes the impossibility of Guatemala to see itself as Indigenous, be it through reconciliation or through disenchantment. Only in the last couple of years have films (that are still in the independent film circuit) explored masculinity through non-heterosexual non-white male characters.

Assuredly, Cortés could not have foreseen that films like *Donde nace el Sol* (2013) or *Ixcanul* (2016) would sway the focus of representations of indigeneity to female Indigenous characters and their struggles.[10] However, my intention in this essay is not to discuss this change of focus. Instead I turn to another film, *El regreso de Lencho* (2010), directed by Mario Rosales. Here, the main character, Lencho, returns to Guatemala after living abroad most of his life. Once in the city and moving through the artistic and leftist circles in Guatemala City, he begins an art project. Lencho is a graffiti artist who wants to showcase graffiti art in the country. They find a space in a school in Rabinal, a town in the interior of the country. In the first meeting we see that Lencho has nothing to say while Manuel, a secondary and Indigenous character, has already had a meeting with the mayor of the town and met four times with local artists. Clearly, Manuel is doing the work of organizing this festival and, for some reason, on the day before the event Manuel thanks Lencho for his leadership and initiative. The film portrays Lencho as somewhat of a *vividor* (a ladies' man, a slacker, an artist), a Ladino, and a masculine leader. However, Lencho's "leadership" is dependent on Manuel's. Moreover, Lencho's masculinity is emphasized by contrast with the Indigenous-looking Manuel, who uses a feminine scarf and has more effeminate mannerisms. Ladino national masculinity then, appears to be a scam, a façade or as Guzmán Böckler notes, a fiction. What *El regreso de Lencho* lets us see is that behind privileged Ladino masculinity we can often find Chun (in *La bodega*) or Manuel (in *Lencho*), Indigenous actors taking an active role in their own destinies.

The presence of Chun and Manuel, as those who do the work that Antonio and Lencho do not, points to a colonial relationship reminiscent of R.W. Connell's description of a gentry masculinity. Connell notes that hegemonic masculinity evolved into two contrasting currently existing modes: the impulsive enforcer and the scientific manager (249). Connell takes this one step further and notes that the rational hegemonic masculinity came to find itself in the metropoles, in the city. Meanwhile, the irrational hegemonic masculinity became confined to the colonies, to the frontier, where acting violently is celebrated and often believed to be necessary. Within this framework, we can look back at Lencho and Antonio, who are both upper-class and embodying a managerial masculinity. This recalls the colonial relationship between the gendered hegemony of managers and that of those who have to act, like Chun and Manuel. In this light, the gendered hegemonic masculinity embodied in these characters necessarily recalls a racial character that cannot be disconnected from the Ladino-Indigenous Guatemalan dichotomy and the racialized violence it implies.

Mara Viveros Vigoya cites the work of Santiago Bastos to underscore that Guatemalan masculinity functions in a double bind, sometimes as a caudillo, sometimes as a sentimental male (Viveros Vigoya). These opposing modes of masculinity seem integral to the colonial masculine Ladino subject. He is the dialectical male who, as Todd Reeser notes, "may go about his life moving back and forth between accepting and rejecting" the characteristics of hegemonic masculinity (Reeser 191). It is of no surprise that many of the male characters in Guatemalan cinema are comedic, slackers, or highly violent, patriarchal *caudillos*. They often will inhabit the same body; they support the same patriarchal system. They do not act against the structure that benefits them and are forgiven for this. More recent films seem to be delving into those questions with pungent critique. More recently, there have been films that step beyond the limits of heteronormativity to discuss homosexuality in the country, like *Temblores* (2019), by Jayro Bustamante, and *José* (2018), by Li Cheng, which are the first two Guatemalan films centered on gay men and their coming out stories, and even films like *Pólvora en el corazón* (2020), which centers around two lesbian women living in Guatemala City. Granja, Espinoza, and List's chapter in this volume details various perspectives on gender and sexuality in Central American film, including gay-themed films. These films are key in further study of gender in Guatemala and Central America and the necessary next step in the critique and depiction of masculinity, patriarchal narratives, and violence. These films may yet open spaces for the creation of masculinities beyond the dialectical and conflicted national character embodied by the Guatemalan Ladino male that we have seen at the center of the national discourse since the work of Asturias and Luis Argueta, until today.

Notes

1 For an analysis of *La jaula de oro*, see María Lourdes Cortés's chapter on immigration and film in this volume.
2 Justo Rufino Barrios would also popularize the term Ladino, which we will explore further ahead.
3 Original quote: "como justificación profunda y ampliamente generalizada se recurre al racismo [. . .]."
4 "De manera que, en la Guatemala colonizada, el racismo y las diferenciaciones raciales son tan importantes como las separaciones calcadas en factores de orden económico."
5 "primitivo-superior, bárbaro-civilizado, prelógico-lógico, mágico-racional, etc. en su forma tecnócrata: subdesarrollado-desarrollado, tradicional-moderno [. . .]."
6 I return to an analysis of Indigenous masculinities further down.
7 "Este *hombre* no es vislumbrado por atributos de virilidad ni se identifica con la figura paternal; mas bien, su imagen se confunde con la del sujeto que humilla, que golpea, que tortura, prevalido del poder y basado en la arbitrariedad. En realidad, no se trata de ningún hombre sino de un *sub-hombre*."
8 This differs vastly from the position of the Mestizo in other Latin American contexts where, although the Mestizo and mestizaje became national policies and representatives of the nation, they did not often come to power or maintained it. Historian Arturo Taracena Arriola points to the use of the term Ladino both as regional identifier and as a term that consolidated power in a group that eventually became hegemonic in Guatemala. In this respect the term Ladino is only understandable within Guatemalan history and underscores how the Guatemalan case differs from masculinity and racial politics in countries like Mexico, where criollo elites remained in power under disguises of Mestizo inclusivity.
9 In identifying with these effeminate martyrs these films recall Laura Mulvey's criticism of the male gaze which ignores the female characters and only sees them as objects to be affected by the men's stories.
10 It is important to note that with the arrival of films that focus on both white and Indigenous female characters, there are other masculinities that appear in the backgrounds of films. This includes *Ixcanul*, which critiques how women often still receive different modes of violence from different types of patriarchal Indigenous masculinity that reinforces traditional heteronormative roles. However, this converstion has been better addressed by Indigenous female scholars who have taken a stance against racial and gendered violence from outside and within Indigenous communities.

Works Cited

Adams, Rachel, and David Savran, editors. *The Masculinity Studies Reader*. Malden: Wiley, 2002.
Aquí me quedo. Directed by Rodolfo Espinosa, Me llega Films, Guatemala, 2010.
Argueta, Luis. *El silencio de Neto: Guión y artículos afines*. Guatemala City: Editorial Universitaria de la U de San Carlos de Guatemala, 2005.
Asturias, Miguel Angel. *El señor presidente*. San José: Editorial de la U de Costa Rica, 2000.

Barillas, Edgar. "El Mundo de Neto en *El silencio de Neto.*" *El silencio de Neto: Guión y artículos afines,* edited by Luis Argueta, Editorial Universitaria de la U de San Carlos de Guatemala, 2005, pp. 11–33.

Böckler, Carlos Guzmán. *Colonialismo y Revolucion.* Guatemala City: Catafixia Editorial, 2019.

———. *Guatemala: Una interpretación histórico-social.* Guatemala City: Cholsamaj, 2002.

Connell, R.W. "The History of Masculinity." *The Masculinity Studies Reader,* edited by Rachel Adams and David Savran, Wiley, 2002, pp. 245–261.

Cortés, María Lourdes. *La pantalla rota: Cien años de cine en Centroamérica.* Ciudad de México: Taurus, 2005.

———. "Vacío, silencio y representación: El indígena en el cine guatemalteco." *Representaciones del mundo indígena en el cine hispanoamericano (Documental y ficción),* edited by Esther Gimeno Ugalde and Karen Poe, Editorial de la U de Costa Rica, 2017, pp. 135–148.

Distancia. Directed by Sergio Ramírez, Casa Comal, Guatemala, 2012.

Donde nace el Sol. Directed by Elías Jiménez, Casa Comal, Guatemala, 2013.

El capitán Orellana y la aldea endemoniada. Directed by Javier Tessari, Oro Puro Producciones, Guatemala, 2012.

El regreso de Lencho. Directed by Mario Rosales, Occularis Films, Guatemala, 2012.

El silencio de Neto. Directed by Luis Argueta, Buenos Días, Guatemala, 1996.

El tamalón navideño. Directed by Rafael Tres, Cinema 502, Guatemala, 2018.

Fe. Directed by Alejo Crisóstomo, Casa Comal, Ceibita Films, Jirafa, Guatemala, 2011.

Figueroa Ibarra, Carlos. *El recurso del miedo: Ensayo sobre el estado y el terror en Guatemala.* San José: Editorial Universitaria Centroamericana, 1991.

Gasolina. Directed by Julio Hernández Cordón, Melindrosa Films, Silvio Sardi Communications, Guatemala, 2010.

Halberstam, Jack. *Female Masculinity.* Durham: Duke UP, 2019.

Hasta el Sol tiene manchas. Directed by Hernández Cordón, Melindrosa Films, Guatemala, 2012.

Historias absurdamente cortas para tardes desesperadamente largas. Directed by Joel López Muñoz and Ivannoe Fajardo Andrade, Colectivo Arrancacebollas, Guatemala, 2012.

Hostal don Tulio. Directed by Rodolfo Espinosa, True Media Company, Guatemala, 2018.

Ixcanul. Directed by Jayro Bustamante, La Casa de Production, Tu Vas Voir Productions, Guatemala, 2015.

José. Directed by Li Cheng, YQstudio LLC, Guatemala, 2020.

La bodega. Directed by Ray Figueroa, Casa Comal, Guatemala, 2010.

La casa de enfrente. Directed by Elías Jiménez Trachtenberg, Casa Comal, Guatemala, 2004.

La jaula de oro. Directed by Quemada-Díez, Animal de Luz Films, Castafiore Films, Consejo Nacional para la Cultura y las Artes (CONACULTA), Mexico, 2013.

La Llorona. Directed by Jayro Bustamante, El Ministerio de Cultura y Deportes de Guatemala, La Casa de Production, Les Films du Volcan, Guatemala, 2020.

Las Cruces: Poblado próximo. Directed by Rafael Rosal, Casa Comal, Guatemala, 2006.

Las marimbas del infierno. Directed by Julio Hernández Cordón, Les Films du Requin, Melindrosa Films, Axolote Cine, Guatemala, 2011.

La vaca—Holy Cow. Directed by Mendel Samayoa, Guatemala, 2011.

Los gigantes no existen. Directed by Chema Rodríguez, Producciones Sin Un Duro, Icónica Producciones, PTP Mundo Maya, Guatemala, 2018.

Maquillaje. Directed by Joel López Muñoz, Guatemala, 2014.

Ovnis en Zacapa. Directed by Marcos Machado, Best Picture System, Guatemala, 2015.

Pol. Directed by Rodolfo Espinosa, Me Llega Films, Guatemala, 2014.

Polvo. Directed by Julio Hernández Cordón, Melindrosa Films, Tic Tac Producciones, Autentika Films, Guatemala, 2012.

Pólvora en el corazón. Directed by Camila Urrutia, Curuxa Cinema, Guatemala, 2019.

Puro mula. Directed by Enrique Pérez Him, Best Picture System, Guatemala, 2011.

Reeser, Todd W. *Masculinities in Theory: An Introduction.* Malden: Wiley-Blackwell, 2010.

Rocha, Carolina, and Georgia Seminet. *Representing History, Class, and Gender in Spain and Latin America: Children and Adolescents in Film.* New York: Palgrave Macmillan, 2012.

Taracena Arriola, Arturo. *Invención criolla, sueño ladino, pesadilla indígena: Los Altos de Guatemala, de región a Estado, 1740–1850.* San José: Porvenir, 1997.

Temblores. Directed by Jayro Bustamante, Tu Vas Voir Productions, La Casa de Production, Memento Films Production, Guatemala, 2019.

Te prometo anarquía. Directed by Julio Hernández Cordón, Interior13 Cine, Fondo para la Producción Cinematográfica de Calidad (FOPROCINE), Rohfilm, Mexico, 2016.

Toque de queda. Directed by Ray Figueroa and Elías Jiménez Trachtenberg, Casa Comal, Guatemala, 2011.

Trip la película. Directed by Fran Lepe, Guatemala, 2011.

Un presidente de a sombrero. Directed by Jimmy and Sammy Morales, Guatemala, 2007.

Viveros Vigoya, Mara. "Contemporary Latin American Perspectives on Masculinity:" *Men and Masculinities,* vol. 3, no. 3 , 2016, pp. 233–260.

V.I.P.: La otra casa. Directed by Elías Jiménez Trachtenberg, Casa Comal, Guatemala, 2007.

14

Film and Gender in Central America

Five Voices

Daniela Granja Núñez

Interviews by Mauricio Espinoza and Jared List

Translated by Mauricio Espinoza, Jared List, and Ana Pérez Méndez

The topic of gender in movies and in the film industry, from the stories that are told to the intricacies of the production process, has been gaining more relevance in the past twenty years. As characters, women have always been a part of the narrative world of cinema. But, as a diverse and complex segment of the population, women have not been represented in a fair or truthful manner for most of the time film as a medium has been in existence. The history of cinema shows us how representations and approaches to dealing with gender portrayals have been evolving, slowly, but surely. As a result, women have seen their own characters change and have also witnessed social movements that push the film industry to include them in more honest and equitable ways. Both in terms of production and representation, women continue the struggle to make themselves more visible in cinema. The same kind of transformation, although more recent and still in its infancy in various cinemas around the world, has also been taking place with regards to sexual orientation and queer depictions in the movies.

In Central America, women play increasingly important roles as screenwriters, directors, producers, and in other facets of filmmaking. As indicated in this volume's introduction, about half of the films being made currently in the region are women-helmed projects (Luna). The centrality of women to Central American film is also gaining the attention of scholars. For example,

Valeria Grinberg Pla highlighted the significant contributions of women directors to the region's cinema in her 2013 article "Mujeres cineastas de Centroamérica: Continuidad y ruptura." Other studies address the construction of female characters, including María Lourdes Cortés's "Mujer y madre en el cine centroamericano actual" (2004) and Andrea Cabezas Vargas's "Las nuevas heroínas del cine centroamericano: De la Historia a la ficción. Transformaciones de los personajes femeninos en las últimas cuatro décadas" (2019). More recently (2020), Ileana Rodríguez published *Modalidades de memoria y archivos afectivos: Cine de mujeres en Centroamérica,* the first monograph dedicated to women filmmakers from the Isthmus—focusing on documentaries by Gloria Carrión, Lucía Cuevas, Tatiana Huezo, Mercedes Moncada, Marcela Zamora, and Leonor Zúñiga, as well as American director Pamela Yates. LGBTQ+ issues, representations, and societal attitudes toward sexual diversity have also been addressed in recent Central American film, including in Laura Astorga's fiction short *Ellas se aman* (Costa Rica, 2008); the features *Abrázame como antes* (Costa Rica, 2016), by Jurgen Ureña, *Temblores* (Guatemala, 2019), by Jayro Bustamante, and Marlén Viñayo's documentary *Imperdonable* (El Salvador, 2020).

Approaches to issues of gender and sexuality are quite diverse in twenty-first-century Central American fiction and documentary film (for example, Arno J. Argueta's chapter in this volume explores representations of masculinity in Guatemalan film). Here, directors Laura Astorga, Ishtar Yasin, Gloria Carrión Fonseca, and Luis Fernando Midence, as well as producer Pamela Guinea, provide their perspectives in the following extracts from personal interviews conducted by Mauricio Espinoza and Jared List between 2017 and 2020.

Laura Astorga Carrera

Astorga is a Costa Rican film director, screenwriter, and activist for human rights, disability, and feminism. Her fiction short *Ellas se aman* (2008) premiered at the Locarno Festival and had a successful run, being featured at festivals such as San Francisco, Mar del Plata, Madrid, Torino, Bilbao, São Paulo, and London; it was also acquired by McGraw-Hill Publishing as part of its selection of Latin American shorts. Her first feature film, *Princesas rojas* (Costa Rica, 2013), had its international premiere at Berlinale and was recognized as Best Opera Prima at several international festivals, including the Los Angeles International Film Festival and the Margarita Latin American and Caribbean Film Festival. Astorga has served as judge for various international film events, including Berlinale, the Ibero-American Platino Film Awards, and the Chicago International Film Festival. She forged her next feature film project (still in the development stages) at Cinéfondation, the Cannes Festival's artist-in-residence program.

Gender issues not only appear in the world of cinema through the representation of women and LGBTQ+ individuals, but also in the stories told in movies. Regarding the incorporation of aspects related to gender and anti-sexism in her films, Astorga points out that it is often a reverse process:

> that is, I constructed these stories and characters and the questions I received from critics and audiences forced me to go back and analyze them, and that's how I discovered that perhaps they do break some stereotypes. For example, in the ending of *Princesas rojas,* Claudia's mother leaves the country and leaves her daughter in the airport. Following the screenings, people would tell me that mothers and/or women just don't do that; that the fact I made a character do such a thing is quite peculiar. I would then feel a bit flustered because I, naively, thought that people and characters can do whatever they want independently of their gender or role. Also, my mom did exactly that. After this experience, I began to study which were those habitual spaces that correspond to each sex and gender in the movies, and that's how the *Sexismógrafo* was born.
>
> The *Sexismógrafo* is a personal research project of mine that is constantly expanding, being fed by the experiences and contributions of other colleagues. It's a pedagogical aggregate tool that detects and redeems sexism in mass media . . . assigning a scale to each audiovisual production. The *Sexismógrafo* combines various tests that measure different types of gender discrimination in a number of cultural products such as film, television, and even literature. The goal is to identify toxic stereotypes and generate criticism. In the scale of the *Sexismógrafo,* Costa Rican and Central American cinema curiously fall within two extremes: sensitive gender or invisible gender. It's the summary of a mathematical and philosophical formula that's very simple and applies to everything: *the more women there are, the less power they have; the more power there is, the fewer women there are,* which demonstrates that despite the fact that academics and journalists point out that Central America is one of the regions of the world with the most women making movies, such observation is naïve or even ignorant.

For Astorga, the problem of gender representation does not lie in the differentiation between commercial cinema and independent cinema. There are commercial films from Hollywood, such as *The Post* (USA, 2018), that:

create an extraordinary female character who also has a very interesting female gaze; we see this very small character grow as a minor character, or rather a shallow character, and she continues growing until the moment of the climax, when the film represents the power that this female character has acquired with a Rembrandt painting. We can see a female character with true power: decision-making power, economic power, political power.

Meanwhile, independent film, with smaller productions, is not able to establish nor develop more well-rounded female characters:

The problem of female representation lies in a social structural element of gender disparity, which not only limits cinema's capacity to create complex and strong female characters but also the hiring of female crew members and team leaders.

In Costa Rica, the conversation around gender representation

is just beginning. For example, the collective presence of women in Costa Rica's film industry has an influence in the allocation of grants and production quotas for women filmmakers. There are conversations with the Film Center so that *El Fauno* fund can establish quotas in its production processes, and we are trying to make it so that quotas are set for having 50% women and 50% female team leaders.[1] My stance is that in order to recover lost time we need to achieve "parity + 1," that is, more than 50%. What happens is that when you have equal groups in terms of men and women, men (because of the confidence gap) and women (because of the imposter syndrome, since we women are the ones who experience it) don't end up interacting in such equal terms. Generally, women don't have the same authority in discourse, in discussions, and in confrontations with others. This is very important, to achieve "parity +1" for a while, so that more women are involved and get to be a majority and put together a political bloc. If we are exactly half or less, we won't achieve a political bloc. And so, all of these elements point to the fact that a conversation is starting to take shape.

An anecdotical situation, in which a female director of photography was not able to take part in the shooting of a film because she needed to stay home with her son, shows us that "it's not a matter of which job a woman holds in a production, but rather that socially we need to generate a safety net so that these women, all of us women, can leave our children and be relaxed working as director of photography for a movie."

Pamela Guinea

Guinea is a Guatemalan producer. She's cofounder of the production company Melindrosa Films, which has been behind films such as *Gasolina* (Guatemala, 2008), *Las marimbas del infierno* (Guatemala, 2010), *Polvo* (Guatemala, 2012), and *Hasta el Sol tiene manchas* (Guatemala, 2012), by Julio Hernández Cordón. She was production manager for the documentary *Lecciones para una guerra* (Mexico, 2012), directed by Juan Manuel Sepúlveda, and line producer in Guatemala for the Mexican film *La jaula de oro* (2013), by Diego Quemada-Díez. In 2013 Guinea moved to Mexico, where she worked as project development coordinator for companies such as Axolote Cine, Circo 2.12, and Agencia Bengala, responsible for films such as *Te prometo anarquía* (Mexico, 2015), by Hernández Cordón; *Extraño pero verdadero* (Mexico, 2017), by Michel Lipkes; *Inzomnia* (Mexico, in production), by Luis Téllez; and *Vaquero del mediodía* (Mexico, 2019), by Diego Osorno. She was producer of the Mexican festival *Distrital, cine y otros mundos* in its 2014 and 2015 editions. She also produced the feature-length film *Tesoros* (Mexico, 2017), by María Novaro, which premiered in the 67th edition of Berlinale. She's coproducer and executive producer of *Nuestras madres* (Guatemala, 2019), by César Díaz, which premiered in the 58th Critics' Week at Cannes in 2019, where it earned the Golden Camera, among other awards. Currently, with her production company Cine Murciélago, she is working on film projects such as *Roza* (Guatemala, 2022) directed by Andrés Rodríguez. She is president of the Guatemalan Association of Audiovisual and Film Production (AGACINE).

As president of AGACINE and producer of more than twelve feature films, Guinea knows well about issues of gender in Central American cinema. She states, "According to a survey we conducted with AGACINE during the beginning of the COVID-19 quarantine in 2020, we saw a huge difference regarding the disparity between men and women who make movies in Central America. I believe more spaces and opportunities are needed for women. And that's something we are working on."

Some of the challenges facing the Central American audiovisual sector also translate into limitations when it comes to gender. Guinea claims:

> We need to create an institutional structure, and for the state to recognize and assume its responsibility in film production. One of those commitments must be the approval of a cinema law and the creation of funds and mechanisms that support the industry's development, as well as respecting and meeting all commitments made. We also need to coproduce in equal conditions. Guatemala does not have co-production

agreements with any European countries; our only legal framework is the Ibero-American Co-Production Accord. This leaves us in a clear disadvantage when the time comes to co-produce with these countries. In the absence of a film institute and a national fund, it's difficult to receive cash and obtain a real assessment of the contribution made by local productions; money always goes back to where it came from, and films always depend on foreign funds, which doesn't allow them to accrue capital to reinvest in the next production.

She adds:

The private sector still doesn't have confidence in film production as an economic engine, there's little investment in movies; this is due to the profitability of movies and entrepreneurs' ignorance of how the film industry works. One of the greater challenges and deficiencies of the Guatemalan audiovisual sector is that it doesn't know itself; there's little concrete information and hard data about how the industry should be developed, about its economic impact as well as its growth and needs.

Thinking about the representation of women in both commercial and independent film, Guinea believes that:

if we were to apply the Bechdel test to any of these two types of cinema, I think few, very few movies would pass. However, I believe that's something that's starting to change, regardless of whether it is commercial or independent film. And it's due, perhaps, also to the fact that now there are more women who are producing, directing, writing, and telling our own stories.

Global movements such as #metoo, that could improve gender representations, "have resonated little in Guatemalan film. There's still a lot of silence and fear. I hope we will soon be able to get started with a protocol or at least a good-practices manual against sexual harassment in spaces related to film and audiovisual products. There's still a lot of work to do in this regard." These ideas also apply to the representation of women in production settings, because:

it's an issue of awareness. In Guatemala there are many very talented professionals, women, in many (if not all) of the areas of film production. But if there isn't full awareness of this fact, it would be hard for there to be true representation of women and/or minorities. It's still so much more common to see crews made up mostly of men.

Ishtar Yasin Gutiérrez

Yasin was born in Moscow to an Iraqi father and a Chilean-Costa Rican mother. After the 1973 military coup in Chile, a young Yasin took refuge with her family in Costa Rica, where she studied at the Conservatorio Castella arts preparatory. At the age of seventeen she traveled to Moscow, where she studied in the State Cinema Institute VGIK. She has worked as a filmmaker and actress in different cities and countries around the world: in Moscow, Kazakhstan, Georgia, Damascus, Lebanon, Chile, Argentina, Costa Rica, Nicaragua, Haiti, and Mexico. In 1999, Yasin founded Astarté Films and directed several movies. In 2004, she obtained a residence in the Centre d'Ecriture Cinematographique CECI in Normandy, France. In 2008, her first feature film *El Camino* (Costa Rica) premiered in the Official Competition of Forum at the Berlin International Film Festival. This film won fifteen international awards and was selected by more than fifty international festivals around the world. In 2010, Yasin traveled to Haiti and filmed the movie *Les Invisibles* (Costa Rica), a month after the earthquake that shook that country. This film was part of the Selection of the International African Film Festival in Spain, the International Cultural Resistance Festival in Lebanon, and the Arts Doc Festival in Mexico City, among others. In 2012, Yasin moved to Mexico, where she made her second feature film, *Dos Fridas* (Mexico/Costa Rica), which premiered in 2018 in the Main Competition of the Tallinn Black Nights Film Festival in Estonia. So far, this film has won ten international awards, including Best Direction at the Gibara International Film Festival, Best Film at the Ícaro International Film Festival, and the Remi Golden Award for Best Experimental Film at the 53rd Annual World Fest in Houston, Texas, in 2020.

As mentioned above, gender representation in cinema occurs at different levels. One of them is the production process, where women may take on positions of power and responsibility (as producers or directors) or where they may occupy roles within the production team (art department, cinematography, editing, sound, pre-production, etc.). As we are talking about a diverse and relatively large production environment, it is normal that the number of women working in the film industry in Central America has increased. Yasin suggests, "It's surprising that in Costa Rica there are so many women directors, many of them with such great talent and sensibility. Women have a great need to express ourselves and cinema is a marvelous medium [to do so], with many possibilities. Luckily, digital film has improved our access to the means of production."

The second important level of representation is the movie itself, which boils down to the characters: women and queer individuals. She adds, "I think it's important to have female characters created by women. We are capable of destroying clichés and stereotypes where women are used as merchandise, occupying the roles determined by the patriarchal system." Stereotypes and the roles of characters, which can be determined a priori by the stories being told, are extremely relevant for the visualization and the representation of gender. Yasin states, "Not long ago I was making a comment about some filmmakers who have said that film is dead. I think they are wrong. We women have much to contribute. The story [of cinema] has been written from a Eurocentric lens or from Hollywood's hegemony, making us undervalue our own [stories] and follow certain rules or trends. We must look from other perspectives, change the angle, achieve a cultural and artistic independence. That is, to decolonize."

In this regard, the treatment of characters in film must be a conscious exercise of fair representation. In this respect, she says:

> In almost all of my movies, the protagonists are females. I cannot generalize in terms of their attributes, as each character has her own peculiarities. But reflecting on them, I could say they are women or girls who have suffered violence, discrimination, abuse, abandonment, and who seek an exit from that pain; they rebel against their own destinies and face the inevitable. We live in a patriarchal-capitalist society, where women fulfill the roles imposed by such system. Their bodies are turned into merchandise, into sexual objects, in subordination to men. This, clearly, manifests itself in cinema. There are filmmakers, especially those doing independent film, who have portrayed women as human beings, with the same rights [as men]. She can be the protagonist and, at the same time, transform reality.

In our current moment, social movements such as #metoo "have given many women the courage to express themselves, tell their stories, sorrows, dreams, struggles; and in this way they can denounce, in an artistic way, the abuse and discrimination we experience on a daily basis. However, we don't yet know the concrete impact of these transformational movements in Central American film." As producer of her own films, Yasin states that "I have never had any problem forming teams made up of people with the best abilities and willingness to pour their hearts and souls into an audiovisual project," always seeking representation from women, "who are not a minority in cinema."

Gloria Carrión Fonseca

Carrión is a Nicaraguan filmmaker who has produced short and feature films of experimental cinema, fiction, and documentaries. Her most recent documentary feature, *Heredera del viento* (Nicaragua, 2017), is an intimate trip to the past—a familiar and national past—to explore and understand the positionality and identity of herself, her parents, and Nicaraguan society during the Sandinista revolution. From an intimate and personal place, the documentary breaks the silence of the past and reflects on the memories of the revolution, giving it a reflective focus, humanizing and democratizing. Her short films include *Fractals* (Nicaragua, 2011), *Rossana en construcción* (Nicaragua, 2013), and others. She earned her master's degree in documentary film from Film University (FUC) in Argentina, aside from her studies and degrees from the London School of Economics and Political Science, New York University, and Trent University. Carrión is director and producer of Caja de Luz production company.[2]

The differences in the way fiction films and documentaries are produced are many, varying in their approaches to the object or subject of study, research methods, pre-production and production methods, and narrative techniques. Positions regarding gender issues can be crucial for the materialization of the final product in either fiction or documentary film. However, such positions do not necessarily dictate the themes, reception, and quality of a movie. Carrión Fonseca explains:

> I don't think there is a "woman's" look in the documentary. Just as I don't think it exists in literature. I think that we, men and women, are marked by many elements throughout our lives, and gender is only one of them. To me it seems that the gaze and the creative vision are born from the complexity of human, social, and existential experience, which includes, but also transcends, the fact that we are men or women. Now, that doesn't mean there are no barriers and inequalities in filmmaking which we confront as female directors, producers, and technicians. Indeed, many of the technicians in filmmaking are men, and sometimes power dynamics emerge that produce inequalities. On a global level, there are even, like in other areas, huge differences among men's and women's pay in filmmaking, which, of course, should change. In Nicaragua, there are several female directors, but this is not the reality across the region. In general, the directors are men.

The construction of identities in film has been linked to various aspects of gender and the depiction of gender identities. Documentary film becomes an excellent tool for the construction of gender identities. Carrión Fonseca adds:

> I think that it definitely has to do a lot with the device. The camera itself introduces an element that in a way calls to performativity because there is staging, a camera setup and the subjects are always being edited, placed on stage, and it seems to me that, in this sense, my role as an observer is just to play this game as well because I also frame ... because I also imprint my subjectivity into what I am looking at. Then, with the short film *Rossana en construcción,* what I was looking forward to do was to make this even more obvious. The fact that the staging of identity is a co-construction. In this sense, the story is co-constructed with what the person is telling about herself and what she is leaving out of this representation. Therefore, I think there is something democratizing in this order to setup a dialogue in which I am not the almighty looking at you, subject, and building what I want from you—but a space in which we are influencing and feeding off each other. When I ask Rossana in the short film to introduce herself, I give the camera to her, I let it go. In other words, I let her interact with that camera and I invite her to play. This is fascinating to me because it addresses a question as eternal as it is inexhaustive: who are we, and how do we construct our own identity?

Luis Fernando Midence

Midence is a Guatemalan filmmaker who specializes in gay-themed short films. His shorts include *One-on-One* (USA, 2010), *Sin ruta* (Guatemala, 2012), *Verdadero-primero-último* (Guatemala, 2017), *Te toca* (Guatemala, 2109), and *Las cosas que no decimos* (Guatemala, 2019). He has a master's degree from the University of Miami in Florida, a second master's degree in theater from Miami University of Ohio, and a third one in humanities from the University of Texas in Dallas.[3]

Midence has produced various short films exploring the experiences of gay characters, who are seldom portrayed in Central American cinema. *One-on-One,* a 2010 short film, was on YouTube the year it debuted. Midence shares, "It [One-on-One] went very well for me, in a matter of perhaps a year and a half, we reached half a million views. But at that time, YouTube's policy was very homophobic, and because we had a kiss, an interracial kiss, someone flagged the video, and it blocked us in almost half of the world. And there was no way of asking YouTube to review it, that the video had absolutely nothing obscene. The film was not against the policy and since there was no way to remove the block, I became frustrated and threw out everything and said to hell with YouTube." One of the challenges of Central American filmmakers in general is the distribution of their products; digital platforms are an alternative.

Many times, as Midence observes, it is the directors who, by their own personal experiences, push topics of gender in their productions. Midence states:

> I am gay and I grew up in the 1990s. In the 90s, if you saw LGBTQ+ representation, they were men dressed as women, but they were not even drag queens or transvestites; they were effeminate men, they were parodies, they were jokes, it was like denigrating them or they had AIDS and they died or they were the girl's best friend and were only in the film for about five minutes. And it wasn't until the film *Threesome* came out that I saw a character completely, I use the word, normal and I realized the power that has. You sit in the audience, and you see some element of you reflected on screen. It has an immense and transformative power; it is a catharsis. I need to see myself reflected on-screen, or if I don't see myself reflected, at least, reflecting some aspect of the community that I know; that is what I am looking for, telling LBGTQ stories. I would like to expand myself more, really tell stories of the entire community, but it costs a lot. There is no budget; there is no interest.

The representation of the LGBTQ+ community in film, in particular in Central American film, is changing. The characters who are developed are more realistic, more honest. The inclusion of characters with different masculinities contributes also to the topic of gender in film. The relationship between characters and actors impacts the quality of the story, and, consequently, its reception in theaters, digital platforms, and film festivals. Midence adds:

> My stories are contemporary; they do not pertain to a magical world. We are living in the real world, and I really like the fact that the actor shows us an extension of themselves, instead of having a character who changes their voice or their way of walking. The beautiful thing about that, or at least here in Guatemala, what I have learned, is that men (despite having to present themselves as very macho), they like physical affection with other men, something that in the United States doesn't happen. In the United States, you hug someone, and they are like "why are you hugging me?" Whereas, here hugging is the most normal thing, giving a kiss to a friend here is the most normal thing. With heterosexual Guatemalan men, I feel, it is a little more difficult to distinguish

who is gay, who is not gay. We are very romantic, sentimental, and that, I don't know, I believe that mix of macho and romantic is very fascinating. I try to take advantage of the characters who are not stereotypes of anything, but rather they feel very real. I play a lot with the actor's own personality because I feel that it gives them a veracity and gives them a realism that you cannot perform.

About other filmmakers whose productions include LGBTQ+ themes, Midence signals:

I cannot honestly speak of Central America, because I hear almost nothing about movies [that are made]. There isn't a lot of noise. It surprises me, Costa Rica has a very good film industry, but I have never seen films from them. Here in Guatemala, up until this moment, I am the only who has been dealing with the LGBTQ+ topic. Jayro Bustamante made a film. He filmed it, I think last year, but it hasn't come out yet.[4] And it deals with the theme of a man who is married with children but discovers that he is gay. It is a feature-length film. If it premieres, it will be the first Guatemalan gay-themed feature-length film. But I am the person, for the moment, who is always making gay-themed movies. That is the association that there is with me and the type of film I make.

As we have seen, multiple challenges exist with the cinematographic task in Central America; the largest being financing. Midence insists:

Look, here in Guatemala, with money you buy whatever you want. The budget really is everything. If you have that budget, there are no obstacles. Fortunately with actors—I am very clear with everyone—I tell them at the beginning, this is gay-themed, but I don't have anything controversial. I don't have sex, I don't have nudity, I don't deal with that in any of my shorts. There is not a problem with the actors, the crew, or anyone. Perhaps an obstacle is the socio-cultural theme, when I am looking for locations. When I film in real locations, sometimes I don't know about informing them that it is a gay film. You say the word "gay" and automatically doors close here in Guatemala. One must learn very well to navigate, so that they give you permission to use locations.

It is evident that financing depends also on other factors, just like it depends on the project's market viability. Unfortunately, many audiovisual products appear difficult to sell or distribute. Audiences always have been a complicated aspect to interpret; audiences in festivals as opposed to audiences in digital platforms, local audiences compared to international audiences. The audience's niches become more evident when the film's themes are more restricted. Midence adds:

> My audience, particularly, are gay men. I want them to identify with the character and so that they can do that, I feel it is important that there is some empathy with the situation that the character is in. Much of what I have learned comes from theater, in the sense of creating empathy between the audience and the character, but also causes a conflict for the audience. You don't want the audience to only fall in love with the character and be blinded by emotions, but rather you want them to be intellectually stimulated with what is happening to the characters, that you begin to put yourself a little bit in the characters' shoes, beyond only creating an empathetic bond with them, but also put yourself in their situation, question their decision. Stimulating yourself intellectually is something that interests me a lot in the stories that I tell, whether it be in film or in theater.

Within LGBTQ+ issues, visual narratives can help demystify the ideas of heteronormative gender roles. Midence suggests:

> Maybe it's just me, but I see many allies of the LGBTQ+ community. You look at men and women who say yes, I am an ally, but then they always commit the error of saying or doing something that goes against being an ally, like bringing up being active or passive. In a certain manner, the desire to be the dominant one is very homophobic. Perhaps not homophobic, but perhaps very anti-gender, to see the feminine sex as the weak sex, to see the dynamic between gay men as masculine or feminine, and to see the feminine as something negative, that is what I am referring to. It is very anti-gender. It is homophobic on its own and ridiculous at the end of the day. If you are heterosexual, surely you have never had to think about your sexual orientation. You don't realize the complication, confusion, and discrimination that people who are LGBTQ+ suffer.

The future of Central American film, in particular LGBTQ+-themed films, is complex. In this respect, he maintains:

> Film in Guatemala is in trouble, I mean, film in general, it doesn't matter the theme. For me, Hollywood is the model to follow. It has more than 100 years of experience. They should have learned something in relation to narrative construction, in relation to distribution, marketing, presentation, etc. In creating the image of the movie star. Here we

do not have movie stars. We do not have famous actors. For that to exist, there must be investment, but here in Guatemala there is no investment. The little investment that there is, is foreign, and the local [investment] is from the most corrupt people there are in the world, and they only want to invest money for themselves. They don't invest in anything local or any movie that has shown positive results at the box office. No movie has shown that it can sell as much locally as internationally, and that is the main point where we fail in Guatemala cinema: that none of the movies have sold. They have won awards but that doesn't sell. The award doesn't reflect anything. You have to demonstrate that you can sell and that you can sell well. The investment is recuperated with capital gains and Central American film has not done that, not a single movie. No one is going to invest locally in cinema if it is not going to earn money in return, or if it is not going to earn more than they invested. That is where we have failed. The stories that we are telling are not the ones the world is asking to be told or with which the world is identifying. If we were to achieve change or implement more of that Hollywood mentality here in Central American cinema, we would change the conversation completely. Now, with respect to LGBTQ+ films, forget it. It is much more difficult.

Notes

1 A fund that supports domestic film productions, provided by the Costa Rican Film Production Center.
2 The interview with Gloria Carrión Fonseca was previously published in Spanish in *Imagofagia* 17 (April, 2018): 299–315. http://www.asaeca.org/imagofagia/index.php/imagofagia/issue/view/7. We thank *Imagofagia* for their permission to use excerpts from the interview in this chapter and thank Ana Pérez Méndez for her English translation of the filmmaker introduction and excerpts from the original interview.
3 Luis Fernando Midence's interview was first published in "Hacia un cine queer centroamericano: Entrevista a Luis Fernando Midence" (List). We thank *Istmo* for their permission to include excerpts of Midence's interview.
4 Midence is referring to the film *Temblores* (2019), which was released after the time this interview was conducted in 2018.

Works Cited

Abrázame como antes. Directed by Jurgen Ureña, Minafilms, Costa Rica, 2016.
Astorga, Laura. Personal interview. 12 September 2020.
Cabezas Vargas, Andrea. "Las nuevas heroínas del cine centroamericano: De la Historia a la ficción. Transformaciones de los personajes femeninos en las últimas cuatro décadas." *Centroamericana*, vol. 29, no. 1, 2019, pp. 33–58.

Carrión, Gloria. Personal interview. 13 July 2017.

Cortés María Lourdes. "Mujer y madre en el cine centroamericano actual." *Cinémas d'Amérique Latine,* vol. 22, 2004, pp. 152–165.

Dos Fridas. Directed by Ishtar Yasin, Producciones Astarté, Mexico/Costa Rica, 2018.

El camino. Directed by Ishtar Yasin, Producciones Astarté/DART/Gedeon Programmes, 2008.

Ellas se aman. Directed by Laura Astorga, Hol y Asociados, Costa Rica, 2008.

Extraño pero verdadero. Directed by Michel Lipkes, Axolote Cine, Mexico, 2017.

Fractals. Directed by Gloria Carrión, Caja de Luz, Nicaragua, 2011.

Gasolina. Directed by Julio Hernández Cordón, Melindrosa Films, Guatemala, 2008.

Grinberg Pla, Valeria. "Mujeres cineastas de Centroamérica: Continuidad y ruptura." *Mesoamérica,* vol. 55, 2013, pp. 103–112.

Guinea, Pamela. Personal interview. 7 July 2020.

Hasta el Sol tiene manchas. Directed by Julio Hernández Cordón, Melindrosa Films, Guatemala, 2012.

Heredera del viento. Directed by Gloria Carrión, Caja de Luz, Nicaragua, 2017.

Imperdonable. Directed by Marlén Viñayo, El Faro, El Salvador, 2020.

Inzomnia. Directed by Luis Téllez, Mexico, in production.

La jaula de oro. Directed by Diego Quemada-Díez, Animal de Luz Films, Mexico, 2013.

Las cosas que no decimos. Directed by Luis Fernando Midence, GuatGuy Productions, Guatemala, 2019.

Las marimbas del infierno. Directed by Julio Hernández Cordón, Melindrosa Films, Guatemala, 2010.

Lecciones para una guerra. Directed by Juan Manuel Sepúlveda, Fragua Cine, Mexico, 2012.

Les Invisibles 2010. Directed by Ishtar Yasin, Producciones Astarté, Costa Rica, 2010.

List, Jared. "Hacia un cine queer centroamericano: Entrevista a Luis Fernando Midence." *Istmo: Revista virtual de estudios literarios y culturales centroamericanos,* no. 43, 2021, pp. 279–293.

———. "Miradas humanizantes, lazos subjetivos, memorias horizontales: Entrevista a la cineasta nicaragüense Gloria Carrión Fonseca." *Imagofagia,* no. 17, April 2018, pp. 299–315, http://www.asaeca.org/imagofagia/index.php/imagofagia/issue/view/7. Accessed May 2021.

Luna, Ilana. "Women Rising: Central American Filmmaking for the 21st Century." 20 November 2017, Invited Lecture, University of Cincinnati.

Midence, Luis Fernando. Personal interview. 16 October 2018.

Nuestras madres. Directed by César Díaz, Need Productions, Guatemala, 2019.

One-on-one. Directed by Luis Fernando Midence, USA, 2010.

Polvo. Directed by Julio Hernández Cordón, Melindrosa Films, Guatemala, 2012.

Princesas rojas. Directed by Laura Astorga, Hol y Asociados, Costa Rica, 2013.

Rodríguez, Ileana. *Modalidades de memoria y archivos afectivos: Cine de mujeres en Centroamérica.* San José: Editorial de la U de Costa Rica, 2020.

Rossana en construcción. Directed by Gloria Carrión, Caja de Luz, Nicaragua, 2013.

Roza, Directed by Andrés Rodríguez, Benuca Films, Guatemala, 2022.

Sin ruta. Directed by Luis Fernando Midence, GuatGuy Productions, Guatemala, 2012.

Te prometo anarquía. Directed by Julio Hernández Cordón, Interior13 Cine, Mexico, 2015.

Te toca. Directed by Luis Fernando Midence, GuatGuy Productions, Guatemala, 2012.
Temblores. Directed by Jayro Bustamante, Tu Vas Voir Productions, Guatemala, 2019.
Tesoros. Directed by María Novaro, Axolote Films, Mexico, 2017.
The Post. Directed by Steven Spielberg, Twentieth Century Fox, USA, 2019.
Vaquero del mediodía. Directed by Diego Osorno, Agencia Bengala, Mexico, 2019.
Verdadero-primero-último. Directed by Luis Fernando Midence, GuatGuy Productions, Guatemala, 2017.
Yasin, Ishtar. Personal interview. 17 August 2020.

Central American Filmography

2000–2021

María Lourdes Cortés, Mauricio Espinoza, and Jared List

The following filmography (organized by countries) includes feature-length and short films, both fiction and documentary, produced during the first two decades of the twenty-first century in Central America. It takes into account Central America's diaspora and includes some films that take place outside of the Isthmus. This filmography is an ongoing endeavor and is not meant to be exhaustive. For some of the entries, production house information is not available.

Costa Rica

A ojos cerrados. Directed by Hernán Jiménez, Miel y Palo Films, 2010.
Abrázame como antes. Directed by Jurgen Ureña, Producciones La Ventana/Mina Films, 2016.
Agua fría de mar. Directed by Paz Fábrega, Tic Tac Productions/Temporal Films/Les Films du Requin, 2010.
Algo queda. Directed by Luciano Capelli and Andrea Ruggeri, Río Nevado Producciones, 2002.
Apego. Directed by Patricia Velásquez, Ceibita Films/Tiempo Líquido, 2019.
Aquí y ahora. Directed by Paz León, Lalala Productions/Miel y Palo Films, 2019.
Asesinato en El Meneo. Directed by Oscar Castillo, Producciones la Mestiza/Producciones OM, 2001.
Atrás hay relámpagos. Directed by Julio Hernández Cordón, De Raíz Productions/Melindrosa Films, 2017.
Aurora. Directed by Paz Fábrega, Temporal Films, 2021.
Caribe. Directed by Esteban Ramírez, Cinetel S.A., 2004.
Casa en tierra ajena. Directed by Ivannia Villalobos, Universidad de Costa Rica/Universidad Estatal a Distancia, 2017.
Cascos indomables. Directed by Neto Villalobos, Cinestación/Sucia Centroamericana Producciones, 2018.

Ceniza negra. Directed by Sofía Quirós, Sputnik Films/Murillo Cine/La Post Producciones, 2019.
Clara sola. Directed by Nathalie Álvarez, Hobab/Laïdak Films/Need Productions, 2021.
Costa Rica S.A. Directed by Pablo Ortega, Nemagon Blues/Fundodo, 2006.
Combo callejero. Directed by Pablo Cardenas, Centro de Imagen del INA, 2003.
Del amor y otros demonios. Directed by Hilda Hidalgo, Alicia Films/CMO Producciones, 2009.
Dos aguas. Directed by Patricia Velázquez, Tiempo líquido/Igolai Producciones, 2015.
Dos Fridas. Directed by Ishtar Yasin, Producciones Astarté, 2018.
El baile de La Gacela. Directed by Iván Porras, Cine Feral/Dos sentidos Producciones/La Feria Producciones, 2018.
El barco prometido. Directed by Luciano Capelli, Río Nevado Producciones, 2000.
El camino. Directed by Ishtar Yasin, Producciones Astarté/DART/Gedeon Programmes, 2008.
El cielo rojo. Directed by Miguel Gómez, Ginaluvosi Productions, 2008.
El despertar de las hormigas. Directed by Antonella Sudasassi, Betta Films/Solita Films, 2019.
El mito blanco. Directed by Gabriel Serra, Betta Films/Ojo de vaca, 2020.
El regreso. Directed by Hernán Jiménez, Miel y Palo Films, 2012.
El sonido de las cosas. Directed by Ariel Escalante, Sputnik Films/Fade In/Miau Films, 2016.
El trofeo. Directed by Miguel Salguero, 2004.
El último comandante. Directed by Isabel Martínez and Vicente Ferraz, Tres Mundos Producciones, 2010.
Ellas se aman. Directed by Laura Astorga, Hol y Asociados, 2008.
El codo del diablo. Directed by Ernesto and Antonio Jara Vargas, Ceibita Films/La Pecera, 2014.
Los Vargas Brothers. Directed by Juan Manuel Fernández, Biofilms Producciones, 2012.
El derecho a elegir. Directed by Juan Manuel Fernández, 2013.
Ergonomía para Diana. Directed by Marcos Machado, Best Picture System, 2013.
Los maes de la esquina. Directed by Juan Manuel Fernández, Biofilm Producciones, 2014.
El compromiso. Directed by Oscar Castillo, Orsay Troupe SRL/INCAA/Programa Ibermedia/ OC Producciones, 2011.
El oro de los tontos. Directed by Pablo Ortega, Universidad de Costa Rica/Vicerrectoría de Unidad Social, 2011.
El pájaro de fuego. Directed by César Caro, Producciones AMI Video, 2021.
El sanatorio. Directed by Miguel Gómez, Ginaluvosi Producciones, 2010.
El tucán que inspiró una nación. Directed by Paula Heredia, 2016.
Entonces nosotros. Directed by Hernán Jiménez, Evoke Productions, LaLaLa Productions, 2016.
Gestación. Directed by Esteban Ramírez, Cinetel, 2009.
Gigi. Directed by Erika Bagnarello, Filmworks, 2017.
Güilas. Directed by Sergio Pucci, Juan Burú Producciones, 2018.
Keylor Navas: Hombre de fe. Directed by Dinga Haines, PCP Productora, 2017.
Italia 90: La película. Directed by Miguel Gómez, Atómica Films, 2014.

Las cinco vidas de María Rodríguez. Directed by Alonso Arias and Gustavo Loría, Fulfierros S.A., 2010.
La Dixon. Directed by Adriana Cordero Chacón, Hormiga Producciones/El Central Producciones, 2017.
La sombra del naranjo. Directed by Patricia Velázquez and Oscar Herrera, Tiempo Líquido, 2016.
La región perdida. Directed by Andrés Heidenreich, Sizigia Films, 2009.
Las 50 vueltas. Directed by Juan Manuel Fernández, Biofilms/Proartes/Cacerola Films/Fundacine, 2011.
Lucía en el limbo. Directed by Valentina Maurel, Geko Films, 2019.
Maikol Yordan de viaje perdido. Directed by Miguel Gómez, Audiovisuales LMD, 2014.
Marasmo. Directed by Mauricio Mendiola, Procines, 2003.
Medea. Directed by Alexandra Latishev, Grita Medios, 2017.
Mujeres apasionadas. Directed by Maureen Jiménez, Producciones la Mestiza, 2003.
NICA/ragüense. Directed by Carlos Solís and Julia Fleming, France-Amérique Latine, 2005.
Nosotros las piedras. Directed by Alvaro Torres Crespo, Betta Films, Neonanacatl Audiovisual, 2018.
Objetos rebeldes. Directed by Carolina Arias Ortiz, El Mito, La Linterna Films, Milagros Producciones, 2020.
Padre. Directed by Alejo Crisóstomo, Ceibita Films, 2013.
Paso a paso: A sentimental journey. Directed by Daniel Ross Mix and Julio Molina, Videos Bicho, 2006.
Password: Una mirada en la oscuridad. Directed by Andrés Heidenreich, Productora audiovisual latinoamericana 2002.
Polvo de estrellas. Directed by Hilda Hidalgo, Tao Films, 2001.
Por las plumas. Directed by Neto Villalobos, Sucia Centroamericana Producciones, 2013.
Presos. Directed by Esteban Ramírez, Cinetel/Ibermedia, 2015.
Princesas rojas. Directed by Laura Astorga, Hol y Asociados/La Feria Producciones/Suécinema, 2013.
Puerto padre. Directed by Gustavo Fallas, Centrosur Producciones/Reeliz Film Producciones, 2013.
Querido Camilo. Directed by Julio Molina and Daniel Ross Mix, Centro de Cine Costa Rica/SINART, 2007.
Río sucio. Directed by Gustavo Fallas, Tresmonstruos Media, 2020.
Se prohíbe bailar suin. Directed by Gabriela Hernández, Arco Arte Audiovisual, 2003.
Se quema el cielo. Directed by Luciano Capelli, Proartes, 2010.
Selva. Directed by Sofía Quirós, Sputnik Films, 2017.
Tres Marías. Directed by Pako Gonzalez, Oveja Negra Producciones, 2010.
Tempo: La Orquesta Sinfónica de Costa Rica. Directed by Nicole Villalobos, Chimbo Films, 2015.
Tercer mundo. Directed by César Caro Cruz, Películas Plot, 2009.
Títiles. Directed by Gabrio Zapelli, ARSCOOP, 2003.
Uranio 238: La bomba sucia del Pentágono. Directed by Pablo Ortega, San José Quaker Peace Center, 2009.

Viaje. Directed by Paz Fábrega, FiGa Films, 2015.
Violeta al fin. Directed by Hilda Hidalgo, Cacerola Films/Producciones La Tiorba, 2017.

El Salvador

Alborada. Directed by Paula Heredia, Heredia Pictures, 2016.
Altares. Directed by Brenda Vanegas, Instituto Salvadoreño para el Desarrollo de la Mujer (ISDEMU), 2020.
Children of the Diaspora: For Peace and Democracy. Directed by Jennifer A. Cárcamo, 2013.
Comandos. Directed by Marcela Zamora, Kino Glaz/El Faro, 2016.
Cuatro puntos cardinales. Directed by Javier Kafie, Tripode Audiovisual, 2014.
El cadáver exquisito. Directed by Victor Ruano, Santasombra Studio, 2011.
El cuarto de los huesos. Directed by Marcela Zamora, Trípode Audiovisual, 2015.
El lugar más pequeño. Directed by Tatiana Huezo, Centro de Capacitación Cinematográfica/Foprocine, 2011.
El Salvador: Archivos perdidos del conflicto. Directed by Gerardo Muyshondt, El Salvador Films, 2016.
El suspiro del silencio. Directed by Alfonso Quijada, Apex Studios/Red Castle Films/Sivela Films, 2021.
El tigre y el venado. Directed by Sergio Sibrián, 2013.
En un rincón del alma. Directed by Jorge Dalton, 2016.
Entre los muertos. Directed by Jorge Dalton. 2006.
Fly so far/Nuestra libertad. Directed by Celina Escher, Debut Feature Film, 2019.
Imperdonable. Directed by Marlén Viñayo, El Faro/La jaula abierta, 2020.
Llevarte al mar. Directed by Jorge Dalton, With a Little Help from My Friends Producciones, 2009.
La batalla del volcán. Directed by Julio López Fernández, Argos Comunicación/Cine murciélago/Trípode audiovisual, 2017.
La frontera del olvido. Directed by Carlos Henríquez Consalvi, 2005.
La palabra de Pablo. Directed by Arturo Menéndez, Firepower Entertainment/Meridiano 89/Sivela Pictures, 2018.
La palabra en el bosque. Directed by Carlos Henríquez Consalvi, Museo de la Palabra y la Imagen, 2011.
La vida loca. Directed by Christian Poveda, Aquelarre Servicios Cinematográficos, 2008.
Las cartas de Lucía. Directed by Brenda Vanegas, Encantada por la vida, 2021.
Los ofendidos. Directed by Marcela Zamora, Kino Glaz, 2016.
Malacrianza. Directed by Arturo Menéndez, Itaca Films/Meridiano 89/Sivela Pictures, 2014.
María en tierra de nadie. Directed by Marcela Zamora, Ruido, El Faro, I(dh)eas, 2011.
Maura Vega. Directed by Marcela Zamora, Kino Glaz, 2018.
Sobreviviendo Guazapa. Directed by Roberto Dávila, DVR Cineworks, 2008.
Tempestad. Directed by Tatiana Huezo, Pimienta Films, 2016.
Tenemos que hablar. Directed by Johanna Alfaro and Jamie Cortez, 2012.
Uno: La historia de un gol. Directed by Gerado Muyshondt and Carlos Moreno, 64A Films/Antorcha Films, 2010.

Volar: La historia del olvido. Directed by Brenda Vanegas, Encantada por la vida/La estación/Relativo Films, 2021.
Víctimas de Guernica. Directed by Ferran Caum, José Lagares Díaz, 2015.
1932: La cicatriz de la memoria. Directed by Jeffrey Gould and Carlos Henríquez Consalvi, Icarus Films, 2003.

Guatemala

Abrazos. Directed by Luis Argueta, Maya Media Corp., 2014.
abUSAdos: La redada de Postville. Directed by Luis Argueta, Maya Media Corp., 2011.
Aquí me quedo. Directed by Rodolfo Espinosa, Me llega Films, 2010.
Cabalgando hacia el trueno: una travesía sobre motocicletas. Directed by Mendel Samayoa, El Angel Producciones, 2014.
Cadejo blanco. Directed by Justin Lerner, La Dante Films, 2021.
Cápsulas. Directed by Verónica Riedel, Anver Films, 2012.
Caudal. Directed by Gladys Tobar, 2001.
Desenredar el ser. Directed by Anaïs Taracena, 2018.
Distancia. Directed by Sergio Ramírez, Casa Comal, 2012.
Donde acaban los caminos. Directed by Carlos García Agraz, Fundación Mario Monteforte Toledo, 2004.
Donde nace el Sol. Directed by Elías Jiménez, Casa Comal, 2013.
El buen cristiano. Directed by Izabel Acevedo, Centro de Capacitación Cinematográfica (CCC)/Foprocine, 2016.
El capitán Orellana y la aldea endemoniada. Directed by Javier Tessari, Oro Puro Producciones, 2012.
El eco del dolor de mucha gente. Directed by Ana Lucía Cuevas, Armadillo Productions, 2015.
Elogio del cine: Pasión por la realidad. Directed by Mario Roberto Morales, 2015.
El mito del tiempo. Directed by Jaguar X, 2010.
El regreso de Lencho. Directed by Mario Rosales, Occularis Films, 2012.
El silencio del topo. Directed by Anaïs Taracena, Asombro Producciones/Colet & Co/El Balam Producciones, 2021.
El tamalón navideño. Directed by Rafael Tres, Cinema 502, 2018.
Entre tejidos y patrones. Directed by Julio Molina, 2009.
Entre voces. Directed by Anaïs Taracena, 2018.
Estrellas de la línea. Directed by Chema Rodríguez, Producciones Sin un duro/Telespan, 2006.
Fe. Directed by Alejo Crisóstomo, Casa Comal, Ceibita Films, Jirafa, 2011.
Gasolina. Directed by Julio Hernández Cordón, Melindrosa Films/Buena onda América/Mediapro Producción Gabriel, 2007.
Hasta el Sol tiene manchas. Directed by Julio Hernández Cordón, Melindrosa Films, 2012.
Hostal don Tulio. Directed by Rodolfo Espinosa, True Media Company, 2018.
Hunting Party. Directed by Chris Kummerfeldt Quiroa, Casa Comal, Hunter 11 Films, New Vision, 2015.
Identidad. Directed by Elliot Morales, 2015.

Ixcanul. Directed by Jayro Bustamante, La Casa de Producción/Tu Vas Voir Productions, 2015.
José. Directed by Li Cheng, YQstudio, 2018.
Kik Vuh–Ala de papel. Directed by Edgar Sajcabún, 2016.
La asfixia. Directed by Ana Bustamante, Cine Concepción/Nanuk Audiovisual, 2019.
La bodega. Directed by Ray Figueroa, Casa Comal, 2010.
La casa de enfrente. Directed by Elías Jiménez Trachtenberg, Casa Comal, 2004.
La casa más grande del mundo. Directed by Ana Virigina Bojórquez and Lucía Carreras, Prisma Cine/Filmadora Producciones/Underdog, 2015.
La compañera Fabiana. Directed by Lucía Reinoso, 2021.
La isla: Archivo de una tragedia. Directed by Uli Stelzner, Iskacine, 2010.
La Llorona. Directed by Jayro Bustamante, El Ministerio de Cultura y Deportes de Guatemala/La Casa de Producción/Les Films du Volcan, 2019.
La prenda. Directed by Jean Cosme Delaloye, JCDe Productions/Radio Télévision Suisse/Tipi'mages Productions, 2015.
Las Cruces: Poblado próximo. Directed by Rafael Rosal, Casa Comal, 2006.
Las marimbas del infierno. Directed by Julio Hernández Cordón, Les Films du Requin/Melindrosa Films/Axolote Films, 2018.
La vaca—Holy Cow. Directed by Mendel Samayoa, 2011.
Los fantasmas. Directed by Sebastián Lojo, A la Deriva Cine/Perro Suelto Cine/Patra Spanou Film, 2020.
Los gigantes no existen. Directed by Chema Rodríguez, Producciones Sin Un Duro, Icónica Producciones, PTP Mundo Maya, 2018.
Luis y Laura. Directed by Sergio Valdés, Producciones Chirripó, 2000.
Lo que soñó Sebastián. Directed by Rodrigo Rey Rosa, El Escarbado Producciones, 2003.
Los ojos de la abuela. Directed by Verónica Sacalxot, Colectivo Lemow/Ix Mayab' Producciones, 2016.
Luz. Directed by Javier Borrayo, Breaker Studios, 2021.
No llores cumbias, cumbias bailarás. Directed by Pablo Rojas, 2020.
Norman. Directed by Julio Hernández Cordón, Melindrosa Films, 2005.
Nuestras madres. Directed by César Díaz, Need Productions/Perspective Films/Proximus, 2019.
Otros 4 litros. Directed by Rodolfo Espinosa, Cinemayic, 2016.
Ovnis en Zacapa. Directed by Marcos Machado, Best Picture System, 2015.
Pol. Directed by Rodolfo Espinosa, Me Llega Films, 2014.
Polvo. Directed by Julio Hernández Cordón, Melindrosa Films/Tic Tac Producciones/Fábula/Autentika Films, 2012.
Pólvora en el corazón. Directed by Camila Urrutia, Curuxa Cinema, 2019.
Por cobrar. Directed by Luis Argueta, Maya Media Corp., 2002.
Primero-Verdadero-Último. Directed by Luis Fernando Midence, GuatGuy Producciones, 2017.
Puro mula. Directed by Enrique Pérez Him, Best Picture System, 2011.
Regresé a la vida. Directed by Rosa Chávez, Actoras de cambio, 2014.
Septiembre, un llanto en silencio. Directed by Kenneth Muller, KraftLogic Studios, 2017.
Sí hubo genocidio. Directed by Julio Hernández Cordón, Melindrosa Films, 2005.

Sin ruta. Directed by Luis Fernando Midence, GuatGuy Producciones, 2012.
Soy de Zacapa. Directed by Mario Enríquez, Luigi Lanuza Presenta, 2014.
Te prometo anarquía. Directed by Julio Hernández Cordón, Interior13 Cine/FOPROCINE/Rohfilm, 2016.
Temblores. Directed by Jayro Bustamante, La Casa de Producción/Tu Vas Voir Productions, 2019.
Territorio liberado. Directed by César Díaz, Kepler 22 Production/Melindrosa Films. 2014.
Toque de queda. Directed by Ray Figueroa and Elías Jiménez Trachtenberg, Casa Comal, 2011.
Trilogía documental sobre Jacobo Árbenz. Universidad de San Carlos de Guatemala, 2014.
Trip la película. Directed by Fran Lepe, 2011.
Un día de sol. Directed by Rafael Tres, Códice, 2010.
Un presidente de a sombrero. Directed by Jimmy and Sammy Morales, 2007.
V.I.P.: La Otra Casa. Directed by Elías Jiménez Trachtenberg, Casa Comal, 2007.
Vuelta en U. Directed by Luis Argueta, Maya Media Corp., 2017.
W2MW: Welcome to My World. Directed by Rafael Tres, Cinema 502, Empire Promotions, 2016.
1991. Directed by Sergio Ramírez, La Casa de Producción, 2021.
20 años después. Directed by Anaïs Taracena, Ek Balam Producciones, 2018.

Honduras

Almas de la medianoche. Directed by Carlos Fanconi, Cana Vista Films/Sigmavision Films, 2002.
Amor y frijoles. Directed by Mathew Kodath, Guacamaya Films, 2009.
Ana Lucía. Directed by Laura Bermúdez, Tercer Cine, 2017.
Anita, la cazadora de insectos. Directed by Hispano Durón, CRA-UNAH, 2002.
Bajo la carpa. Directed by Laura Bermúdez, 2013.
Berta vive. Directed by Katia Lara, Oxfam/Terco Producciones/Tercer Piso, 2016.
Brigada. Directed by Mario Ramos, Cabezahueca Films/Full String Pictures, 2017.
Corazón abierto. Directed by Katia Lara, Terco Producciones, 2005.
El paletero. Directed by Michael Bendeck, HonduFilms/Eduardo Andonie Enterprise, 2016.
El porvenir. Directed by Oscar Estrada, Marabunta Films, 2008.
El Xendra. Directed by Juan Carlos Fanconi, Cana Vista Films, 2012.
Espejos. Directed by Jennifer Ávila, Los amigos de la plaza/Planned Parenthood, 2018.
Fantasmas del huracán. Directed by Elizabeth Figueroa, Centro de Recursos de Aprendizaje (CRA) de la Universidad Nacional Autónoma de Honduras (UNAH), 2000.
Fuerzas de honor. Directed by Tomás Chi, Newalk Productions, 2016.
Garifuna in Peril. Directed by Ali Allie and Rubén Reyes, Aban Productions, 2012.
Los hijos del Tomán. Directed by Gerardo Aguilar, 2014.
Más allá de una esperanza. Directed by Francisco Andino, 1999.
Más allá del árbol. Directed by Juan Carlos Fanconi, Cana Vista Films, 2014.
Merlo. Directed by Samanta Hernández, 2016.
Morazán. Directed by Hispano Durón, Fundaunpfilms, 2017.

Negra soy. Directed by Laura Bermúdez, Jablo Productions/Tercer Cine, 2017.

No amanece igual para todos. Directed by Francisco Andino, Manuel Villa and Ramón Hernández, Acracia Films, 2011.

No hay tierra sin dueño. Directed by Sami Kafati, Alta Loma Films, 1986–2002.

Olancho. Directed by Chris Valdés and Theodore Griswold, Olancho Movie/Tercer Piso, 2017.

¿Quién dijo miedo?: Honduras de un golpe . . . Directed by Katia Lara, Terco Producciones/INCAA, 2010.

¿Quién paga la cuenta? Directed by Benji López, Guacamaya, 2013.

Se lo dije Lucecita. Directed by Rafa Rivera, Fundaunpfilms, 2015.

Toque de queda. Directed by Javier Suazo Mejía, Aura Creativa, 2012.

Un lugar en el Caribe. Directed by Juan Carlos Fanconi, Cana Vista Films, 2017.

¿Y los tamales? Directed by Tomás Chi, Sula Studios, 2017.

11 cipotes. Directed by Tomás Chi, Enserio Producciones, 2014.

90 minutos. Directed by Aeden O'Connor, Pulsar, 2019.

100 horas de furia. Directed by Alejandro Irías, B'alam Entertainment, 2020.

Nicaragua

Antojología de Carl Rigby. Directed by Eduardo Spiegeler and Maria José Alvarez, Luna Films/Tanacatana, 2019.

A quién le importa. Directed by Rossana Lacayo, Gota Films, 2009.

Belén en Nicaragua. Directed by Rossana Lacayo, Gota Films, 2009.

Brisa nocturna. Directed by Rossana Lacayo, Gota Films, 2006.

Daysiry. Directed by Rossana Lacayo, Gota Films, 2008.

De macho a macho. Directed by Rossana Lacayo, Gota Films, 2011.

De niña a madre. Directed by Florence Jaugey, Camila Films, 2004.

Desde el barro al sur. Directed by Maria José Alvarez and Martha Clarissa Hernández, Luna Films, 2002.

Días de clase. Directed by Florence Jaugey, Camila Films, 2013.

El canto de Bosawas. Directed by Camilo Castro and Brad Allgood, Calé Producciones, Fall Line Pictures, 2014.

El choguí. Directed by Félix Zurita, Alba Films, 2001.

El día que me quieras. Directed by Florence Jaugey, Camila Films, 2000.

El diálogo permanente. Directed by Rossana Lacayo, Gota Films, 2008.

El engaño. Directed by Florence Jaugey, Camila Films, 2012.

El inmortal. Directed by Mercedes Moncada, Zafra Video, 2005.

El valor de las mujeres: La lucha por el derecho de la tierra. Directed by Rossana Lacayo, Gota Films, 2009.

Equívoco. Directed by Rossana Lacayo, Gota Films, 2007.

Exiliada. Directed by Leonor Zúniga, Coproducción Nicaragua-Costa Rica, 2019.

Festival de poesía de Granada. Directed by Rossana Lacayo, Gota Films, 2008.

Fuerza bruta. Directed by Laura Baumeister de Montis, Centro de Capacitación Cinematográfica, 2016.

Funerales en el porvenir. Directed by Rossana Lacayo, Gota Films, 2009.

Girasoles de Nicaragua. Directed by Florence Jaugey, Camila Films, 2017.
Hasta con las uñas: Mujeres cineastas en Nicaragua. Directed by Tania Romero, Blink Production Films, 2017.
Heredera del viento. Directed by Gloria Carrión, Caja de Luz, 2017.
Historia de Rosa. Directed by Florence Jaugey, Camila Films, 2005.
KAOS experimental. Directed by Rossana Lacayo, Gota Films, 2009.
Laberinto. Directed by Rossana Lacayo, Gota Films, 2012.
La hija de todas las rabias. Directed by Laura Baumeister de Montis, Felipa Films.
La isla de los niños perdidos. Directed by Florence Jaugey, Camila Films, 2001.
La pantalla desnuda. Directed by Florence Jaugey, Camila Films, 2014.
La parka. Directed by Gabriel Serra, 2013.
La pasión de María Elena. Directed by Mercedes Moncada, IMCINE, 2003.
La sirena y el buzo. Directed by Mercedes Moncada, Amaranta/IMCINE/La Zanfoña Production, 2009.
La Yuma. Directed by Florence Jaugey, Camila Films/Ivania Films/Wanda Visión, 2009.
Lih Wina. Directed by Dania Torres, 2012.
Los amantes de San Fernando. Directed by Peter Torbiornsson, Gota Films, 2002.
Lubaraun. Directed by Maria José Alvarez Sacasa and Martha Clarissa Hernández Chávez, Luna Films, 2016.
Minguito el Señor de los Milagros. Directed by Rossana Lacayo, Gota Films, 2008.
Miskito. Directed by Rebeca Arcia, Imaginarte Films, 2014. Nicaragua.
Ombligo de agua. Directed by Laura Baumeister de Montis, Tanacatana Films, 2018.
Palabras mágicas (para romper un encantamiento). Directed by Mercedes Moncada, Producciones Amaranta/Bambú Audiovisual, 2012.
Paraíso perdido. Directed by Rossana Lacayo, Gota Films, 2010.
Pikineras. Directed by Rossana Lacayo, Gota Films, 2012.
Raúl y Emir. Directed by Rossana Lacayo, Gota Films, 2004.
San Francisco en La Chureca. Directed by Rossana Lacayo, Gota Films, 2014.
Sembrando esperanzas. Directed by Rossana Lacayo, Gota Films, 2013.
The Black Creoles. Directed by Maria José Alvarez and Martha Clarissa Hernández, Luna Films, 2011.
Verdades ocultas. Directed by Rossana Lacayo, Gota Films, 2003.
YCAZA. Directed by Rossana Lacayo, Gota Films, 2007.
1, 2, 3 . . . a bailar. Directed by José Wheelock, Imaginarte Films, 2016.

Panama

A la deriva. Directed by Miguel I. González, Contraplano Films, 2016.
Algo azul. Directed by Mariel García Spooner, Clap Studios, 2021.
Caja 25. Directed by Deflina Vidal and Mercedes Arias, Besteda Films/Jaguar Films, 2015.
Caos en la ciudad. Directed by Enrique Pérez Him, CIMAS, 2012.
Chance. Directed by Abner Benaim, Apertura Films/Río Negro, 2010.
Cimarronaje en Panamá. Directed by Toshi Sakai, 2017.
CURUNDú. Directed by Ana Endara Mislov, Cinergia, 2007.
Diciembres. Directed by Enrique Castro Ríos, Milagros Producciones, 2018.

El último soldado. Directed by Luis Romero, Bolero Films/Citera/DocTV, 2010.

Empleadas y patrones. Directed by Abner Benaim, Aperatura Films/Barackacine Producciones/INCAA, 2010.

Familia. Directed by Enrique Castro Ríos, Asociación Cinematográfica de Panamá, 2007.

Héroe transparente. Directed by Orgun Wagua, Marina Productions/SerTV, 2014.

Hidden. Directed by Guillermo Bárcenas and Frank Spano, Cow Lamp Films, 2017.

Historias del canal. Directed by Pinky Mon, Pituka Ortega-Heilbron, Abner Benaim, Luis Franco, Carolina Borrero, Hypatia Films/Manglar Films, 2014.

Ilegítimo. Directed by Juan Camilo Gamba, EGM Producciones, Juguar Films, Silver Productions, 2017.

Invasión. Directed by Abner Benaim, Ajimolido Films/Apertura Films, 2014.

Kimura. Directed by Aldo Rey Valderrama, Tiempo Real, 2017.

La estación seca. Directed by José Canto, CIMAS/Tiempo Real/Jaguar Films, 2018.

La felicidad del sonido. Directed by Ana Endara Mislov, Mansa Producciones, 2016.

La fuerza del balón. Directed by Alberto Serra, WP Films, 2016.

La Matamoros. Directed by Delfina Vidal, Jaguar Films, 2017.

La ruta. Directed by Pituka Ortega-Heilbron, Hypatia Films/Manglar Films, 2016.

La ruta de la luna. Directed by Juan Sebastián Jacomé, Abaca Films/Jaguar Films, 2012.

Los agustines. Directed by Roberto Latorre, Cinesucio, 2013.

Liza . . . como ella. Directed by Anne Canavaggio, Marina Productions, 2005.

Los puños de una nación. Directed by Pituka Ortega, Hypatia Films, 2005.

Luciamor. Directed by Ana Elena Tejera, Mestizo Cinema/Too Much Productions/Cine animal, 2018.

Memorias del hijo del viejo. Directed by Enrique Castro Ríos, Save the Children Norway/Universitetet i Bergen, 2004.

Panquiaco. Directed by Ana Elena Tejera, Too Much Panama, 2020.

One dollar (El precio de la vida). Directed by Héctor Herrera, ABS Productions/Genco Films/Magma Films, 2001.

Reinas. Directed by Ana Endara Mislov, Cinergía, 2011.

Rompiendo la ola. Directed by Annie Caravaggio, Marina Productions/Tres mundos, 2014.

Salsipuedes. Directed by Ricardo Aguilar and Manolito Rodríguez, Viceversa Productions, 2016.

Todos cambiamos. Directed by Arturo Montenegro, GC Films/Q Films/Freedom Films, 2019.

Costa Rica, Panama, Honduras, El Salvador, Nicaragua, Guatemala

Días de luz. Directed by Gloria Carrión Fonseca, Julio López Fernández, Enrique Medrano, Mauro Borges Mora, Enrique Pérez Him and Sergio Ramírez, Chicken Bus/Dos Sentidos Producciones/Mente Pública, 2019.

Costa Rica, Guatemala, Honduras

Nina y Laura. Directed by Alejo Crisóstomo, Ceibita Films, 2014.

Contributors

Arno Jacob Argueta is assistant professor at California State University, Bakersfield. His field of study includes the cultures and cinemas of Central America, Mexico, and Brazil.

Tomás Arce Mairena is a PhD student and a Taft Research Center Dissertation Fellow (2021–2022) in the Department of Romance and Arabic Languages and Literatures at the University of Cincinnati. He obtained his MA in Spanish and Latin American literature in 2018 from the University of Cincinnati. He is the director of the short documentary *Si buscabas* and has published reviews and articles in the anthology *Flores de la Trinchera,* as well as in literary magazines and journals such as *El Hilo Azul, Latin American Today, Carátula, Cincinnati Romance Review,* and *Revista de Historia IHNCA.*

Patricia Arroyo Calderón is assistant professor in the Spanish and Portuguese Department at the University of California, Los Angeles (UCLA), where she also cofounded and was the first faculty chair of the Central American Studies Working Group (2018–2020) at the Latin American Institute. She has published extensively on topics of Central American history, literature, and visual culture, with a special emphasis on late nineteenth-century women's cultural production, as well as contemporary Central American film. Her latest work has appeared in journals such as *Entre Diversidades* and *Lectora: Reviste de dones i textualitat,* as well as in collective volumes such as *Teaching Central American Literature in a Global Context* (edited by Gloria Elizabeth Chacón and Mónica Albizúrez Gil).

María Lourdes Cortés is a historian of Central American cinema and professor at the University of Costa Rica. She was director of the first Central American school of Cinema and Television (Veritas University) and the Costa Rican Center for Cinematographic Production. She has won the Joaquín García Monge Prize and the Aquileo J. Echeverría Essay Prize twice, for the books *Amor y traición: Cine y literatura en América Latina* and *La pantalla rota: Cien años de cine en Centroamérica.* For this last book, she also received the Ezequiel Martinez Estrada award bestowed by the Casa de las Americas (Cuba) to the best published essay of the year. Her essay "Amores contrariados. García Márquez y el cine" received the best essay award for film presented by the Fundación del Nuevo Cine Latinoamericano. In 2017 she was designated the Humboldt professor and recognized as the University of Costa Rica researcher of the year in 2020. Currently she is researching a project on Central American cinema in recent decades.

Mauricio Espinoza is assistant professor of Spanish and Latin American literature at the University of Cincinnati, where he is also affiliate faculty with the Niehoff Center for Film and Media Studies. He holds a PhD in Latin American Literatures and Cultures from The Ohio State University. His scholarship focuses on Latinx media and popular culture, Central American literary and cultural studies, migration, and translation. His articles have appeared in *Istmo: Revista virtual de estudios literarios y culturales centroamericanos, Revista Ístmica, Post Script: Essays in Film and the Humanities,* and *Studies in 20th & 21st Century Literature,* among others. He is also a poet and a translator of several Central American and Central American-American poets.

Lilia García Torres is a PhD student at the Universidad Nacional Autónoma de México, where she received a master's degree in history and a bachelor's degree in Latin American studies. She is the coproducer of the documentary film *Trinchera sonora. Voces y miradas de Radio Venceremos* (2017). She belongs to the ReDoc Documentary Research Network. In 2020 she launched the Wiki editathon for women documentary filmmakers. Appointed to Insituto Mora's Audiovisual laboratory of Social Research, she is currently researching audiovisual productions generated by the Salvadoran guerrilla and Mexican women documentary filmmakers (1975–1985).

Juan Pablo Gómez Lacayo is a lecturer in the Department of Modern Languages, Literatures and Linguistics at the University of Oklahoma. He has a PhD in Latin American cultural and literary studies from The Ohio State University. He is the author of *Autoridad/Cuerpo/Nación. Batallas Culturales en Nicaragua, 1930–1943* and coeditor of *Políticas encadenantes: sobre cuerpos y violencias en Centroamérica; Recordar el pasado para imaginar otro futuro: artes y políticas de la memoria en Centroamérica* (*Revista de Historia*); and *Antología del pensamiento crítico nicaragüense contemporáneo.*

Jennifer Carolina Gómez Menjívar is associate professor of media arts at the University of North Texas. Gómez Menjívar's publications have appeared in the *Journal of Pidgin and Creole Languages, Applied Linguistics, Chasqui, Diálogo, A contracorriente, Hispanófila, NAIS Journal,* and *Mesoamérica,* among others. She is coauthor of *Tropical Tongues: Language Ideologies, Endangerment, and Minority Languages in Belize* and coeditor of *Indigenous Interfaces: Spaces, Technology, and Social Networks in Mexico and Central America*, as well as *Hemispheric Blackness and the Exigencies of Accountability*.

Júlia González de Canales Carcereny is a postdoctoral researcher at the University of Vienna. Previously she taught Spanish and Latin American literature at the University of Neuchatel, Switzerland. She holds a PhD in organizational studies and cultural theory from the University of St. Gallen and is the author of *Releyendo a Enrique Vila-Matas. Placer e irritación*. Her articles have been published in *Romance Studies*, *Hispanic Research Journal*, and *Studies in Spanish and Latin American Cinema*. She has coedited the book *Metamedialidad. Los medios y la metaficción*, as well as the special issue "Estéticas globales hispánicas."

Daniela Granja Núñez is a PhD student in the Department of Romance and Arabic Languages and Literatures at the University of Cincinnati where she has taught Spanish and is currently teaching Introduction to Screenwriting. She has an MA in Spanish, an MFA in screenwriting, a certificate in visual anthropology, and a bachelor's degree in sociology. She is the cowriter of the Ecuadorian film *Sumergible* and is working on two feature film projects. She has also worked as a reader in screenwriting labs and production companies. Her creative writing work has been published by *Revista Temporales* and *This is WAAC* magazine.

Liz Harvey-Kattou is senior lecturer in Hispanic studies at the University of Westminster (UK) where she has taught and researched since 2016, having completed her BA, MA, and PhD in Spanish and Latin American studies at University College London (UCL). Her current research project focuses on gender and the family in contemporary Central American cinema, while her past research projects have analyzed identity and nationhood in Costa Rican literature and film. She is the author of *Contested Identities in Costa Rica* and has had articles on Costa Rican cinema published in the *Journal of Romance Studies* and *Studies in Spanish and Latin American Cinema*, where she edited a special edition on Central American cinema.

Jared List is associate professor of Spanish at Doane University in Nebraska. His research and publications cover topics related to Central American literature and film. Currently his research includes representations of life, death, relationality, and memory in contemporary Central American documentary film. His essays have appeared in *Kamchatka: Revista de análisis cultural*, *Istmo: Revista virtual de estudios literarios y culturales centroamericanos*, *Imagofagia*, *Revista Ístmica*, and *Middle Atlantic Review of Latin American Studies*, among others.

Esteban E. Loustaunau is professor of Spanish at Assumption University in Worcester, Massachusetts. His main areas of research focus on contemporary Latin American and Latinx film, narrative, music, and art as these intersect with issues related to migration, dispossession, and human rights. His research has been published in several book collections and in peer review journals such as *Revista Iberoamericana, CR: The New Centennial Review, Revista de Literatura Mexicana Contemporánea, Diálogo: An Interdisciplinary Studies Journal,* and *Latino Studies,* among others. He is coeditor of the book *Telling Migrant Stories: Latin American Diaspora in Documentary Film.*

Carolina Sanabria obtained her PhD in audiovisual communication from the Autonomous University of Barcelona and is now full professor at the University of Costa Rica, where she lectures on film and visual culture. She has published numerous journal articles and book chapters in the fields of literature and film studies, including, most recently, a contribution to *Spanish Erotic Cinema*. Her monographs include *Bigas Luna. El ojo voraz; Contemplación de lo íntimo; Las adaptaciones subliminales. Tres obras maestras de Alfred Hitchcock;* and *Ofelia fementida.*

Index

Page numbers in *italics* refer to illustrations.

Abrázame como antes (film), 293
Abrego, Leisy, 156
Acuña, Victor Hugo, 35–36, 198, 200, 202–203
Adams, Rachel, 280
Affect (Affect studies), 37–38, 40–41
Affiliative models of memory transfer, 153, 163, 167–168n16, 169n26
African diaspora, 11, 178, 182, 184–185
Afro-Indigenous cultures, 18–19, 251–268
AGACINE (Guatemalan Association of Audiovisual and Film Production), 296
Agamben, Giorgio, 137, 143
Agua fría de mar (film), 6
Agudelo, Irene, 104
Aldana, Thelma, 132
Alemán, Arnoldo, 102
Alfaro Córdoba, Amanda, 5, 11, 12
Allie, Ali, 253–254. See also *Garifuna in Peril* (film)
Alsino y el condor (film), 4
Althusser, Louis, 235
Alvarado, Karina Oliva, 153, 155, 157
Amoretti, María, 200, 201
A ojos cerrados (film), 8
Aquí América Latina (Ludmer), 70
Aquí me quedo (film), 285
Las Aradas: Masacre en seis actos (film), 53
Arbena, Joseph, 213
Árbenz Guzmán, Jacobo, 4, 10, 275, 280, 281
Arcel, Ray, 217, 220
Arce Mairena, Tomás, 96–108
Arce Zablah, Rafael, 48, 59
Archives, social dimension of, 54–55

ARENA (Alianza Republicana Nacionalista) party, 49, 52
Argueta, Arno Jacob, 19, 275–288, 293
Argueta, Luis, 1, 275, 276, 280, 281–282
Arias, Arturo, 155, 156, 157, 280
Arroyo Calderón, Patricia, 16, 89, 152–164
Articulatory practices, 31–32
Asesinato en el Meneo (film), 8–9
Asociación General de Estudiantes Universitarios Salvadoreños, 163
Astorga Carrera, Laura, 19, 293–295
Asturias, Miguel Ángel, 275, 280–281
Atrás hay relámpagos (film), 8
Austin Powers (film), 197
Avalas, Aníbal, 87

Baldizón, Manuel, 242, 283
"Bare life," 16, 137, 139–140
Barillas, Edgar, 276, 282
Barilli, Ademar, 147
Barnet, Darren, 8
Barrios, Rufino, 278
Barrios de Chamorro, Violeta, 96, 102
Bastos, Santiago, 288
La batalla del volcán (film), 14, 49–50, 61
Bauman, Zygmunt, 126
Beasley-Murray, John, 40
Benaim, Abner, 14, 17, 29, 30, 33–41, 177, 180–182, 219
Beverley, John, 133
Bhabha, Homi, 122–123
Billig, Michael, 212
The Birth of a Nation (film), 175
Blades, Rubén, 218, 219
La bodega (film), 284

Bong Joon-ho, 8
Bonilla, Alcira Beatriz, 118
Border imagery, 121–123. *See also* Migration to U.S.
Borrero, Carolina, 17, 177, 178
Borrows, John, 263
Bourdieu, Pierre, 135, 197, 198
Bourke-White, Margaret, 160
Boyarin, Daniel, 280
Brantley, Luis Franco, 17, 177, 179–180
Brecht, Bertolt, 157, 235, 236–237, 242
Bridges, Beau, 8
Brondo, Keri Vacanti, 264
Brown, Alfonso Téofilo, 213
Burton, Julianne, 27, 29
Bustamante, Jayro, 6, 8, 10, 276, 288, 293
Butler, Judith, 124, 135–136, 144

Cabezas, Yazlin, 200
Cabezas Vargas, Andrea, 11, 83, 293
Cabrera, Estrada, 275
Cabrera, Manuel, 278
Cáceres, Berta, 268
Cálix, Juan, 224
Calveiro, Pilar, 33, 47
Caminata de la esperanza (Walk of Hope), 135
El Camino (film), 6, 15, 115, 298
Campos, Sandra, 139–140, 144–145
Canto a la patria que ahora nace (short film), 179
El capitán Orellana y la aldea endemoniada (film), 284
Caravana de Madres de Migrantes Desaparecidas, 134, 137
Cárcamo, Jennifer A., 16, 152–164; *Eternos Indocumentados*, 153, 164–165n2
Cárdenas, Maritza, 155
Carib Wars (1769–1797), 253
Carrera y Turcios, Rafael, 278
Carrión Cruz, Carlos, 105–106
Carrión Fonseca, Gloria, 14–15, 19, 93n15, 97–98, 103–108, 293, 300–301
Carta de Morazán (film), 58
Carter, Jimmy, 181, 218
Carter, William, 180
Casa Comal (Guatemalan film school), 284
La casa de enfrente (film), 284
Casaús Arzú, Marta, 277
Castillero, Enoch, 179

Cayasso, Juan, 226
El Centerfielder (film), 210
Centroamérica (Acuña), 35–36
Chacón, Fernando, 89
Chacón, Mario, 195
Chang, Augusto, 282
Chávez, Daniel, 100–101, 102
Cheng, Li, 288
Chi, Tomás, 210
Children of the Diaspora (film), 16, 152–164
Chinchilla, Maya, 155
Chinchilla, Nora Stolz, 155
Chomsky, Noam, 9
Christian Base Communities (CEB), 48
El cielo rojo (film), 193
El cielo rojo 2 (film), 193
Cine centroamericano y caribeño siglo XXI (García Diego), 12
El cine hondureño (Inczauskis), 12
Cinema of marginality, 16, 115–116, 124–126
The Cinema of Poetry (Pasolini), 96
Cinema Paradiso (film), 180
Cine Murciélago, 296
Cinergia Foundation, 6
Clark, Ramsey, 32
Colonialism: colonial discourses, 239; and Indigenous languages, 252; and masculinity, 277–278; of Panama Canal Zone, 176, 181, 184–185, 189; in postmodern era, 131–132; and power relationships, 8–9; and racism, 279; settler colonialism and *Garifuna in Peril* (film), 263–268
Colonialismo y revolución (Guzmán Böckler), 279
Coming to Our Senses (Reber), 41
Cómprame un revólver (film), 8
"III Conferencia vienesa" (Kapuściński), 62
Connell, R. W., 277–278, 280, 288
Constituting Central American-Americans (Cárdenas), 155
Cortés, María Lourdes: Cinergia Foundation, 6; countryside and city contrasted in *Maikol Yordan*, 196, 204; on *El silencio del Neto*, 281; on female characters, 293; on Indigenous peoples in cinema, 286–287; on *Italia 90*, 225; migration represented in cinema, 15–16, 47, 113–127; *El nuevo cine costarricense*, 3–4; *La pantalla rota*, 1, 12, 28–29, 275; on twentieth-century developments, 239

Cortez, Beatriz, 11, 237–238
Las cosas que no decimos (film short), 301
Costa Rica: Costa Rican exceptionalism, 202–205; creation myth of, 198, 199–200; growth of cinema, 2; nostalgia and patriotism, 195–198, 202; World Cup soccer, 222, 224–228
Costumbrismo, 4, 17, 198–202
Counter cinema, 234–244
Counterhegemony, 39
Crisóstomo, Alejo, 284
Cristiani, Alfredo, 49
Crosson, Séan, 214, 216
Las Cruces: Poblado próximo (film), 284
Cuando el río y el mar se unieron (film), 257
Cuarón, Jonás, 122
Cuban cinema, influence of, 5, 100, 176, 177
Cuevas, Lucía, 293
"Cultural memory work," 153, 157
Cultural resistance, regional cinema as, 115
Cumes, Aura, 277
Cuvardic García, Dorde, 198–199

Da Silva Catela, Ludmila, 72
D'Aubuisson, Roberto, 52, 60
Davis, Nick, 236
De Armas, Ana, 218
La decisión de vencer, los primeros frutos (film), 58
De Garay, Graciela, 57
De Genova, Nicholas, 137
De la Fuente, Anna Marie, 2
Del amor y otros demonios (film), 2
Delefoco (magazine), 204
De Lesseps, Ferdinand, 176, 178
Deleuze, Gilles, 236, 239
Delgamuukw v. British Columbia, 263
De Niro, Robert, 217
Derrida, Jacques, 57
Desierto (film), 122
Díaz, César, 296
Díaz, Enrique, 225
Díaz, Júnior, 225
Didi-Huberman, Georges, 127
Distancia (film), 287
Distrital, cine y otros mundos (film festival), 296
D'Lugo, Marvin, 239
Documentary film: and archival sources, 57–61, 99–100, 107, 218–219, 224–225; cinematic poetry/prose balance, 103; and collective memory, 37, 71–73, 87–90; development in region, 3–4, 13–14; emotional response to, 79–81, 107; and gender identities, 300–301; inquiry and interrogation, 76–77; interactive documentary, 133; oral history and memory, 54–55, 56–57, 73–76; preservation as function of, 84; as provider of tools for evaluation, 78–79; social actors and testimony of survivors, 34–36, 51, 60, 83–86; and social memory, 69–70, 90–92; soundtracks, 162, 168n21, 241; story and history, 29–30; and *testimonios*, 133–134, 135, 139–140, 146–147; as treatment of reality, 50; voice-over techniques, 83–84, 86
Donde nace el Sol (film), 284, 287
Donoghue, Michael, 217
Dos Fridas (film), 298
Duarte, José Napoleón, 60
Durán, Felicidad, 218, 220
Durán, Roberto, 13, 18, 34, 210, 215, 217–220
Durón, Hispano, 2–3, 8–9
Dying from Improvement (Razack), 263

Eco-cinema, 256–257
Eco-fourth film, 257, 263
Edison, Thomas, 209
Eisenstein, Sergéi, 175
Eleta, Carlos, 219
11 cipotes (film), 210
Ellas se aman (film), 293
Elsaesser, Thomas, 234, 235
El Salvador: Cinquera massacre, 240–241; civil war (1980–1991), 10, 46; film production and distribution, 61; Football War with Honduras, 210; General Amnesty, 47; *Libro Amarillo (Yellow Book)*, 53; Peace Accords (1992), 46; testimonies condemning state violence, 47–48; Truth Commission, 46–47; USEU (Unión Salvadoreña de Estudiantes Universitarios), 154, 165n5; World Cup soccer, 222
El Salvador: archivos perdidos del conflicto (film series), 14, 49, 60, 61
Elsewhere (film), 8
Elsey, Brenda, 229
"El encuentro con el Otro como reto del siglo XX" (Kapuściński), 62
"The End of Hegemony? Panama and the United States" (Sanchez), 32

En sentido opuesto (film), 284
Entonces nosotros (film), 8
Entrepreneurs of memory, 36–37
ERP (People's Revolutionary Army), 48
Escalón, Guillermo, 58
Escobar, José, 198
Espinosa, Rodolfo, 285
Espinoza, Mauricio, 13, 18, 181, 193, 209–229, 288, 293
El espíritu de mi mamá (film), 253–254
Estrada, Alicia Ivonne, 155
Estrellas de la línea (film), 210
Eternos Indocumentados: Central American Refugees in the U.S. (film), 153, 164–165n2
Ethnogenesis, 253
Ethnohistory, 253
Euraque, Darío, 266
Excitable Speech: A Politics of the Performative (Butler), 124
Extraño pero verdadero (film), 296

Fábrega, Paz, 6
Fabulaciones del nuevo cine costarricense (Cortés), 12
Fajardo Andrade, Ivanhoe, 285
Falicov, Tamara L., 243
Familial models of memory transfer, 153, 163
Fanon, Frantz, 126
Fe (film), 284
Figueroa, Ray, 284
Figueroa Ibarra, Carlos, 278–279
Film festivals, 6
El fin (film), 193
The First Maus (Spiegelman), 159–160
Fleming, Robert, 179
FMLN (Farabundo Martí National Liberation Front), 46, 49, 57, 58, 88, 154
Focus of images, 157–158
Football (short film), 209
Foucault, Michel, 54
Fractals (film), 300
Freire de Carvalho Frey, Aline, 257
La fuerza del balón (film), 210
Fukunaga, Cary Joji, 15, 115
Fumero, Patricia, 12
Funes, Mauricio, 154
Futbolera: A History of Women and Sports in Latin America (Elsey & Nadel), 229

Gabriel, Teshome, 239
Galt, Rosalind, 236
Gamboa, Dannia, 205
García, Salvador, 77
García Diego, Charo, 12
García Espinosa, Julio, 237
García Granados, Miguel, 278
García Torres, Lilia, 14, 46–63
Garifuna in Peril (film): background and overview, 18–19, 252–253; land and tourism, 263–268; land as heritage, 257–263; water and eco-cinema, 253–257
The Garifuna Journey (film), 257
The Garifuna Nation Across Borders (Palacio), 252
Garifuna people and language, 252, 254–255. See also *Garifuna in Peril* (film)
Garifunas Holding Ground/Lucha garifuna (film), 257
Gasolina (film), 6, 7, 285–286, 296
Gay-themed films, 288, 301–305
Gender issues: alternate masculinities in Guatemalan cinema, 275–288; domestic labor, 227; effeminacy and alternative masculinity, 281–283; gender representation in cinema, 19, 294–295; Gloria Carrión Fonseca interview, 300–301; Ishtar Yasin Gutiérrez interview, 298–299; Laura Astorga Carrera interview, 293–295; LGBTQ+ issues, 293, 301–305; Luis Fernando Midence interview, 301–305; Pamela Guinea interview, 296–297; queer cinema, 236, 244n8; and sports, 214, 229; women's precarity on migrant journeys, 136, 140–142, 144–145
The Generation of Postmemory (Hirsch), 152–153, 159–160
Gestación (film), 9
Getino, Octavio, 236, 237, 239
Los gigantes no existen (film), 284
Godard, Jean-Luc, 234
Goethals, George Washington, 179, 190n4
Gomberg-Muñoz, Ruth, 137
Gómez, Miguel, 193–195, 210, 224–228. See also *Maikol Yordan de viaje perdido* (film)
Gómez Lacayo, Juan Pablo, 14, 69–92, 98, 107
Gómez Menjívar, Jennifer Carolina, 18–19, 251–268
González, Jorge "El Mágico," 222

González, Julia, 83
González, Nancie, 252, 253
González de Canales Carcereny, Julia, 18, 234–244
Gorgas, William Crawford, 179, 190n5
Gould, Jeffrey, 14, 48, 52, 55, 59
Gramsci, Antonio, 31
Gramscian framework, 33, 38
Granito (film), 15
Granja Núñez, Daniela, 288, 292–305
Graves, Lester León, 180
Grierson, John, 50
Griffith, D. W., 175
Grinberg Pla, Valeria, 80, 81, 103, 242, 293
Grupo Experimental de Cine Universitario (GECU), 3, 28–29, 176
Guatemala: Casa Comal film school, 284; cinema, 275–288; dictatorships, 10, 278–280; *ladinidad,* 279; presidential elections (2019), 132; revolution, 242–243
Guattari, Félix, 236
Guerra, Ramón, 133
"La guerra de los nombres" (Mazariegos), 29–30
Guimaraes, Alexandre, 226
Guinea, Pamela, 19, 283, 293, 296–297
El guión para cine documental (Mendoza), 58
Gutiérrez Alea, Tomás, 238–239
Guzmán Böckler, Carlos, 277, 279

Haines, Dinga, 210
Halberstam, Judith, 278
Halbwachs, Maurice, 72
Hale, Charles, 277
Hamilton, Nora, 155
Hands of Stone (film), 13, 18, 210, 215–220
Harvey-Kattou, Liz, 4, 5, 12, 17, 193–205, 227
Hasta el Sol tiene manchas (film), 13, 18, 234, 240–244, 286, 296
Hegemony: concept of, 31, 37–38; contrasted with domination, 33; and counternarratives, 39; and metonymy, 39
Hegemony and Socialist Strategy (Laclau & Mouffe), 31
Henríquez Consalvi, Carlos, 14, 48, 51–52, 55, 58–59, 62
Herbert, Jean-Loup, 279
Heredera del viento (film), 14, 15, 93n15, 98, 103–106, 107–108, 300

La herencia colonial de América Latina (Stein), 84
Hernández, Esther, 155
Hernández Cordón, Julio, 6–8, 13, 19, 234, 240–244, 245n11, 285–286, 296
Hess, John, 238
Hidalgo, Hilda, 2
Hirsch, Marianne, 16, 152–153, 159–160, 163, 164, 167–168n16
Historias absurdamente cortas para tardes desesperadamente largas (film), 285
Historias del Canal (film). See *Panama Canal Stories* (film)
History: archives used in documentary, 99–100; control of historical narrative, 32–33; education in El Salvador, 48; intersectional historiography, 36; relational history, 36; and story, in documentary, 29–30
Hok-Sze Leung, Helen, 239–240
Hollywood, influence of, 177
Honduras: coup d'état (2009), 132; Football War with El Salvador, 210; Garifuna community, 254; rimlands and Garifuna people, 251–252, 254, 263; tourist industry, 263–264
La Hora de Los Hornos (film), 238
Huezo Mixco, Tatiana, 15, 69, 81–87, 234, 240–244, 245n11, 293
Hybrid cinema, 177, 179

Ibarra, Epigmenio, 60
Images, focus of, 157–158
Imperdonable (film), 293
Inczauskis, David, 12
Independent film production model, 5
Indigenous and Tribal People's Convention (1989), 168
Indigenous peoples: languages, 252; representation in cinema, 10–11, 286–287
Instituto Nicaragüense de Cine (INCINE), 3, 5, 80, 100–101
Intangible Cultural Heritage of Humanity (UNESCO), 18, 252, 260, 268
Intersectional historiography, 36
An Introduction to Female Masculinity (Halberstam), 278
Invasión (film), 14, 29, 30, 33–41, 181, 219
Les Invisibles (film), 298
Inzomnia (film), 296

Irías, Alejandro, 210
Istmo (journal), 11–12
Istmo Film, 3
Italia 90: La película (film), 18, 193, 210, 222, 224–228
Italian neorealism, 238
Ixcanul (film), 6, 7, 8, 10, 19, 276, 287, 289n10

Jaeck, Lois Marie, 280
Jakubowicz, Jonathan, 13, 210
Jara, Claudio, 226–227
Jaugey, Florence, 210
La jaula de oro (film), 16, 19, 115–116, 118, 119–127, 276, 296
Jelin, Elizabeth, 37, 70, 73
Jeong, Ken, 8
Jiménez, Elías, 284
Jiménez, Hernán, 8
Johns, Christina Jacqueline, 32
Johnson, P. Ward, 32
José (film), 288

Kampwirth, Karen, 102
Kapuściński, Ryszard, 62
Kehde, Suzanne, 204
Kelz, Rosine, 1336
Keylor Navas: Hombre de fe (film), 210
Kimura (film), 210
Kinloch, Frances, 71, 76
Kino Glaz, 54
Klein, Naomi, 131
Kristeva, Julia, 126
Kroshus Medina, Laurie, 266

Lacayo, Ramiro, 210
Laclau, Ernesto, 31, 33, 38, 39, 40–41
Ladinidad, 279
LaFrance, David, 213
Languages, Indigenous, 252
Latinamericanism, 203
Lecciones para una guerra (film), 296
León, Christian, 16, 116, 124
León, Claudia, 134
Leonard, Sugar Ray, 215, 217, 218, 230n9
Levinas, Emmanuel, 98, 104–105, 106
LGBTQ+ issues, 293, 301–305
Liberalism in postmodern era, 131–133, 143
Liberation theology, 48, 84–85

Lipkes, Michel, 296
List, Jared, 14, 27–41, 181, 219, 288, 293
Littín, Miguel, 4
La Llorona (film), 4, 8, 10, 276
López, Ana M., 27–28, 243
López, Julio, 14, 48, 53, 54, 56–57, 60–61, 63
López González, Augusto, 77–78
López Muñoz, Joel, 285
Lorenzana, Guillermo, 223
Los puños de una nación (film), 13, 18, 181, 210
Loustaunau, Esteban, 16, 47, 115, 131–147, 164
Love Hard (film), 8
Lubaraun (film), 257
Ludmer, Josefina, 70, 89, 90
El lugar más pequeño (film), 15, 18, 69, 81–90, 91, 234, 240–244
Lumiere Brothers, 209
Luna, Alfonso, 163, 169n25

Mabo (film), 257
Maikol Yordan de viaje perdido (film), 9, 17, 193, 194–195; and Costa Rican exceptionalism, 202–205; and costumbrismo, 198–202; nostalgia and patriotism, 195–198, 202
Mandoki, Luis, 16, 115
Maquillaje (film), 19, 285
La Mara (Ramírez Heredia), 117
María en tierra de nadie (film), 15, 16, 47, 115, 134–147; still photos, *138, 141, 145, 146*
Las marimbas del infierno (film), 7, 286, 296
Martí, Farabundo, 163, 169n25
Martin, Michael T., 28
Martín-Baró, Ignacio, 82, 86, 88–89
Martínez, Emetria, 134, 142, 144, 148n3
Martínez, Óscar, 143
Martínez Hernández-Mejía, Iliana, 134
Martínez Rivas, Carlos, 108
Las masacres del Mozote (film), 53
Massumi, Brian, 38
Maus (Spiegelman), 159–160
Mazariegos, Juan Carlos, 29–30
McCullough, David, 176, 178
Meiselas, Susan, 14, 69, 70–79, 91
Melindrosa Films, 296
Memoria, olvido, silencio (Pollak), 33
Memory: affiliative memory transfer, 153, 163, 167–168n16, 169n26; collective, 87–90; democratization of memory, 36; domi-

nant contrasted with hegemonic, 36–37; entrepreneurs of memory, 36–37; familial memory transfer, 153, 163, 166n10; family and generational violence, 89–90; framing of memory, 33; intergenerational traumatic memory, 152–153, 167n13; labor of memory, 79; linear contrasted with circular, 80; multiplicity of memory, 35–36; postmemory, 16, 159–160, 167n13; postwar and memory, 14–15; social memory, construction of, 79–81

Méndez, María Inés, 137–138, 142
Mendoza, Carlos, 58
Meneses, Vidaluz, 75
Menjívar, Élmer, 60
Mesoamerican ballgame, 211, 229–230n5
Midence, Luis Fernando, 19, 293, 301–305
Migration to U.S: *María en tierra de nadie* (Zamora): as act of resistance against state power, 137; adolescent migrants, 116–118; La Arrocera crossing, 143–144; border imagery, 121–123; context and theory, 10, 15–16, 118–121; marginalization of migrants, 124–126; migrant shelters, 139; overview, 113–114; treatment in cinema, 114–115; *via crucis* caravans, 134–135, 137, 143–144. See also *Children of the Diaspora* (film)
Milutinović, Velibor "Bora," 227–228
Mitchell, W.J.T., 117, 126
Miyoshi, Masao, 131
Modalidades de memoria y archivos afectivos (Rodríguez), 12, 70
Mon, Pinky, 17, 177, 178–179
Moncada, Mercedes, 14–15, 69, 79–81, 97–99, 102–103, 107, 293
Montero, Mauricio, 225, 226, 227
Moore, Davey, 215
Morales, Jimmy, 132, 283
Morales, Sammy, 283
Morazán (film), 2
Moreno, Carlos, 210
Moreno, Hortensia, 229
Morgan, Michael L., 106
Mouffe, Chantal, 31, 33, 38, 39, 40–41
Movimiento Migrante Mesoamericano, 134, 142–143
Muñoz, Marta, 139–140, 144–145
Murillo, Rosario, 108
Muro, Diego, 195–196, 204
Murphy, Kaitlin, 83, 240
Museo de la Palabra y la Imagen (MUPI), 52, 54, 58–59, 162
Muyshondt, Ernesto, 52
Muyshondt, Gerardo, 14, 48, 52–53, 55, 59, 210

La Nación (newspaper), 195
Nadel, Joshua, 212, 229
Nagib, Lúcia, 243
Nationalism and sports, 211–215
Nava, Gregory, 152
Navas, Keylor, 210
New Latin American Cinema (NLAC), 3, 27–29
Nicaragua: Alemán presidency, 102; Esquipulas Agreements, 76; FSLN (Sandinista National Liberation Front), 74, 77, 79, 96, 98, 107; insurrection (1979), 70–71, 82; post-war trauma, 87–90; Sandinista revolution, 71, 82, 96–102; Somoza regime, 10, 97–98
Nicaragua, June 1978 to July 1979 (Meiselas), 70–71, 73, 74
Nichols, Bill, 51, 133
1913 (short film), 178, 183–186
1932 Cicatriz de la memoria, 52
1950 (short film), 178–179, 186–187
1964 (short film), 179–180, 187–188
1977 (short film), 180–182, 188–189
2013 (short film), 182–183
90 minutos (film), 210
Noriega, Manuel, 10, 219
El Norte (film), 152
Northern Triangle nations, 128n4, 132–133, 164–165n2
Novaro, María, 296
Nuestras madres (film), 296

O'Connor, Aeden, 210
Oettler, Anika, 76, 77
Los ofendidos (film), 14, 49, 56, 61
100 horas de furia (film), 210
One-on-One (film short), 301
Ortega, Daniel, 96, 97, 102, 106, 108
Ortega-Heilbron, Pituka, 13, 17, 177, 181–183, 210, 216, 218
Ortiz Wallner, Alexandra, 11
Osorno, Diego, 296

Osorto, Pancho, 223–224
Osuna, Steven, 165–166n7, 166n10
Ovnis en Zacapa (film), 19

La palabra en el bosque (film), 14, 48–49, 61
Palabras mágicas para romper un encantamiento (film), 14–15, 69, 79–81, 91, 98–99, 102–103, 107
Palacio, Joseph O., 252
Palacios, Adriana, 99
Palmer, Steven, 198, 200
Panama: background and overview, 175–176; canal construction, 176; Canal Zone as contact zone, 183–189; cinema movement, origins of, 28–29; Day of the Martyrs, 179–180; Torrijos-Carter Treaty, 181, 182, 211, 218; U.S. invasion and occupation, 9–10, 30, 31–33, 215, 216–218
Panama Canal Stories (film), 17, 29, 176–190; Canal Zone as contact zone, 183–189; *1913*, 178, 183–186; *1950*, 178–179, 186–187; *1964*, 179–180, 187–188; *1977*, 180–182, 188–189; *2013*, 182–183
The Panama Deception (film), 38, 39
Panama International Film Festival, 2
La pantalla rota (Cortés), 1, 12, 28, 115, 275
Pantoja, Pedro, 146, 147
Parasite (film), 8
Pasolini, Pier Paolo, 96, 103
Patriarchal structure and alternative masculinity, 19, 275–288
Las Patronas, 147
Pérez, Yansi, 241
Pérez Him, Enrique, 285
Pérez Molina, Otto, 283
Perpich, Diane, 106
Pickering, Jean, 204
Pictures from a Revolution (film), 14, 69, 70–79, 91
Pol (film), 285
Poll, Claudia, 225, 229
Pollak, Michael, 33, 37
Polvo (film), 286, 287, 296
Pólvora en el corazón (film), 288
Pontes, Bahia, 50
Posey, Parker, 8
The Post (film), 295
Postmemory, 159–160, 163, 164, 167n13
Pratt, Mary Louise, 184, 189

Precarious Life: The Powers of Mourning and Violence (Butler), 136
Precarity, concept of, 16, 135–137, 145–146
Presos (film), 7
Princesas rojas (film), 4, 293
El Profe Omar (film trilogy), 284
Psicología social (Martín-Baró), 88
Pulido Ritter, Luis, 183–184, 185
Los puños de una nación (film), 215–220
Puro mula (film), 19, 285

Queer cinema, 236, 244n8
Quemada-Díez, Diego, 16, 115, 121, 276, 296
Quesada Soto, Álvaro, 199, 201, 202
Quílez, Laia, 87
Quiñones, Néstor, 219

Ramírez, Édgar, 217
Ramírez, Gilberto, 29
Ramírez, Sergio, 210, 287
Razack, Sherene, 263
Reagan, Ronald, 219
Reber, Dierdra, 41
Reeser, Todd, 288
Regarding the Pain of Others (Sontag), 56
El regreso (film), 8
El regreso de Lencho (film), 287–288
Reichenbach, Marcel, 3
Reinterpreting the Banana Republic (Euraque), 266
Renov, Michael, 76, 78–79, 84
El retorno (film), 4
Reyes, Dagoberto, 157
Reyes, Rubén, 253–254, 267. See also *Garifuna in Peril* (film)
Rich, Ruby B., 234, 235–236
Ricoeur, Paul, 89
Ring (magazine), 215, 218
Ríos Montt, Efraín, 278
Rivera, Alberto, 179
Rivera, Arnoldo, 226
Roach, Jay, 197
Rocha, Glauber, 237
Rodríguez, Ana Patricia, 153, 156, 165–166n7
Rodríguez, Andrés, 296
Rodríguez, Chema, 210, 284
Rodríguez, Dimas, 50
Rodríguez, Ileana, 12, 70, 86–87, 90, 91, 131–132, 293

Rodríguez, Mauricio, 223
Rodríguez, Silvio, 157, 158
Romero, Óscar, 54, 60, 168n20
Rosales, Mario, 287
Rossana en construcción (film), 300
Rowe, David, 209
Roza (film), 296
Rubén Blades Is Not My Name (film), 29
Rushton, Richard, 235

Sacasa, Juan Bautista, 98
Saito, James, 8
Salas, Bértold, 4–5
Salguero, Miguel, 210
Salmon, William Noel, 252
Samayoa, Mendel, 284
Samora, Marcela, 48
Sanabria, Carolina, 17, 175–190, 217
El sanatorio (film), 193
Sánchez, Diana, 6
Sánchez, Hugo, 224
Sanchez, Peter, 32
Sánchez Méndez, Sandra Mabel, 138, 142
Sánchez Soler, Martha, 134, 142, 147
Sanctuary movement, 165–166n7
Sandino, Augusto César, 97
Sandoval García, Carlos, 220
Santí, Enrico, 203
Sassen, Saskia, 132
Savarn, David, 280
Schoonover, Karl, 236, 241
"Second-hand identities," 153, 156–157
La semilla y la piedra (film), 54
Semprún, Jorge, 241
El señor presidente (Asturias), 275–276, 280–281
Sepúlveda, Juan Manuel, 296
Serra, Alberto, 210
Settler colonialism, 263–268
Sexual exploitation of migrant women, 136, 140–142, 144–145
Shohat, Ella, 6, 8, 176, 177, 238
Shum, Harry, Jr., 8
Silence: and forgetting, 33, 35–36; official silence, 36–37, 77; of voices in diaspora, 156, 159, 166n8
El silencio de Neto (film), 1, 4, 19, 275–276, 280–283
Simán, Ricardo, 59

Sin nombre (film), 15, 115, 116, 117–118, 119, 121, 122
Sin ruta (film short), 301
Sistema Radio Venceremos (SRV), 58–59
Smart, Ian, 251
Soccer films, 220–228. *See also* Sports films
The Social Documentary in Latin America (Burton), 27
Sojourners of the Caribbean (González), 252
Solalinde, Alejandro, 138, 147
Solanas, Fernando, 236, 237, 238–239
Solís, Ottón, 201
Somoza Debayle, Anastasio, 98
Somoza Debayle, Luis, 98
Somoza García, Anastasio, 97–98, 101
Sontag, Susan, 56
Sorto, Manuel, 58
Soundtracks, 241; documentary film, 162, 168n21; genre film, 181
Speed, Shannon, 252–253, 268
Sports films: background and overview, 209–211; *Hands of Stone,* 215–220; *Los puños de una nación,* 215–220; soccer, 220–228; sports and national identities, 211–215; underdog theme, 211, 222, 227
Sprenkels, Ralph, 79
Stam, Robert, 6, 8, 176, 177, 238
State Crime, the Media, and the Invasion of Panama (Johns & Johnson), 32
Stein, Barbara, 84
Stein, Stanley, 84
Studies in Spanish & Latin American Cinemas (journal), 12
Swier, Patricia Lapolla, 280

Taking Their Word (Arias), 157
El tamalón navideño (film), 283–284
Taylor, Chris, 264–265
Téllez, Luis, 296
Temblores (film), 8, 276, 288, 293
Te prometo anarquía (film), 7, 296
Terra Vermelha (film), 257
Tesoros (film), 296
Testimonios in documentary film, 133–134, 135, 139–140, 146–147
Te toca (film short), 301
Third Cinema, 235–236, 237–240, 243
Thoburn, Nicholas, 37–38
La tierra prometida (film), 238

Tomás, Consuelo, 220
Toque de queda (film), 284
Tornatore, Giuseppe, 180
Torrijos, Omar, 215, 217–218, 219
Los trabajos de la memoria (Jelin), 70
Tres, Rafa, 284
El trofeo (film), 210
Tropical Tongues (Salmon & Gómez Menjívar), 252
Truth Commission (El Salvador), 46–47

Ubico, Jorge, 278
UN Declaration on the Rights of Indigenous Peoples (2007), 168
United States, interventionist history, 9–10
Uno, La historia de un gol (film), 18, 210, 222–224
Ureña, Jurgen, 293
USEU (Unión Salvadoreña de Estudiantes Universitarios), 154, 165n5

La vaca (film), 284
Valderrama, Aldo Rey, 210
Vannini, Margarita, 71, 76, 77, 91
Vaquero del mediodía (film), 296
Vayamos jubilosos (film), 59
Venegas, William, 195, 201, 203
Ventura, Miguel, 48
Verdadero-primero-último (film short), 301
Verfremdungseffekt (distancing effect), 236, 242
La vida precoz y breve de Sabina Rivas (film), 16, 115, 117, 119, 121, 124–126

Viñayo, Marlén, 293
Violencia, marginalidad y memoria en el cine centroamericano (Cortés), 12
Violeta al fin (film), 2
V.I.P.: La otra casa (film), 284
Viveros Vigoya, Mara, 288

Walker, William, 9
Wasted Lives: Modernity and Its Outcasts (Bauman), 126
Wheatley, Abby, 137
White settler myth, 198
Wolfe, Patrick, 266
Wollen, Peter, 234, 235, 240, 243
Wright, James Charles, 179
Wright, Patsy, 179

Yasin Gutiérrez, Ishtar, 6, 15, 19, 115, 293, 298–299
Yates, Pamela, 293
Ydígoras Fuentes, Miguel, 278
La Yuma (film), 210
Yurumein (film), 257

Zamora, Rubén, 49, 53
Zamora Chamorro, Marcela, 14–16, 47, 53–54, 56, 60–61, 62–63, 115, 293; *María en tierra de nadie,* 134–147
Zapata, Mario, 163, 169n25
Zapata, Pelé, 223
Zúñiga, Leonor, 293

Reframing Media, Technology, and Culture in Latin/o America

Edited by Héctor Fernández L'Hoeste and Juan Carlos Rodríguez

Reframing Media, Technology, and Culture in Latin/o America explores how Latin American and Latino audiovisual (film, television, digital), musical (radio, recordings, live performances, dancing), and graphic (comics, photography, advertising) cultural practices reframe and reconfigure social, economic, and political discourses at a local, national, and global level. In addition, it looks at how information networks reshape public and private policies, and the enactment of new identities in civil society. The series also covers how different technologies have allowed and continue to allow for the construction of new ethnic spaces. It not only contemplates the interaction between new and old technologies but also how the development of brand-new technologies redefines cultural production.

Telling Migrant Stories: Latin American Diaspora in Documentary Film, edited by Esteban E. Loustaunau and Lauren E. Shaw (2018; paperback edition, 2021)

Mestizo Modernity: Race, Technology, and the Body in Postrevolutionary Mexico, by David S. Dalton (2018; first paperback edition, 2021)

The Insubordination of Photography: Documentary Practices under Chile's Dictatorship, by Ángeles Donoso Macaya (2020)

Digital Humanities in Latin America, edited by Héctor Fernández L'Hoeste and Juan Carlos Rodríguez (2020)

Pablo Escobar and Colombian Narcoculture, by Aldona Bialowas Pobutsky (2020)

The New Brazilian Mediascape: Television Production in the Digital Streaming Age, by Eli Lee Carter (2020)

Univision, Telemundo, and the Rise of Spanish-Language Television in the United States, by Craig Allen (2020)

Cuba's Digital Revolution: Citizen Innovation and State Policy, edited by Ted A. Henken and Sara Garcia Santamaria (2021; first paperback edition, 2022)

Afro-Latinx Digital Connections, edited by Eduard Arriaga and Andrés Villar (2021)

The Lost Cinema of Mexico: From Lucha Libre to Cine Familiar and Other Churros, edited by Olivia Cosentino and Brian Price (2022)

Neo-Authoritarian Masculinity in Brazilian Crime Film, by Jeremy Lehnen (2022)

The Rise of Central American Film in the Twenty-First Century, edited by Mauricio Espinoza and Jared List (2023)